ECONOMICS

Themes and Perspectives

G. B. J. ATKINSON

Causeway Press

Kirsty Holmes.

Cover photograph by Walter Wick, provided by The Telegraph Colour Library
Cover design and graphics by Susan and Andrew Allen
Cartoons by Ian Traynor and Alan Fraser

Acknowledgements
The publishers are grateful to the following for permission to reproduce photographs.

Andrew Allen pp. 39, 90, 201, 202; Ford Motor Company pp. 49, 64; Sally and Richard Greenhill; p. 135 (left); Ian McAnulty pp. 121, 128; Popperfoto pp. 4, 5, 7, 9; Public Relations Office, Liverpool University p.117; Sefton Photo Library p. 255 (right); Topham Picture Source p. 119; Travel Photo International p.22.

British Library Cataloguing in Publication Data
A catalogue record for this book is available from the British Library.

ISBN 1-873929-27-7

Causeway Press Limited
PO Box 13, Ormskirk, Lancs, L39 5HP

First Edition 1989 (reprinted twice)
Second edition 1994
Reprinted 1997

Origination by Image Setting, Ormskirk, Lancs L39 4RT.
Printed and bound by Alden Press, Oxford.

Contents

Preface

This book was written in the belief that economics is interesting. Many economics texts give the impression that the student needs to memorise lots of facts and complex diagrams. In this book, economics is presented as a subject in which competing schools of thought contend. This reflects the reality of the subject.

Each chapter is organised so that there is a logical development of understanding. Though there are a few variations, each chapter follows a similar pattern.

- A short introduction outlines the area.
- Themes and debates which set the topic in context are then dealt with. Thus the chapter on unemployment begins with a discussion on the measurement and extent of unemployment.
- The competing perspectives which relate to the topic are discussed. At the end of each perspective there is a brief summary.
- The policies which result from a particular analysis follow these summaries where appropriate.
- The chapter concludes with an 'evidence' section. This section includes the application of perspectives to economic issues, for example an examination of recent experience.

The book has been written to cover examination syllabuses at A and AS level, professional courses and introductory courses in higher education. Recent developments in A level syllabuses have been taken into account. For example, areas such as environmental and development economics are emphasised. The book is also very suitable for modular courses and it has proved to be an ideal introductory course book for higher education because its approach is to concentrate on issues, debates and perspectives whilst developing critical analysis - a feature of such courses - whilst covering the main areas usually taught on such courses.

The book could not have been written without the help of many people. My colleagues at the University of Central Lancashire have been extremely supportive and I would like to thank those students who read various chapters and made valuable suggestions. My wife has improved my English and I would also like to thank Mike Kidson for all his efforts and suggestions which have proved invaluable. Many of the ideas in the book have been adapted from various chapters in *Developments in Economics* (published annually by Causeway Press), which I find is the best way to keep up to date. I am grateful to all these people, and in particular to Dave Gray, my editor, who has made huge improvements to the book. Despite all this help, there are doubtless errors and omissions; these are my responsibility.

Brian Atkinson

Introduction and First Principles

Who reads introductions? Reviewers hoping for a quick quotation, insomniacs wanting something to send them to sleep, and the hyper-conscientious who read everything. Sensible people, knowing that time is scarce, often skip to the first chapter. Nevertheless this introduction is probably the most important part of the book because it introduces the basic ideas of economics.

Economics has been called 'the dismal science'. One reason for this (if you think about certain parts of economics syllabuses you may think of another!) is that without scarcity the subject would not exist. If we could all have our wants satisfied there would be no need for economics. A flick of the fingers and a Rolls Royce would appear, another flick and a villa on the Riviera would be mine, another and a machine would do the chores. There would be no need for production or distribution. Money would be irrelevant. Unfortunately the world is not like that.

Every society has to face three basic economic problems, since we cannot produce everything that everyone would like:

- What should we produce?
- What methods should be used to produce these goods and services?
- Who should receive the goods and services that are produced?

Economics is the study of how people and societies choose to employ scarce resources which have alternative uses to produce goods and services, and how to distribute them. Economists analyse the costs and benefits of alternative ways of using resources.

By 'resources', economists mean land, labour and capital, such as machines and raw materials, which can be used in production. (These are also known as factors of production). Resources are used to produce everything from apples to zoos, and it is because resources are scarce relative to wants that the economic problem arises.

Economists make use of concepts, and three in particular underlie much economic thinking: **opportunity cost, marginality** and **efficiency.** Even when these words are not specifically used in the text, the ideas they embody will be relevant to the analysis.

The opportunity cost of any action is the value of the forgone alternative action. All through life, individuals, firms and governments have to make choices. Choosing one alternative means that other alternatives have to be given up. Therefore the real cost of an action is the value of the most attractive alternative. In this sense all costs are opportunity costs. If a child is offered an ice cream or an ice lolly and chooses the latter, its real cost is the ice cream forgone. The real cost to Mary of kissing Peter is that she cannot kiss Paul (at least not at the same time!). If a plot of land could be used for playing fields, but instead the council decides to

One view of the opportunity cost of building the Channel Tunnel

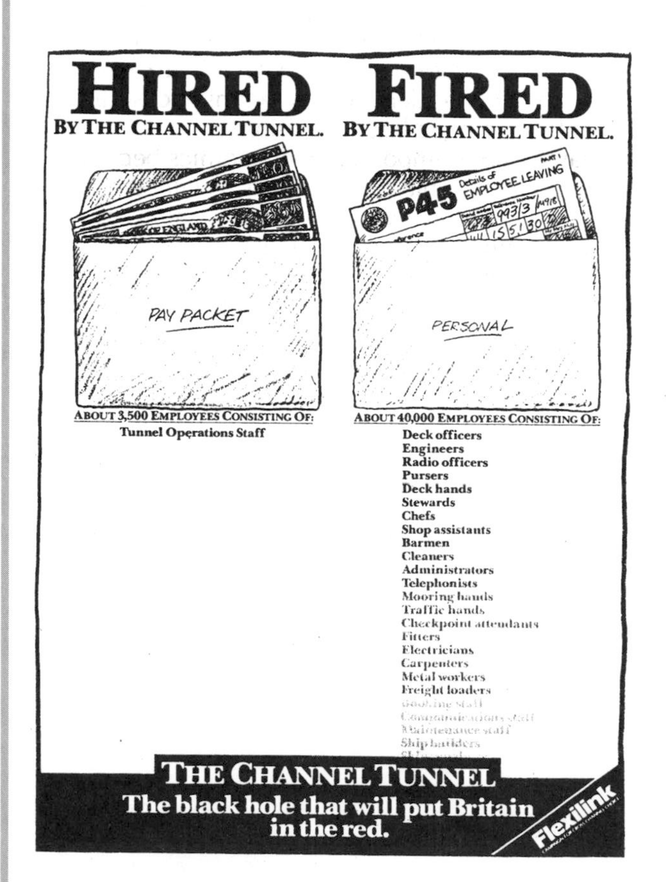

Source: Flexilink, The Campaign for Cross Channel Choice.

use it for parking, the real cost of the car park is the playing field forgone.

The central assumption underlying opportunity cost is that each act excludes other possible acts at any moment in time. In some cases the opportunity cost can be measured in monetary terms. Often it cannot. Whatever the difficulties of measurement, opportunity cost is probably the most fundamental concept in economics, and is applicable in a wide range of circumstances. It explains why some teachers rush off home as soon as school ends (home is preferable to school) – and why some are reluctant to go home. It helps us realise that the real cost of putting up old age pensions may be that child benefit cannot be increased. Similarly, if resources are used to develop a third London airport, provincial airports such as Manchester may suffer restricted growth.

The second fundamental concept is that of the margin. Marginal analysis is the analysis of the relations between increments or decrements of the total quantity of some economic variable.

The idea of the margin is frequently used in everyday life. A cook deciding to add a little more salt to the soup is undertaking marginal analysis. So too is an athlete who wonders whether or not an extra training session would be beneficial, and the student who considers the (opportunity) costs and benefits of an extra hour's revision.

Marginality is important in economics because the appropriate unit of appraisal is usually the increment. That is because we rarely start from scratch. A business person calculates the consequences of employing extra workers or installing a few more machines. Will the extra costs of production be covered by the extra revenue obtained when the product is sold? Similarly, the Chancellor of the Exchequer starts from the position that the rate of income tax is (say) 25 pence in the pound and therefore calculates the effects of a (marginal) change in the rate of tax to 26 pence in the pound.

Our third basic concept is efficiency. Efficiency means that it is not possible to maintain the present level of output with less input, or that it is impossible to get more output of a good from given inputs.

Efficiency therefore has a fairly specialised meaning in economics. In everyday life it sometimes seems to mean cutting costs, such as wages. For the economist, however, a rise in cost may mean greater efficiency if it causes revenue to rise by a greater amount. Efficiency provides a criterion by which we can judge the success or otherwise of any act. When economic circumstances change, so will efficiency. Thus if people work harder or longer this may increase efficiency, but it may reduce it because output will also change.

In economic analysis these three concepts often interact. Thus in **micro-economics** (the study of individual institutions such as firms), economists analyse such questions as the effect on efficiency if a firm makes a decision to increase output (a marginal decision). This will also involve consideration of the opportunity cost. These three concepts also underlie **macro-economics** (the study of the economy as a whole).

The theoretical framework of economics is one which seeks to improve the allocation of resources. This often involves comparing the costs and benefits of actions and drawing appropriate conclusions, making use of concepts such as opportunity cost, marginality and efficiency. The costs and benefits may be measurable in money terms, but this can sometimes be impossible or difficult. For example, how is the loss evaluated when a factory is built which ruins a beautiful view?

The basic concepts discussed in this introduction underlie the whole of economics. They will frequently re-appear in the rest of the book because they are used by economists of all perspectives to develop economic arguments.

For Rachel Atkinson: greatly loved, because greatly loving.
(1966-1985)

1 Why Economists Disagree

'If all the economists in the world were laid end to end they wouldn't reach a conclusion.' Economists disagree for a very good reason; no one possesses ultimate truth. Like other people, economists tend to associate with those who share their own values and opinions and hence various schools of thought develop. This chapter identifies three main perspectives which are referred to throughout the book.

- One group who, for the moment, will be referred to as free market economists, focus their attention on the individuals who provide goods and services, and argue that governments should give more incentives to such individuals. They believe that markets are the best way to allocate resources and that government intervention should be limited.
- Interventionists argue that there is a greater role for government, for example, in combatting unemployment. They believe that, whilst markets are important, they often fail to allocate resources in a satisfactory way.
- Marxists argue that in a capitalist system economic crises are inevitable and so a change in the entire system is needed.

Although many economic debates can be approached through these three perspectives, there are others which cannot. Debates about the size of firms, for example, involve other groups. Where appropriate, debates will focus on these other viewpoints.

Reasons for disagreement

It is only in the worlds of dreams or dictators that everyone agrees. In such realms either everything is perfect and all 'truths' are known, so there is nothing to disagree about, or the dictator lays down 'the truth' and everyone is forced to agree. Fortunately there is no dictator of economic theory. Economists believe that they live in the real world and not in the land of dreams. Hence they disagree with each other and occasionally with their own previously expressed opinions. This disagreement is a virtue. Since no economist would claim to have discovered the ultimate truth about the subject, it follows that what is written and spoken by economists is less than the whole truth. Therefore criticism of such untruths or partial truths is necessary, for it is only by rigorous criticism that the subject will progress.

Some economists claim that economics is a science and uses scientific methods of enquiry. There are various ways in which scientific knowledge develops. One which is often fruitful is based on the gradual development of understanding. Scientists build on their knowledge of what has gone before. X puts forward a theory, Y points out a flaw and Z improves the theory. Hence the development of understanding depends on criticising the work of others.

There are several reasons why economists disagree.

Ignorance

Economists disagree because they are ignorant. This statement applies to scholars of all disciplines. Until ultimate truth is known, if it ever is, people will make false statements which reflect their ignorance. Consequently economics books, like those of other subjects, cannot be regarded as conveying 'ultimate truth'.

Particular difficulties facing social scientists

If all scientists face the problem of ignorance, those working in social sciences, such as economics, face particular difficulties. One reason is that the focus of their attention is people and people's behaviour changes. The same family will save this year, but decide to spend next year. At another time they will want work, but as time passes they may be content to stay at home. If taxes are increased, some people will decide to work more in order to maintain their income after tax, whilst others will work less because they decide work is no longer worthwhile. Moreover, people's behaviour changes over time because they learn from their experiences. An atom of hydrogen will always act like an atom of hydrogen, but people will sometimes change their actions when faced with a similar situation. This makes it very difficult, perhaps even impossible, to derive any general laws of human behaviour. An economic 'law' which seems to operate in one country, or at one period of time, may prove to be quite inadequate elsewhere or at other times. Human beings are complex creatures, so it is not surprising that academics who try to derive laws which will predict their actions are often wrong.

Inadequate methods

Economists also disagree because their methods are not good enough to reveal the whole truth. Economic theory is an attempt to explain and interpret economic data, for example, to determine the causes and effects of economic events. These explanations are often expressed in terms of 'if this, then that'; for example, if the price of fish rises then people will eat less fish, or if the government increases its spending then there will be a fall in unemployment. However, in complex societies such predictions can never be absolute; the demand for fish may not fall, even if its price does rise, if there is a shortage of meat or if there is a successful advertising campaign for fish.

Such predictions depend on the assumption of *ceteris paribus* – that other things remain equal. In real life, however, other things do not remain equal. A prediction that was previously successful may not be so at another time or in another place.

Testing theories

The only way to test economic theories is to match them against the evidence. This may seem obvious, but in practice evidence cannot prove a theory to be true. That is because facts do not speak for themselves, but have to be interpreted. Which facts should be used? There are millions of economic 'facts', so the ones which are chosen will depend, in part, on the purpose of the investigation and also on the values and attitudes of those undertaking the investigation. For example, there may be disputes between economists over whether the people in a particular area are really poor. How do we decide who is 'poor'? Concentration camp inmates and famine victims are certainly poor, but there is room for considerable disagreement about which people in any particular country can be called poor. Even if this could be agreed, differences of opinion would emerge as to the causes of the poverty.

Some may argue that poverty is caused because:

- people are lazy;
- people are unlucky;
- of ignorance;
- of family background;
- people are the victims of social forces, such as declining industries;
- of bad government policies.

Evidence could be found to support all these possible causes of poverty. Those researchers who believe that the real reason why some people are poor is that they are lazy or ignorant will certainly be able to find examples to support their case, as will those who favour other causes, such as unsatisfactory government policies.

Values

People tend to seek out evidence to support their beliefs and so substantiate their opinions. We can easily find examples of this in other areas of life. Manchester United football fans often talk to other United supporters and reinforce each other in their belief that theirs is the best team. Similarly, people who believe that poverty is a severe problem in the UK may often associate with others who hold similar beliefs and so strengthen this belief. If such people then decide to research the extent of poverty in the country it is not surprising if they find many examples of people living in poverty.

When Manchester United supporters see their striker fall in the opposing team's penalty area, they interpret this fact to support their belief that the striker was fouled and that a penalty is justified. So it is in economics. People who support or oppose trade unions tend to interpret the facts about unions in ways which will support their beliefs.

There is strong disagreement in economics as to whether or not it is possible to develop economic theories which are entirely value free – where the economist's opinions make no difference to the argument or to the evidence which is presented to support or oppose the argument. This 'value free' approach is called **positive economics** and dominated the subject for many years. The positive approach is discussed further in the concluding chapter. Whether or not it is possible for economics to be value free, it is certainly true that in some cases the values and opinions held by economists influence their findings and cause them to disagree with other economists. For example, economists are sometimes paid to investigate a problem and this can influence their findings. A leading American economist, J.K. Galbraith, claimed in his autobiography *A Life in our Times* (1981):

'Economics professors often seek outside income, and one obvious place of resource is the big corporation. This is not good. When an economist argues for lower taxes on the affluent, people should be right in believing that he is speaking out of economic perception or compassion and not because he has been bought.'

A perspective approach assumes that there are a variety of ways of seeing an economic problem and that the particular approach adopted will depend on the views of the individual economist.

Two quotations illustrate this point. The first is from a Nobel prize winning economist called Milton Friedman, a passionate supporter of the use of markets to allocate resources. 'I find it hard... to see any justification for graduated taxation solely to redistribute income' *(Capitalism and Freedom,* 1962). On the other hand, Galbraith, an interventionist, argues that '...progressive taxation is indispensable in the civilising effort to attain a greater measure of equality' *(Economics and the Public Purpose,* 1974). Clearly there is a strong probability that the value differences represented by these quotations will lead to different policy prescriptions.

Key ideas

1. The root cause of all disagreement is ignorance. Without ultimate truth, people will disagree.
2. Social scientists face particular difficulties because they study people and people are inconsistent.
3. Economic theories and models are not adequate for the task they face.
4. Economists' values affect their investigations.

Three schools of thought

There are thousands of economists in the world, so any attempt to divide economists into groups is bound to be a rough and ready division. Nevertheless, economists are often divided into three groups, each of which has its own set of beliefs and attendant arguments. However, there are disagreements within each group, just as Christians, Moslems and Hindus each have common underlying beliefs, yet also disagree with others of the same faith.

Economists also share some beliefs with those from other schools of thought, just as some Christians might accept ideas from other religions. Hence the following description of three groups of economists should not be interpreted to mean that there is complete agreement within, or disagreement between, each school of thought. Economists disagree even with those who have quite similar views!

The free market perspective

Many of the ideas of this group of economists derive from the work of Adam Smith (1723-90), whose book *An Enquiry into the Nature and Causes of the Wealth of Nations* (1776) is a masterpiece which has stimulated many later economists. Smith was born in Kirkcaldy in Scotland and later attended the universities of Glasgow and Oxford, where he found the teachers scandalously idle and incompetent (how different from teachers today!). *The Wealth of Nations* was an immediate success. It was published at the beginning of the Industrial Revolution and provided a guide to policies in this new world, for example, advocating free trade and less state control.

Supply side economists focus their attention on the factors which encourage people to produce and exchange more goods and services. Although this title is relatively new, the approach of these economists represents an updating of **classical economics**. Classical economists, such as Adam Smith, were the first to emphasise the use of markets to allocate resources. Their ideas were refined by **neo-classical** economists who developed important concepts such as demand and supply. In the 1970s, a group of economists worried about inflation built on the ideas of the neo-classical economists and stressed the importance of controlling the money supply. Consequently they are sometimes called **monetarists**. The position is even more complicated because some of these economists advocate **new classical macro-economics**. This implies that they take the values and approaches of classical economists and apply them to modern macro-economic problems, such as inflation and unemployment. Such a diversity of names is an indication that this is not a single coherent group, but one which contains a variety of views. In this book, we choose not to explore their detailed differences. Instead, where a specific emphasis is required, such as the view of monetarists, then the appropriate name will be used. In most cases, however, we will use the terms 'market economists' or 'supply side economists' to describe this group.

Adam Smith (1723-1790)

Free market ideas

Despite the differences, the work of economists within this group has a common focus. Their ideas focus on the beliefs and actions of individuals. They believe that individuals know what is in their own interest and are competent to choose wisely. The only exceptions are those who are not able to look after themselves. Milton Friedman, one of the leading economists in the group, wrote that:

'freedom is a tenable objective for responsible individuals. We do not believe in freedom for madmen or children'.

This may seem a reasonable approach, but its consequences are far reaching. Countries such as the United Kingdom have compulsory insurance schemes for illness and old age. Some of the economists in this group believe this should be stopped because it restricts the freedom of the individual. If people want to spend all their money when young and healthy they should be free to choose this option, even if it means that they will be unable to pay for treatment when they are ill and may starve when they become old.

Similarly, it is the responsibility of individuals to seek employment. If people really want work, they can find it. Jobs are always available, but people have to accept lower wages in order to obtain them.

Freedom to choose is a central feature of this approach. Charles Rowley (1978), a leading British supply sider, argues that:

'freedom to choose is an end in itself... The freedom is negative and not positive, ensuring an individual of no particular opportunities, but leaving him free to choose among such alternatives as are available to him without restrictions'.

If individuals are to have the maximum freedom, it follows that the state should play a crucial, but smaller, role in society, particularly in economic affairs. At present the state plays a major role in economic life. To give just a few examples, it spends huge amounts of money on social security, health and education. It subsidises certain goods, such as some bus services, and gives mortgage tax relief to those buying their own homes. It also provides money to encourage industries to move to areas of high unemployment. Free market economists would try to reduce or eliminate many or all of these activities because they limit the freedom of individuals to do what they want.

Put another way, they believe that the best way to allocate resources is to leave it to the market. This is the subject of other chapters. Here it is enough to say that they want to limit the activities of the state to such things as defence, law and order, and the protection of those who are unable to look after themselves because they are children or mentally incompetent. The state should also give top priority in economic policy to the elimination of inflation because this harms individuals.

'In everything we seek to do we must recognise the unique importance of each individual in the scheme of things... We shall look to people, not corporate bodies and institutions, to individual flair and drive... to spearhead our industrial and commercial recovery'

proclaimed Angus Maude (1977), an early supply sider.

Key ideas – summary of the free market approach

1. Economies develop because of the actions of individuals.
2. Individuals are rational and know their own best interests. If individuals are unemployed it is usually because they are not willing to work at prevailing wage rates.
3. The role of the state is important, but it should concentrate on a limited range of activities, such as providing an environment in which individuals can flourish.
4. Market forces are the best way to allocate resources. Trade unions interfere with markets and so are to be discouraged.

Policies

If this belief in individualism, markets and limited government is accepted, then certain policies follow. Individuals are responsible for their own actions, so state spending on social security should be reduced and targeted on those who are unable to help themselves. If individuals are without jobs this is usually because they choose to be unemployed; they could always get work if they were willing to accept lower wages. State 'interference' in business, such as the need for planning permission before building a new factory, should be cut. Legislation to protect workers' rights should be reduced, so employers can make workers redundant more easily, and trade union power weakened because this interferes with market forces. Taxes should be cut, particularly income tax, because this reduces the incentive to work.

At the heart of these policies is individual motivation and the encouragement of incentives to work, innovate and compete in markets.

'The aim should be to promote free markets throughout the world and maximum reliance by all countries on free enterprise in an environment favourable to competition and to individual initiative'

urges Milton Friedman.

The focus of interest of this group of economists can be illustrated by the titles of the books published by the Institute of Economic Affairs, an organisation specialising in the study of markets:

- *The Fallacy of the Mixed Economy.*
- *Too Much Money.*
- *Experiment with Choice in Education.*
- *Shoppers Choice.*
- *What Right to Strike?*
- *The Birth of Enterprise.*

The Interventionist perspective

If supply side economics developed out of the work of Adam Smith and the classical economists of the nineteenth century, interventionist economics can best be illustrated by the ideas of a man who challenged that tradition, John Maynard Keynes.

John Maynard Keynes (1883-1946)

Keynes was born in 1883, the son of a Cambridge University lecturer. He went to a preparatory school and won a scholarship to Eton where he was encouraged by his father's stream of letters, which included such comments as 'Why did you let Smith minor beat you in the Maths test last week?' From Eton he went to Kings College Cambridge where he studied Maths. The rest of his life was spent between Cambridge and London. Keynes was one of the few rich economists. In one summer in the 1920s he made £200,000 tax-free by speculating in international currency markets and used the money to finance his passionate interest in the arts. He founded the Cambridge Arts

Theatre and was later responsible for the formation of the Arts Council. He was an active member of the Bloomsbury group of writers and artists, which included E.M. Forster, Virginia Woolf and Duncan Grant. Bertrand Russell wrote:

'Keynes' intellect was the sharpest and clearest that I have ever known. When I argued with him I felt that I took my life in my hands and I seldom emerged without feeling something of a fool.'

During the Second World War, Keynes was responsible for British economic policy and was the prime mover in the creation of the International Monetary Fund and the World Bank. He died in 1946.

Interventionist ideas

Interventionists believe that although market forces have some virtues, they can also have many undesirable consequences. For example, interventionist economists believe that without some kind of government intervention market forces may lead to:

- persistent unemployment on a large scale, as happened in the 1930s and 1980s;.
- industrialists polluting the atmosphere;
- too many cars in the cities, leading to congestion and accidents;
- sick people being unable to afford medical care.
- young people receiving an inadequate education;
- some regions of the economy facing long-term decline;
- poor housing for some people;
- certain groups in society, for example, the old, those with large families and the handicapped living in unacceptable poverty.

Hence interventionists argue that the government must intervene in the economy to prevent or remedy the undesirable consequences which can result from unregulated market forces. Roy Hattersley, though not an economist, puts the case clearly in his book *Choose Freedom* (1987). He argues that although markets must determine the allocation of resources for many goods and services, they may have to be regulated in various ways, such as by price controls and subsidies or by regulations to protect workers, consumers and the environment.

He continues:

'The pattern of distribution which unrestricted market forces produce automatically and inevitably creates a hierarchical society, in which the needs of the less well-off are neglected in the interest (the immediate financial interest) of the prosperous. A hierarchical society will not create or sustain an adequate health service; nor will it provide all the nation's families with adequate housing or education.'

Note that although Roy Hattersley is a Labour Party politician, people from other political parties would also accept Keynesian arguments.

Key ideas – summary of the interventionist approach

1. Individuals cannot always be self-reliant and often need the help of the state. The old, the sick and the poor are examples. Similarly, if people are unemployed it is usually not their own fault but the result of the system. If one person gets a job, it may be at the expense of others unless more jobs are created.
2. Markets have considerable defects, but are still an important way of allocating resources.
3. Governments should play an active role in economic life to remedy these defects, often by increasing government spending to remedy the inability of individuals to afford desirable goods or to regulate the activities of industry.

Policies

Interventionist policies derive from the basic assumption that governments need to intervene in the economy. Keynesian economists argue that if there is large-scale unemployment, then the government should stimulate the economy by increasing government spending on goods and services. Employers in industries where sales increase will then take on more workers, so reducing unemployment. Similarly, the government should increase spending in the poorer regions of the country and subsidise industries moving to these areas. They also argue that the government should regulate industry, for example, in order to reduce pollution and protect workers against exploitation. Interventionists also favour policies which help disadvantaged groups in society, such as the expansion of the National Health Service, higher social security payments to those in need and greater spending on foreign aid to poorer countries.

Unlike free market economists, interventionists argue that people are sometimes unable to make rational choices and therefore the state must intervene to protect them, for example, by passing laws which stop people selling dubious 'medicines'.

The Marxist perspective

Although Marxist economics has never been dominant in countries such as the UK, it does offer valuable insights and acts as a counterweight to the acceptance of more conventional theories.

Marxist economics derives largely from the work of one person, Karl Marx, who was born in 1818 in Germany and died in 1883 – the year in which Keynes was born. When he was 17 he went to the University of Bonn to study law and took an active part in student life; on one occasion he was imprisoned for a night for drunkenness and on another he was wounded in a duel. He had a long and happy marriage and five children, though three of these died while Marx was still alive. His political views made it difficult for him to obtain work and he was usually hard up. He was forced to leave Germany and spent the latter half of his life in Britain. Marx wrote newspaper articles to raise money and was also active in left wing political activities. With Friedrich Engels he wrote *The Communist Manifesto* (1848), but his economic ideas are to be found in the volumes of *Capital* (Vol. 1 1867, Vol. 2 1885, Vol. 3 1894).

Marxist ideas

The collapse of communist regimes in Eastern Europe in the late 1980s and early 1990s led some people to believe that Marxist ideas had become obsolete. However, modern Marxists in the West argue that these regimes did not really apply Marxist ideas, and that these ideas are still relevant to the analysis of contemporary society.

Marx's economic ideas derive from his political/philosophical analysis. These ideas are very complex, but at the risk of over-simplification it is possible to say that Marx believed he had discovered a universal theory of history. He argued that throughout history societies had been run in the interests of those who owned the dominant means of production. Thus in medieval times the most important means of production was the land and so laws were passed in the interest of the landowners, for example, making poaching punishable by death. He argued that in modern society the dominant means of production is capital, so society is run in the interests of those who own factories and banks. For example, laws are passed attacking trade unions; the media are owned or controlled by the rich and so praise those who make profits and attack those who threaten the status quo. Marx believed that capitalism could not last.

Karl Marx (1818-1883)

'Society as a whole is splitting up into two great hostile camps, into two great classes facing each other'

he wrote in *The Communist Manifesto.* He believed competition between capitalists would cause large firms to take over small ones, so the economy would be characterised by a few giant organisations and these would be opposed by a growing number of workers. In this system conflict and crisis would be inevitable. If firms paid high wages then crises would result because profits would be too low. There would also be a crisis if wages were low because then the workers would not be able to buy enough goods and services to maintain full employment.

Key ideas – summary of the Marxist approach

1. Crises are inevitable in capitalist countries. This means that unemployment will be a recurrent feature of such societies.
2. In the long run, economic crises can only be overcome by a complete change in the system – by a revolution.
3. In the short run, appropriate policies can ameliorate the adverse consequences of the system. These involve greater use of state power, either to nationalise privately owned firms or to make them behave in socially desirable ways, such as undertaking functions which are beneficial but not profitable.
4. Markets have a part to play, but these can lead to undesirable consequences, such as unemployment and shortages of desirable goods. Hence the government should intervene to improve the position.

Policies

Marxist economic policies derive from this basic analysis. Economic crises are inevitable and in the long run only a complete change of the system will solve the problems of capitalism. In the short run, however, Marxist economists argue that appropriate policies can improve the economy. These policies usually involve a greater role for the state. Markets have a part to play, but need to be managed so they work in the interests of people and not the capitalists. 'Production for need, not profit' would be accepted as an appropriate slogan by modern Marxists. They also believe that, left to itself, a capitalist system will lead to greater divisions in society. Therefore the government should increase taxes on the rich and improve welfare benefits for the disadvantaged.

Marxists believe that the state needs to own and run the most important industries in the economy, such as banking. Only in this way can the country be sure that there will be high levels of investment, that useful goods and services which are not profitable will be produced and that industries will continue to produce in declining regions. Thus Marxists would tend to keep unprofitable coal mines open in some areas because they serve as a focus for community life and because profit is not a valid way to estimate the contribution of an industry to the community. Marxists also advocate the use of subsidies to persuade privately owned firms to act in socially desirable ways. Firms might be given grants to encourage them to move to areas where unemployment is high or to maintain unprofitable services, such as rural bus routes. To combat unemployment, Marxists argue that the government should increase its spending along the lines which Keynesian economists advocate, but they tend to suggest that greater amounts of money should be spent. Many Marxists would also support controls on imports to protect domestic industries.

Conclusion

No economist possesses ultimate truth. Economists disagree because the world is so complex that we can only hope to understand small parts of how an economy works. Moreover, our inability to understand complex problems is compounded by inadequate methods; complex problems require complicated methods of analysis and all the computers in the world are insufficient to master its economic problems.

People differ in their values and attitudes; this affects the way people see the world and its problems. Often the way economists approach a problem will reflect their underlying beliefs and, because these differ, so will their economic analyses. An economist who believes that contraception is wrong will have a very different approach to the analysis of population to one who favours the use of contraceptives. These differences between economists lead to different schools of thought or perspectives.

Three main perspectives have been outlined in this chapter, each with its own ideas and policies. Others will be examined, where appropriate, in later chapters. However, the following should always be taken into account.

- There is some agreement between economists from different groups, for example, that rising living standards depend on making the economy more efficient.
- There are differences between economists in the same group, for example, about the precise policies needed to bring down the rate of inflation. More dramatically, Trotsky, a leading Marxist, ended up with an ice pick in his head, put there by another Marxist. Fortunately, few disagreements end up this way or there would be a considerable shortage of economists!

Many of the disagreements between these groups of economists focus on the use of markets to allocate resources and this is the concern of the next two chapters.

Data questions

The case for an active industrial policy

The call for a more active industrial policy rests on a different understanding to that current in government circles on the nature and place of market forces in industrial reconstruction and on a different set of attitudes to the importance and role of trade unions. 'Leaving things to the market' will not produce in the UK the scale, quality and competitiveness of manufacturing industry required to sustain employment and living standards. We need a more active partnership between industry, labour and the state so that we have a policy of sharing industrial power under active state leadership.

Source: Adapted from Centre for Industrial Policy and Performance, Bulletin No. 2, University of Leeds, Summer 1993.

The Welfare State

Is the Welfare State a monumental achievement by a socially aware, democratic government? Or is it a necessary requirement for the perpetuation of a capitalist system? Some speak with reverence about the achievements of the Welfare State – the support for the needy, the care given to those who are ill and the benefits for the deprived. It could, however, be seen as an essential tool of a capitalist system. After all, doesn't the state service the reproduction of capitalism? Doesn't the system of social security produce a reserve army of labour and ensure that labour is controlled? State power is the power of capital. It serves capital's interests and has been captured by it.

Source: Adapted from Brown C. V. & Jackson P.M., *Public Sector Economics* 4th ed., Basil Blackwell, 1990.

Question 1

1. Identify the perspectives illustrated in the above articles. Justify your choices.
2. Outline the policies that each perspective would advocate to solve (i) lack of economic growth and (ii) inflation.

Agriculture

Since the late 1920s farm protection has taken root. Barriers to trade in some farm commodities have climbed tenfold. Farm protection is now out of hand. American farmers top up every dollar of their earnings from farming with nearly 50 cents in handouts from American taxpayers and consumers. Subsidies double the incomes of their cousins in the EC. In Japan twice as much of farmers' money comes from the state as from the land. Arguments for free trade have fallen on stony ground. It seems not to matter that a world in recession throws away $100 billion by government interference in markets.

Source: 'A survey of agriculture', *The Economist*, 12 December 1992.

2 Allocating Resources: Market and Command Economies

No society can supply all the goods and services which people would like. That is because resources of land, labour and capital are scarce relative to society's desires for goods and services. Consequently difficult decisions have to be made. Since we cannot produce all the goods and services people would like, we need to decide what we should produce (the allocation problem), what methods should be used to produce these goods (the production problem), and who should receive the goods and services which are produced (the distribution problem).

● There is no perfect way to solve these problems. In command economies the major economic decisions, such as what to produce, are made by the government. Examples of command economies are China, Cuba, Burma, North Korea, and the UK during the Second World War.

● However, command economies have a number of limitations – they are often rigid and bureaucratic. Consequently many economists favour market forces as a way of solving the economic problems arising from scarcity.

How should economic systems be judged?

If we want to judge someone's height we have a universally accepted criterion and method. We simply measure the person using a unanimously accepted scale, such as inches or centimetres.

Making judgements on economic systems is a different proposition because there is no generally accepted measure, and because some ways of organising the economy produce good results in one area but not in another. Moreover, there are no generally accepted criteria for deciding what an economic system should achieve. Despite the difficulties, it is probably true to say that for many economists, and perhaps the majority of people in countries such as the UK, the desirable characteristics of an economy are:

- rapid economic growth;
- low levels of unemployment;
- no inflation;
- efficiency;
- equity (fairness);
- a satisfactory composition of output – for example, resources are used to produce those commodities which people want;
- a satisfactory balance of payments.

Note that this list would not be accepted by all economists. For example, some people believe that we put too much emphasis on economic growth and too little on the conservation of natural resources. This would be the view of Green Party supporters in many countries.

Different types of economy attempt to achieve these goals in different ways. In this chapter we will examine two important types – the **command economy** and the **market economy**. In practice these two types of economic system do not exist in a pure form, so that all modern economies are a mixture of the two types.

Nevertheless it is useful to consider these 'ideal

types' because they enable us to examine the economic problem in two contrasting contexts.

The command economy

A command economy is one where the allocation of resources is decided by a centralised administrative process.

The command economy is so called because economic decisions are made by commands from authorities who are responsible for planning the economy; consequently this system is sometimes also called a planned economy. This type of system was used in countries such as the UK in the Second World War, when the government took powers to order factories to produce certain goods and the Minister of Labour had power to direct labour – men and women – into particular occupations or into the armed forces. Consumers may have wanted chocolates or bananas, but the country needed weapons of war; central planning ensured that these goods were produced.

Command economies are closely associated with the Marxist perspective. This is because Marxists advocate the abolition of capitalism, and in existing command economies most of the means of production are owned by the state so that there is only a small capitalist class.

Because of the link between Marxism and command economies, the best examples of command economies used to be the socialist states of Eastern Europe and the Soviet Union. Now that these countries are becoming market economies countries such as China, Cuba and Burma provide the best examples, but even here considerable use is made of market mechanisms. Command economies, however, are not always Marxist. They include any economy where the basic decisions about resource allocation are made by the state.

The idea of a command economy is relatively simple and is illustrated in Figure 2.1. The authorities – usually the government – decide the priorities of the system. This is necessary because no country can provide all the goods and services that are desirable. In the Soviet Union in the 1930s, the leader Joseph Stalin decided that the top priority should be given to heavy industry. This means that resources were targeted at industries such as coal, steel and electricity, and these industries expanded quickly. The consequence was that few resources were then available for consumer goods such as furniture, carpets or clothes, so living standards remained low.

Figure 2.1: *Allocating resources in a command economy*

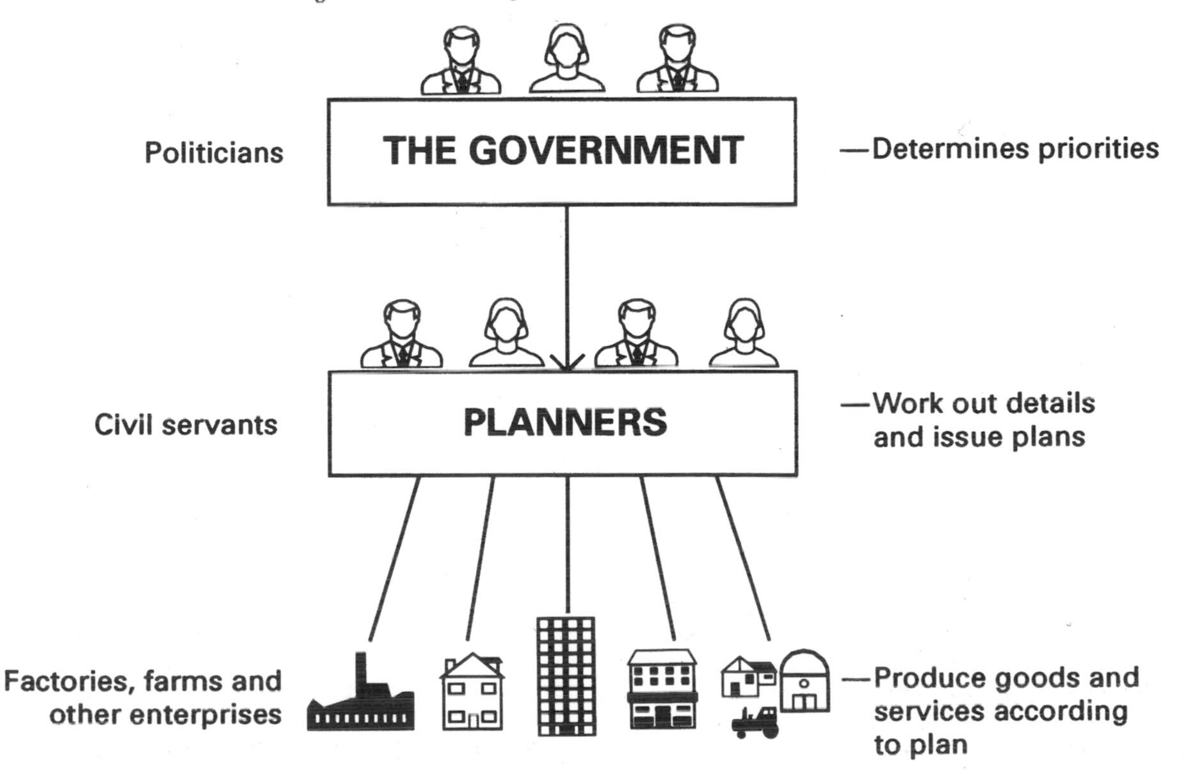

Once the priorities are decided, they have to be translated into orders. This is often done through a series of plans, often carried out over five or ten years, although plans for such long periods have to be adjusted in the light of changing circumstances. This is done by a planning organisation and is a complex job. For example, if one of the priorities decided by the government is to improve housing, then the planners will have to expand the output of cement, steel and wood since these are all used in building. In turn more electricity will be needed to produce the steel and in turn this will require more coal or oil. Thus a decision to expand one sector necessitates changes in many other parts of the economy and these have all to be planned. Moreover, the planners also have to plan the supply of labour. Will there be enough electrical engineers, secretaries or carpenters? Eventually, the plans are refined and individual factories and farms receive their targets. If the plan has been well drawn up, and if there are no hitches, then the national targets will be met and the plan deemed a success. Indeed, sometimes factories will exceed their targets and the plan be overachieved.

In particular countries the details of the command economy will vary. For example, the plan can be of variable lengths. In some countries agriculture is a central part of the plan; in others there is little government regulation of farmers. Also, in some countries such as China there are areas where planning is supreme whilst in other areas there is little planning. This has been called 'One country, two systems'.

Despite these differences, the central features of a planned economy are clear.

The government decides the priorities – what shall be produced – and individual factories are set targets. If these are accomplished, the Plan will be successful. In practice, the system is more complex. The manager of a factory or farm knows the problems and possibilities of the organisation and this information is fed up the hierarchy. If managers think that their target is impossible they will say so and the target will then often be adjusted. Thus to some extent orders are written by those who receive them. Influences such as the weather, which cannot be planned, also affect the system, so that plans cannot be rigid and inflexible but are constantly adjusted in the light of changing circumstances. Moreover, although the authorities can plan production, they cannot really plan consumption. If families do not wish to buy a particular product they cannot be forced to do so.

In this system the authorities make relatively little use of prices to influence production or consumption, though if they wish to discourage consumption of a particular product (such as tobacco) they will put up the price. Prices, however, do also play a part in the private sector of the economy. Many people have small plots of land on which they grow produce to sell and prices do influence what will be grown. High prices for a particular product will persuade people to produce more of it next year. In general, however, the role of the price system is one of the fundamental differences between a planned economy and a market system. The private producers just described are characteristic of the market system rather than the planned economy, but they do not change the nature of the system because they produce only a small proportion of total output in most planned economic systems.

In command economies prices are fixed by the state and are usually based on the cost of production, plus a 'profit' margin, though prices for favoured goods such as public transport and housing are kept deliberately low. Once prices have been decided they are then only changed at infrequent intervals.

The planned economy in China

In practice, the operation of a planned economy will differ from one country to another. In some, use will be made of market forces. In China, for example, the First Five Year Plan was introduced in 1953 and based very closely on the Soviet model. It gave priority to heavy industry, and resulted in rapid growth in this area of the economy. Over time the system was modified. It was found impracticable to develop a plan covering a number of years, for example, because the system could not collect the detailed economic statistics which were necessary for detailed long term planning. Consequently, five year planning was abandoned and the economy was directed by annual plans together with several hundred industrial projects which were implemented as the opportunity arose, without any date being given for their initiation or completion.

Ultimate power in preparing the plan belongs to the central party committee, though the actual work is done by others. The plan is the result of a dialogue. The central planners pass down targets, but these are then altered as a result of discussions, both at the level of the individual production unit, and by district and state authorities. The plan is then finalised by the State Economic Commission, which coordinates the plans. These include production and marketing targets, by value and volume, for essential commodities, and plans for foreign trade, investment and wages. Regional authorities plan local transport, housing and local consumer goods.

The Chinese found that an all-inclusive plan was impracticable in such a large country. This is because there are hundreds of thousands of products and many more variations of these products; these cannot be covered by a single plan. Consequently only a few hundred products (about half the output of the economy) are covered by the State Planning Commission. Detailed planning was found to damp enthusiasm in agriculture, so agricultural collectives are given quotas of products they must produce and sell to the state; but they can decide to produce more than the quota, and also produce different foods. They can then benefit from selling this extra production through the market.

The Chinese economy also deviates from a narrow command economy model because it makes considerable use of prices to influence the allocation of resources. The central planning authority uses prices to control consumption, the distribution of income, and the rate of inflation. For example, prices of basic foods are kept low in order to ensure that even the poorest families can buy necessities. Public transport is also very cheap, but prices of luxuries are kept high to discourage consumption.

Advantages of a command economy

A command economy can have substantial benefits. If the priorities of the people are those of the planners, then resources can be concentrated to satisfy these priorities. This was the case in the UK in the Second World War. Although people would have liked more consumer goods, it was generally realised that priority had to be given to the war effort and the result of planning was a huge increase in the production of weapons of war. In the USSR priority was given to goods and services such as public transport and housing, classical music, basic foodstuffs and approved books. The prices of these were kept low and most were in abundant supply, though housing, particularly in the big cities, remained a problem area. Education and health were also given priority. In East Germany, sport was given a high priority and the result was that this small country was the most successful in the world in many sports.

Unemployment ceases to be a major problem in command economies. That is because the state planning organisations plan labour as well as production. If the planners decide to expand the motor vehicle industry, for example, they have to ensure that sufficient workers with the right skills are available. Moreover, the managers of individual units try to ensure that they have sufficient workers to fulfil their targets. Although workers can be sacked for breaches of labour discipline, they seem to be able to find other jobs quite easily. Although this is an advantage to the individual workers, it can lead to labour inefficiency because idle workers know that other work is available should they be sacked. Full employment does not mean that people always get the job they would like; as in other societies, they have to take what is on offer.

Disadvantages of command economies

Despite its undoubted benefits, the command economy contains many drawbacks. If the planners determine priorities, these may not be what ordinary people would want, so that individual choice is subordinated to that of society. Command economies tend to restrict consumer choice by providing only a limited range of goods and services. People who like chewing gum, drinking genuine champagne, wearing jeans or driving their own car would tend to be frustrated because goods such as these tend to have a low priority.

Moreover, many products are of low quality. In a command economy an organisation which produces goods where quality is low cannot go bankrupt, so that the consequences of producing faulty products are less drastic than in a market economy. Whilst it is possible for the planners to specify that goods should be produced up to a certain standard, it is difficult to ensure that they do meet these standards. Planning services is particularly difficult. It is hard to plan how many lifts will need repairs, how many pipes will burst or how many cars will break down, or to ensure that the quality of such repairs will be satisfactory. Consequently services such as these are often undertaken through a 'black market' which operates outside the official system.

In many planned economies there are shortages of goods. For example, a correspondent in *The Times* wrote that the planned economy in Burma did not succeed in producing the goods which people want. This led to goods as diverse as cement and deodorants being smuggled in from Thailand, making them very expensive. The correspondent found a deodorant on a market stall

which in the UK would have cost about 75 pence. At the official Burmese rate of exchange the cost in Rangoon would have been £75.

One reason for these deficiencies is that the planners suffer from information overload. This makes them slow to respond to deficiencies. Detailed plans have to be drawn up for thousands of factories and farms and then co-ordinated. The co-ordination of such plans for an entire economy is clearly an immense task and the bureaucracy is frequently overwhelmed.

At the level of the individual plant there are often considerable inefficiencies. Managers want to ensure that their part of the plan will be fulfilled. This means that they try to negotiate easy targets so that these can be achieved. In turn, Ministers go along with this so that their Ministry can achieve its targets. This means that even when targets are achieved or surpassed there may still be a considerable amount of inefficiency in the system. Moreover, in order to achieve their targets managers often try to ensure that they have hidden reserves of labour and raw materials. Since shortfalls and delays in supplies will occur, the careful manager will try to keep spare supplies knowing that these can always be used to bargain with other units if shortages do occur. A unit with a shortage of buttons but a surplus of cloth may be able to arrange a swap. The existence of these excess supplies means that the system is inefficient; the ratio of inputs to outputs is higher than it need be.

Some incentives can easily be incorporated into the working of a command economy. Higher productivity can be rewarded by higher wages. It is much more difficult to introduce incentives for new products. Bacon flavoured crisps or video recorders would probably never be invented in a planned economy because there are no rewards for doing so and because goods such as these would receive a low priority. Production units are often slow to introduce new technologies because improved performance may lead to higher targets in the next period and to different requirements for raw materials, which might not be available. Consequently, technology has tended to follow that in the West.

Key ideas – command economies

1. Command economies are sometimes called planned economies because the crucial economic decisions are planned by a central authority.

2. They are often associated with a Marxist approach because they often feature public ownership of the means of production.
3. Supporters of command economies say that they can ensure resources are used to produce the most desirable goods and that unemployment can be reduced or eliminated.
4. Disadvantages of command economies can include lack of incentives for producers and choice for consumers, poor quality of goods, bureaucracy and shortages.

The market economy

Opposing the ideas of the command economy is the market economy, sometimes called the free enterprise system. In a market economy resources are allocated by the operation of market forces of demand and supply working through the price system. In this system no individual or organisation consciously seeks to solve the basic economic problems of what to produce, how to produce, or for whom should production be organised. Instead economic agents such as families or firms seek to promote their own self-interest. This system was first analysed by Adam Smith (1776) in *The Wealth of Nations:*

'It is not from benevolence of the butcher, the brewer or the baker that we expect our dinner but from their regard to their own self-interest'.

In other words, all the participants in the system – workers, employers, consumers – try to maximise their own utility. Consumers will try to buy goods and services as cheaply as they can. Producers will try to charge high prices and pay low wages so that they maximise their profits. Workers will aim to obtain high wages. Through all this self-seeking develops a system which needs no planning, but which works as if an 'invisible hand' was guiding the economy.

How a market system works

Let us take a few examples to show how such a system might work. We can start with an increase in demand. Assume that for some reason there is an increase in the birth rate. Other things being equal, this will mean that producers of products used by babies, such as nappies, cots, push chairs and baby foods, will find that they sell more products. If production does not rise then shortages will develop. Rational producers and shopkeepers seeking to maximise their incomes will respond to these shortages by putting up prices in order to increase profits. Manufacturers of similar products will note these higher profits and diversify into the market for childcare products. Some shops which sold cycles will now sell push chairs; some which traded in teenage clothes will change to maternity wear. In this way resources – labour, land and capital – will be re-allocated to produce the goods and services which consumers want. The wishes of consumers will have led to changes which help satisfy these wishes. Indeed, the extra supplies may force down prices so that consumers not only benefit because they have increased supplies of goods which they want, but also because these may cost less.

Figure 2.2: *Consumer sovereignty*

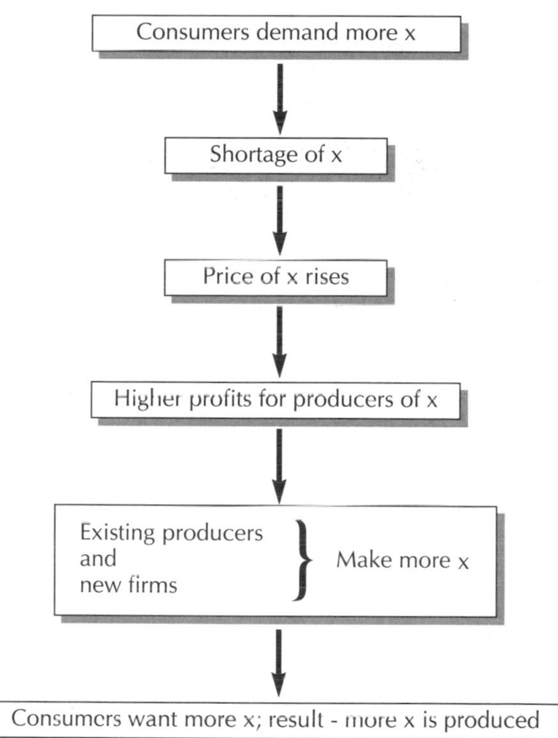

Resources are also re-allocated if consumers choose less of a product. If men want fewer hats, ties or suits, the market responds by producing fewer of these commodities. Shops which sell these commodities will have to cut their prices to clear their stocks and either go bankrupt or else diversify into selling clothes that people want. Producers will similarly be forced to respond to the dictates of market forces. If they continue to produce clothes which consumers are unwilling to buy they will soon go out of business. Their factories and workers will become available to make products which consumers wish to buy.

These changes in consumer demand will also affect wages. Workers in industries where there is a rising demand for the products that they make will be able to benefit by negotiating higher wages. Those in declining industries will find that their wages fall relative to those in other sections of the economy. Some workers will respond to this by changing jobs. In this way consumer preferences for particular products will encourage labour to be re-allocated, so that workers are available to produce the goods that people want.

The system also responds to changes in the supply of goods. For example, if bad weather in Brazil cuts the supply of coffee, this will lead to a shortage. Producers and shopkeepers, being rational, will respond by putting up the price. In the long run this may stimulate producers in other countries to increase production. The rise in coffee prices may also encourage some consumers to switch to other drinks such as tea. If tea producers believe that the switch is likely to be long lasting they will increase production.

Thus the system works to allocate resources whether the impetus for change is a movement in demand or in the supply of goods. Markets are able to function in this way because of the operation of the price system.

The price system

A price system enables people to co-operate in attempting to solve economic problems even though they do not know each other. Millions of economic transactions take place each day and the prices that result from these voluntary transactions co-ordinate the activities of producers and consumers in such a way that everyone benefits – if the system works well. In order to do this the price system must perform three functions.

Information

It must transmit information to the people who need to know. If there is a boom in one sector of the economy, shopkeepers selling these products will increase their orders to the manufacturers and, in order to persuade manufacturers to supply more goods, they will probably have to pay higher prices. This will induce the suppliers to increase their workforce – or make it possible for them to pay overtime rates of pay. All the people involved in this market will be aware of the change in prices. The information will be of no interest to those in different markets and will be ignored by them.

Incentives

The price system must provide incentives to people to act in certain ways. If the price of a product is rising it will pay producers to increase output because this will cause their profits to rise. If wages in one occupation are rising it will pay some workers to shift jobs. If one shop sells a product at a lower price than its competitors then it will pay consumers to buy at that shop (though there are costs involved in changing jobs and in shopping around, particularly the time involved). To give a real example, in 1979 the price of oil doubled and then doubled again. This had many effects on the world economy. It provided an incentive for producers to explore potential oil fields and for consumers to use less oil. People stopped buying oil fired central heating. Electricity producers used more coal fired stations and decided to build nuclear powered generating plants. Consumers bought fewer large cars, whilst sales of cars giving more miles per gallon increased, so encouraging producers to introduce new models which used less petrol. All these changes occurred without central direction because of the information and the incentives provided by fluctuations in price.

Income distribution

The price system must also influence the distribution of income. People's earnings depend on the price they receive for their services. In the case of employed workers, wages will depend largely on the success of their employer's business and on the demand and supply of people with their particular skills. A 'striker' for Glasgow Rangers will receive very high earnings because he has very scarce skills which are needed by a wealthy employer. People with skills that are not required by employers receive low earnings. Someone who is good at sweeping the streets will receive low earnings because there are many people with this ability relative to the demand for them.

Advantages of markets

The central belief of many economists is that markets offer the best way of allocating resources.

In the first place, they give consumers enormous choice. Whether we want to buy a radio, a pen or a haircut, the market will provide a wide range of alternatives. The goods will vary in quality, in design and in price, so that knowledgeable consumers can maximise their satisfaction by buying goods and services that suit their particular purposes. The choices offered by a modern market economy are so familiar that we tend to take them for granted, but no society in history has offered so many alternatives to consumers as does the modern market economy.

Moreover, the discipline of the market works to ensure a high quality of goods. A producer who makes shoddy products may be able to sell them once, but the rational consumer will not succumb twice. Good products drive out bad ones and therefore business people who produce poor products go out of business. Firms making quality goods will be rewarded with high profits.

Another feature of markets is that they provide incentives to desirable behaviour. If a firm can organise so that it makes its product at less cost than its competitors, it will be rewarded by higher profits. Thus built into the system are features that encourage efficiency. Business people are therefore constantly searching for ways to cut costs by introducing new techniques of production and better management of resources. The firm benefits because profits rise, but consumers also benefit because competing firms become more efficient and competition keeps down prices.

The market rewards those who provide what consumers want. Hence it encourages innovation. People who make new or better products desired by consumers benefit from larger sales and profits. Every year thousands of new products are marketed. Many are rejected by consumers, but others increase consumer choice and satisfaction.

All this takes place without any great bureaucracy to organise it. The system is decentralised. Decisions are made by millions of consumers and thousands of producers and co-ordinated through the invisible hand of the price system. The mass of civil servants and government planners required by the command economy are not needed in a market economy. This not only makes available the services of thousands of workers who can produce goods for the consumer rather than spending their time passing paper, it also means that the system is very flexible and responds quickly to changes. A bad harvest, a strike, a new discovery – those interested will be made aware by changes in price and will take appropriate action without any need for government action.

Some supporters of markets believe the system has close affinities with democracy; Enoch Powell, in *Freedom and Reality* (1969), claims:

'The free enterprise economy is the true counterpart of democracy; it is the only system which gives everyone a say. Everyone who goes into a shop and chooses one article rather than another is casting a vote in the economic ballot with thousands or millions of others. That choice is signalled to production and investment and helps to mould the world just a tiny fraction nearer to people's desire. In this great and continuous general election of the free economy, nobody, not even the poorest is disenfranchised; we are voting all the time.'

Thus its supporters claim that a market system is characterised by **consumer sovereignty,** where the wishes of consumers are translated into action by producers.

Market failure

Criticisms of the pro-market argument

Those economists who believe that markets have only a limited part to play in allocating resources advance a number of arguments. In the first place they claim the analogy with democracy is misleading. In a democracy each person has only one vote; each person's wishes carry equal weight. In a market economy the reverse is true. The system does not provide what the majority of people would choose, but what the people with money would choose. A millionaire has far more preferences satisfied than does a pauper. Put another way, the argument for markets assumes that the existing distribution of income is satisfactory. To this criticism, some pro-marketeers would respond that if the distribution of income is not satisfactory it should be corrected by tax and social security changes and not by government interference in the goods market.

Some critics argue that the apparent choice provided by markets is largely an illusion. Choice depends on knowledge. Unless consumers are well informed, they may choose poor quality products at a high price. Many competing consumer goods are complex and technical so that only a few people are really competent enough to understand the differences between them. In addition, better goods may be available elsewhere, but nobody has complete knowledge of what products are available in every shop.

Choice is limited in another way. Advertisers spend large amounts of money to influence consumers. If this is successful then spending represents not consumer choice, but the influence of the advertising agency. Rather than consumer sovereignty we would have producer sovereignty. Instead of the sequence:

consumers choose → producers respond

which is supposed to happen in a market system, we would have:

firms plan production and marketing → consumers respond

Supporters of this line of argument point to the huge size of firms in the modern economy and claim it is naive to expect giants of industry to respond passively to the whims of consumers. Instead they plan their production, often years in advance, and then carefully market their products to try to ensure that their plans are successful.

Weaknesses of markets

Critics of markets point out that unemployment is common in such systems. Whilst the level of unemployment varies over time, it is never totally absent and sometimes reaches very high levels. It is therefore necessary for governments to intervene in order to reduce the level of unemployment. The existence of unemployment is a specific example of a more general argument; that there seems to be a tendency for markets to break down in disorder. Marxists would argue that this is an inherent tendency. The sequence of events depicted earlier in Figure 2.2 can break down in various ways:

- There can be volatile swings caused by overshooting. The traditional example is the 'pig cycle'. If there is an increased demand for pork or bacon the price of pigs will rise. This will cause more farmers to breed pigs and in time these will come on to the market. This excess supply will force down the price and cause many farmers to switch to other products. Eventually a shortage will occur causing the price to rise and encourage more farmers to breed pigs. So the cycle can continue without demand and supply ever reaching a stable equilibrium.
- All markets are related – some more closely than others – so that instability in one market will affect others. Thus large changes in the foreign exchange market will affect domestic prices, cause firms to postpone investment and create unemployment.
- Markets depend on money. Because people may at one time choose to spend and at another to save, markets are often subject to disruption.
- Markets are not always competitive. They are often dominated by a few firms so that competition may be limited. If this is so, consumers will not receive the full benefits of choice and low price which markets are supposed to confer. This is discussed in more detail in Chapter 6.

Public goods

A specific limitation of markets is that they are not able to supply the most desirable quantity of **public goods**. These have two characteristics. One is non-rivalry in consumption. This means that any individual can consume the good without reducing the quantity available for others – if I listen to the radio, it does not prevent anyone else from listening to the same programme. The other characteristic of public goods is that they are non-excludable. This means that they cannot be withheld from one person without withholding them from everyone. A lighthouse is a good example. Once it is built the owner cannot stop passing ships from seeing it and being warned away from any danger. Other examples of public goods include defence, street lighting and flood defence systems.

Since public goods are available to all, they are not provided in the right quantities by markets because businesses cannot charge all those who benefit. Some people would have a free ride – that is benefit without paying. In the case of a private good, such as ice cream, this does not happen. The producer can ensure that only those who pay get the goods. Consequently whilst private goods are provided by markets, public goods are usually provided by the state because otherwise too few of these goods would be produced. A complication of this argument is that the distinction between private and public goods is not always clear, particularly in areas such as health and education. The existence of these semi-public goods means that economists who believe most strongly in market forces argue that services such as education, health and housing are not pure public goods and so should be left largely to market forces, whilst other economists believe the state should intervene on a substantial scale to ensure that an appropriate level of services is supplied.

Merit goods

Merit goods pose a similar dilemma. These are goods which the community believes would be consumed in too small a quantity if left to market forces. If people had to pay an economic price for goods such as classical music concerts, using swimming pools, education or roof insulation, the quantity demanded would be much smaller than at present. Consequently the state intervenes in these markets, either to provide the goods or to pay or subsidise provision by others.

The state also intervenes to discourage or prohibit economic 'bads' such as the consumption of cigarettes or heroin. Some extreme proponents of market forces would argue that the state should not intervene in this way because it restricts the choice of rational consumers who desire such goods.

Externalities

Another reason why markets may fail is that externalities are present. These occur when the activities of producers or consumers affect third parties other than through the normal working of the price system. Externalities are sometimes known as spillovers because the effects of an action spill over on to others. There are lots of examples.

- Throwing take away containers into the street.
- Releasing industrial waste into the river or air.
- Night flights by aeroplanes.
- Commuters or lorries causing congestion.

These are all negative externalities. There are also some positive ones.

- Beekeepers whose bees pollinate nearby flowers.
- An attractive garden which gives pleasure to others.
- Clearing a rubbish-filled site to build a well-designed factory.

Because people usually only take account of their own costs and benefits, these spillover effects are usually ignored. If these effects are negative, it is argued that society ought to intervene to restrict the freedom of those undertaking the activity (for example, to force firms to reduce pollution) or to take other appropriate action, such as subsidising public transport in order to reduce congestion on the roads. These issues and policies to deal with them are discussed in Chapter 11.

Information

Markets also fail because people do not have the information they need to make the best choices. Hence the state needs to intervene to protect the

consumer. For example, the government intervenes in the market to ensure that taxis are licensed. If anyone could operate a taxi some vehicles would be unsafe, some drivers be violent criminals. Consumers have no way of judging this when they hire a taxi. The state will therefore impose restrictions on vehicles and on who can work as a taxi driver. Similarly, customers cannot judge the usefulness of drugs or the safety of buildings, so the government intervenes by setting regulations which firms in these areas have to satisfy.

Key ideas - summary of the case for and against markets

1. Market systems allocate resources through the interplay of consumer demand and producer supply, with consumer sovereignty being the driving force.
Supporters of markets would claim:
2. The system provides a huge range of consumer choice.
3. It rewards efficient producers and penalises inefficient ones.
4. Markets provide incentives to innovate and to improve existing products.
5. The system adapts quickly to changing circumstances and requires no bureaucracy to administer it.
Critics of unrestricted markets would claim:
6. Whilst choice is important, it is often more apparent than real because producers manipulate consumers, for example, through advertising.
7. Markets often fail to ensure desirable results; for example, unemployment is common.
8. Markets also fail because consumers and producers have imperfect knowledge and because some producers have monopoly power.
9. Instability in one sector (for example, the money market) often spreads to affect others.
10. Markets often do not provide the optimum amount of public and merit goods.
11. Governments should intervene to correct for externalities.

Transition from command to market economies

It is difficult for countries to change systems. That is because institutions, laws and ways of thinking are adapted to a particular environment. Thus when the USSR switched to a command economy it required strong leadership from Lenin and Stalin, together with considerable use of force. They used this to take industries and agriculture into public ownership and to change the ideology of the people. Even so, it was not until a decade after the Revolution that the first Five Year Plan was instituted.

Many countries in the late 1980s and early 1990s began to move from command to market economies. This was partly because of the collapse of the Communist ideology, and partly because of the relatively poor economic performance of command economies over a number of decades.

The process of change

Change from a command to a market economy is difficult. Various reforms need to be undertaken. Laws concerning business have to be changed. For example, Poland passed laws setting up a stock exchange, laws setting out various forms of ownership and laws liberalising foreign investment and trade.

The most obvious changes concern ownership. For example, in 1989 there were 8,000 state owned institutions in Poland and to transfer these to the private sector was a huge task. A popular procedure for large organisations is to transfer state owned enterprises into companies with 100 per cent state ownership of capital. These can then be sold to private investors in the form of shares. Smaller enterprises can be sold directly to private investors. Some state enterprises are so unprofitable that they cannot be sold to the private sector and so have to remain in state ownership or be closed down.

Problems

Privatisation gives rise to problems. For example, many state owned enterprises were monopolies. Are these to be allowed to continue as private monopolies which might exploit consumers? Moreover, many traded extensively with state owned enterprises in other Eastern European countries. These markets have now been much reduced, so the large enterprise is now faced with falling sales.

The change to a market economy has led to large rises in unemployment as newly privatised firms have laid off excess labour. For example, between June 1990 and March 1991, unemployment in Bulgaria rose from only 2,400 to 124,000, in Hungary from 41,000 to 150,000 and in Poland from 568,000 to 1,322,000. This is a shock to people accustomed to lifetime security of employment. The rise in unemployment was accompanied by a fall in output. Thus in 1991 output in Bulgaria fell by 9 per cent, in Poland by 11 per cent, in Romania by 7 per cent and in the former USSR by 4 per cent.

Inflation also accompanies the change to a market economy, partly because governments have printed money to shore up loss-making state enterprises which cannot compete. Consequently, in 1991 prices rose by 128 per cent in Romania, 474 per cent in Bulgaria and 585 per cent in Poland.

The transition to a market economy is accompanied by considerable social changes, often undesirable. Poverty and homelessness increase, and there are rises in the crime rate as people try to adapt to lower incomes and higher prices.

Benefits

These undesirable features may or may not be short term. That will depend in part on the ability of people to change their values and develop an enterprise culture. The hope of those involved is that the problems are transitional, the benefits long term.

However, even in the short term some benefits are apparent. The removal of controls has led to a large increase in the variety of goods available – for those with the money to buy them. For example, in the past tropical fruits such as bananas and oranges were largely unobtainable in many parts of Eastern Europe; now they are widely available, even in winter.

In the longer term, people in these countries hope that the benefits associated with market economies such as greater consumer choice and improvements in the quantity and quality of consumer goods will improve the quality of life. Moreover, they hope that competition between firms will make industry more efficient and that the incentives which market systems provide will lead to rising living standards.

Whatever the success or failure of these economies to adapt to a market economy, the basic argument will remain. What is the most desirable mix of market and state allocation of resources?

Conclusion

At the heart of economics is the problem of scarcity. No society can produce all the goods and services which its citizens would like. Hence disagreements arise about how to choose what goods and services to produce.

Some economists favour command economies, where the most important economic decisions are made by the government and orders are sent to factories and farms telling them what to produce. This system has advantages – it concentrates resources on producing the goods which are thought desirable. However, such systems are often inefficient and bureaucratic. An alternative way to allocate resources is to use markets. Some economists believe these are a marvellous way to allocate resources because they are efficient and reflect the wishes of consumers. Critics – often interventionists or Marxists – believe markets often fail to allocate resources in a satisfactory way and that therefore the government should intervene on a substantial scale to correct these failures. Both command and market systems have limitations. Modern economies are, in practice, mixed economies containing elements of both systems and argument centres on the composition of the mixture. Most Western economies have a market system with some government intervention in order to deal with the criticisms made of markets. The extent of such intervention will depend on the extent to which the market is seen to fail. This is the subject of the next chapter, which concentrates on the market mechanism and the consequences of intervention.

The argument about markets also reflects differing values and political positions. Left wing economists have usually favoured intervention because they believe markets tend to favour the better off sections of society. Those on the right dispute this, or else argue that incentives are necessary and that markets spur the poor to improve their position. In judging this argument, the reader should be aware that writing about markets reflects not only economic judgements but also political beliefs.

Data questions

The command economy in China

'China has a planned economy based on public ownership. Planned production and circulation cover the main body of our national economy. At the same time, the production and circulation of some products are allowed to be regulated through the market without being planned... This serves as a supplement to planned production and circulation, subordinate and secondary to it but essential and subordinate nonetheless. The state secures proportionate and co-ordinated growth of the national economy through overall balancing by economic planning and a supplementary role of market regulation.'

Source: Hu Yaobang, speech to the Twelfth National Congress of the Party, quoted in Xue Muqiao, *China's Socialist Economy*, Foreign Languages Press, Beijing 1986.

Question 1

1. Explain the main features of 'a planned economy'.
2. What part do market forces play in the Chinese economy?

Hungary's transition to a market economy

Hungary has come closer than most East European countries to the point of self-sustaining economic growth and irreversible reform. But this perception appears to be more widespread among foreigners who have invested more than $4 billion over the last three years than among Hungarians, many of whom have seen their living standards drop and social security eroded. Apart from the dozen or so large investments by US and European multinationals, Hungary now has 13,000 joint ventures with foreign companies. More than 10% of exports come from companies with a turnover of less than $1 million, the activities of which are often neither reported in official statistics nor effectively taxed.

Delays in implementing tax reforms and slower than expected privatisation have deprived the treasury of income at a time when expenditure on unemployment pay and modernisation of the structure of government have increased expenditure.

Foreign investment has been crucial in facilitating structural change in the economy. In the past Hungary concentrated on producing buses for the entire region; now it has put itself in a position to become a leading producer and exporter of GM cars as well as up to 60,000 Suzuki cars a year and motor components made by Ford and other multinationals with new plants in the country.

Source: Adapted from 'Recent economic developments in Hungary', Farkas F., *Developments In Economics Vol. 8*, Causeway 1992.

Question 2

1. Explain what is meant by 'multinationals', 'privatisation', and 'structural change in the economy'.
2. Explain the possible (i) advantages; (ii) disadvantages that foreign investment might bring to a former command economy that has introduced a market system.
3. Why do you think that Hungarians should be more pessimistic than foreigners about their future economic position?

THE MARKET IN BRITAIN

* In 1991 one person in twelve in the labour force was unemployed; for males aged 16-19 it was nearly one in five
* The poorest half of the population has only 7% of the wealth of the country
* The UK has the highest mortality rate for breast cancer of any country in Europe
* 260,000 old people were in residential accommodation
* In 1991 there were 170,000 homeless people; of these two thirds had dependent children
* Four in every ten people do not take a holiday of any kind

Source: *Social Trends*, 1993, HMSO.

Question 3

1. To what extent are these facts caused by the operation of the market system?
2. Should the government intervene to change this position? If so, how?
3. How do you think that a command economy would deal with these problems?

3 Demand, Supply and the Market

The previous chapter discussed the relative merits and problems of market and command economies. This chapter focuses on the market economy and particularly on the working of the market mechanism. This is one of the key areas of economics; perhaps **the** key area. In modern countries such as the United Kingdom, markets are used to allocate most resources and to decide what goods and services are produced. The forces of demand and supply interact through the price system in order to allocate these resources. There are, however, instances where government intervention in markets is necessary.

- Supporters of markets would argue that, left to itself, the market will usually allocate resources efficiently. Government intervention should be restricted, for example, to the provision of services such as defence.
- Critics would suggest, as outlined in the previous chapter, that governments need to intervene in order to deal with the consequences of market failure. Intervention can take many forms, including levying taxes, giving subsidies, and fixing maximum and minimum prices. The Common Agricultural Policy of the European Community is another example of government intervention.

In order to examine the role of governments and markets we need first to consider the factors which determine demand and supply, and to show how these interact to bring about market equilibrium, where demand equals supply.

Market equilibrium

A market exists when buyers wishing to exchange money for a good or service are in contact with sellers wishing to exchange goods or services for money.

Markets need not be confined to a single place. They can occur without the buyer and seller actually meeting. This can happen, for example, when people buy and sell shares, or when they buy goods by post or telephone. In a market economy, prices are determined by the interaction of demand and supply.

Demand

By 'demand' economists mean the willingness and ability to pay money for some amount of a particular good or service.

'Demand' in economics has a precise meaning. It is a **desired** quantity, how much of a commodity or service households would wish to purchase at differing prices if the commodity were available. It does not necessarily measure how much they are actually able to purchase. If there were a strike or a crop failure, consumers may wish to buy but not be able to do so. Note that economists distinguish between 'demand' and 'quantity demanded'. 'Demand' describes the behaviour of consumers at every price – so much will be demanded at one price, rather less if the price is higher. 'Quantity demanded' refers to a particular price: 'At a price of £50 consumers will demand a thousand units a week.'

There are several factors which influence how much of a good consumers will demand. The level of consumers' incomes, an advertising campaign and the price of competing products are just three of these factors. In order to analyse the effect of changes in these variables we will make use of a technique much used by economists, namely to assume *ceteris paribus* – that all factors except one remain unchanged. This enables us to estimate the effect of a change in one variable.

We will first examine the relationships between price and demand. The other influences will be examined later. For most items the relationship is clear; demand will rise as price falls. The promoter of a CD may sell a million if the price is £5, at £25 sales may fall to a few thousand. Similarly, a chip shop which charged a penny a portion would have queues outside the door; at £5 trade would be zero. This inverse relationship between price and demand applies to almost all products, though there are a few exceptions. For example, firms selling goods with a 'snob value' sometimes find they sell more when they put up the price. Another exception from the general rule is a 'Giffen good', where demand varies directly with price. The classic example is that of the potato famine in Ireland. At that time, potatoes were the staple food, and so when their price rose people could not afford other foods and so bought more potatoes.

Supply

The comparable concept to demand is supply. Supply is the quantity of a good or service which sellers will wish to sell at various prices.

As with demand, 'supply' measures not how much firms actually sell, but how much they would like to sell at a range of prices. There are a number of influences on supply; for example, the price of raw materials, the state of technology, the availability and cost of labour, and, for particular products, the weather. Again we will make use of *ceteris paribus* and consider only the most important determinant of supply, that is price. The relationship will differ for particular products, but in general we may expect that the higher the price the more profitable it will be to make the good or provide the service.

At high prices firms will be able and willing to put workers on overtime rates and so increase output whilst still making a good profit. When prices are low, some firms may be unable to cover their costs and therefore supply may be zero. In the case of fish and chips, if a customer walked into a shop and asked 'How many portions of fish and chips will you sell me at £5 a portion?' the proprietor would presumably be willing to supply all that it was physically able to produce; at 5 pence a portion the supply might be zero. Consequently we may expect supply to rise with price.

Equilibrium

Table 3.1 shows hypothetical demand and supply schedules for jeans. In both cases we assume that factors other than price remain unchanged. The Table shows that firms will be willing to supply more jeans at high prices than when the price is low. Conversely consumers will be willing to buy more when the price is low. Thus at low prices demand will exceed supply. For example, at a price of £16 per pair, consumers would like to buy 60,000 pairs a month but firms are only willing to supply 25,000. At a high price, such as £26, firms are willing to supply 80,000 pairs but consumer demand is only 20,000 per month. It follows that at some price between these two the quantity demanded will just equal the quantity supplied. This is the equilibrium price (£20).

Table 3.1: *Demand for, and supply of, jeans*

Price (£ per pair)	Demand (Thousand pairs per month)	Supply (Thousand pairs per month)
12	100	15
14	80	20
16	60	25
18	50	30
20	40	40
22	30	50
24	25	60
26	20	80

A market is in equilibrium when the quantity of the product which consumers wish to buy at the prevailing price exactly matches the quantity producers wish to sell.

At the equilibrium price the market will **clear**. This means that there will be no scarcity and no surplus. At prices higher than equilibrium, firms will have unsold stocks; a sign of excess supply. When the price is below equilibrium, shortages will occur; a sign of excess demand.

An alternative presentation of the data in Table 3.1 is given in Figure 3.1. This shows the equilibrium price of £20 and the excess demand which exists at a price of £16. At the low price demand will exceed supply by A – B, that is 60,000 – 25,000 = 35,000 pairs of jeans a month.

The forces of demand and supply usually cause markets to move towards equilibrium. In the cases just described, where demand is greater than supply, shortages will occur. Shopkeepers will be faced by consumers wanting jeans but be unable to supply them. They will pass on extra orders to manufacturers. The response of rational firms in this situation will be to raise prices and hence profits. The increase in price will cause some consumers to leave the market and it will also induce firms to supply more. This will continue until the equilibrium price is reached and the market clears.

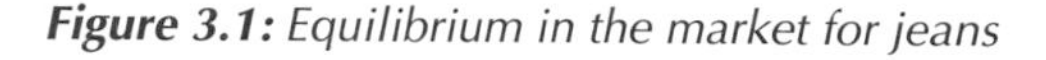

Figure 3.1: *Equilibrium in the market for jeans*

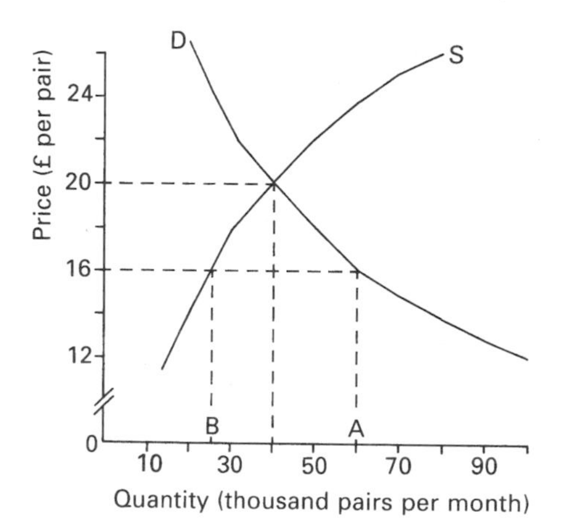

In the opposite case, where price is higher than equilibrium, firms will be left with rising stocks which they cannot sell at the prevailing price.

Sometimes they may store the excess in the hope of better times, but unless some other factors change, at some point of time they will be forced to cut prices in order to clear stocks. The process of adjustment will be quicker for perishable goods, such as strawberries, than for goods which can be easily stored, such as diamonds or spoons. The cut in price will induce more consumers into the market and it will also cut supply; at lower prices manufacturers will be unwilling to pay overtime rates. Eventually demand will equal supply, other factors remaining unchanged.

Note that at any particular time the market may not be in equilibrium. Moreover, in the real world other factors are constantly changing so that equilibrium may never be reached.

Key ideas

1. Markets exist whenever buyers wishing to exchange money for goods and services interact with sellers wishing to exchange goods and services for money.
2. By 'demand', economists mean the willingness and ability of consumers to pay for a good. Consumers will usually demand more when price falls.
3. 'Supply' is the quantity of a good which firms wish to sell at various prices. They will usually be willing to sell more when price rises.
4. When demand equals supply the market is in equilibrium. At the equilibrium price the market will clear.

Shifts in demand and supply

So far we have held constant all factors except price and considered what happens when this changes. As we have seen, when the price of a good rises or falls there is movement along the demand or supply curve. However, when there is a change in factors other than price there is a movement of the whole curve. It is now time to explore what factors will cause the demand and supply curves to shift.

Other factors affecting demand

There are many factors, other than price, which could affect demand, but we will consider four: advertising and fashion, complementary goods, substitute goods and income. The relationship between demand and these other factors can be shown in a demand function:

Demand = f (Price, Advertising, Complementary goods, Substitute goods, Income...)

(The dots in this equation indicate that some other unlisted variable may affect demand.)

Demand for some goods is hardly affected by advertising or fashion. The amount of chalk teachers use is not affected by adverts on TV, and film stars do not try to persuade us to use more blotting paper. Nevertheless, for many goods and services advertising does have a considerable effect; if it did not firms would not spend large sums of money on it. Similarly, fashions change, particularly for products such as records or clothes. If a manufacturer decides to have an advertising campaign for jeans and this is successful (or jeans have become more fashionable), what effect will this have on the price and quantity of jeans bought and sold?

The result of a successful advertising campaign is shown in Table 3.2 and Figure 3.2. Consumers are willing to buy more jeans at every price. This is represented graphically as a **shift** in the demand curve from D_1 to D_2. the supply curve is not affected; this continues to show how many pairs of jeans firms are willing to supply at each price and is not affected by an advertising campaign.

Table 3.2: *The effect of a successful advertising campaign for jeans*

Price (£ per pair)	Original demand (Thousand pairs per month)	Demand after advertising (Thousand pairs per month)
12	100	120
14	80	100
16	60	80
18	50	70
20	40	60
22	30	50
24	25	45
26	20	40

The effect of a shift in the demand curve is that a new equilibrium is reached where the supply curve intersects with the new demand curve D_2. The price of jeans has risen from £20 to £22 and the quantity has also risen, from 40,000 pairs a month to 50,000. At any other price there will be excess demand or supply. At the original price, for example, demand will be 60,000, supply 40,000, and shortages would occur, forcing up the price.

Figure 3.2: *A shift in demand*

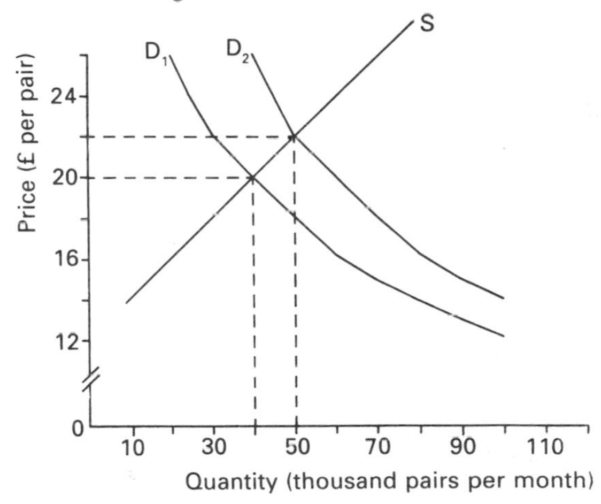

A second factor which affects demand is what happens to **complementary goods**. These are goods which 'go together'. Examples are cars and petrol, fish and chips, squash courts and squash balls. The relationship is significant because if a factor changes which influences one good, the complementary good will also be affected. For example, if there is a rise in the price of potatoes fewer people will go to chip shops and hence the demand for fish will fall. This is illustrated in Figure 3.3 which shows that the demand curve for the complementary good – in this case fish – moves to the left, resulting in a price fall from p_1 to p_2. The quantity bought and sold also falls from q_1 to q_2. A fall in the price of potatoes would have the opposite effect, leading to an increase in demand for fish and hence a rise in price and quantity.

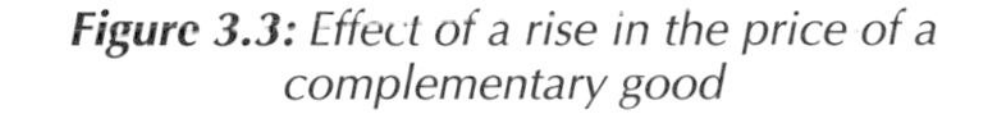

Figure 3.3: *Effect of a rise in the price of a complementary good*

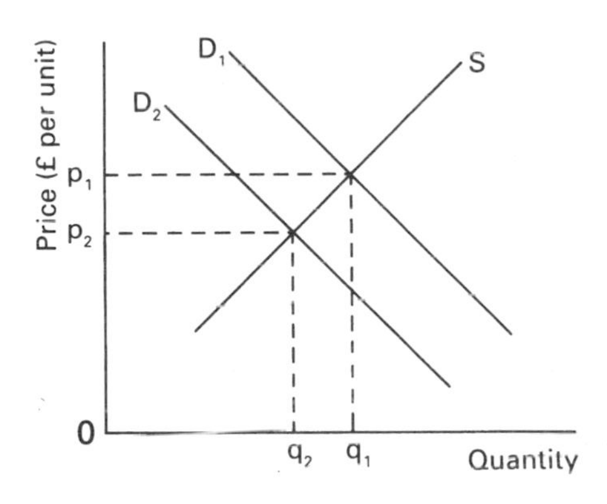

As their name implies, **substitute goods** offer an alternative to the consumer. If we want a cold drink we may not mind if it is lemonade or a cola; nor whether we drive a car made by Ford or Vauxhall, or whether we eat beef or pork. In all these cases a rise in the price of one will lead to an increase in demand for the other. Thus if the price of beef rises, some shoppers in the butchers or supermarkets will choose to buy pork instead. The amount of substitution will vary according to the particular alternative and the preferences of the consumer; some people would not buy pork whatever happened to the price of beef. When substitution does occur, a rise in the price of beef will cause the demand curve for pork to shift to the right, the extent of the shift depending on the amount of substitution. This shift will lead to an increase in the price of pork and in the quantity bought and sold.

Changes in income also affect demand. As incomes rise we tend to buy more of some goods, such as records or clothes. This will also cause a shift in the demand curve leading to a rise in price and quantity. However, for some goods such as salt or nails, a rise in income will have little or no influence on demand. The effect of a change in income is important and is discussed further in a later part of this chapter.

This discussion of the factors which affect demand is far from complete and particular products may be affected by specific influences. Sales of flowers and cards rise before Mother's Day; the demand for toys rises before Christmas, and we buy more ice cream in August than in January. Similarly, the weather ensures that we buy more winter coats in November than in June. Changes in the birth rate would cause changes in the demand for baby care products such as nappies. These factors all cause a shift in the demand curve.

Shifts of a curve and movements along a curve

It is important to understand the difference between a shift in the demand curve and a movement along the demand curve. The two are very different as can be seen in Figure 3.4. Other things being equal a change in price from p_1 to p_2 leads to a movement along a curve, for example from A to B.

This is quite different from an increase in demand which occurs, for example, when there is a favourable change in fashion or tastes. This causes the whole demand curve to shift so that more is demanded at each price, for example, at price p_1 demand will rise from A to C. If the change in tastes is unfavourable then less will be demanded at each price.

Figure 3.4: *Shifts in demand curves and movements along a curve*

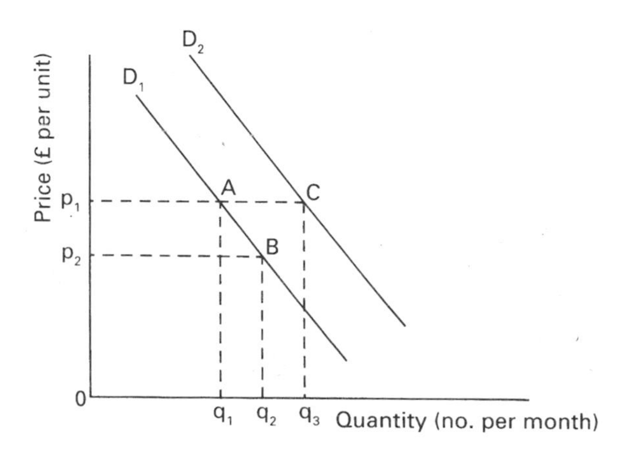

Other factors affecting supply

The supply curves we have drawn so far have been based on the assumption that factors other than price remain constant. It is now time to relax that assumption and to examine what will occur when these other factors change.

Changes in the price of inputs will affect the quantity of goods which firms are willing to supply. If raw material prices fall, then manufacturers will be willing to supply more at each price and the supply curve will move to the right as shown in Figure 3.5. The result is a fall in price from p_1 to p_2 and a rise in quantity bought and sold from q_1 to q_2. A rise in the price of inputs would have the opposite effect. If wages go up or there is an increase in the cost of raw materials, business people (often called entrepreneurs or decision makers in economics) will then wish to supply less at each price and the supply curve will shift to the left, leading to a rise in prices and a fall in quantity.

Technology affects the position of the supply curve. An entrepreneur who was willing to supply (say) a thousand telephones per week at a certain price may be willing to supply more at that price if new techniques of production mean less labour or raw materials are needed to produce each telephone.

Figure 3.5: *Shifts in the supply curve*

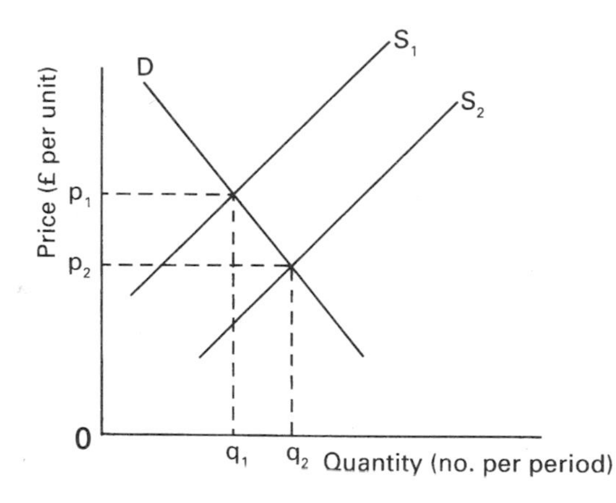

A **firm's goals** will also affect the extent to which it is willing to supply goods at particular prices. A change in management may make the firm more aggressive, for example, making it eager to capture a larger slice of the market. This would shift the supply curve to the right. Conversely, an ageing management may be less willing to compete and be content to supply less.

The **actions of governments** also have a considerable effect on supply. If a government imposes regulations on an industry this will affect the amount of goods which firms are willing to supply at particular prices. A notable example is car manufacturing. Governments in many countries have imposed detailed regulations about safety and pollution control, and these have the effect of shifting the supply curve to the left.

The government also influences supply when it imposes taxes on a good. For the manufacturer this has the same effect as a rise in the price of inputs. If the government imposed a tax of £10 on each micro computer, manufacturers would be forced to hand over this amount to the government and its effect would be exactly the same as if the manufacturer had to pay component suppliers an extra £10. The result will be that the supply curve moves to the left. Similarly, the imposition of VAT on hot food takeaway meals caused a fall in the supply of fish and chips.

A subsidy has the opposite effect. If the government decides to improve house insulation and give a subsidy to the producers of such material, then firms will be willing to supply more at each price because they will receive a hand-out from the government as well as receiving money from the consumer. The supply curve will shift to the right.

Key ideas

1. The demand curve for a good will shift when there is a change in variables such as advertising, consumer incomes, complementary or substitute goods. For particular goods other influences, such as the weather, will shift the demand curve. A shift in the demand curve means that more or less is demanded at each price.

2. The supply curve for a good will shift when there is a change in variables such as the cost of raw materials or in wages. Changes in technology and the weather will also move the supply curve, causing more or less to be supplied at each price.

Elasticity

So far we have considered movements along curves and why curves shift. It is now time to discuss the **shape** of demand and supply curves, because this has a considerable effect on the price and quantity of goods bought and sold.

Imagine that you are in charge of a business and have to decide what price to charge for your product. Will the firm benefit if you cut the price, keep it unchanged, or raise it? The answer will largely depend on how consumers respond to changes in price.

Price elasticity of demand

For some goods a change in price will make little difference to demand. If manufacturers doubled the price of paper clips, halved the price of candles, or trebled that of toilet paper, demand for the products would hardly change. For other goods the position would be very different and consumers would be very sensitive to changes in price. The responsiveness of the quantity demanded to price changes is measured by the price elasticity of demand, often abbreviated to just the elasticity of demand:

The price elasticity of demand

$$= \frac{\text{\% change in quantity demanded}}{\text{\% change in price}}$$

We can examine elasticity both arithmetically and graphically. If the price of a good falls from £100 to £50 and demand rises from 10 to 30 items then:

$$\text{Price elasticity} = \frac{+200\%}{-50\%} = -4$$

For another good the same fall in price may lead to a much smaller rise in demand, say from 10 to 12 items. In this case:

$$\text{Price elasticity} = \frac{+20\%}{-50\%} = -0.4$$

Although price elasticity is negative (since a rise in price leads to a fall in demand and vice versa), the minus sign is often omitted for the sake of brevity.

When the price elasticity of demand for a good is higher than one we say that it is **elastic**. This indicates that demand for the good is very sensitive to changes in price. Demand is **inelastic** when its price elasticity is less than one, showing that changes in price have relatively little effect on consumer purchases. When the elasticity of demand equals one we say that it is **unitary**.

***Figure 3.6:** Price elasticity of demand*
(i) Elastic

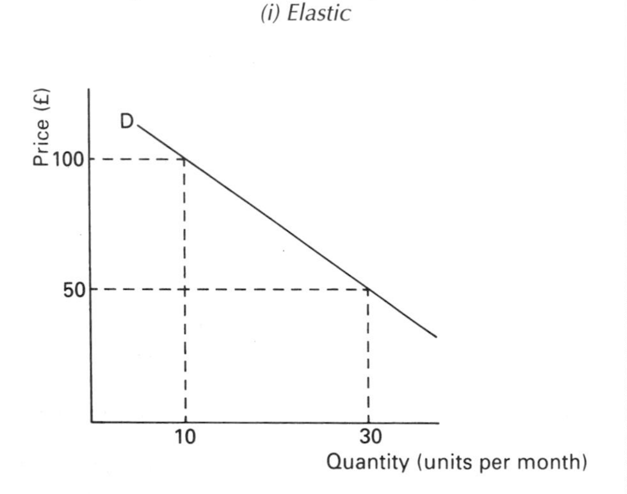

(ii) Unitary

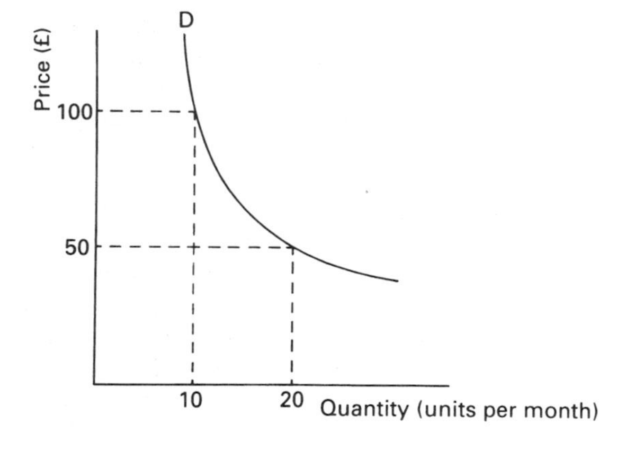

(iii) Inelastic

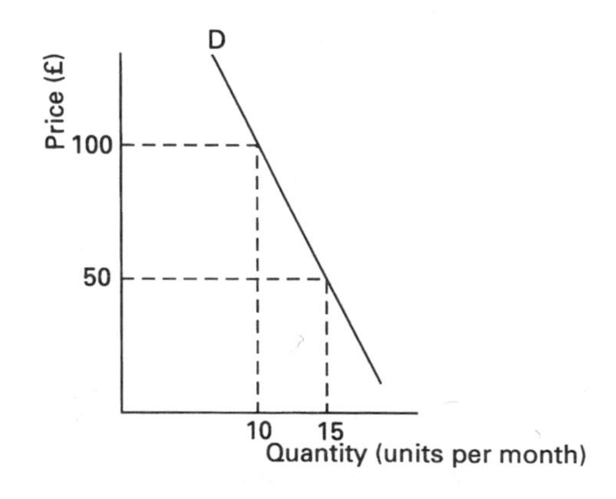

The three conditions are shown in Figure 3.6. This shows that when demand is elastic, a small fall in price leads to a large rise in quantity. Since the total revenue received by a firm is price x quantity, the total revenue will rise when the price is cut. In the case of Figure 3.6(i), a total revenue at the higher price of £100 is £100 x 10 = £1,000. When the price is cut to £50 total revenue rises to £50 x 30 = £1,500. It is therefore not surprising that firms in this position try to keep their prices below those of their competitors. A good example is a petrol station along a road where there are several other petrol stations; if it sells its petrol for a penny a litre less than its competitors, sales will rise substantially. That is why pricing is so keen that prices are signposted in fractions of a penny.

When demand is unitary the firm's revenue is the same at all prices. This is shown in Figure 3.6(ii) where the firm's revenue is always £1,000. This is clearly a statistical freak. Of more importance is the case where demand is inelastic. A large cut in price will only lead to a few more sales so that total revenue falls. In the case of Figure 3.6(iii), total revenue falls from £1,000 to £750 when price is cut from £100 to £50. Consequently markets for products where demand is inelastic will not be characterised by price cutting. Indeed, firms will seize every chance to put up prices because total revenue will also rise.

At the two extremes demand can be perfectly elastic or perfectly inelastic. These are shown in Figure 3.7. When demand is perfectly inelastic a rise or fall in price will make no difference to sales. When demand is perfectly elastic demand would fall to zero if price was raised by even a penny. These are theoretical extremes and do not exist in everyday life.

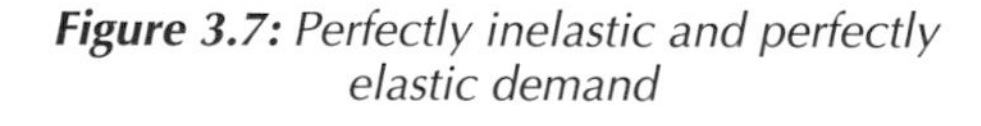
***Figure 3.7:** Perfectly inelastic and perfectly elastic demand*

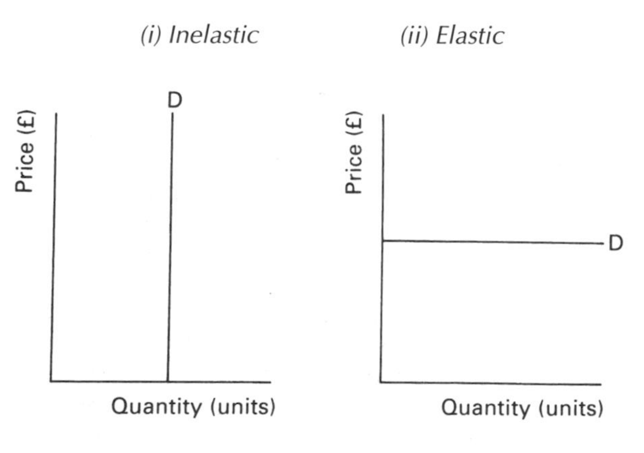

What determines price elasticity of demand?

The most important determinant of price elasticity of demand is the extent to which consumers can find acceptable substitutes. Goods such as salt, light bulbs, cigarettes or drawing pins have no close substitutes. Consequently it is not difficult to predict that if the price of these products were raised by say 10 per cent then sales might fall as a result, but probably by much less than 10 per cent. In other words, these goods are characterised by inelastic demand. Other examples of goods in this category are alcoholic drinks, toilet paper and rulers – goods with no close substitutes and which are either habit forming, or where expenditure on the good is only a small part of total spending.

Where goods have close substitutes demand becomes elastic. This occurs where the term 'good' is narrowly defined. Demand for oil is inelastic; demand for Esso or Shell is elastic because there are close substitutes.

***Table 3.3:** Estimates for price elasticity of demand for selected household foods in the UK**

Milk	0.19
Cheese	1.53
Carcass meat	1.17
Chicken, uncooked	0.55
Other poultry	1.26
Frozen convenience meat and meat products	1.08
Fresh potatoes	0.14
Frozen chips and other convenience potato products	0.37
Frozen peas	0.75
Bread	0.25

*Calculated from monthly survey data.

Source: Adapted from *Household Food Consumption and Expenditure,* HMSO.

Price elasticities of selected household foods are given in Table 3.3. The table shows that demand for milk is clearly less likely to respond to a change in price than that for cheese, for example.

Estimates of price elasticity are of considerable interest to firms because they make it possible to calculate what will happen to sales and total revenue if prices are raised or cut. For example, if the manager of a firm calculates that the price elasticity of demand for a product is -0.5, it is possible to calculate that if prices are raised by 10 per cent then sales will fall by only 5 per cent:

Price elasticity of demand

$$= \frac{\text{\% change in quantity demanded}}{\text{\% change in price}}$$

$$-0.5 = \frac{\text{\% change in quantity demanded}}{10\%}$$

therefore change in quantity = -5%

Since total revenue is price x quantity, the firm's total revenue will rise as a result of the price increase.

It is difficult to make accurate estimates of price elasticities. The most usual approach is to use experience; that is, to look back on what happened to sales of the product when prices were altered in the past. Of course, since then other factors will have changed; new products may have appeared, existing products been redesigned and advertising campaigns undertaken. All of these factors may have affected the price elasticity of demand. A specific example of the complexities of the real world occurred in 1993 when *The Times* cut its price from 45p to 30p; sales increased by 26 per cent giving a price elasticity of demand of 26/33 = 0.78. This means that *The Times'* revenue from the sale of papers fell as a result of the price cut. However, the cut may have been worthwhile for two reasons. Newspapers also get revenue from advertising, and the higher sales may have enabled *The Times* to have put up its advertising rates. The other reason is that in the long run a price cut may cause a rival paper to collapse. It may have been this possibility that led *The Independent* to put up its price from 45p to 50p. The difficulty of calculating elasticity is shown by the fact that sales of this paper then **rose** by 2 per cent; but this was not because consumers were irrational, but because the product had changed – *The Independent* increased its size and spent more on advertising. Simple textbook analysis is easier than real life application!

***Table 3.4:** Price, elasticity and total revenue*

Price	Elasticity	Total revenue
Rises	Inelastic	Rises
	Elastic	Falls
Falls	Inelastic	Falls
	Elastic	Rises

When demand is unitary, total revenue is unchanged.

Cross-elasticity of demand

The cross-elasticity of demand is a measure of the effect on one good when the price of another changes:

Cross-elasticity of demand

$$= \frac{\text{\% change in quantity demanded of good X}}{\text{\% change in the price of good Y}}$$

For substitute goods the cross-elasticity will be positive. A rise in the price of tea will lead to an increase in the quantity of coffee which consumers demand. Similarly, an increase in the price of bitter will lead to a rise in demand for lager.

For complementary goods the cross-elasticity will be negative. Thus we may expect a rise in the price of fountain pens to lead to a fall in the demand for ink. Similarly, a fall in the price of video recorders would be expected to lead to a rise in the demand for video cassettes.

Income elasticity of demand

It is now time to examine in more detail the relationship between income and demand. Earlier we suggested that as incomes rise more will be demanded. That is true for many goods, but not for all. Again we make the usual assumption that factors other than income remain unchanged:

Income elasticity of demand

$$= \frac{\text{\% change in quantity demanded}}{\text{\% change in income}}$$

For most goods income elasticity will be positive, showing that a rise in consumers' income will lead to a rise in quantity demanded. For example, if incomes rise by 5 per cent and as a result spending on meals in restaurants rises by 10 per cent we can calculate that the income elasticity of demand is +2. This is an example of a **normal good**.

A normal good has a positive income elasticity of demand whilst an **inferior good** has a negative income elasticity of demand.

For a few goods the quantity demanded will fall as incomes rise. Examples are coal, journeys by bus, cheap clothes and cuts of meat. As their incomes rise consumers will buy less of these goods and substitute others; for example, spending on coal will fall as consumers install central heating and instead of travelling by bus people will buy cars. Table 3.5 illustrates the close link between income and the ownership of various consumer durables. In all cases except one, households with higher incomes own more consumer durables. The exception is that the number of families owning black and white TVs falls as incomes rise (though of course families with high incomes may purchase a black and white TV as a second set).

Table 3.5: *Income and percentage of households owning particular consumer goods*

	Usual weekly gross income (£)		
	0-50	150-200	350-400
Video recorder	47	63	81
CD player	16	16	32
Dishwasher	6	5	12
Telephone	63	82	95
Microwave oven	34	48	67
Washing machine	64	86	93
Black & white TV only	9	4	2

Source: *General Household Survey*, HMSO, 1993.

The difference between normal and inferior goods is shown in Figure 3.8. When the good is normal, as incomes rise more will be demanded at each price; in other words the demand curve will shift from D_1 to D_2. When the good is inferior less will be demanded at each price and the curve will shift from D_1 to D_3.

Figure 3.8: *Normal and inferior goods*

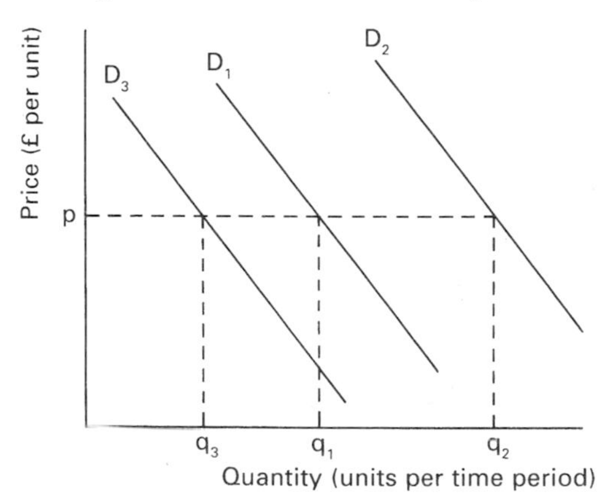

The importance of income elasticity

Income elasticity of demand is an important concept. Over a number of years incomes tend to rise. When the income elasticity of demand is positive and also greater than one (sometimes used as a definition of luxury goods) spending will rise considerably and the industry will expand. Examples are holidays abroad, microwave ovens, detached houses, wine and various recreational activities, such as squash, surfboarding and sailing.

For some industries income elasticity will be

positive but less than one (sometimes used as a definition of necessities). Most food is in this category. Such industries will not be substantially affected by changes in incomes. Shoe laces, toothpaste, washing up liquid and light bulbs are other examples. When the income elasticity of demand is negative (inferior goods) then spending will fall as incomes rise and producers will see their industries decline. This is what has happened to coal and also to bus travel and is the reason why governments have had to subsidise this form of transport in order to ensure that services continue.

One of the problems of the UK economy is that it exports goods which have a low or even negative income elasticity of demand and imports goods with a high income elasticity. That means that as world incomes rise UK exports of manufactured goods tend to be static whilst imports to the UK rise. This leads to balance of payments problems, to industrial decline and to high unemployment. The problem is easy to recognise, but it is less easy to devise a strategy which would lead to such a substantial change in the structure of the British economy that the position would be reversed.

Elasticity of supply

Just as the elasticity of demand measures the responsiveness of demand to changes in price, so the elasticity of supply shows how the supply of a particular good or service will be affected by changes in price:

Elasticity of supply

$$= \frac{\text{\% change in quantity supplied}}{\text{\% change in price}}$$

Because the supply curve (almost) always slopes upwards the elasticity of supply is positive; higher price leads to a rise in quantity supplied.

When elasticity is greater than one, we say supply is **elastic**. When the change in quantity is less than one we say that it is **inelastic**.

In a few cases supply will be perfectly inelastic, showing that whatever happens to price the supply will not vary. That is the case for new paintings by Leonardo, new songs by John Lennon, seats at the F.A. Cup Final or commercial flights to the moon this year. This position is illustrated by a vertical supply curve. At the opposite extreme we can imagine a horizontal supply curve showing perfectly elastic supply; in this case a slight fall in price would cause supply to fall to zero and a slight rise in price would lead to an infinitely large supply. These are extreme cases.

The crucial factor influencing the elasticity of supply is **time**. We can distinguish between two periods.

- The short run. This is when firms can produce more with existing plant. Workers can be put on overtime, or shift work introduced, but no major reconstructions take place. In this case it may be impossible to produce much more however high the price rises. This is the case with most agricultural products; during any one season, little can be done to increase the quantity of produce which can be grown. In the case of coconuts, the 'short run' can be a very long period of time. By the same reasoning, the supply of rubber is inelastic!
- The long run. Existing firms can build new factories and new firms can enter the industry. In the long run a rise in price will tend to call forth proportionately greater quantities so supply is elastic.

Figure 3.9: *The effects of an increase in demand under different supply conditions*

(i) Perfectly inelastic supply

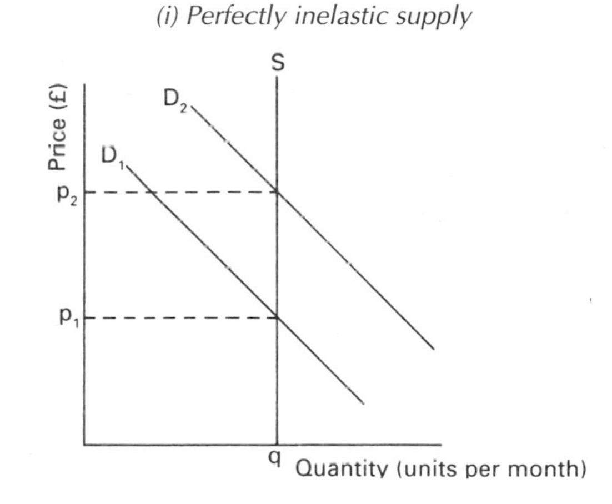

(ii) Inelastic supply

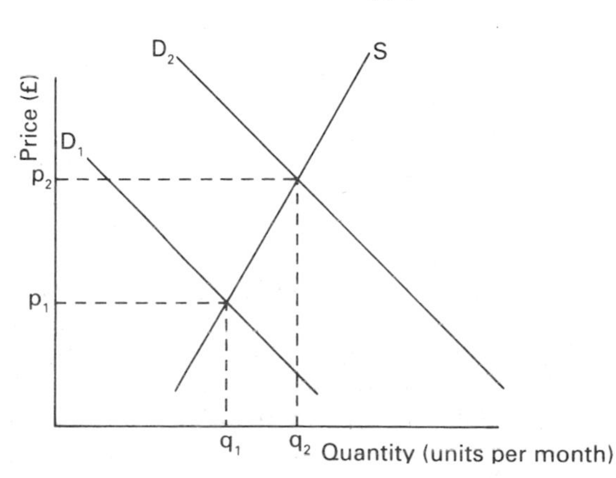

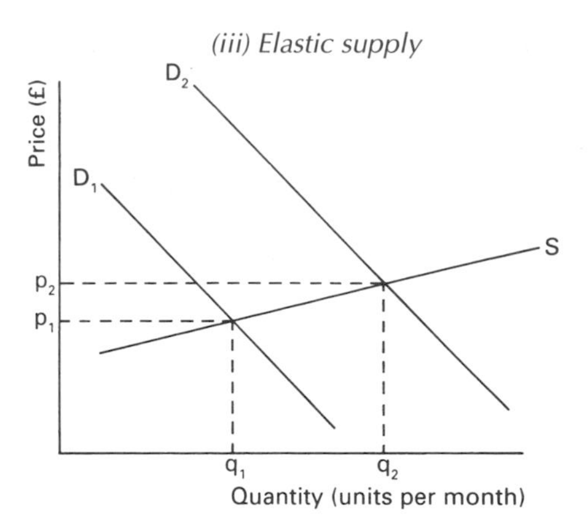

The shape of the supply curve will determine how much effect a change in demand will have on price.

Three possible cases are shown in Figure 3.9. In each, an increase in demand leads to a rise in price, but this is much less when the supply curve is elastic. This is the usual long-run equilibrium condition.

Key ideas

1. Price elasticity of demand measures the responsiveness of demand to changes in price.
2. When demand is responsive to price changes we say that it is elastic. When it is not responsive to price changes, demand is said to be inelastic.
3. The main determinants of price elasticity of demand are the existence of substitutes, whether goods are habit forming and the proportion of total expenditure which is spent on the good.
4. When demand is elastic, producers will attempt to cut prices because this will increase total revenue.
5. Income elasticity of demand measures the responsiveness of demand to changes in income. For normal goods a rise in income will lead to an increase in demand and the demand curve will move to the right.
6. Elasticity of supply measures the responsiveness of supply to changes in price. Time is the crucial factor influencing elasticity of supply. In the long run, firms can increase supply by building new factories; hence in the long run, supply tends to be elastic.

The need for government intervention

The previous chapter discussed the reasons why markets might fail. These included the existence of public and merit goods, externalities and unsatisfactory distribution of income. Consequently governments intervene in order to correct these failures, and it is possible to use the analysis we have developed to investigate the consequences of various forms of intervention.

The imposition of a tax

Governments impose taxes for a number of reasons. One is to raise revenue, but taxes on goods such as cigarettes can be used to discourage consumption. The effects of a tax on a particular product are shown in Figure 3.10.

Figure 3.10: *Effect of an indirect tax on price and quantity*

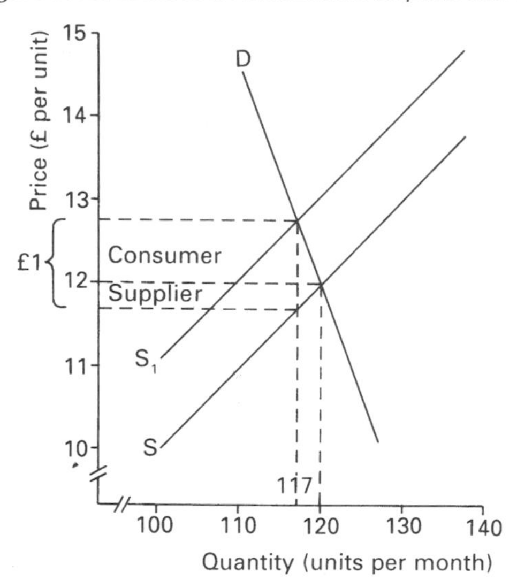

This shows the effect of a tax on price and quantity. Original equilibrium is at a price of £12 and a quantity of 120. When a tax of £1 per item is imposed, firms will supply fewer goods at the original price (so far as firms are concerned, a tax is equivalent to a rise in the price of labour or raw materials) so the supply curve shifts to the left giving a new equilibrium price of £12.75 – a rise of 75p, and a fall in quantity to 117 items. Note that the vertical distance between the two supply curves shows the amount of the tax.

In this way, the producer has managed to shift most of the burden to the consumer. As a result of the tax, the consumer pays £0.75 x 117 = £8.75 to the government, whilst the supplier pays £0.25 x 117 = £29.25. Note that only 75% of the tax rise has been passed on to the consumer, so that the price does not rise by the full amount of the tax.

The ability of the producer to shift the burden depends on the elasticity of demand. When demand is inelastic, the producer will be able to shift most of the burden because people will continue to buy the product even at a higher price. When demand is elastic, the imposition of a tax will lead to a large fall in quantity demanded, the price will not rise by much, and the producer will be forced to pay most of the tax (to check this try drawing Figure 3.10 with a very elastic demand curve). Consequently governments usually tax goods with inelastic demand because this has relatively little effect on the quantity of goods bought.

Thus we can conclude that a tax on a product raises the price and cuts the quantity, the extent depending on the price elasticity of demand.

Because habit forming goods, such as cigarettes, are assumed to have inelastic demand they have been subjected to relatively high taxes on the grounds that most of the burden would be carried by the consumer and that the industry would not suffer unduly.

Subsidies

There are various reasons why a government may wish to subsidise a particular product.

- To help the producer. Before Britain joined the EC, farm incomes were lower than non-farm incomes and governments helped farmers by paying a subsidy so that, in addition to money received from the consumer, farmers received money from the government.
- To increase consumption of a particular good. For example, the government may wish to encourage house insulation in order to reduce energy consumption. A subsidy will increase the quantity bought and sold, the extent depending on the price elasticity of demand.
- To help customers, particularly the poor. In many countries governments subsidise basic foodstuffs in order to help those with low incomes. A subsidy will bring down the price, the extent depending on the price elasticity of demand.

The analysis of the effects of a subsidy is similar to that showing the effects of a tax, except that the subsidy causes producers to supply more at each price causing the supply curve to shift to the right. Consequently we can conclude that a subsidy on a product cuts the price and increases the quantity, the extent depending on the price elasticity of demand.

Economists often argue against subsidies for two main reasons. In the first place, they interfere with the working of the price system. The equilibrium price of a good measures the extent to which consumers are willing to pay; if they are not prepared to pay this price then it follows that they would rather spend their money on something else. Consequently it is argued by some economists that subsidies lead to the misallocation of resources because they lead to an increase in the consumption of the subsidised goods and a fall in demand for other goods (since consumers cannot spend the same money twice).

Secondly, someone has to pay the subsidy; in most cases this is the taxpayer. Consequently those who pay taxes face additional costs whilst those who receive the goods benefit. Depending on the circumstances, this may or may not be fair.

Fixing a maximum price

Another way in which governments intervene in markets it to fix the maximum price at which particular products can be sold. This is often done to help poorer sections of the community who may not be able to afford basic foodstuffs. Governments intervene in this way in many Third World countries and it was the practice in the Second World War in Britain.

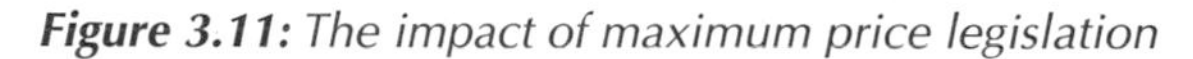

Figure 3.11: *The impact of maximum price legislation*

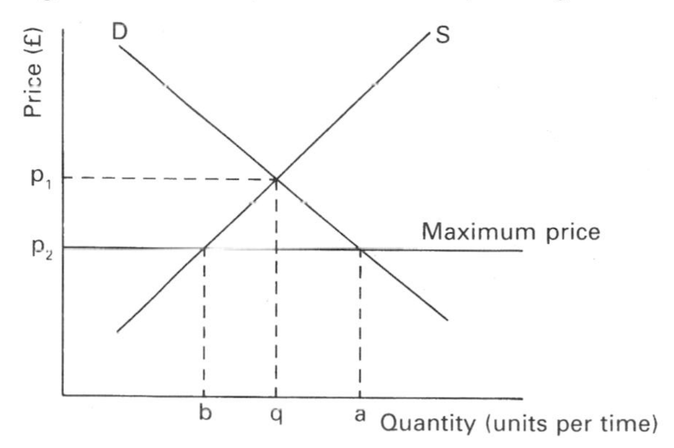

Figure 3.11 shows how maximum price legislation operates. Original equilibrium is at price p_1, and quantity q_1. The government believes this price is too high – perhaps unscrupulous merchants are exploiting the poor. They therefore pass a law which fixes the maximum price at which the

product can be sold at p_2. At this price the quantity demanded rises to a, but supply falls to b. The result is a shortage equal to a – b. This may lead to a black market because, as the demand curve shows, some people are willing to pay much higher prices than p_2. Hence some shopkeepers hide stock, tell ordinary customers that they have sold out, and then secretly sell at much higher prices to special customers.

There are various possible government responses to this position. Shooting a few shopkeepers has been tried in some countries, but is undesirable! The solution in the Second World War in the UK was to introduce a rationing system which divided up the available supply fairly among the population. The price system 'rations' a given supply by using price, and a rationing system does this more fairly – or so it can be argued. Against this a rationing system can be very bureaucratic and expensive to operate and the maximum price may cut down the quantity which is available for purchase.

Note that Figure 3.11 may exaggerate the problem. If demand and supply are both inelastic the quantity demanded will not rise much when price is cut and the quantity supplied will only fall slightly. Consequently the shortage may be very small and the black market problem insignificant.

Minimum wage legislation

Similar analysis can be used to study the effect of legislation to fix a minimum wage. Many workers are low paid; poverty is a social problem which society should alleviate. Therefore it is argued that laws should be passed forcing employers to pay all their workers at least a minimum wage.

The result is shown in Figure 3.12(i). Original equilibrium is at wage w_1, and the quantity of labour employed is q_1. The government believes that this wage is too low and fixes a minimum wage of w_2. The diagram shows that the higher wage will increase the supply of labour to point a – some existing workers will want to work longer hours and new workers will enter the labour market. However, the higher wage will force some employers to cut down on the quantity of labour they wish to employ, so the quantity of labour in employment falls to point b. Thus, it is argued, minimum wage legislation will lead to a rise in unemployment equal to a – b.

However, a note of caution needs to be sounded. Firstly, the diagram has been drawn with fairly elastic demand and supply curves; the rise in unemployment would be much less if these were inelastic. This would be the position if higher wages did not cause many more workers to seek jobs and if only a few employers laid off workers at the higher wage level.

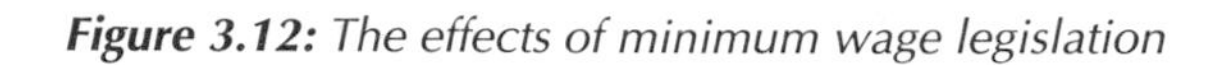

Figure 3.12: *The effects of minimum wage legislation*

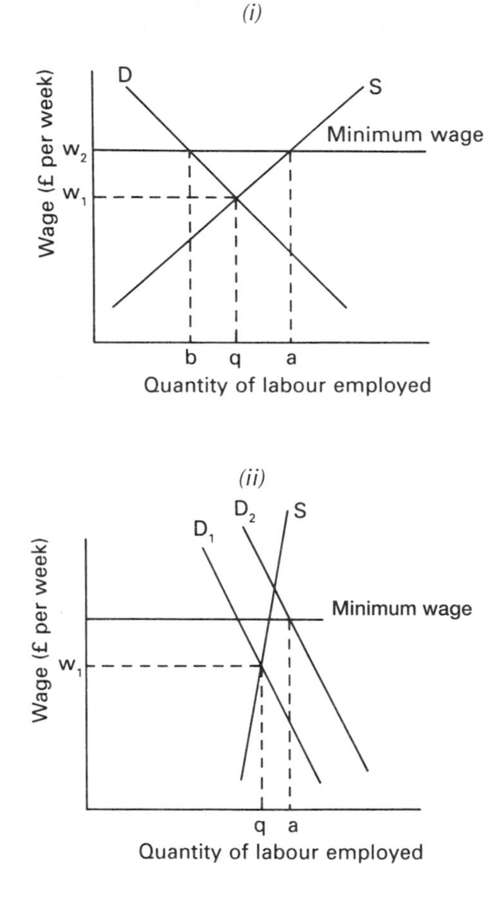

Secondly, the workers receiving higher wages will spend some of their extra money. This will lead to higher demand for some products and to more jobs in these industries; that is the demand curve for labour will move to the right as shown in Figure 3.12(ii). Whilst the extra spending by workers with higher incomes may not be sufficient to move the demand curve by much, changes in other factors may do this. For example, if the government were to increase its spending (on say education, health and construction) this would increase the demand for labour in certain industries causing the demand curve to move to the right so that the quantity of labour employed was a. Thus whilst minimum wage legislation will tend to increase unemployment if **other things remain equal**, appropriate measures by government may be able to override this effect.

The Common Agricultural Policy of the EU

Article 39 of the Treaty of Rome sets out the objectives of the CAP. These are to increase agricultural efficiency, stabilise markets, secure food supplies, increase farm incomes and ensure reasonable prices for consumers. There are various methods used to achieve these goals, but the main one is shown in Figure 3.13. The free market price within the European Union is given by the intersection of the demand and supply curves. However, world prices are much lower than this at $0p_1$. If foreign supplies were able to enter freely, European farmers would only supply 0a at this price, but EU demand would be 0b and imports would fill the gap ab.

Figure 3.13: *The CAP price support system*

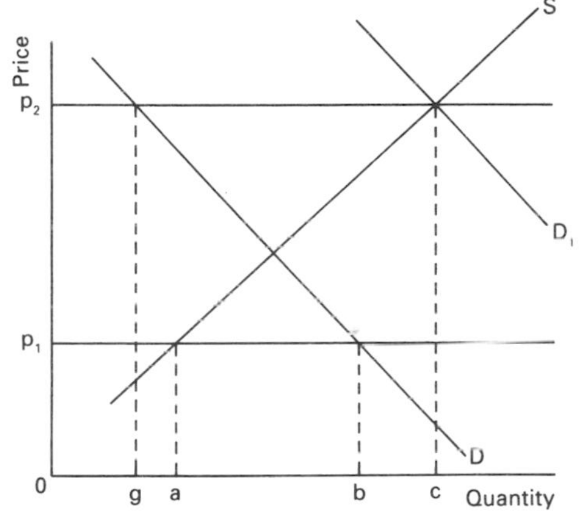

In order to achieve its objectives the Union imposes a levy on imports equal to price p_1-p_2. The high price stimulates European farmers to supply quantity 0c, but the high price also cuts demand down to 0g. The problem is 'resolved' by community administrators entering the market and buying up the surplus gc, in effect shifting the demand curve to D_1.

Of course this creates a new problem – what to do with all the produce that has been purchased? They can put it into store, thus creating the famous butter mountains and wine lakes. Alternatively they can sell the surplus at very low prices in world markets, or seek new uses for particular products. None of these solutions is very satisfactory. An alternative suggestion is that European surpluses should be given away to help people in poor countries. However, this may cause greater poverty, because the increase in supply will force down the local price for food, making it uneconomic for local farmers to grow food so that more shortages occur.

In recent years the size of some surpluses has been reduced by imposing a quota on farmers, so limiting supply. This is unpopular with farmers and rather bureaucratic. Whilst the agricultural policy enables some of the EU objectives to be realised, it is expensive and inefficient. The obvious solution is to bring down prices closer to the market equilibrium, but this is politically very difficult since farm lobbies are very powerful in all EU countries. However, in 1993 an agreement was reached during the GATT Uruguay Round (see Chapter 19) to review thoroughly the CAP in 2003.

Key ideas

1. Governments intervene in the economy in various ways to correct market failure.
2. A tax on goods raises the price and reduces the quantity bought and sold, the extent depending on the price elasticity of demand.
3. A subsidy may be imposed to help producers or consumers. Subsidies lead to falls in price and to increases in the quantity of goods bought.
4. Governments sometimes fix the maximum price at which a product can be sold in order to help poor consumers. However, this may lead to shortages.
5. Governments sometimes fix minimum wage levels in order to help low paid workers. Critics say this causes unemployment.
6. The CAP aims to help farmers and stabilise prices. However, price guarantee schemes like CAP can lead to surplus production.

Should the government intervene in the housing market?

No government can give everyone all the housing that they would like. Large numbers of people would like better housing – in a nicer area, with more rooms, a bigger garden or a garage. Some would like a second house to use as a holiday cottage. It is impossible to satisfy all these wishes because the cost would be too high – for example, large amounts of unspoilt green areas would be required. Moreover, houses have a high and positive income elasticity of demand so that as living standards improve people want better and better housing. Consequently, desires for better housing will continue to outstrip the supply. Since everyone cannot have the housing that they would like, the question arises – how should we decide the quantity and quality of housing?

At present, the housing market in the UK is provided by a mixture of market forces and government intervention. Market forces are dominant when houses are bought and sold; for example, through estate agents. However, even here there is considerable government intervention since house buyers can claim relief on their income tax on the interest payments they make on the mortgage taken out to buy a house. The government also intervenes by requiring planning permission to be obtained before houses can be built – this is to protect areas from undesirable development. Government intervention is also widespread in the rented sector. Here the government provides council houses and it also intervenes by helping housing associations. Even in the private rented sector the government intervenes, for example, by passing laws concerning fair rents. Finally, the government intervenes by providing accommodation to homeless people.

The argument for a free market in housing

Free market economists would argue that all this is unnecessary. Whilst the housing market may have some characteristics which may make it special, market forces of demand and supply will allocate resources in this market efficiently, just as they do in others. They would argue that the best way to decide if people really want some good or service is if they are willing to pay for it. Consequently, the best way to decide the quantity of housing that people want is to let them choose; if people want better housing then they will be willing to pay for it. If they are not willing to pay the market price it is a misallocation of resources to provide it.

According to the market perspective, if demand rises, then prices should also rise and this will lead to an extension of supply. If demand falls, then so should prices, and this would be accompanied by a fall in the number of houses built. Evidence suggests that this does happen. The UK economy was booming between 1983 and 1988; this led to a rise in incomes and house prices doubled in this period. There was also an increase in the number of houses built. In the recession at the beginning of the 1990s, unemployment rose, leading to a fall in demand for housing. As market supporters would predict, this led to a fall in house prices and in the number of houses built, particularly in those regions where the recession was most severe.

The policy implications of this argument are that the government should stop subsidising housing. It should also stop requiring planning permission, except in very special cases. Only in the rare cases of people unable to help themselves – for example, those who are handicapped – should the government intervene to provide or to subsidise housing. They argue that this would lead to a better allocation of resources because society would be providing the quantity and quality of housing that people really wanted.

Reasons for intervention

Interventionists argue that this would be unsatisfactory. Ending the requirement for planning would mean that beautiful areas of countryside would be filled with houses. Instead the state should continue to require planning permission before development. Moreover, they argue that the characteristics of housing mean that it is a special case. If there is a shortage of shoes in a particular place, the shortage can quickly be remedied by transporting shoes from elsewhere. Moreover, the supply of shoes can quickly be increased by raising output. Housing is different; it is not mobile, and the supply cannot be increased quickly.

They would also argue that housing is a merit good – that in a civilised society people have a right to a reasonable standard of housing and that left to the market many people cannot afford this. Thus a survey of housing in the mid 1980s found that over a million houses in the UK were in serious disrepair; another million were classed as unfit for human habitation and over half a million lacked basic amenities such as an indoor WC or hot and cold water. Another indication of market failure is the number of homeless; between 1989 and 1991 the recession led to an increase in the number of homeless people from 130,000 to 160,000. Consequently, interventionists argue that the state must intervene in order to correct market failure in the housing market.

Conclusion

Markets, operating through the forces of demand and supply, have many advantages as a way of allocating resources. But as the last chapter shows, markets also have disadvantages. Consequently governments sometimes intervene. Some of these interventions, such as the imposition of taxes, are accepted as necessary by all economics. Other interventions, such as government action to fix prices or wages, are more controversial. Demand and supply analysis allows the effects of such intervention to be studied, but the results of the analysis often reflect the values of the researcher. For example, different assumptions about elasticity can lead to very different conclusions about the effect of any intervention.

Data questions

Price elasticity of demand for cars

The main independent variables determining car demand are prices and incomes. Estimated price elasticities of demand for cars vary from -0.1 to over -3.0, whilst estimates for particular models vary from -2.0 to -7.0. Income elasticity of demand varies from 1.1 to 4.2.

Source: Rhys G., 'Competition in the car industry' in G.B.J. Atkinson, ed., *Developments in Economics,* Causeway Press 1993.

Question 1

1. Why should price elasticity of particular models be higher than that for cars as a whole?
2. What effect on the sales of cars would you expect to result from a rise of 10%?
3. If incomes rise by 5%, what will the effect be on car sales?

Newspapers' story of VAT woe is not backed by facts

The idea that the Treasury might consider imposing VAT on newspapers, magazines and books has, predictably, raised howls of protest from the companies which produce (you guessed it) newspapers, magazines and books.

The latest in a series of salvoes was launched yesterday by the Newspaper Society, representing the provincial press, which last year commissioned a study by Price Waterhouse of the likely effect of introducing VAT on newspapers at Britain's full 17.5%. There are two key unknowns. First, if VAT is put on papers, who would bear the pain: would newspaper groups try to absorb some of the cost themselves? And if some of the cost increase was passed on to customers, would people buy fewer papers?

Price Waterhouse suggest that the elasticity of demand for regional morning and Sunday newspapers is perhaps -0.3, whilst that for evening papers might be -0.4 and for paid weeklies -0.5. The problem with trying to guess such figures is this: no one has ever before tried putting up the price of all newspapers on the same day. Evidence of what happened in the past when one paper put up its price is not relevant, because the elasticity of demand for a single newspaper is bound to be higher than the figure for newspapers as a whole.

Source: *The Guardian*, 5 February 1993.

Question 2

1. Explain what is meant by 'price elasticity of demand'. Why should this be a minus figure?
2. Why should the price elasticity of demand for a single paper be higher than that for papers as a whole?
3. Why do you think the elasticity of demand for different groups of papers will vary?
4. Sales of provincial morning and evening papers are 6 million, provincial Sunday papers 500,000 and paid-for weeklies 6.7 million. If the estimates of price elasticity are correct, what will be the effect of the imposition of VAT?

4 Behind the Demand Curve: The Theory of Consumer Choice

The demand curve is so crucial in economics that it is useful to analyse the reasoning which explains the slope of the curve. Consumer theory attempts to explain why the curve slopes down from left to right and also the situation where, when faced with a choice of goods, a consumer will maximise satisfaction (utility).

There are several ways in which the theory of consumer choice can be analysed. This chapter looks at two alternatives, which both fall within the neo-classical approach.

- The marginal utility approach uses a cardinal measure of utility to explain consumers' behaviour. This theoretical model assumes that a numerical value can be placed on the amount of utility gained from the consumption of a good.
- Indifference curve analysis rejects this idea and attempts to explain consumer behaviour using an ordinal measure of satisfaction. In this theory, consumers state that they prefer one quantity of goods to another rather than placing an actual value on the amount of satisfaction gained.

Marginal utility analysis

Diminishing marginal utility

Consumers buy goods and services because of the utility (satisfaction) which they receive from the goods. A bag of fish and chips or a bottle of cola will give a certain amount of satisfaction to someone who is hungry or thirsty. A second helping may also increase utility, but perhaps not by very much. A third helping may not increase utility at all and indeed may make the consumer sick – an example of negative utility. This is an example of the law of diminishing marginal utility.

Marginal utility can be defined as the extra utility obtained from the consumption of one more unit of a good. The law of diminishing marginal utility states that as the amount of a good consumed increases, the marginal utility tends to decrease, though total utility may continue to rise.

A simple example of the law of diminishing marginal utility is given in Table 4.1. In this case, marginal utility at first rises, but then the fall sets in after the consumption of the second good. Note that this example assumes that utility can be given a numerical value.

Table 4.1: *Diminishing marginal utility*

Quantity of the good consumed	Total utility	Marginal utility
0	0	—
1	5	5
2	12	7
3	16	4
4	18	2
5	17	-1
6	16	-2

The law of diminishing marginal utility can be used to explain the slope of an individual's demand for a single good. As more units are consumed, marginal utility falls, hence the price which consumers are willing to pay will also fall to compensate for this loss of satisfaction. An alternative way to look at the slope of a demand curve is to say that when only a small quantity of a good is consumed, an extra unit gives a relatively high marginal utility; hence consumers are willing to pay a high price. When a number of units have been bought, an extra unit yields only a small amount of satisfaction, hence only a low price will be paid.

A rational consumer, when faced with deciding what quantity of this good to consume, will aim to maximise total satisfaction. In the example illustrated in Table 4.1, the consumer will buy 4 goods. At this point, total satisfaction is maximised. However, in practice, consumers are faced with a choice from a number of goods and are constrained by a limited income, and by the price of the goods.

The equi-marginal principle

In order to maximise satisfaction a consumer should arrange expenditure so that the marginal utility of a particular purchase is proportional to its price. Let us examine this idea. Assume that the satisfaction a person obtains from going to a disco is greater than that resulting from a visit to a cinema. If the satisfaction obtained from the disco is five times that obtained from the cinema, it is reasonable that the person should spend five times as much on discos as on films. If the person had been spending ten times as much on discos as on visiting the cinema, it would be rational to switch some expenditure from discos to cinemas since discos only give five times the satisfaction (assuming that the cost of the two is the same).

We can generalise from this example. If a particular good gives less marginal utility than goods as a whole, we should switch the expenditure away from that product, until the marginal utility of a good, relative to its price, rises to equal that of other goods. In the example in Table 4.1, it would be foolish to buy 4 items of that particular good when this has a marginal utility of only 2 if purchases of other goods had a higher marginal utility – say 4 (again assuming that the price of each good is the same). If that was the case we should buy three items of the good to equalise marginal utility between this good and others.

The fundamental condition of consumer equilibrium can be expressed as:

$$\frac{MUx}{Px} = \frac{MUy}{Py} = \frac{MUz}{Pz}$$

where MU = marginal utility, P = price and x, y and z are goods.

When the price of a good such as x falls the value of $\frac{MUx}{Px}$ will rise and more should be spent on x.

In other words, when the price falls the ratio of marginal utility to the price will rise. This will cause the rational consumer to buy more, causing the demand curve to slope downwards.

Since more money is spent on x, less can be spent on y and z. Given the law of diminishing marginal utility, the reduced consumption of these goods will raise their marginal utilities until the ratio of marginal utility to price is equal for all goods. This is the equilibrium condition which maximises consumer satisfaction.

This equilibrium will be disturbed if there is a change in income. A rise in income will allow more goods to be bought, though consumers will not buy more of all goods. The way a particular good is affected will depend on how consumer preferences change as a result of income.

Substitution and income effects

An alternative way of analysing the downward sloping demand curve makes use of substitution and income effects. We can use these effects to show how, when the price of a good rises, the quantity demanded falls, or how, when the price of a good falls, the quantity demanded rises. If the price of beef rises whilst other prices do not, then beef has become relatively more expensive and its marginal utility will fall compared to other goods. It will therefore pay consumers to substitute other products for beef. Similarly, if train fares rise, rational consumers will substitute other services for this form of travel. The substitution effect will be large when a product has close competitors.

When incomes are fixed and the price of a product rises, the effect is the same as a cut in real incomes. With a lower real income, consumers will cut their expenditure on many products, including the good whose price has risen. (The exception to the general rule occurs with **inferior goods** when a fall in income will cause consumers to buy more of that product.) The income effect will be large when spending on the product takes a high proportion of income. It will have little or no effect for products such as pencils, calendars or plastic bags, where expenditure takes only a minute part of total spending.

The substitution and income effects together

explain why some goods have elastic and some inelastic demand. When both income and substitution effects are strong, a rise in price will have a considerable effect on consumer spending and demand will be elastic. When the effects are small, demand will be inelastic.

Consumer surplus

On hot days people are thirsty and would be willing to pay much more for a cool drink than the price actually charged. The difference between the price paid and the utility obtained by the consumer is a measure of consumer surplus. Because of the law of diminishing marginal utility, the surplus will diminish as more drinks are bought, and it will eventually disappear.

Consumer surplus can be defined as the difference between the total amount of money a person would be prepared to pay for some quantity of a good and the amount actually paid.

Figure 4.1: *Consumer surplus*

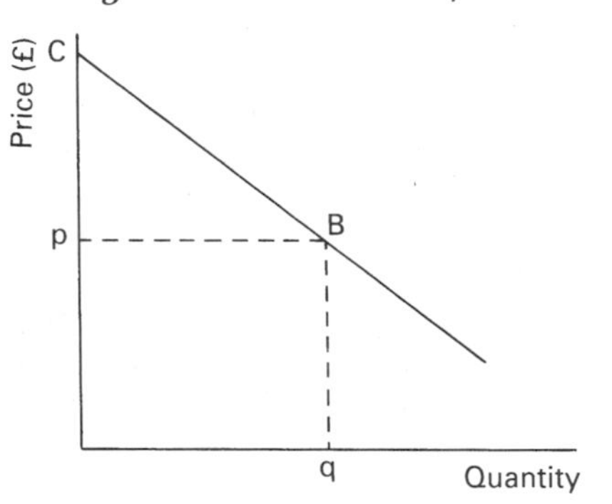

In Figure 4.1 equilibrium is at price p and quantity q. However, some consumers are willing to pay much higher prices – even as high as C. Consumers' surplus is measured by pBC. This is the area above the price, but below the demand curve.

Cardinal and ordinal utility

So far this analysis has implicitly assumed that utility can be measured. The term used for this is cardinal utility. A cardinal measure of utility assumes the consumer can compare the increase in utility obtained from (say) consuming two apples instead of one, with the increase in utility obtained from increasing the consumption of pears from two to three.

This assumption that utility can be measured has been criticised on the grounds that such measurement is not possible in practice. Centimetres can be used to measure length, but there is no scale to measure changes in the satisfaction obtained by consuming different goods. Despite this disadvantage, the marginal utility approach can still be used to make useful predictions about consumer choice.

An alternative approach is to use ordinal utility. This assumes a person can say that he or she prefers three pears to two pears, but not by how much more. An approach based on ordinal utility is used in indifference curve analysis.

Key ideas – summary of marginal utility

1. Marginal utility is the extra utility obtained from the consumption of an additional good. The law of diminishing marginal utility states that as more of a good is consumed, marginal utility will eventually decrease.
2. Since marginal utility falls as consumption increases, consumers will be unwilling to pay for more of the good, i.e. the demand curve will slope to the right.
3. Consumers will maximise satisfaction when the marginal utility obtained from buying a good is proportional to its price.

Indifference curve analysis

Indifference curve analysis offers an alternative approach to the analysis of consumer choice.

An indifference curve joins together all the combinations of two goods which yield the same utility.

Assume a consumer buys only two commodities, bread and apples, and that their relative value is as shown in Table 4.2. The Table shows that the consumer is indifferent if offered the choice between 1 loaf of bread and 6 apples, or between 2 loaves and 3 apples. 'Indifferent' in this context means that it does not matter one way or another; the alternatives have equal value. These points can be linked up to form an indifference curve as shown in Figure 4.2. In the example illustrated in this figure, the consumer is indifferent between combinations A and B, but would prefer A (with 6 apples and 1 loaf) to another alternative such as 3 apples and 1 loaf.

***Table 4.2:** Indifference combinations*

Bread	Apples	
1	6	A
2	3	
3	2	B
4	1.5	

***Figure 4.2:** An indifference curve*

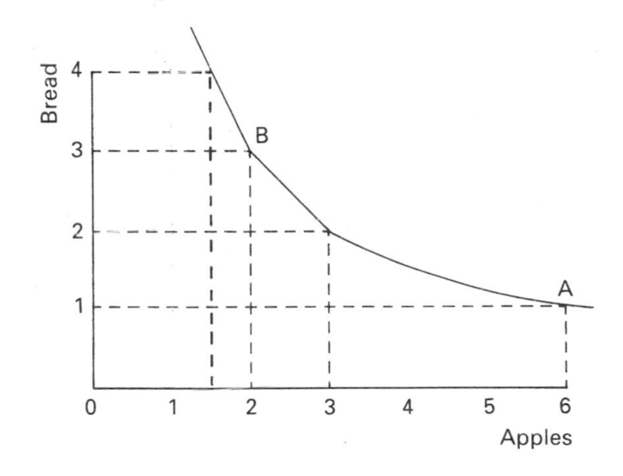

The curve illustrates the law of substitution; that the scarcer the good the greater its relative value. In other words as a good becomes scarcer its marginal utility rises relative to the marginal utility of the other good. Thus at point A the consumer would be willing to give up three apples in order to obtain an extra loaf of bread because bread is relatively scarce. However, at B the consumer would only be willing to give up half an apple to obtain a loaf of bread because bread is plentiful. If we compare two points on an indifference curve in this way, we obtain the **marginal rate of substitution**. This shows the amount of one commodity a consumer would be willing to give up in order to obtain one more unit of another commodity, leaving the overall level of satisfaction unchanged. Indifference theory assumes the marginal rate of substitution is negative and diminishing. This means that to gain an increase in the consumption of one good, a consumer is prepared to reduce consumption of another commodity. It also means that if there are two goods, x and y, as consumers obtain relatively large quantities of good x they will only be willing to give up smaller and smaller amounts of y to obtain more x.

If more resources become available the consumer may be able to choose more of each good as shown in Figure 4.3. Here I_3 offers a higher level of utility than I_2 and I_2 than I_1, because they offer a greater quantity of either or both goods. Indifference curves never cross because each offers a combination of more goods or fewer goods, depending on the distance from the origin.

***Figure 4.3:** Indifference curves*

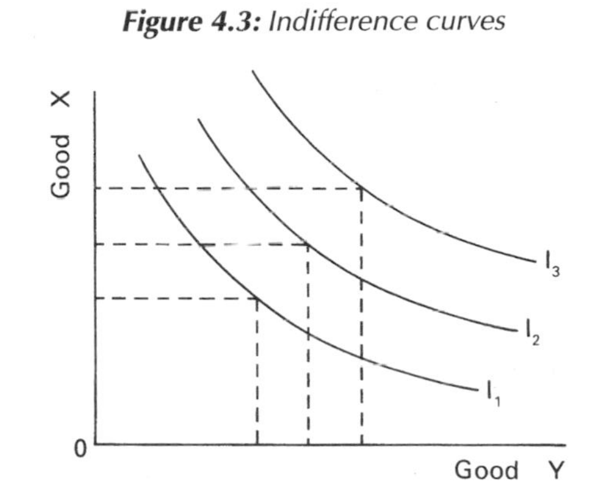

The budget line

A budget line indicates what combination of goods a consumer can buy when resources are limited. Assume that our imaginary consumer has £5 a week to spend and can choose whether to spend this money on apples or on bread. In Figure 4.4(i) the budget line shows the alternatives; at X all the money goes on apples, at Y all goes on bread. The position between these extremes shows various combinations of possible expenditure, such as £3 on bread and £2 on apples. The consumer cannot choose a position such as C because this would require £8, more money than is available.

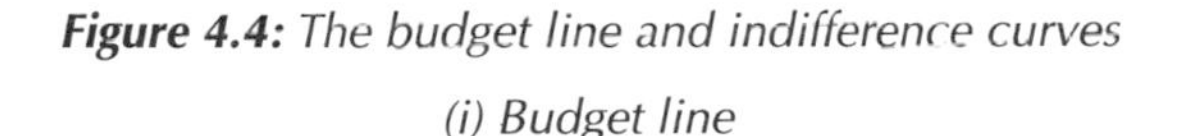

***Figure 4.4:** The budget line and indifference curves*

(i) Budget line

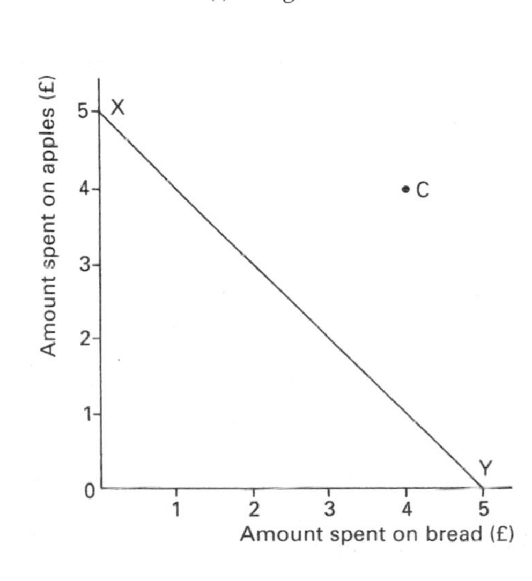

(ii) Consumer's optimal equilibrium

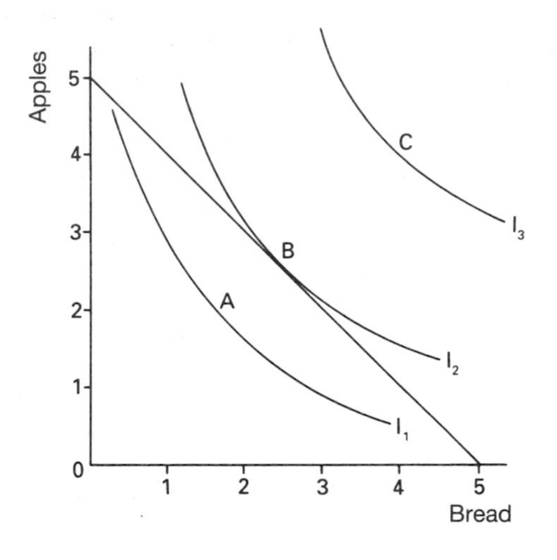

Consumer's equilibrium

The consumer's optimal equilibrium position will be at B in Figure 4.4(ii) where the indifference curve touches the budget line. This is the point where the consumer's substitution ratio is just equal to the ratio of bread prices to apple prices, and where the marginal utilities of both goods are equal.

Points such as A and C do not give optimal equilibrium. A is not acceptable because, although the ratio of apples to bread is acceptable, more of both goods are available on higher indifference curves. C is not possible because the money available does not permit the purchase of this quantity of goods.

Here position B gives the highest combination of goods which the budget will allow the consumer to buy. This is usually explained as being the position where the ratio of marginal utilities is equal to the ratio of prices.

A rise in income

A rise in income will change the position as shown in Figure 4.5. When income rises, a new budget line is drawn and makes possible a position on a higher indifference curve parallel to the original. This is because, with a higher income, the consumer can buy more of both goods (assuming that the price of the goods is unchanged). In this particular example income rises to £8 so that the consumer could spend this amount on various combinations of apples and bread. The rise in income will cause more of each good to be bought (unless one is an inferior good), but the exact proportion of the income will depend on the relative income elasticities. In the example of Figure 4.5. the new equilibrium is at C. The points A, B and C show the **income expansion path**.

Figure 4.5: *Effect of a change in income on equilibrium*

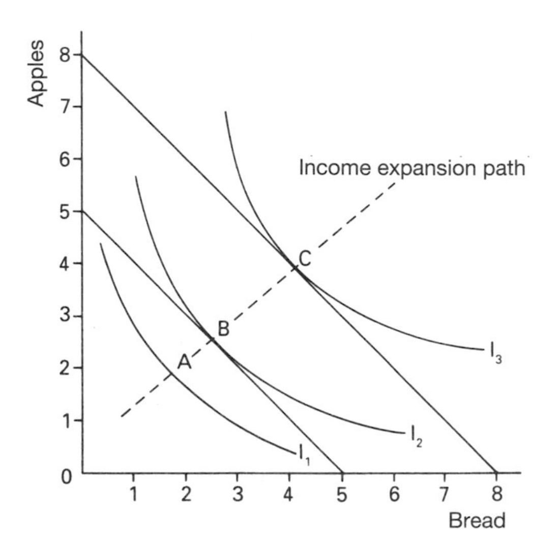

A change in price

A fall in the price of pears, while the price of apples is unchanged, will cause the budget line to shift as shown in Figure 4.6. The line shifts in this way because with an unchanged income the consumer will be able to buy as many apples as before, and more pears. Initially consumer satisfaction would be maximised at point Z on indifferent curve I_1. The fall in pear prices shifts the budget line from AB to AC so that the consumer will be able to choose a point on indifference curve I_2.

Figure 4.6: *The effect of a change in price*

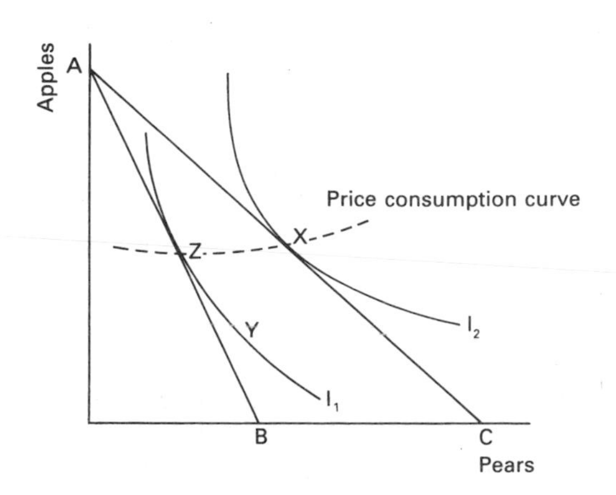

The final result will depend on the sum of two effects – a substitution effect, and an income effect. The substitution effect will mean a move along the indifference curve from point Z to say point Y, showing an increase in consumption of pears and a reduction in the consumption of apples. The income effect will mean a move from indifference curve I_1 to curve I_2 and a final position at X. A line joining points such as X and Z is called a price consumption curve. This analysis shows that a fall in price leads to an increase in the quantity demanded – the demand curve will slope down.

Indifference curve analysis and the demand curve

Indifference curve analysis can be used to show why the demand curve usually slopes down. To do this, we will analyse one commodity, beer, and assume that consumer income and the price of all other goods remains constant.

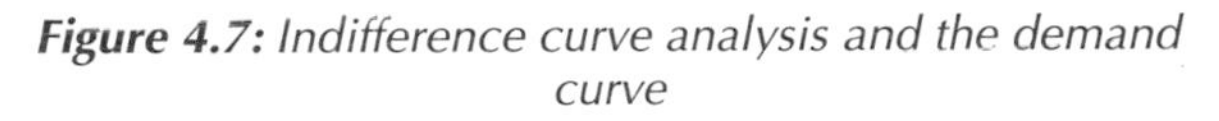

***Figure 4.7:** Indifference curve analysis and the demand curve*

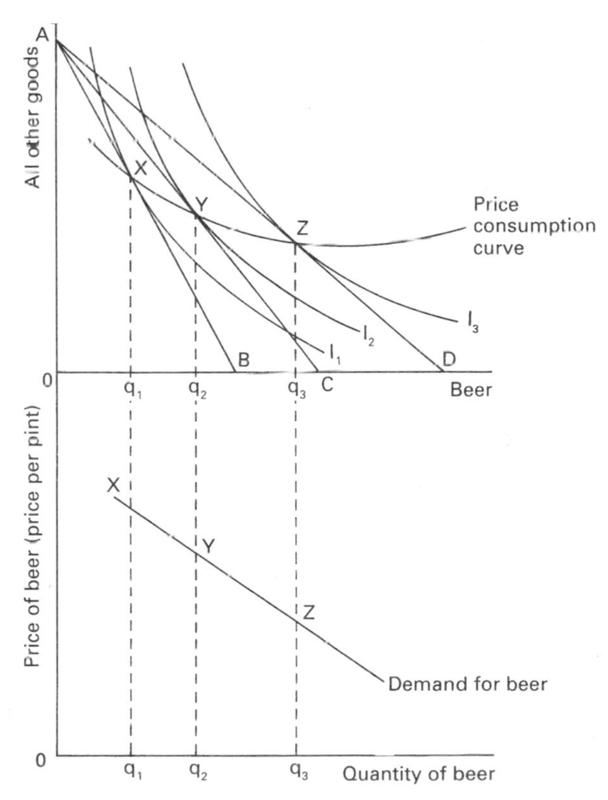

The top part of Figure 4.7 is a conventional indifference curve diagram. The budget line AB shows that the consumer can buy 0B pints of beer, or quantity 0A of all other goods. When the price of beer falls, the budget line will move to 0C and then 0D. Originally the consumer would be at position X on indifference curve I_1, but as the price of beer falls the consumer will be able to move to higher indifference curves I_2 and I_3. Points X, Y and Z show successive places on the price consumption curve corresponding to changes in the price of beer.

The bottom part of the Figure is derived from the top part. In both parts, the horizontal axis shows the quantity of beer which will be bought, but in the bottom part of the diagram, the vertical axis shows the price of beer. As you can see, this part of the diagram is a conventional demand curve diagram. At the original price of beer, the consumer's preference for this drink will be at point X, and quantity q_1 will be consumed. This is shown in both parts of the Figure. The budget line AB also corresponds to a particular price of beer, and is shown in the bottom part as point X.

If the price of beer then falls to that shown by budget line 0C, the consumer will maximise satisfaction at point Y, and this corresponds to point Y in the bottom part of the Figure. If we move along the price consumption curve to position Z, we will find the quantity of beer which will be consumed when the price falls to 0D. This gives us point Z in the bottom part of the Figure. Joining together these points gives us the demand curve for beer, which slopes down to the right. The slope of the curve – the elasticity – will depend on the consumer's preferences as shown in the top part of the diagram. If a fall in the price of beer caused very little more to be consumed, then 0B, 0C and 0D would be closer together, giving a steeper (inelastic) demand curve.

Key ideas – summary of indifference analysis

1. An indifference curve joins together all the combinations of a good which yield the same utility. The slope of the curve shows the marginal rate of substitution.
2. Indifference curves can never intersect.
3. A consumer's optimum equilibrium position will be where an indifference curve touches the budget line.
4. A rise in income will make possible a position on a higher indifference curve.
5. A price rise will involve both substitution and income effects.

Work and leisure

Indifference curve analysis can be used to analyse the effects of an increase in wages on an individual's choice of whether to work more or less.

In Figure 4.8, 0L represents the amount of time that a person can devote to either work or leisure and 0W shows the pay received if the person works all the time available and has no leisure. The line WL shows the marginal rate of substitution between work and leisure and I_1 is an indifference curve. The rational individual will be in equilibrium at A_1 and will do Q_1L amount of work and have $0Q_1$ leisure. If the person then receives a pay rise, the income received if all the time available was used for work would rise to $0W_1$ and the slope W_1L would show the opportunity cost of leisure. The individual would move to indifference curve I_2 and respond to the increase in wages by working longer hours LQ_2 instead of LQ_1. The amount of leisure taken would fall by Q_1 - Q_2.

Figure 4.8: *An increase in wages leads to a fall in income*

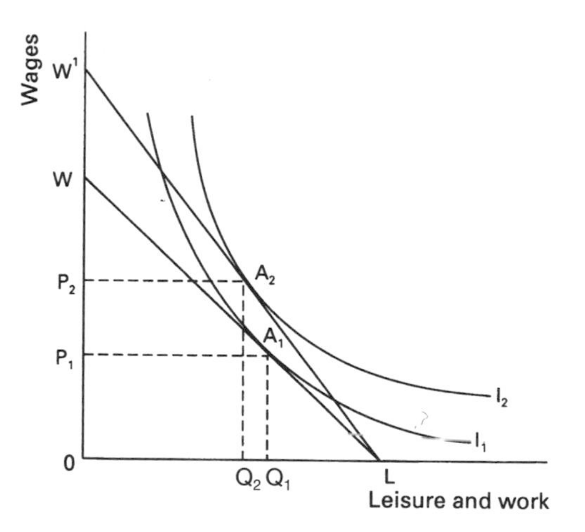

However, it is possible to use indifference curves to put forward a different argument. As before, the substitution effect will encourage an individual to work more hours and have less leisure time. But now this effect is overcome by the income effect. The rise in wages makes the person better off and this rise in income will cause an increase in the demand for leisure. The new effect is shown in Figure 4.9. The original position is the same, but the increase in wages causes our

Figure 4.9: *An increase in wages leads to a rise in leisure*

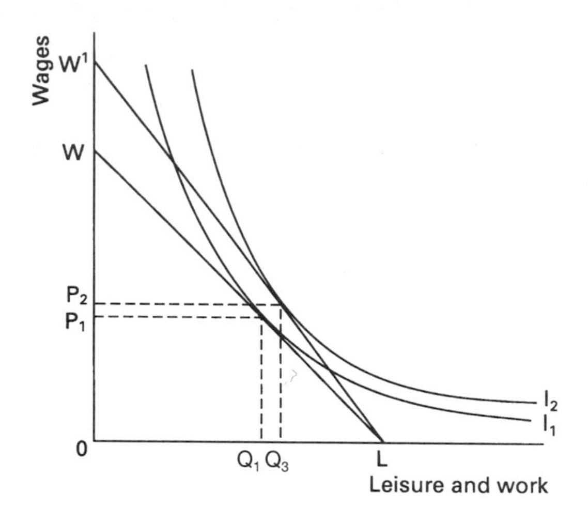

individual to choose more leisure and to work less. The result is that the amount of time spent working falls from LQ_1 to LQ_3, i.e. by Q_1 - Q_3. A real life example of this happened in the past when coal miners received an increase in wages. They often decided that their income was now sufficiently high that they did not need to work full time, so they reduced the time at work by missing a shift. This caused the Coal Board to change the payment system so that miners' income depended less on time worked and more on productivity bonuses.

This theoretical analysis has considerable practical importance. If the government cuts income taxes, the effect will be the same as an increase in wages. But will it cause people to work more – as the government would hope – or will they follow the path outlined in Figure 4.9 and instead increase their leisure? There is no certain answer to this question, but empirical evidence suggests that the two effects might balance out, so that tax cuts have little effect on the amount of time worked.

Conclusion

The theory of consumer choice is a rather technical way to analyse the demand curve. An approach using marginal utility is useful, but sometimes criticised because it assumes utility can be measured in a cardinal way. Indifference curve analysis does not have this disadvantage and can be used to show the effects of changes in prices and in incomes.

Data questions

Spending on food

Unfortunately for food producers, the human stomach has a limited capacity for food. The world being what it is, farmers throughout the world try to produce more, but the more they produce the lower the price that they receive for their produce. There are exceptions, of course. At one end of the spectrum, in poor countries where food is scarce, the population is rising, and where people are hungry, the price of food may rise. This is also the position at the other end of the spectrum, where in rich countries such as Britain people are willing to spend more money on exotic foods such as tropical fruits and vegetables. However, these exceptions are relatively unimportant. The overall picture is clear; without government intervention the price of basic foods will fall. The position is made worse because as incomes rise people spend proportionately less of their income on food, and more on other goods.

Question 1

1. Using either of the two approaches to consumer theory outlined in this chapter, explain the effect on consumers' equilibrium of:
   (i) the change in the price of food and
   (ii) the change in income
   as discussed in the article.
2. Explain what is meant by income and substitution effects and relate these concepts to the changes in the price of food.

5 Size of Firm: Big is Best – or is Small Beautiful?

Two hundred years ago production was organised on a small scale. Whilst a few merchants and manufacturers employed comparatively large numbers of people, most production was organised round the home. Moreover, the public sector was tiny and composed largely of the armed forces and a minute civil service. Today the position is very different. Millions of people work in the public sector and many large firms employ thousands of people. There are two conflicting opinions on these changes.

- On the one hand some economists believe that large-scale production is more efficient because it allows firms to take advantage of economies of scale.
- On the other hand critics of this view believe that these economies can be exaggerated and argue that large-scale organisation breeds bureaucratic inefficiency and often dehumanises the workers. Moreover, it is held that if economic power is concentrated in the hands of a few large firms, these will also have a great deal of political power and this will weaken the democratic rights of ordinary people.

Consequently there is considerable debate about the most desirable size of firm. However, before we can participate fully in that debate, we need to discuss the relative importance of small and large firms in the UK, and also how firms grow.

How important are large and small firms in the UK?

Is the UK economy dominated by a few large firms or is economic power evenly spread throughout the economy? One way to examine this question is to see what proportion of total manufacturing output is produced by a certain number – usually 100 – of the largest firms and the extent to which this has changed over the years. The degree of concentration rose until the depression of the 1930s and then fell until the end of the Second World War. Then there was a huge rise in concentration which seems to have levelled out in recent years. Ignoring short-term variations, there is no doubt that over the long period there has been a great increase in the economic importance of large manufacturing firms. One example of this increasing concentration is the brewing industry. At the beginning of the century there were nearly 1,500 brewing companies in the UK; now the number is down to about 60, though the total production of beer has hardly changed.

This evidence is supported by looking at what has happened to small firms. In the forty years following 1930 the number of very small firms (in this case those employing less than 10 people) fell by a half, though in the last few years there appears to have been a recovery in the importance of these firms. One reason for this is the fall in the size of some large firms as they laid off workers in response to the decline in economic activity after 1979.

A similar pattern emerges if we look at small but slightly larger firms – in this case those employing less than 200 workers. In 1935 these were responsible for 38 per cent of jobs in manufacturing. By 1968 their contribution had fallen to 19 per cent, but it then rose to 31 per cent by 1987.

In recent decades the service sector has grown in importance and this has had an important effect on the overall picture. However, data for this sector is not easily available. What is clear is that in the service sector there is great disparity in size, often depending on the particular industry. In banking and air transport, for example, the industry is dominated by a few large firms, whilst in hair-dressing and shoe repairs the typical firm is very small.

Figure 5.1: *Share of UK car production by firm, 1991*

Is Rover bigger than Ford?

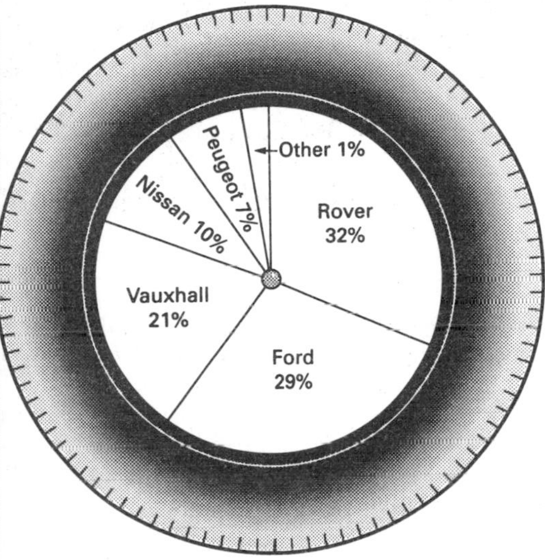

Source: Adapted from *Motor Industry of Great Britain*, Society of Motor Manufacturers and Traders, 1993.

The size of firms in manufacturing

Measurement

There are a number of ways in which the size of firms can be measured. Perhaps the most common is to use the number of people employed by the firm, but some economists prefer to use the value of the output produced or the level of profits. Each method has its problems. For example, the number of people employed by a firm may vary considerably over a year, so that arbitrary decisions have to be made about which figure to use. Moreover, most firms employ part time workers and it is not always obvious how many part timers equal a full time worker. Similar problems arise if output or profitability are used. Should these be measured inclusive or exclusive of taxes such as VAT or corporation tax?

There are problems which arise whatever the method. Many large firms have overseas subsidiaries. Should these be included when estimating the size of UK firms? There is no correct answer to questions such as these. What is clear is that different methods will give different results. Using the value of output will increase the relative importance of firms making products, such as tobacco or petrol, where the retail price includes a large tax element. Using the number of workers will increase the relative importance of labour intensive firms. Table 5.1 illustrates this point. What order would you put the firms in if you were arranging them in order of size?

Table 5.1: *Which firm is biggest?*

Company	Turnover (£ million)	Profit (£ million)	Employment	Equity (£ million)
Shell	52,166	7,445	135,000	31,291
BP	29,641	2,533	119,850	11,441
BAT Industries	21,636	2,041	311,917	5,089
Unilever	21,521	1,802	296,000	3,194
BT	12,315	2,302	24,200	14,251
British Gas	7,983	1,051	79,000	19,487

Source: European Business Top 500, 1991-92.

Moreover, figures which give the size of firms in one country can be very misleading. Figure 5.1 shows manufacturers' share of car production in the UK. The largest firm is Rover, which produces about a third of the total. But this could be misleading because all of the firms are part of large car manufacturing groups with massive production outside the UK. Hence Rover may appear to be a dominant firm in the industry, but it is possibly smaller in world terms than, for example, Ford.

Evidence

Whatever the criteria used, the same pattern emerges when manufacturing industry is analysed: there is a large number of small firms and only a few very large firms. However, these large firms are very important in the UK economy. This is also true in other advanced industrial countries.

Table 5.2. shows the size distribution of manufacturing enterprises in the United Kingdom. It is clear that the vast majority of firms are small – if up to 100 employees can be regarded as small – but these companies account for only 25 per cent of employment and 18 per cent of output. At the other extreme there are less than 300 firms employing over 2,000 workers, but these employ 43 per cent of the workers in manufacturing and produce just over half of the output. These figures apply to activities in the UK. If foreign sales and output were included, the importance of these giants would be even more marked.

Table 5.2 gives the picture for manufacturing industry as a whole, but the general picture conceals considerable variations between industries. These are illustrated in Figure 5.2. In 1992 small businesses were particularly important in agriculture, where a third of farmers had a turnover of less than £25,000. Perhaps rather surprisingly, in the catering industry only 3 per cent of establishments had turnover of this size.
At the other extreme, large firms were particularly important in wholesaling.

Table 5.2: *Size distribution of manufacturing enterprises in the UK, 1990*

No. of Employees	No. of enterprises	Total employment (000)	Gross output (£ million)
1- 99	127,998	1,204	56,455
100- 199	2,342	324	17,308
200- 499	1,482	454	27,272
500- 999	538	378	25,669
1000-1999	286	397	26,942
over 2000	294	2,053	164,464

Source: *Business Monitor* PA 1002, HMSO, 1992.

There is also considerable variation between different industries within the manufacturing sector. This is shown in Table 5.3, which makes use of a measuring device often used by economists – **the five firm concentration ratio**. This shows the share of output and employment of the five largest firms in the industry. In the tobacco and steel industries the ratio was well over 90 per cent. Clearly, these are industries dominated by a few large firms. At the other extreme, in sawmilling the share of the five largest firms was less than 20 per cent.

Figure 5.2: *Relative contributions by small and large businesses*

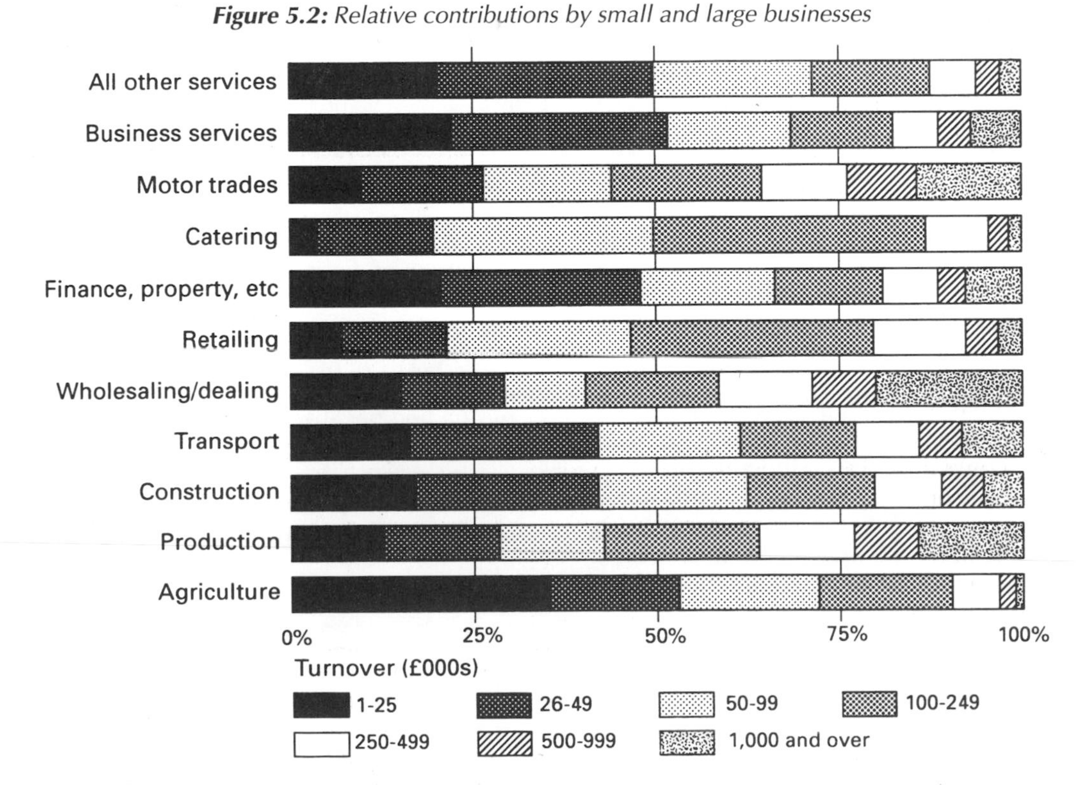

Source: Adapted from *Business Monitor* PA 1002, HMSO, 1992.

***Table 5.3:** Share of the largest five firms*

Industry	% share of Employees	% share of output
Non-ferrous metals	36	38
Iron and steel	92	95
Paint	32	34
Man-made fibres	89	91
Clocks & watches	34	24
Tobacco	98	99
Sawmilling	16	19

Source: *Business Monitor* PA1003, HMSO 1991-92.

The public sector

Most of this chapter will focus on the private sector, but the picture would not be complete without giving a brief survey of the position in the public sector. This includes a very wide range of activities including the work of teachers, soldiers, police officers and civil servants as well as those working in nationalised industries such as the Post Office. In some cases the employers are responsible for thousands of workers, yet the individual operates in a small environment. An example of this would be teachers working in small village schools. This example illustrates an important point to be made when discussing the scale of operations. In some cases people work in small units even though they are part of a large organisation. The size of the unit in the public sector is often determined by the nature of the job. If the town is small, then the library and the local sports centre will also be small. For nationalised industries, the factors governing their size are often the same as those affecting private sector firms, for they are influenced by similar – though not identical – economic factors.

Key ideas

1. Over the long term, there has been an increase in the importance of very large firms.
2. In manufacturing there are only a few large firms, but they have considerably economic importance.
3. In some industries the typical firm is very large, in others small firms are more common.
4. In the public sector organisations tend to be large, but individual work units may be small.

Revenue and costs

How do firms decide how much to produce? One major influence in making this decision will be the profit that they expect to make at various levels of output. In order to examine the effects of firm size we need to examine in some detail two important economic concepts: revenue and costs.

Total revenue and total costs

Profit = Total revenue – Total cost

***Table 5.4:** Total revenue, total cost and profit*

(1) Output (units per month)	(2) Price (£ per unit)	(3) Total revenue (QxP) (£ per month)	(4) Total cost (£ per month)	(5) Profit (TR-TC)
10	50	500	450	50
11	49	539	486	53
12	48	576	516	60
13	47	611	541	70
14	45	630	550	80
15	43	645	560	85
16	40	640	575	65
17	36	612	620	-8
18	32	576	680	-104

The total revenue received by a firm depends on two factors: the number of items sold and their price. In most cases the demand curve slopes down, showing that firms which wish to sell more have to cut the price. In the hypothetical example given in Table 5.4, ten items can be sold at a price of £50, but to sell eighteen the price has to be cut to £32. Multiplying price by quantity gives total revenue as shown in column 3. Total cost also depends in part on the number of items produced. It costs more to produce eighteen items than ten because more raw materials and more labour are needed. However, costs may not rise proportionally with quantity because at some point the firm will have to pay overtime rates and perhaps hire extra machines which will push up costs. For this reason costs in the Table are shown as rising faster than output.

Column 5 shows profits. In this hypothetical example they rise with output, reaching a maximum when fifteen items are produced. Profits then start to fall, and the firm would make a loss if it produced seventeen or more items. The fall in profits at high levels of output reflects the high cost of producing this number of goods and also that the price has to be cut if large numbers are to be sold.

Average and marginal revenue and costs

Marginal cost is the cost of increasing output by one extra unit. Average cost is found by dividing total cost by the quantity produced.

Table 5.5: *Total, average and marginal costs*

(1) Output (units per month)	(2) Total cost (£ per month)	(3) Average costs (TC+Q) (£)	(4) Marginal cost (£)
10	450	45.0	–
11	486	44.2	36
12	516	43.0	30
13	541	41.6	25
14	550	39.3	9
15	560	37.3	10
16	575	35.9	15
17	620	36.5	45
18	680	37.8	60

In the example given in Table 5.5, when ten items are produced the total cost is £450 and consequently the average cost is £45. If output is increased to eleven items the total cost rises from £450 to £486, an increase of £36. This figure of £36 is the marginal cost of producing the eleventh item. Similarly, the marginal cost of producing the twelfth item is £516 – £486 = £30. These figures can be used to draw an average cost curve and a marginal cost curve, as in Figure 5.3. Note that it is the convention to draw the marginal cost curve **between** outputs. For example, the marginal cost of the 11th unit (£36) in Figure 5.3 is drawn between 10 and 11 on the graph.

Figure 5.3: *Average and marginal costs*

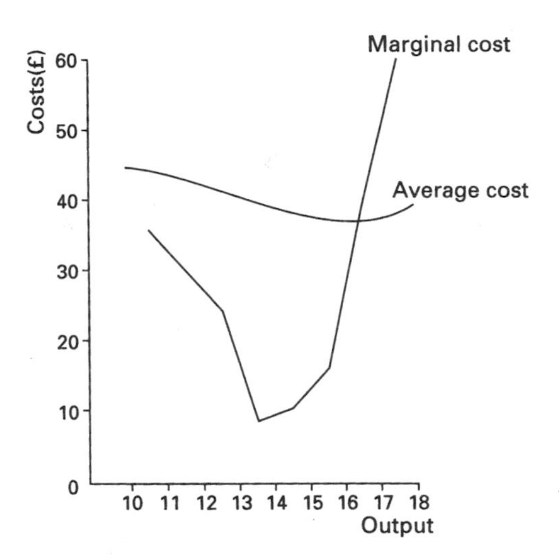

The average cost curve is usually drawn with a 'U' shape. That is because it is influenced by what is happening to marginal cost. When marginal costs are falling it pulls down the average (just as when a cricketer with a batting average of 50 is out for 10 in his next innings). In the example illustrated in Table 5.5 and Figure 5.3, marginal cost at first falls as output expands. The reason for this is explored in more detail later; for the present we can say it is because the firm can use more specialised techniques as output expands and this brings down the cost. However, at higher levels of output the marginal cost may rise quickly, perhaps because the firm is forced to take on untrained labour or pay overtime rates. This rise in marginal cost will pull up average cost (just as a batsman's average will rise if he has a big score in his next innings).

Marginal revenue is the extra revenue generated by the sale of an extra unit. In Table 5.6 total revenue is £500 when the quantity sold is ten; when this rises to eleven total revenue rises to £539. Consequently the marginal revenue is £539 – £500 = £39.

Table 5.6

(1) Quantity	(2) Price (£ per unit)	(3) Total revenue (£ per) month)	(4) Marginal revenue (£)
10	50	500	–
11	49	539	39
12	48	579	37
13	47	611	35

Table 5.7: *Marginal cost and marginal revenue*

(1) Quantity	(2) Marginal cost (£)	(3) Total revenue (£)
10	–	–
11	36	39
12	30	37
13	25	35
14	9	19
15	10	15
16	15	-5
17	45	-28
18	60	-36

Figure 5.4: *Marginal cost and marginal revenue*

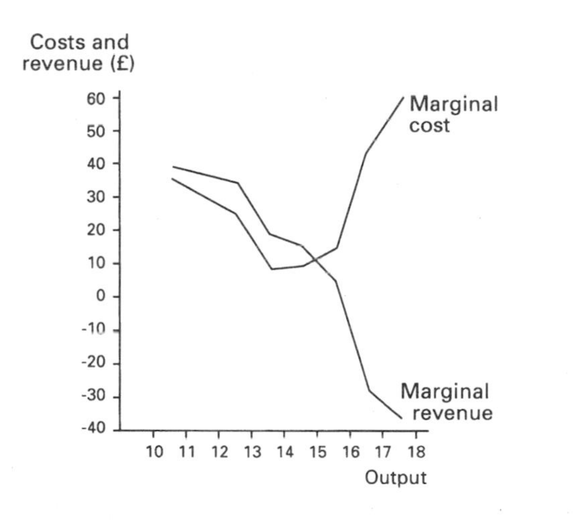

As Table 5.7 and Figure 5.4 show, if the firm increases its output from thirteen to fourteen, its costs rise by £9 and its revenue by £19. Clearly it will pay the firm to expand its output from thirteen to fourteen items. Similarly, when output rises from fourteen to fifteen, costs rise by £10 and revenue by £15. Again it will be profitable to increase output. However, if output was increased to sixteen, costs could rise by £15 whilst revenue would actually fall by £5. Hence if the firm wishes to maximise profits it will produce 15 items. This marginal analysis has confirmed the result we obtained by looking at total costs and revenue. In marginal analysis the general rule, of which this is a contrived example, is that **a firm will maximise profit if it expands output up to the point at which marginal revenue (MR) equals marginal cost (MC).**

Normal profit

This rule can only be explained in full if we bring in a slight complication. You may wonder why the firm should expand output until marginal revenue **equals** marginal cost. If increasing production raises both revenue and costs by the same amount, why bother to increase output? The answer is that the economist's concept of cost differs from that of the accountant and also from that used in everyday life. Economists include in 'costs' a notional element of profit needed to keep the firm in business. If the firm received less than this notional amount, it would be rational for the firm to close down the business and invest the money somewhere else. Hence if the firm produces at the level of output where marginal revenue equals marginal cost it will be making just enough profit to stay in business. This notional amount of money needed to keep a firm in business is called 'normal profit'. Any profit greater than this is called excess or abnormal profit.

Fixed and variable costs

An alternative way to analyse costs is to distinguish between fixed and variable costs. 'Fixed' costs are

Table 5.8: *Costs of a firm in the short run*

(1) Output (units)	(2) Total fixed costs (3)	(3) Total variable costs (£)	(4) Total costs (£)	(5) Average fixed costs (£)	(6) Average variable costs (£)	(7) Average costs (£)	(8) Marginal costs (£)
0	100	0	100	–	–		
1	100	10	110	100	10	110	10
2	100	15	115	50	7.5	57.5	5
3	100	19	119	33.3	6.3	39.6	4

those which the firm has to pay whether or not it produces any goods. Examples of fixed costs are rent, rates, bank charges, security costs and some salaries.

'Variable' costs do vary with output. Examples are wages, raw materials and the power used for machinery. These costs will normally rise as output expands:

Total costs = Fixed costs + Variable costs

In Table 5.8, column 2 gives total fixed costs; these do not vary with the level of output. Column 3 shows total variable costs; these do increase as output rises. Column 4 shows that total costs are the sum of fixed and variable costs. Columns 5 and 6 give average fixed and average variable costs. In the case of average fixed costs, these are obtained by dividing total fixed costs by output. Average variable costs are obtained in the same way, by dividing total variable costs by output. The last two columns in the Table show average costs and marginal costs. These are calculated as shown in the last section.

These relationships can be shown diagrammatically and Figure 5.5 does this for marginal cost (MC), average fixed costs (AFC), and average variable costs (AVC).

Figure 5.5

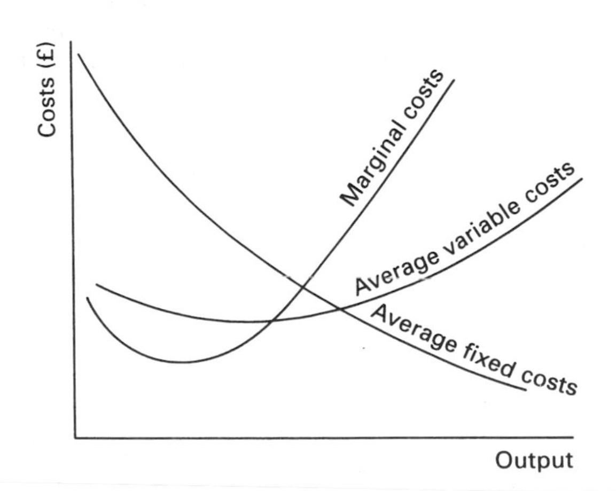

Average fixed costs fall as output rises, because at low levels of output these costs are very large for each item produced, but as output expands the fixed costs can be spread over more items. If a factory produced a hundred thousand tins of baked beans a week, the rent bill would only add a minute cost to each tin.

Diminishing returns

In Figure 5.5 the average variable cost curve and the marginal cost curve are drawn sloping down and then rising up again. One explanation of this rise derives from **the law of diminishing returns**. This says that if all factors of production except one are held constant, then increases in the variable factor will eventually lead to declining average and marginal products.

An example will clarify this law. If we have fixed inputs of land (say 100 acres) and capital (say 2 tractors and a given amount of seed), but can vary the quantity of labour, what will happen to output as the number of workers increases? At some point the marginal product of labour will start to fall. Workers will start to get in each others' way, and some will have no tools. If more workers are added there will be growing management problems and at some point the amount produced may actually fall as the number of workers increases.

Two points about the law of diminishing returns should be noted. Firstly, the word 'eventually' makes it clear that at first output may rise as additional units of the variable factor are added. Two people building a house may be more than twice as productive as one because they can specialise and also help each other with heavy jobs. Time is also important. In the short run firms cannot build new factories and so we may expect the law of diminishing returns to operate. This will mean that at some point output per worker will fall, thus explaining why marginal costs eventually rise.

Figure 5.6: *Long-run average cost*

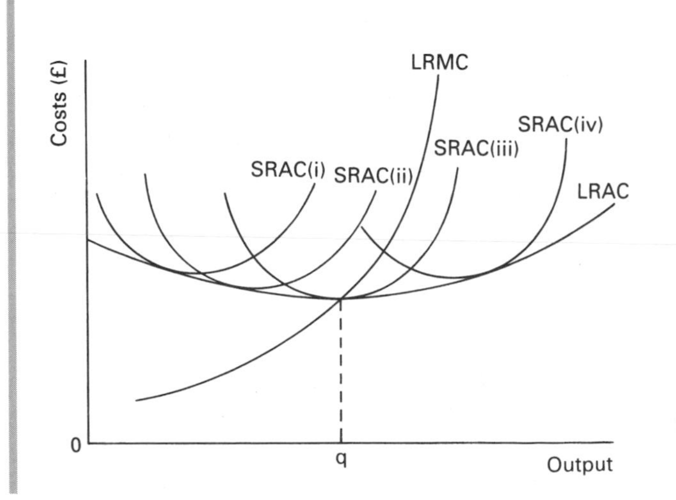

In the long run the position is different because firms can vary all the factors of production. In particular they can build new factories. This means that the firm's long-run average cost curve will be made up of a series of short-run average curves as shown in Figure 5.6. In the long run the firm can choose to produce anywhere on this long-run curve. The most efficient place will be at q where average cost is lowest. (This is also the place where the long-run marginal cost curve intersects the long-run average cost curve.)

A word of caution is needed here. The analysis of costs presented here is very theoretical. This has advantages; it enables us to develop a framework of analysis. However, real life is often more complicated. Two examples will illustrate this. Firstly, firms may not seek to **maximise** profits; instead they may be content to make reasonable profits. If this is so, they may produce at a range of places on the cost curve. This issue is examined in more detail in Chapter 6. Secondly, in practice cost curves may not always rise and fall in the 'U' shape shown in most diagrams. For example, average costs may not rise when output expands (this is illustrated in Figure 5.9). Their actual shape will vary considerably between firms because some will have lower costs than others.

Key ideas

1. Marginal cost is the cost of increasing output by an extra unit. Marginal revenue is the extra revenue obtained when output is increased by one unit.
2. Profits will be maximised when a firm produces where marginal revenue equals marginal cost.
3. Fixed costs do not vary with output; variable costs do.
4. The law of diminishing returns says that if all factors of production except one are held constant, then increases in the variable factor will eventually lead to declining average and marginal products.

How do firms grow?

Firms grow in two ways: by internal growth and by merging with others.

Internal growth

Many firms become large by generating internal growth. Marks and Spencer is an example. It started as a market stall selling clothes and still does this, though it has also diversified into other products. Other firms have also grown by diversifying within the same industry. The Ford Motor Company started by producing only one car model; now it produces not only a wide range of cars, but also trucks and other related products. Such diversification makes it possible for firms to become large while still remaining in the same business.

One reason why firms grow large is that, in some cases, their average costs fall in the long run as the firm produces more. This was illustrated in Figure 5.6. When the cost curve is this shape, any firm producing only a few goods will be at a disadvantage compared to its competitors because its costs will be higher. Where costs vary with output in this way, firms tend to grow until they produce a level of output where costs are low.

Mergers

Some firms are content to remain small. Their owners are satisfied with reasonable profits and are not willing to deal with the problems which may arise if the firm is to grow. On the other hand some entrepreneurs want to be big. They are constantly seeking new opportunities for growth and are willing to struggle in order to take over other firms, even though these may resist. For this group big is beautiful.

Figure 5.7: *Types of integration*

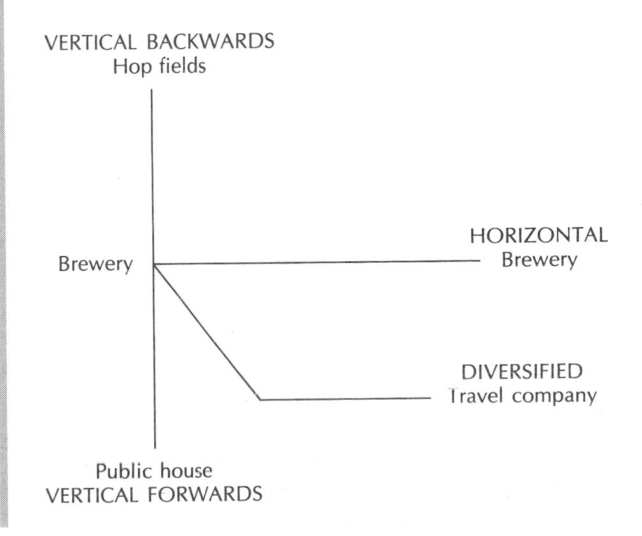

Mergers can take several forms. Sometimes firms take over their suppliers or their customers. This is called **vertical integration**. Examples would include a brewing company which bought hop fields or took over a firm owning pubs. Vertical integration can be either forward or backward. Firms integrate backwards to obtain control over the raw materials and components they need. Forward integration gives them control over marketing the products they make. Another reason for vertical integration is that it reduces transactions costs. As the phrase implies, these are the costs involved in buying and selling goods. Uncertainties over demand and supply conditions can lead to costly haggling over the terms of a contract between firms. This haggling can be eliminated if one firm merges with the other. For example, Stuckley (1983) examined vertical integration in the American aluminium industry. The basic raw material used in this industry is bauxite, which varies in quality. This leads to uncertainty, haggling and high transactions costs when trade takes place. Consequently aluminium producers seek to reduce these costs by backward vertical integration.

Horizontal integration occurs when a firm buys another at the same stage of production. Examples include a brewer buying another brewer or one publisher taking over another. One reason firms do this is that it gives them an element of monopoly power. This may allow them to put up prices. It can also increase their bargaining power with suppliers who may be forced to cut the price they charge a large customer.

The other form of merger is sometimes called **diversified integration** and occurs when a firm merges with another in a completely different industry as, for example, when a tobacco company buys an insurance company or an engineering firm joins a company building houses. Mergers between very different firms lead to the formation of **conglomerates**. For example, what have the following in common: Ashanti Goldfields, Mufundi Tea Co., Volkswagen UK, Scottish Farmer Publications, Dutton-Forshaw, Princess Casinos? The answer is that they are all part of a conglomerate called Lonrho. Another example of a conglomerate is Hanson plc. This owns Beazer Homes, Berec Batteries, Bulldog Insurance Co., Consolidated Gold Fields, Portland Chemicals, Hanson Bank, Imperial Tobacco and Jacuzzi.

One reason for diversified integration is that it reduces risk. If one product or firm within the conglomerate fails, profits from the others will allow the firm to continue in business. Another reason is that diversified firms within a conglomerate possess assets which can be shared. One may have technological know-how, another spare physical capacity and a third may have marketing or managerial expertise. Sharing such assets can bring substantial benefits to the group. Moreover, diversification can reduce transactions costs if quick managerial decisions within a firm replace expensive negotiations with other firms.

Key ideas

1. Many firms grow through internal growth. One reason is that costs may fall in the long run as the firm grows.
2. Alternatively firms grow through mergers. These can take the form of vertical, horizontal or diversified integration.

Big is best

No one believes that in every case large firms are better than small ones; but many economists do argue that in numerous industries large firms will have a significant advantage. They therefore advocate that government policies should recognise this advantage, for example, by encouraging firms to merge or at least refraining from restricting firms' growth. One reason for this belief is the existence of economies of scale.

Economies of scale

Economies of scale exist when long-run average costs fall as output expands. Sometimes these occur as the **firm** grows, sometimes they result from growth in the individual **factory or plant**.

Plant economies of scale

As the name implies technical economies arise out of the techniques of production. Some occur because of specialisation of both labour and machines. When plants operate on a large scale they can make use of specialised equipment which would be too expensive for small operations. A good example is the robots used on car production lines.

Specialised machinery often goes hand in hand with the use of specialised labour, that is with the division of labour. Over two hundred years ago Adam Smith described the spectacular results that could be achieved in a pin factory when each worker concentrated on one task. In modern factories, as in those described by Smith, workers who concentrate on one task become expert and highly productive.

Another related economy of size arises from increased dimensions. A large truck and a small van can both be driven by one person, but the larger vehicle can carry far more goods. Moreover, as units are built on a larger scale the construction costs may rise proportionally less than the building size. Engineers have a rule of thumb which suggests that the cost of a building increases by only two-thirds of the increase in the size of the building. Some machines and techniques of production are indivisible. It is not possible to build a small nuclear power station or a tiny plant making jet engines for aeroplanes. Another economy accruing to large-scale plants sometimes arises in the use of stocks. Small workshops need spare parts for all the processes; a much larger plant may also require only the same quantity of spares.

Figure 5.8: *Economies of scale*

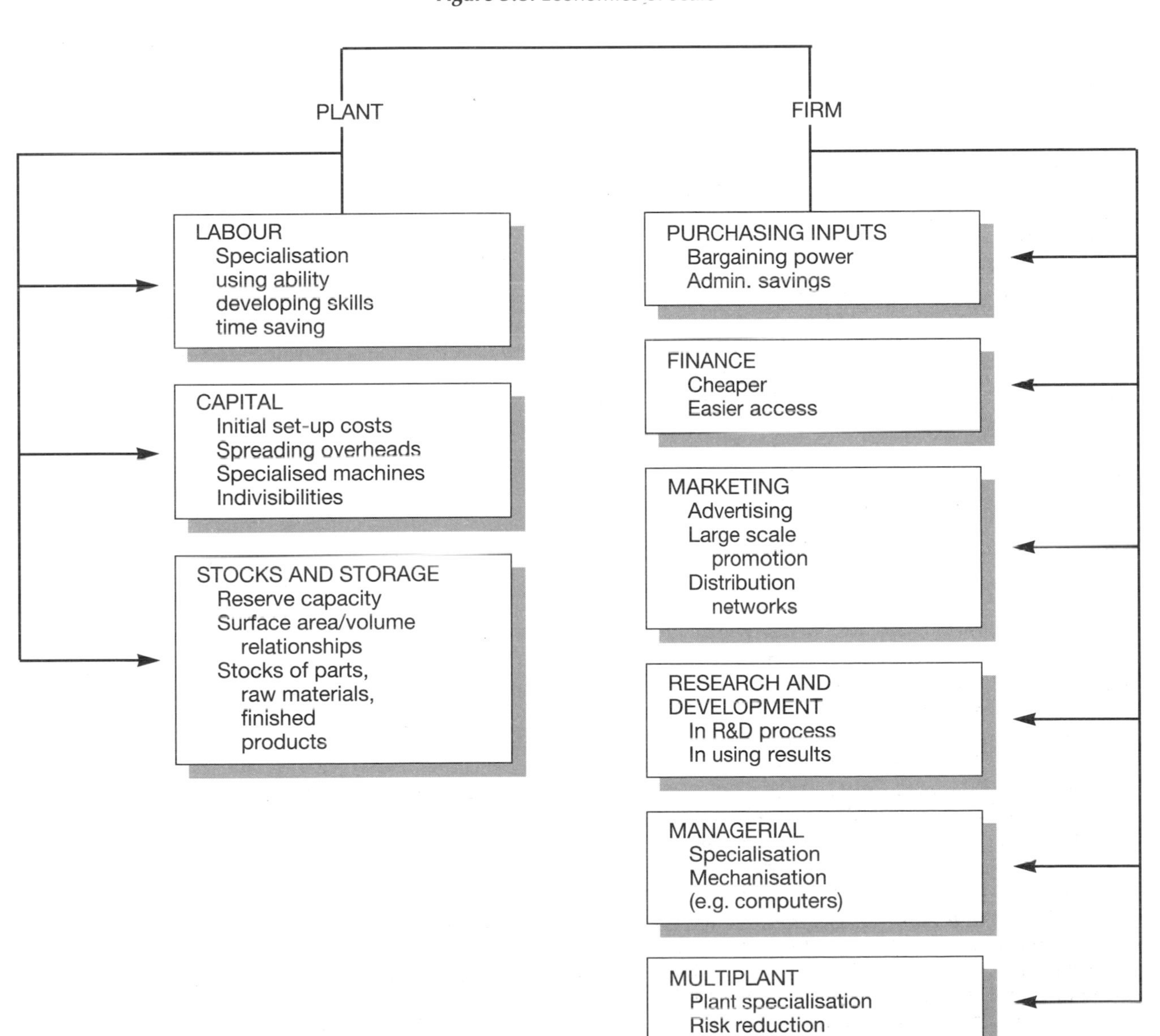

The existence of plant economies of scale means that factories are inefficient if they do not reach a certain size. Table 5.9 gives estimates of this minimum efficient size for a number of products.

Table 5.9: *Some estimates of minimum efficient plant size*

Product	Minimum efficient plant size
Beer	1 million barrels per annum
Commercial vehicles	30,000 units per annum
Electric cookers	30,000 units per annum
Sugar refining	45,000 tonnes
Diesel engines	10,000 units

Note: This is a simplified extract; the original contains several estimates for some items.
Source: Adapted from *A Review of Monopolies and Mergers Policy*, HMSO.

Firm economies of scale

Risk bearing economies arise because a large firm which produces many products can stand the loss if one product does not sell. Table 5.10 illustrates this economic version of the adage: 'Don't put all your eggs in one basket'. Hence B.A.T., which makes many of the cigarettes sold outside the UK, bought an insurance company in order to reduce the risk associated with the production of only one commodity. This is an example of diversified integration discussed earlier.

Table 5.10: *Multi-plant and firm economies*

Industry	Source of economies
Beer brewing	Advertising, co-ordination of new plant investments
Cement	Risk spreading and raising finance
Refrigerators	Long production runs, advertising, transplantation
Cigarettes	Advertising and product differentiation

Large firms can have **financial advantages** compared to small ones. They can afford to employ financial specialists. In addition, financial institutions often prefer to lend to large organisations, so these find it easier to borrow money. Moreover, they can often borrow more cheaply. Thus a firm such as Sainsburys can borrow money more easily and cheaply than could a village shop.

Large firms may also have advantages in both **buying and selling**. Big firms can buy in bulk and hence buy at lower cost. Often they can also sell more cheaply because they can spread their marketing costs over a larger output. A firm with a hundred shops can advertise them all on television for the same price that a small firm can advertise one shop. **Research and development** can be expensive. To introduce a new medicine, for example, can involve large teams of highly trained – and expensive – people, and even when the drug has been created it needs expensive testing. Small firms cannot afford such costs.

Some evidence on economies of scale

The supporters of large-scale production can produce evidence to support their claims. Pratten (1971) investigated the minimum efficient scale of plants and concluded that in some industries, such as aircraft production, electronic data processing and equipment, steel rolling mills and electric motors, there were significant advantages in producing in large plants. Put another way, the slope of the long-run cost curve in Figure 5.7 was steep so that firms producing quantities less than q in that diagram would face much higher costs. Other evidence was provided by Scherer (1980) who investigated the minimum efficient size of plants in the USA. His evidence is presented in Table 5.11.

Table 5.11

Industry	Minimum optimal scale
Cigarettes	36 billion cigarettes a year, 2,275 employees
Glass bottles	133,000 tons per year, 1,000 employees
Refrigerators	800,000 units a year
Shoes	1 million pairs a year
Paints	10 million gallons a year

Source: Scherer, F.M. *Industrial Market Structure and Economic Performance,* Rand McNally, 1980.

These are only examples and changes in technology over time alter the precise point at which plants reach their greatest efficiency.

Another example of the efficiency of large-scale production occurs in the steel industry. In the mid-1950s half the plants in Japan had a capacity of less than half a million tons. By the end of the decade almost all these plants had been closed and replaced by larger ones so that nearly half of the plants had a capacity of five million tons or more. This development enabled Japan to dominate the

world steel market and by the early 1980s one Japanese plant was so large that it could produce more than the entire British Steel Corporation whilst using far fewer workers.

Experience curves

Another argument in favour of large-scale operation derives from the notion of experience curves. The long-run average cost curve shows how costs behave at a particular moment in time; but there is some evidence which suggests that costs can fall over time as the volume of output increases over the life of a product. It is suggested in management literature that costs will decline by a constant percentage each time the accumulated production or experience of the firm doubles. Such a curve is called an 'experience curve' and one example taken from the government Green Paper on mergers and monopolies suggested that as Pilkington Glass increased their experience of producing float glass on a large scale, total cost per square foot fell by over 40 per cent. If falls in real costs are common they are a good reason why firms should try to increase the volume of production.

Key ideas – summary of the argument in favour of large-scale production

1. As living standards have increased over the years, firms have grown larger. This suggests that further increases in size will lead to greater rises in living standards.
2. As factories grow in size they can make use of specialised machinery and extend the division of labour.
3. As firms grow in size they can enjoy other economies of scale in areas such as finance, marketing, purchasing and in risk bearing.
4. Experience curve arguments suggest that costs fall as the volume of production rises.

Small is beautiful

It is clear that there is a powerful set of arguments to suggest considerable advantage from large-scale production. Yet there are strong competing arguments which emphasise the advantages of small organisations.

Criticisms of the economies of scale argument

In the earlier section we emphasised the economies to be gained from large-scale production. Many of these arguments are open to criticism.

In the first place, in many industries there may be either no economies of scale, or these may be of negligible importance. This is the case in many service industries where personal attention is needed. That is why there are no enormous hairdressing shops employing hundreds of assistants. Similarly, there are few economies of scale in other jobs that require individual attention, such as roof repairs, plumbing, or painting and decorating. In all these cases firms tend to be small; indeed, they are often owned and operated by only one person.

Even in manufacturing, economies of scale are often small. In industries as diverse as the production of shoes, bricks, bread, beer, cotton spinning and weaving, and book printing, it is possible to produce economically on a small scale. Put another way, the minimum efficient size of plant is relatively small and once this is reached there are few economies to be obtained by growing bigger. Hence the long-run average cost curve quickly becomes flat as shown in Figure 5.9. This line of argument is supported by the work of Pratten (1971), who estimated that only in a few cases would costs rise by more than 10 per cent if the firm operated at half the optimum capacity. Similarly, Scherer (1980) analysed American industries and concluded that the long-run cost curve was similar to that shown in Figure 5.9 and that:

'the minimum optimal plant scale revealed in studies of American manufacturing industries has been small relative to industry size'.

Figure 5.9: *Few economies of scale*

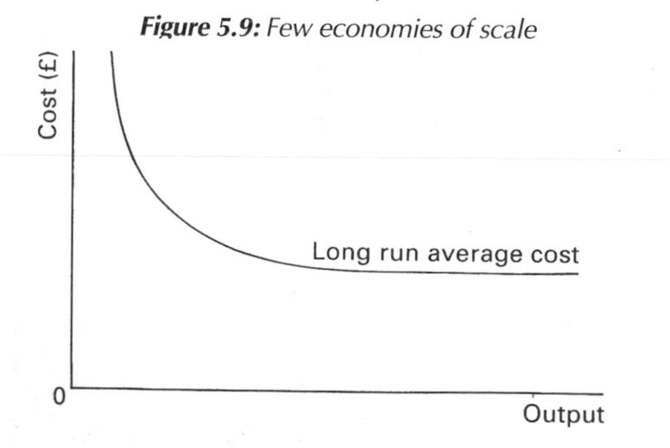

Similar arguments can be used to suggest that there are few economies accruing to large-scale firms. Profits are one possible measure of efficiency. Buzzel and Gale (1987) investigated the relationship between size and the rate of return on investment. They found an inverse relationship; rates of return were far higher in small market segments. This confirmed earlier research by Whittington (1976) which found that small firms had a rate of return of 17 per cent whilst for large firms it was only 15.8 per cent.

Even where firms do benefit from being large, this may not be in the interest of the consumer. In some cases large firms may use their large size to dominate the market and reap monopoly profits by exploiting the consumer. Similarly, where there are economies in size these may not benefit the consumer. Advertising may protect the positions of established firms and reduce competition. Firms which borrow money more cheaply may not pass the benefits on to the consumer and, if the supply of funds is scarce, large firms may obtain loans at the expense of small ones, who may be unable to borrow.

Diseconomies of scale

Even where economies of scale do exist, they have to be balanced against the possibility that diseconomies of scale may also exist. The main reason for this is that management is more difficult in large firms. Managers spend lots of time in meetings and much effort goes into ensuring satisfactory communications. Decision making may be slow, so that the firm takes time to adapt to change. In addition, one characteristic of large-scale organisations is that parts of the whole develop their own goals which may be at variance with the needs of the whole. The managing director may wish to maximise profits, but the manager of a particular department may be more concerned to increase the size and influence of that department.

Moreover, large firms may have poorer labour relations than small ones. Workers may feel that they are just tiny cogs in a huge wheel and be more likely to strike or take other forms of industrial action than workers in small firms.

Advantages of small firms

Small firms sometimes have positive advantages over large ones or else devise methods which minimise their disadvantages. For example, they sometimes buy in expertise and so take advantage of other firms' specialities. This is common in the building industry, where the main contractor for a development may hire specialists, such as architects or scaffolders. They sometimes buy in semi-finished products and so take advantage of the economies of scale enjoyed by their suppliers. Above all, small firms can offer personal service and can react quickly to changing opportunities in the market.

Small is beautiful

A rather different line of argument in support of smallness is taken by a group inspired by the writings of E.F. Schumacher, whose book *Small is Beautiful* (1974) is subtitled 'a study of economics as if people mattered'. He argues that large-scale methods often de-humanise workers and quotes Gandhi:

'I want the dumb millions of our land to be healthy and happy, and I want them to grow spiritually... If we feel the need for machines, we will certainly have them. Every machine that helps every individual has a place, but there should be no place for machines that concentrate power in a few hands and turn the masses into mere machine minders.'

Schumacher argues in favour of 'technology with a human face' – small-scale machines that give workers a feeling of satisfaction. He argues that:

'The technology of mass production is inherently violent, ecologically damaging, self-defeating in terms of non-renewable resources, and stultifying for the human person'.

What is needed is **intermediate technology**, superior to the primitive technology of old, but without the destructive qualities of super-technology. This intermediate technology should be located in small-scale organisations which promote individual dignity. Critics of this approach suggest that international competition forces firms to search for ways to cut costs so that they are 'locked into' particular methods of production and cannot adopt a more humane approach because the risks would be too great.

Key ideas – summary of the argument in favour of small size

1. In many industries there may be few – if any – economies of scale.
2. Large firms may use their size to exploit the consumer.
3. There are diseconomies of scale, such as bureaucracy.
4. Small firms have positive advantages such as personal service and flexibility.
5. Schumacher argues that large organisations de-humanise people, while small ones using intermediate technology can promote health and happiness.

Innovation in large and small firms

One of the advantages often claimed for large firms is that they can afford to spend more on research and development and that therefore large firms are more innovative and efficient.

The reality may be more complex. For example, according to its Annual Report, in 1992 IBM spent $6,522 million on research and development. Research on this scale gave IBM thousands of patents and made it the first to develop and produce four consecutive generations of memory chips. This deep R&D background made it possible for a new IBM company formed to manage its PC business to introduce more than 80 new products in only a few weeks.

On the other hand relatively small firms can also innovate. At the beginning of the 1980s Apple Computer was a $100 million company; by the end of the decade its turnover was $5 billion. One reason for this growth was its emphasis on innovation; for example, spending 8.5 per cent of sales on R&D. One result of this spending was the elimination of CFCs (which cause global warming) in all of its manufacturing plants round the world.

Table 5.12 summarises the advantages and disadvantages of small and large firms in introducing innovation. The table shows that innovations can originate and be developed in all sizes of firm. One suggestion is that the advantage may lie with large firms in established industries, but that in rapidly developing industries, such as computers, small firms can be more innovative.

Table 5.12: *Advantages and disadvantages[1] of small and large firms in innovation*

	Small firms	Large firms
Marketing	Ability to react quickly to keep abreast of fast changing market requirements. *Market start-up abroad can be prohibitively costly.*	Comprehensive distribution and servicing facilities.
Management	Lack of bureaucracy. Dynamic, entrepreneurial managers react quickly to take advantage of new opportunities and are willing to accept risk.	Professional managers able to control complex organisations and establish corporate strategies. *Can suffer an excess of bureaucracy. Often controlled by accountants who can be risk-averse. Managers can become mere 'administrators' who lack dynamism.*
Internal communication	Efficient and informal internal communication networks. Affords a fast response to internal problem solving; provides ability to reorganise rapidly to adapt to change.	*Internal communication often cumbersome: this can lead to slow reaction to opportunities.*
Qualified technical manpower	*Often lack suitably qualified technical specialists. Often unable to support a formal R&D effort on an appreciable scale.*	Ability to attract highly skilled technical specialists. Can support the establishment of a large R&D laboratory.

External communication	*Often lack the time or resources to identify and use important external sources of scientific and technological expertise.*	Able to 'plug-in' to external sources of scientific and technological expertise. Can afford library and information services. Can buy crucial technical information and technology.
Finance	*Can experience great difficulty in attracting capital, especially risk capital. Inability to spread risk over a portfolio of projects.*	Ability to borrow on capital market. Ability to spread risk over a portfolio of projects. Better able to fund diversification into new technologies.
Economies of scale and the systems approach	*In some areas scale economies form a substantial entry barrier to small firms.*	Ability to gain scale economies in R&D, production and marketing. Ability to offer a range of complementary products.
Growth	*Can experience difficulty in acquiring external capital necessary for rapid growth*	Ability to finance expansion of production base. Ability to fund growth via diversification and acquisition.
Patents	*Can experience problems in coping with the patent system. Cannot afford time or costs involved in patent litigation.*	Ability to employ patent specialists. Can afford to litigate to defend patents against infringement.
Government regulations	*Often cannot cope with complex regulations. Unit costs of compliance for small firms often high.*	Ability to fund legal services to cope with complex regulatory requirements.

[1]The statements in *italics* represent areas of potential disadvantage.
Source: Adapted from Rothwell R., 'Innovation and firm size', *Journal of General Management,* 1983.

Conclusion

In a modern industrial economy there is a huge diversity in the size of firms and factories. That is because, in some cases, economic forces encourage the growth of large units, whilst in others these forces are weak or non-existent. On one side of the argument there are good examples to show that costs sometimes fall as the scale of organisation increases. Large firms can undoubtedly benefit from economies of scale.

On the other hand it is argued that these economies may be exaggerated and that small-scale organisations have positive advantages.

The balance of the argument seems to depend on the particular circumstances; there is no overall ideal size of firm or factory.

Data questions

Economies of scale in the motor industry

Optimum scale in various car making activities	Output per year (volume)
Casting of engine block	1,000,000
Casting of various other parts	100,000 - 750,000
Power train (engine, transmission etc) machining and assembly	600,000
Pressing of various panels	1-2,000,000
Paint shop	250,000
Final assembly	250,000

Non-technical economies of the firm	Optimum number of cars per year
Advertising	1,000,000
Sales	2,000,000
Risks	1,800,000
Finance	2,500,000
Research and development	5,000,000

Source: Adapted from Dunnett, P.J.S., *The Decline of the British Motor Industry*, Croom Helm.

Question 1

1. Explain what is meant by the various non-technical economies of scale.
2. In order to minimise costs, (a) what should be the optimum size of plant; (b) what should be the optimum size of firm?
3. Given that there seem to be considerable economies of scale in the car industry, how do relatively small firms continue to exist?

Private contractors in the construction industry (Great Britain) 1991

Size of firm (by number employed)	Number of firms	Number employed (000)	Work done (£ million)
1	103,169	94	809
2-3	70,452	147	883
4-7	21,664	91	754
8-13	4,981	49	436
14-80	6,097	169	1892
80-299	803	108	1447
300-1199	195	103	1647
1200 and over	39	100	1369
All firms	207,400	861	9237

Source: *Housing and Construction Statistics 1981-1991*, HMSO 1992.

Question 2

1. What percentage of firms employ less than 25 people? What percentage of total employment and output are these firms responsible for?
2. Calculate the value of work done per person employed in these small firms and compare this with the value of work done per person in very large firms employing over 1200 people. Comment on your results.
3. Why do you think this industry has such a wide variation in the size of firms?

6 Monopoly, Competition and the Theory of the Firm

This chapter has two themes. The first is concerned with the advantages and disadvantages of competition compared to those which arise when competition is limited. The second theme is concerned with the merits of the neo-classical approach to the theory of the firm compared to those which have developed more recently.

Neo-classical theory has largely been concerned with explaining the price a firm should charge and the output it should produce. A prime determinant of firms' behaviour will be the market structure in which it operates.

- At one extreme is perfect competition. This is a hypothetical situation where firms face vigorous competition and individual firms have little influence. 'Market' economists agree that competition has considerable benefits for the consumer, so that any restriction of competition is undesirable.
- At the other extreme is monopoly – where the firm is the industry. In between these two extremes there are other forms of market structure, such as monopolistic competition and oligopoly, where some market control exists. It can be argued that these market structures do bring benefits to the consumer.

A further debate concerns the extent to which these theories give a realistic account of the way firms operate. Other developments in the theory of the firm have attempted to give a more true to life explanation.

Defining and measuring market structure

A major theme in the economic analysis of markets is that the structure of an industry affects the conduct and performance of firms in terms of the price they charge, the level of output produced and the amount of profit made. Several aspects of market structure have a particular effect on the way firms operate.

- Seller concentration – the number of firms in an industry and their relative size.
- Buyer concentration – the number of customers for a product. For many consumer goods there are potentially millions of customers, but for products such as telephone exchanges or tanks the market is limited. Similarly, most coal in the UK goes to the electricity industry.
- Barriers to entry – how easy it is for new firms to enter the industry.
- Product differentiation – whether or not products in the same market are regarded as perfect substitutes.

Here we will focus on two of these, seller concentration and barriers to entry.

Seller concentration

As we saw in the last chapter, five firm concentration ratios may vary considerably between industries. At one extreme an industry may be made up of thousands of small firms – hairdressing and roof repairs are examples. At the other extreme a single firm may dominate the industry as the Post Office dominates letter delivery. Between these two extremes lies a huge range of differing concentrations. However, there is some evidence of increasing concentration. Curry and George (1983) analysed UK industry over a long period (1935 - 1968) and concluded that on

Table 6.1: *Types of industrial structure*

Structure	Number of producers	Product differentiation	Firm's control over price	Example
Perfect competition	Many	Identical products	None	Wholesale market
Monopolistic competition	Many	Products differ	Some	Hairdressers
Oligopoly (i)	Few	Little or no differentiation	Some	Petrol
Oligopoly (ii)	Few	Some differentiation	Some	Cars
Monopoly	One	Unique product	Considerable	Post Office

average the level of concentration had increased. Table 6.2 shows the five firm concentration ratios for certain UK industries. If concentration continues to increase it has implications for policy; if large firms dominate an industry they may be able to exploit the consumer so government action may be needed to stop this from happening.

Table 6.2: *Five firm concentration ratios for certain industries*

Motor vehicles and engines	87.3
Man-made fibres	94.8
Building products (e.g. concrete)	32.3
Pharmaceuticals	48.3
Agricultural machines	60.5
Iron and steel	95.6

Source: Adapted from *Business Monitor*, PA 1002.

Barriers to entry

The level of competition in an industry does not only depend on the number of firms operating in an industry at any one time, but also on the ease with which new firms can enter the market. If barriers to entry are high, then existing firms may be able to exploit their position; if these barriers are low, then firms in the industry may modify their behaviour – for example, by keeping down prices and profits – in order not to attract new firms. Barriers to entry are costs which any new firm entering an industry will have to bear. They were first analysed in depth by Joseph Bain (1958), who distinguished three types.

Economies of scale barriers

In some industries firms have to be big to survive. Only a huge firm could construct a nuclear energy plant or build a commercial aeroplane. Sometimes existing firms try to create barriers; for example, the advertising costs needed to get a substantial share of the detergent market are so large that they deter possible new entrants. Similarly, in industries such as electricity and water supply, the costs of connecting millions of houses are sufficient to deter new firms from entering the market.

Absolute cost barriers

These barriers are often related to knowledge. New entrants may lack experience so that their costs are higher than those of existing firms. Moreover, these firms may protect their position by patents which prevent new entrants using existing methods. Thus Polaroid patented methods of taking instant photographs which prevented potential competitors such as Kodak from entering this market. Finally, firms already in the industry may have control of sources of raw materials and this makes it difficult for new firms to join the industry.

Product differentiation

This occurs when a firm makes several products which appear to the customer to be competing against each other. If a single firm makes ten varieties of soap powder, then any potential entrant would be faced by this range of competing products and, on average, would only be likely to capture one tenth of the market. This may not be enough for the product to be viable and so potential entrants are deterred. Where barriers to entry are high, we may expect competition to be at a low level; if these barriers are low then new firms will tend to be drawn to profitable markets and so increase competition. However, it remains to be seen if competition is necessarily desirable.

The case for competition

Perfect competition

The argument for competition is most clearly approached by using theoretical models of differing market structures. These may not exist in 'real life', but they set out various assumptions and show what the results will be if these assumptions are satisfied. This is the case with perfect competition.

In order for a market to be perfectly competitive, several conditions have to be met. There have to be large numbers of buyers and sellers so that even if one firm increased production considerably or one customer bought many more goods, it would have no effect on total supply or on the price at which the product sold. In addition, all the firms in the industry are assumed to make an identical product so that customers do not mind from which firm they buy. Moreover, the model assumes perfect knowledge so that everyone – buyers and sellers alike – knows what is going on. This means that if one firm attempted to put up its price no one would buy its product because an identical product could be bought from many other firms. Hence firms have to accept the going price and are called **price takers** – they charge the same price as everyone else.

Figure 6.1 shows the position of the industry and the firm in perfect competition. For the industry as a whole, the forces of demand and supply lead to an equilibrium price for the product. This is shown in the left part of the diagram. At this price the market clears – there is no shortage and no surplus; every consumer willing to pay this price will be able to purchase goods and every firm willing to supply will sell all its products. The individual firm takes this price as given and is unable to influence the price it charges for its goods. Consequently, this is the price at which every firm has to sell its product. Since there are many firms in the industry, each can sell as much as it likes at this price because none is large enough to have significant influence on total sales. Because firms can sell all they produce at the same price, the demand curve will be perfectly elastic and the average revenue received from sales will equal the marginal revenue – the price received from selling an additional unit.

The figure also shows the costs of the firm. The average cost curve is the familiar 'U' shape shown in the last chapter and the marginal cost curve has also been included. This is the cost of producing an extra unit. The marginal cost curve falls for a while as the output increases, but then rises as diseconomies of scale set in. As the last chapter showed, the firm will maximise its profits if it produces where marginal cost equals marginal revenue. In Figure 6.1 the firm will maximise profits when it produces quantity q. If it makes more or less than this quantity, costs will exceed revenue. Only at q will the firm cover its costs. This is an efficient quantity to produce, because average costs are at a minimum. Moreover, the consumer benefits from the lowest possible price – firms are charging a price which only just covers their costs. These characteristics of low cost, low price and no excess profits suggest that competition is desirable in an economy.

The short and long run

Figure 6.1 shows the long-run equilibrium position. In the short run, however, firms can make excess profits as shown in Figure 6.2. In this Figure, profits

Figure 6.1: *The industry and firm in perfect competition*

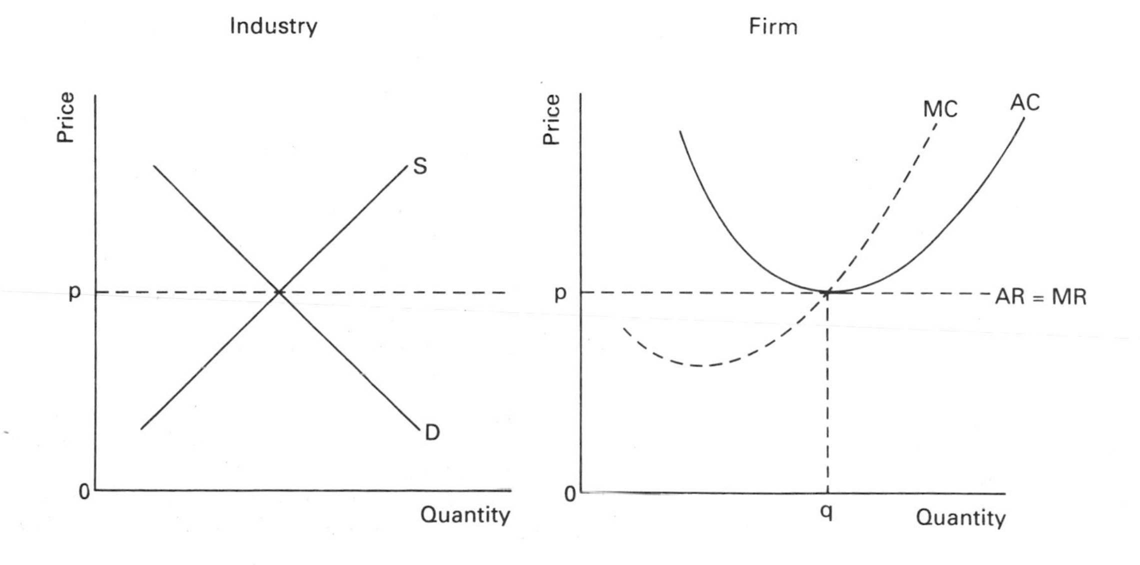

are shown by the difference between the average revenue and average cost curves multiplied by the quantity of goods. This is only a short-run position and cannot last in perfect competition. That is

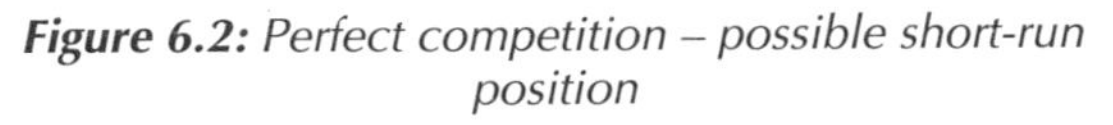

Figure 6.2: *Perfect competition – possible short-run position*

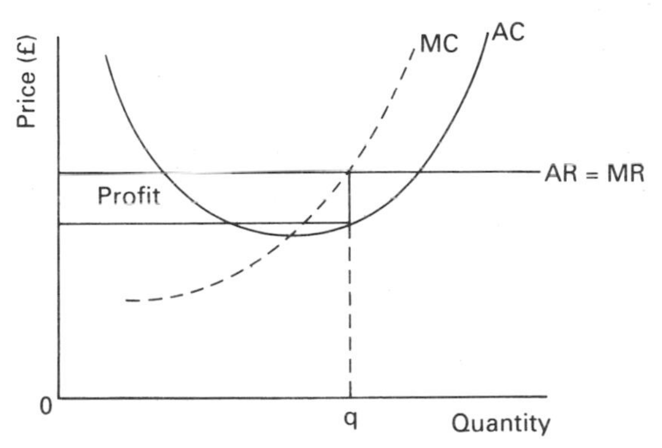

because the model assumes perfect knowledge so everyone knows about these profits. The model also assumes that it is easy to enter the industry. Hence new firms will move in and this will force down the price until it reaches the long-run equilibrium position shown in Figure 6.1. Here the firm is making just enough profit to stay in business and is not making excess profits as described in the last chapter. The main features of perfect competition are listed in Table 6.3.

Table 6.3: *Perfect competition*

1 Assumptions	Many buyers and sellers Identical product Easy entry and exit Perfect knowledge
2 How firm is affected	Firm is price taker Demand curve is horizontal (AR=MR) Firm attempts to maximise profit and produces where MR=MC
3 Result	Low price Firm produces at minimum average cost Firm makes only normal profit in the long run

Monopoly

Monopoly is at the opposite end of the spectrum from perfect competition. In economic theory it exists when there is only one firm in the industry. Pure monopoly is very rare. The Post Office comes close, but it faces competition in some parts of its activities. Because there is only one firm in the industry the firm's demand curve is also the industry demand curve. This will normally slope down to the right, showing that if the monopolist wants to sell more it has to cut its price. Hence the monopoly has a choice; it can sell more – but at a lower price. Alternatively it can charge a higher price, but then will only be able to sell a smaller quantity. Consequently the monopolist is a **price maker**; unlike the firm in perfect competition it can choose its price.

Figure 6.3: *Monopoly equilibrium*

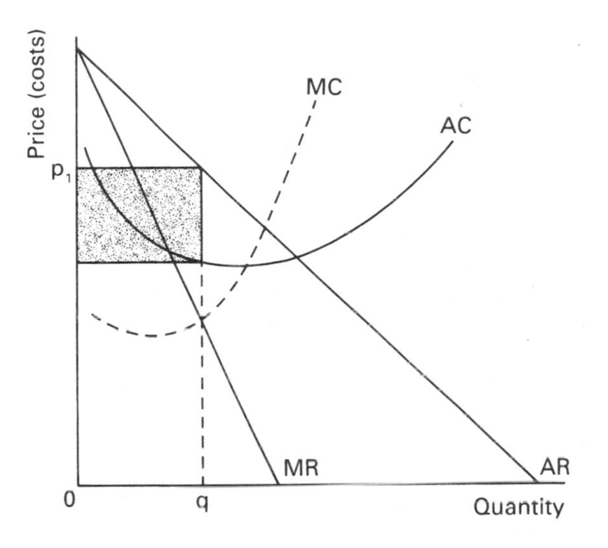

Critics of monopoly argue that this means that monopolists often choose to fix a high price. Figure 6.3 shows the equilibrium position of a monopolist. The marginal cost and average cost curves are the usual shape. The demand curve (which is also the average revenue curve) slopes down because to sell an extra good the firm will have to cut its price, and the marginal revenue curve slopes more steeply because to sell an extra good the firm will have to cut its price still more.

The firm will maximise profits when marginal revenue equals marginal cost, that is at quantity q. At this level of output the firm will be making excess profits. These are shown by the difference between the average cost and average revenue multiplied by the quantity and are shaded in the diagram. Note that at output q the firm will not be producing as efficiently as it could (at the lowest point on the average cost curve) – average cost would fall if it produced more goods. This would also benefit consumers because they would gain both from lower costs and from the availability of a greater quantity of goods. The firm does not expand output to this level because to sell these extra goods it would have to cut prices to such an extent that profits would fall. Hence supporters of competition oppose monopoly because they associate it with inefficiency, low output and high prices. The long run features of monopoly are shown in Table 6.4.

***Table 6.4:** Monopoly*

1 Assumptions	Only one firm in the industry Barriers to entry prevent competition Firm attempts to maximise profit and produces where MR=MC
2 How firm is affected	Firm is price maker Demand curve slopes down
3 Result	High price Firm makes excess profit Inefficient firm does not produce where average cost is lowest Excess capacity – firm could produce more at lower cost

Discriminating monopoly

In some cases a monopolist can charge consumers different prices for what is essentially the same service. Consider a British Rail train. Some of the passengers will be travelling first-class and paying a high fare. Some will be paying full standard class fare. Sitting next to them may be someone with a saver ticket and paying a much lower price. There may also be someone with a railcard paying an even lower fare. Under what circumstances can a producer charge different prices for the same service?

In the first place, the producer must be a monopolist, otherwise another producer might offer a cheaper service. The other essential characteristic is that different groups of people must have different elasticities of demand. Those travelling first-class have a very inelastic demand. Either they are 'rich', or the firm is paying. In either case, the price makes little difference to their decision to travel. At the other extreme, someone with a Young Person's Railcard has a very elastic demand curve. This is because there are other close alternatives, in particular travel by bus – or not making the journey at all. A high price would deter such travellers. The third characteristic is that it must be possible to separate these different groups. This can be done on a train. Some seats can be limited to first-class passengers and some trains forbidden to people with saver tickets.

Other examples of discriminating monopoly are first and second-class letters which can be treated differently by the Post Office, telephone calls at different times of day, and aeroplane flights. Where these conditions apply, a firm will maximise its profits when it charges different prices to the different groups. The highest price will be charged to those with inelastic demand, the lowest to those whose demand is elastic.

Since discriminating monopolies charge different prices for essentially the same service, they are criticised for being unfair. However, they do offer advantages. Since the essence of a discriminating monopoly is that it splits up the market, this means that if one group of people stop buying the service, the firm can still continue in business, supported by the other groups. Moreover, people with low incomes can benefit since they can obtain essentially the same service as richer people, but at a lower price.

Perfect competition and monopoly are theoretical models at opposite ends of a spectrum. In between are two forms of imperfect competition which are much more common. One is called monopolistic competition, the other, oligopoly. Supporters of competition criticise both these forms of market, suggesting they result in an unsatisfactory allocation of resources.

Monopolistic competition

Monopolistic competition is so called because it combines some features characteristic of monopoly and some which resemble competitive industry. It has monopolistic features in that its products are not identical. Company X and company Y make **similar** products, but they do differ, for example, in design, quality, after sales service, or as a result of advertising. This **product differentiation** means the firm is faced with a downward sloping demand curve; if it wants to sell more goods it will have to cut its price.

However, other characteristics are similar to those found in competitive industry. There are many firms in the industry and it is relatively easy for new ones to enter.

Monopolistic competition is frequently found in a modern economy. Public houses, hairdressers, roof repairers and pop records are examples.

This combination of competition and monopoly leads to some results which are desirable and some which are not in the public interest. The competitive elements, such as freedom of entry, mean that firms do not make excess profits – if they did new firms would enter the industry and force down the price. Consequently monopolistic competition is characterised by normal profit. However, the fact that firms are faced by a downward sloping demand curve means that some firms will choose to sell smaller quantities at a higher price; hence some consumers who would like the product will not be able to afford the goods. This restriction in quantity is undesirable. It means that, as in monopoly, firms in this kind of industry will have substantial excess capacity; they could produce more and if they did so their average costs would be lower. Firms do not follow this desirable path because they would have to cut their price to sell these extra goods and this would result in a fall in profits.

Oligopoly

Oligopoly is also a form of imperfect competition and is usually defined as an industry with many buyers but only a few sellers. Examples are the manufacture of a wide range of products as diverse as cigarettes, cars, newspapers and detergents. The distinguishing characteristic of all these industries is that there are only a few firms in the industry because there are significant barriers to entry; for example, enormous building and machinery costs for a firm wishing to mass produce cars and high expenditure on advertising in the cigarette industry.

Because there are only a few firms in the industry, all firms have to consider the response of competitors to any change in price or output. In some cases firms will collude – act as if they were a single firm. The most famous example of this occurred in 1973/74 when the oil producing countries doubled the price of oil, and then doubled it again a few months later. There are more recent examples of collusion; for example, the manufacturers of polypropylene tried to limit production and put up prices but were stopped by the EU in 1986.

In some cases collusion is less formal; for example, small firms may just follow the example of dominant firms. It is not always easy to say whether price changes are co-ordinated. For example, if several firms in the oil industry put up prices at about the same time, is this due to collusion, or is it because they are all affected by similar economic forces which force them to put up prices?

If firms do collude, the analysis is similar to that of monopoly and critics say the result will be high prices, excess profits, a reduction in the quantity of goods produced, and excess capacity, with the typical firm not producing at minimum average cost.

In other cases of oligopoly the firms may not collude; indeed they compete vigorously. This competition may take the form of **non-price** competition. Firms spend a lot of money on product differentiation – a glance at the local supermarket will show a huge variety of crisps, for example, and car manufacturers try to build in features which cause customers to prefer their cars to those of competitors. They also spend large sums of money on advertising and special offers.

The kinked demand curve

Where oligopolistic firms may not compete is on price. Some firms may fear that if they cut their price their competitors will follow suit so that all the firms may be worse off. If they put up prices, competitors may not change theirs so that the firm making the change will lose sales and be worse off. This line of argument has led to the suggestion that oligopoly will be characterised by stable prices, shown in Figure 6.4 by a kinked demand curve. If the firm moves from the price at the kink its revenue will fall. If the firm puts up its prices, competitors may not follow suit so its sales revenue will fall. On the other hand, if it cuts prices, competitors may also cut their prices so that the original price-cutting firm does not sell much more. Consequently firms may prefer to keep prices stable.

Figure 6.4: *A kinked demand curve*

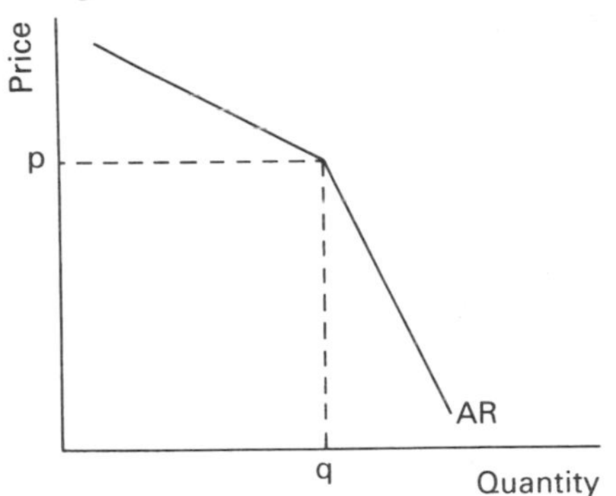

However, research evidence tends to suggest that most oligopolies are not characterised by stable prices, showing that persuasive arguments are not always correct. For example, oil companies frequently change the prices that they charge for petrol and banks often vary the interest they charge borrowers.

Critics of oligopoly argue that its results are unsatisfactory. It can lead to collusion, high prices and lower quantities of goods being put on the market than would be the case in perfect competition. Even where firms do not collude, there may be undesirable results since competition may take forms which do not really benefit the consumer, such as advertising and 'free' gifts which the consumer would not choose to buy.

Moreover, oligopolistic firms often produce a wide range of slightly differentiated products. They argue that this gives consumers more choice. However, critics would say that they do this because it makes it difficult for new firms to enter the market. If a firm makes ten varieties of shampoo or toothpaste then a potential entrant would face ten competitors and probably decide that it was not worth the risks involved. Hence existing firms can avoid further competition.

Key ideas – summary of the pro-competition argument

1. Perfect competition leads to low prices, low profits, no excess capacity, and production is efficient in that firms produce at minimum average cost. Hence competition is the most desirable form of market structure and any deviation from this is to be deplored.
2. Monopoly is characterised by high prices, excess capacity and high profits, the extent depending largely on the strength of the barriers which prevent new firms entering the industry.
3. Monopolistic competition is characterised by many firms which practice product differentiation. The result is normal profits, but excess capacity.
4. An oligopolistic industry is one with few sellers. The consequences will depend on whether firms collude.

Policy recommendations

The group of economists who emphasise competition put forward policies which they believe will strengthen competition and weaken monopolistic elements in the economy. They argue that nationalised industries should be split into separate competing firms. Thus they suggest that the coal industry should be privatised and its assets split up into several competing firms. In the private sector they want policies which would reduce the number of mergers because these restrict competition. Also they would like tough policies on monopolies. They support the breaking up of monopolies and, where a degree of monopoly is unavoidable (as with British Telecom, for example), they want strong controls to prevent such firms exploiting their monopoly position (as, for example, when laws were passed which forced British Telecom to face competition from firms such as Mercury). Similarly, in industries characterised by oligopoly they want firms to be punished when they collude.

The argument against competition

Few economists would deny that there can be considerable merits in competition. However, some economists argue that there are limits to these benefits and that monopolies can sometimes be beneficial.

Criticism of the case for competition

The case for competition is often derived from the theoretical analysis of the benefits of perfect competition or the disadvantages of monopoly. However, these theoretical results depend on the assumptions underlying the analysis; if these assumptions do not hold, then neither do the results. Since the assumptions underlying the perfect competition model are so stringent that they are not found in the real world, it is argued that the supposed benefits are also unlikely to be realised. For example, perfect competition assumes perfect knowledge, but since this does not exist, firms may be unaware of profitable opportunities and may not move in to new markets, thus allowing existing firms to continue to charge high prices and make excess profits.

How firms really operate

Economists who are critical of the case for competition argue that theoretical analysis ignores the way in which firms really operate. For example, they argue that the theoretical analysis assumes firms attempt to maximise their profits, whereas in real life firms may have different objectives. If this is so, then the theoretical analysis given earlier is invalidated.

Cost plus pricing

Surveys of how firms fix their prices suggest they do not attempt to maximise profits by producing at the level of output where marginal revenue equals marginal cost. Instead they tend to adopt a strategy of cost-plus pricing, sometimes called full cost pricing. To give just one example, Skinner (1970) surveyed 170 firms on Merseyside and found that 70% used cost-plus pricing. There are a number of varieties of cost-plus pricing, but typically price is decided by adding a percentage profit margin to unit costs. In some cases firms vary the profit margin to take account of demand conditions. Where this is done, the results would be similar to those predicted by the marginal analysis discussed earlier. However, overall the evidence is sufficient to cast doubts on the view that firms will attempt to maximise profits.

Satisficing

One reason for this is that decisions in firms are taken by managers rather than shareholders. Although the legal position is that shareholders own the firm, there are often so many shareholders that individually they hold little power and only a tiny minority attend the annual general meeting of their company. Consequently the relationship between owners and managers is like that of principals and agents. The principals – the shareholders – do not have full information so managers are often free to pursue their own interests, which may be different from those of the shareholders. Different groups within the firm will have their own objectives; some managers, for example, may be more interested in enlarging their own department than in maximising profits. This line of argument suggests that conflicts are inevitable inside firms and that these are often resolved by 'satisficing' – compromises within the firm so that different groups get something of what they want. This is an 'organisational' approach to the firm and, to the extent that it represents reality, it weakens the theoretical arguments which suggest that competition is better than monopoly.

Contestable markets

An alternative critique reinforces this conclusion. The disadvantages of monopoly depend on the assumption that monopolies attempt to maximise profits. However, there are various reasons which suggest that they may not do this. For example, Baumol (1958) suggested that firms do not attempt to maximise profits, but instead try to maximise sales revenue, even though this means that profits are not as high as they could be. These arguments suggest that firms may be content with 'reasonable' profits, that is a level of profits which gives shareholders a satisfactory return on their capital. One reason for this, pointed out earlier in the chapter, is that high prices and profits may encourage competitors to enter the market. If the barriers to entry are not impenetrable, then the lure of high profits may give an incentive to new firms to breach these barriers. Lower profits may reduce this incentive. Moreover, the managers would then benefit from a quiet life; they would be able to get on with the job of running the firm without worrying about the actions of rivals. Hence the high prices predicted by the assumption that firms attempt to maximise profits may not be realised in practice. Instead firms may cut prices and increase production in order to reduce the likelihood of new firms entering the market. An example often quoted is the ability of many financial institutions to offer services, such as mortgages, loans etc., which were previously the province of banks, building societies, etc.

Countervailing forces

Another defence of monopoly was put forward by Galbraith (1952) when he introduced the concept of 'countervailing power'. This suggested that monopolists were often prevented from exploiting their position because they were faced by a countervailing power – other firms which had the power to resist them. Thus a large monopoly such as British Coal sells most of its output to the electricity generating companies, which also possess monopoly power and can resist any attempt by British Coal to exploit them.

Positive advantages of monopoly

In addition to criticising the theoretical case for competition, there are some positive points to be made in favour of monopoly. In the first place, some monopolies are 'natural' in the sense that huge quantities of capital are needed to start the business. Hence it is logical that there should only be one organisation responsible for the national grid distributing electricity, and only one organisation laying water pipes down any particular street. In cases such as these competition would be wasteful.

Moreover, monopolies are often (but not necessarily) large and can take advantage of the economies of scale discussed in the last chapter. If this is so their costs will be lower than would be the case if there were several small competing firms in the industry. In particular, large firms may be able to spend more on research and development than could small firms. This line of argument was developed by one of the great Austrian economists, Joseph Schumpeter. (Like many economists Schumpeter was not noted for his modesty. He once remarked that in his youth he had had three ambitions – to be the greatest lover in Austria, the greatest horseman in Europe and the greatest economist in the world. He regretted that he had failed in his second ambition.) In his book *Capitalism, Socialism and Democracy* (1943) he wrote:

'"Restraints of trade" of the cartel type, as well as those which merely consist in tacit understandings about price competition, may be effective remedies under conditions of depression...they may in the end produce not only steadier but also greater expansion of total output than could be secured by an entirely uncontrolled onward rush that cannot fail to be studded with catastrophes.'

In Schumpeter's view there are two reasons for this. One is the belief that market forces, depending on competition, do not always represent a satisfactory way to allocate resources. Secondly, Schumpeter introduced the concept of 'creative destruction'. By this phrase he meant that innovation led to the destruction of traditional techniques and their replacement by more efficient ones. He argued that monopolists were more likely to undertake creative destruction, partly because they had the resources needed and partly because innovation – helped by patents – would help them maintain barriers to entry.

Since Schumpeter's time there has been a good deal of research into innovation. However, this evidence has proved to be inconclusive. On the one hand many inventions originated with small-scale operators, while some monopolies were lazy. On the other hand there have been dynamic monopolies and many innovations have originated within large firms.

Transactions costs

An alternative line of support for large organisations such as monopolies is that they are efficient because they reduce transactions costs. Traditional textbooks focus on the market as the way in which resources are allocated. However, some economists believe that in markets substantial costs arise in buying and selling raw materials and equipment used in the manufacture of goods, and that these costs can be minimised if organisation takes place inside firms rather than through the market. Consequently a large firm, such as Ford, will allocate capital and labour within the firm in several countries in order to produce cars efficiently. If large firms do reduce transactions costs, consumers may benefit, even though the firm is a monopoly.

Benefits of oligopoly

Oligopoly has its merits. Cynics may sneer at the 'special offers' which characterise this type of industry, but firms would not offer them if they were not attractive to customers. Moreover, it is possible to argue that oligopolists can only keep out competitors because they offer their customers a good service. These satisfied customers are the best indication of the merits of oligopoly. In addition, oligopolies also keep out competitors because they are efficient. If they were not, new firms would enter the market.

Key ideas – summary of the case against competition

1. The theoretical case for competition depends on unrealistic assumptions; if these are not met then the conclusion that competition is best also fails.
2. Monopolies may not exploit their position and may choose to make only reasonable profits.
3. Monopolies may be more efficient because, if large, they can enjoy economies of scale, spend more on research and development, and incur lower transactions costs.
4. Similarly, oligopolies can often only restrict entry by satisfying customers and by being efficient.

Policy recommendations

The line of argument followed here leads to policies based on the assumption that whilst competition may have its virtues, so do less competitive forms of market structure. Whilst in some cases monopolies may exploit their position, in others they may be beneficial and policies should reflect this. They therefore advocate that each case should be judged on its merits with an independent body considering the advantages and disadvantages of a particular monopoly or proposed merger. This approach lies behind UK policy on monopoly.

These arguments about competition and monopoly overlap with those about markets and also those concerned with size. Those economists who favour markets as a way of allocating resources tend to be critical of monopolies, which they believe hamper the efficient allocation of resources. Similarly, those economists who favour small-scale production are critical of monopolies because they argue that these tend to be large-scale bureaucratic organisations.

Research evidence on monopoly

Several researchers have attempted to measure the actual costs of monopoly to society. This is not an easy task, because it is not possible to calculate exactly what would be the result if a monopoly was replaced by competitive firms.

The pioneering research was done by an American called Harbinger in the 1950s. His calculations suggested that the welfare loss arising from monopoly was very low – about 0.1 per cent of national income – which amounted to the cost of a good steak dinner for every family. If that estimate is correct, then it is a waste of time putting much effort into controlling monopoly because the costs of enforcement would exceed the benefits arising from the reduction in monopoly. However, Harbinger obtained his results by making some extreme assumptions. For example, he assumed that marginal costs were constant and that the price elasticity of demand for all products was -1. Relaxing these assumptions gives a considerably larger loss; perhaps 3 per cent of national income. On the other hand, in 1978 Cowling and Muller estimated the costs of monopoly in the UK and concluded that the welfare loss amounted to about 4 per cent of national income. If this is the case, a reduction in the extent of monopoly would give substantial benefits to consumers. This suggests that a vigorous pro-competition policy is necessary.

Competition policy in the UK and the EU

Competition policy in the UK and the EU takes a pragmatic approach. It recognises that monopolies may exploit their power, but that they may not; indeed that monopoly may sometimes bring benefits. Hence each case must be judged on its merits. For example, in 1988 Rentokil, with 60 per cent share of the market in pest control services and making high profits, was judged to be operating against the public interest. On the other hand two companies, Tambrands and Southalls, supply almost 100 per cent of the market for tampons, and in spite of making high profits it was judged that they were not exploiting their monopoly power. One reason for this was that they faced some competition from retailers' own brands. This can be regarded as an example of contestable markets preventing consumers from being exploited.

Competition policy has a number of aspects. One concerns monopoly; in UK law this occurs when a company (or group of companies acting together) has over 25 per cent of the market for a product. When this situation arises, the Monopolies and Mergers Commission can be asked to investigate whether this is in the public interest. 'Public interest' is not defined, but the Commission has to take account of such factors as efficient production and distribution, employment and the encouragement of new enterprise. Many industries are in the position where one firm has more than 25 per cent of the market but are not investigated because there are no complaints, and little evidence of exploitation. When firms are investigated it is often for such practices as refusing to supply retail outlets unless they refuse to stock competitors' goods, or for excessive prices and profits. A particular problem in monopoly policy concerns the recently privatised utilities. Firms such as British Gas have a monopoly position, and to prevent these utilities exploiting their position regulatory agencies such as OFGAS have been appointed. These are discussed in more detail in the next chapter.

The Monopolies and Mergers Commission can also investigate proposed mergers of firms. For example, ten companies set up and owned a company called British Posters Ltd. This would have dominated the industry and the Commission recommended that the company be disbanded. This was carried out. Similarly, the Commission investigated a proposal by P&O and Sealink to provide a joint car ferry service on short crossing routes across the Channel. The companies argued that this was needed if they were to be able to compete successfully against the Channel Tunnel. However, the Commission concluded that the proposal would reduce competition and the Secretary of State (who makes the final decision) accepted the recommendation.

The Commission also investigates mergers which, although small, might have a significant local effect. For example, in 1993 they investigated the £12.5 million purchase by Trinity International of Joseph Woodhead of Huddersfield. That was because Trinity owns newspapers in North West England and Wales whilst Woodhead publishes the Huddersfield Daily Examiner. The Commission can also make conditions before it will permit a merger. For example, Grand Metropolitan wished to acquire the William Hill Organisation. The Commission decided that the merger would restrict competition in some areas because the merged firm would own most of the betting shops. It therefore recommended that some shops be sold before the merger could proceed.

A second aspect of competition policy concerns restrictive practices. This includes such matters as agreements between firms to fix prices or to divide up a market. Here the body responsible for enforcing legislation is the Restrictive Practices Court. Under the Restrictive Trade Practices Act (1976), details of certain kinds of agreements between firms must be reported to the Court. Currently, approximately one thousand agreements a year are reported, about half relating to goods and half to services. The Act provides that an agreement shall be deemed to be against the public interest unless the court is satisfied that the agreement has positive advantages to the public. Advantages may arise, for example, if the agreement protects the public against injury, or if its removal would have a serious effect on the level of unemployment, or if the restriction does not restrict competition. One of the few examples of a successful defence of an agreement was the Association of British Travel Agents (ABTA). They argued that the arrangement whereby members of ABTA would only deal with other members of ABTA was in the public interest because it protected the consumer from dealing with unreliable travel firms.

In recent years the European Union has taken a more active role in developing competition policy. The EU is mainly concerned with activities of firms which have a European dimension; monopolies which affect only one country would normally be dealt with by national legislation. The aim of the policy is to encourage competition throughout the EU; the single market cannot be a reality if monopolistic practices restrict trade. Their powers derive largely from Articles 85 and 86 of the Treaty of Rome. Article 85 is concerned with agreements between firms which are likely to affect trade between countries and which are likely to result in a restriction of competition. It therefore includes agreements to fix prices, to limit production, or to share out markets. For example, in 1986 a group of 15 multinational companies were fined ECU 58 million (= £40 million) for operating a price fixing and market sharing cartel in the polypropylene market. More recently, fourteen firms were fined for operating an agreement to share out the market for wire mesh (widely used in the building industry).

Article 86 of the Rome Treaty deals with the abuse of market dominance. 'Dominance' includes consideration of both market share and of actual practices. It therefore is concerned with abuses such as imposing unfair selling prices or limiting production. Sometimes the Commission uses its power to persuade a dominant firm to stop an uncompetitive practice. For example, Coca Cola in Italy had concluded distribution agreements with distributors which gave them a fidelity rebate if they agreed not to sell other cola drinks. The Commission felt that this was unfair to other producers since Coca Cola had such a large share of the market. Coca Cola agreed to stop the practice.

For many years there was no specific provision for controlling mergers. This weakness was ended in 1990 when a Merger Regulation was introduced which gave the Commission power to control the largest mergers; for example, those involving firms with a total world turnover which exceeds £3.5 billion. Under the Regulation, mergers are appraised to see whether they create or strengthen a dominant position which would hinder competition. If so, they can be banned or conditions imposed so that the merger would not have serious effects on competition. For example, the Commission approved the takeover by Nestlé of Perrier, but felt that this would give the new firm too much market power. In order to obtain clearance, Nestlé had to agree to sell Vichy and other brands to a single buyer in order to create a viable competitor. The Commission has powers to suspend mergers whilst it investigates their effect. Thus in 1993 it delayed for four months the proposed acquisition of Societa Italiana Vetro, the Italian state glass company, by Pilkington, the UK glass group and Techint Finanziaria, its Italian-Argentine partner. During this period the Commission's merger control task force assessed its impact on competition in the EU.

One feature of EU competition policy which differs from national policies concerns public procurement. All governments try to favour domestic firms; for example, police forces in a country usually drive cars made in that country. This reduces competition, so the EU has insisted that companies throughout the Community should be able to bid for large public contracts and it forbids discrimination in favour of domestic producers.

Monopoly legislation illustrates the link between economic analysis and policy. Economists who believe that there are often advantages to be derived from monopoly are, by and large, content with the legislation; those who favour more competition would like to see the law revised to discourage mergers and to do more to weaken monopolistic elements in the economy.

Key ideas – competition policy

1. Competition policy in the UK works on the principle that each case should be judged on its merits.
2. In the privatised utilities, regulatory bodies such as OFGAS have been established.
3. The Monopolies and Mergers Commission (MMC) investigates established dominant firms and can forbid proposed mergers.
4. EU competition policy is concerned with the activities of firms which have a European dimension.

Developments in the theory of the firm

So far this chapter has been mainly using what might be called 'neo-classical theory', though some more modern concepts have been used. Neo-classical theory assumes firms try to maximise profits and uses marginal techniques to analyse firms' decisions. The theory treats the firm as an individual decision maker, as if a single person in a firm made all the decisions.

In recent years there have been a number of developments in the way that economists analyse firms, and some of these are considered here.

Managerial models

Although managerial models are not really new, they do represent a development in the traditional model of the firm. These models start with the recognition that in most modern firms shares are owned by very many people who have little real power. Consequently decisions are made, not by owners, but by managers. This means that decisions are not aimed at maximising profits. Instead they try to maximise the utility of managers. This may involve maximising other objectives such as sales, or the firm's growth. One conclusion of this line of approach suggests managerial desire for growth will encourage firms to merge, since this will increase promotion opportunities and give managers increased status. The model also explains the existence of extensive managerial 'perks' such as company cars. These often reduce profits, but benefit managers.

Why do firms exist?

One answer to this question was given in 1937 by R.H. Coase. He suggested that in some circumstances there are costs involved in using markets which make it cheaper to organise production within a firm. To use his own words:

'Firms arise voluntarily because they represent a more efficient method of organising production.'

One reason for this is the existence of transactions costs, which were explained earlier in this chapter. Coase suggested that in some circumstances markets will be used to allocate resources. In others, these will be allocated within firms because this will reduce costs. The crucial factor will be the extent of transactions costs. When these are high, resources will be allocated within firms. The same principle can be used to explain the size of firms. Firms will grow until the costs of organising an extra transaction within the firm are equal to the costs of using the market. Thus a firm such as Ford will constantly ask if it should produce this new component itself, or if it should buy it in the market?

Principal-agent theory

Another recent development in the theory of the firm is principal-agent theory. This does not draw a sharp distinction between 'market' and 'firm' ways of organising resources. Instead it suggests that inside firms people must often be left to decide for themselves how to behave. The same is true outside firms in relationships, such as those between an estate agent (the agent) and a principal selling a house. In principal-agent relationships, agents choose their own behaviour within the terms of a contract.

In a principal (P) - agent (A) relationship, P's welfare depends on what A does. P wants A to do what is best for P, but A will be self-interested and do what is best for A. This causes problems, particularly as A often has hidden information since P cannot always supervise A. Within firms this leads to principals, i.e. the owners, giving share incentive schemes to their agents, the managers, in order to encourage them to take risks. Without such schemes, managers would be too cautious since their reputations would suffer if things went wrong, and they would not benefit much from success.

Performance-related pay schemes are another example of P-A relationships. Workers often have scope to make their own decisions, and performance-related pay schemes provide an incentive for effort, especially in cases where the workers' actions cannot be closely supervised.

Key ideas – summary of recent developments

1. The new approach is more realistic and aims to give better explanations of how firms really operate.

2. One emphasis in this approach is to recognise that managers may run firms in their own interest, which is not necessarily the same as that of the owners.

3. Firms exist because it is more efficient to organise production within firms than through markets.

4. Firms grow to reduce transactions costs.

5. Principal-agent theory offers explanations of behaviour both inside and outside firms where one person is contracted to carry out actions for another.

Conclusion

The traditional theory of the firm is concerned with questions such as the consequences of different forms of market structure. If certain rigorous assumptions are fulfilled, then perfect competition will have desirable consequences, such as low price. However, these conditions are not found in the real world and there is a vigorous debate about the advantages and disadvantages of competition. More recently, economists have asked more basic questions such as: 'Why do firms exist?; What causes them to grow?' This new approach offers the potential for greater understanding of the nature of large firms which organise resources within the firm and not through the market. Similarly, work on transactions costs and on principal-agent theories can offer ideas to improve organisational relationships, for example, by providing appropriate incentives.

Data questions

People of the same trade seldom meet together, even for merriment and diversion, but the conversation ends in a conspiracy against the public, or in some contrivance to raise prices. It is impossible indeed to prevent such meetings, by any law which either could be executed or would be consistent with liberty and justice. But though the law cannot hinder people of the same trade from sometimes assembling together, it ought to do nothing to facilitate such assemblies; much less to render them necessary.

Source: Adam Smith, *Wealth of Nations*, First published 1776.

The introduction of new methods of production and new commodities is hardly conceivable with perfect – and perfectly prompt – competition from the start. And this means that the bulk of what we call economic progress is incompatible with it. As a matter of fact, perfect competition is and always has been temporarily suspended whenever anything new is being introduced – automatically or by measures devised for the purpose – even in otherwise perfectly competitive conditions.

Source: Schumpeter, J. *Capitalism, Socialism and Democracy*, Allen and Unwin, 1943.

Question 1

1. Summarise the economic arguments which lie behind the quotations.
2. What types of economic policy would follow from the views expressed in these articles?

EC blocks Franco-Italian bid for de Haviland

The European Commission yesterday blocked a Franco-Italian bid for Canadian aircraft maker de Haviland on the grounds that it would have stifled competition in the market for small turbo-prop aircraft. Sir Leon Brittan, the EC's competition commissioner said the deal could have driven competitors, which include British Aerospace, out of the market for commuter aircraft. The case involved a bid by Aerospatiale of France and Alenia of Italy, which already produce a small aircraft, the ATR, to buy de Haviland from Boeing. Sir Leon said that the merged companies would have had half the world market for commuter aircraft and 67% of the EC market.

Several Commissioners opposed the decision and argued that the deal would enable European companies to compete internationally and disputed Sir Leon's contention that the relevant market was 20 to 70 seater planes. Sir Leon, however, said that the decision followed 'an exhaustive analysis' which concluded that the merger would 'create a powerful and unassailable dominant position in the world market for turbo-prop aircraft'. His decision was supported by other companies, including BAe and Fokker of the Netherlands who had written to complain about the bid.

Source: Adapted from *The Guardian*, October 3, 1991.

Question 2

1. What is meant by 'a dominant position'? Why is this considered to be undesirable?
2. Who might benefit and who might suffer from the EC decision to block the proposed merger?
3. The passage refers to the problem of deciding what is 'the relevant market'. Illustrate, with examples, the problem of deciding exactly what constitutes a market.

Barriers to entry

Entry barriers play a central role in both the theory of industrial economics and the market analysis carried out by competition authorities. Between July 1980 and March 1992 the Monopolies and Mergers Commission (MMC) identified barriers to entry in thirty seven reports in industries as diverse as soluble coffee (1991), new motor cars (1992) and artificial lower limbs (1989).

Their investigation into the market for white salt (1986) illustrates many of the barriers to entry. The industry was dominated by two firms; ICI had a 45% market share and British Salt (BS) 50%. Two small firms and imports accounted for the remaining 5%. Entry was made difficult because there was excess capacity in the industry so that any firm trying to gain entry would expect to face price cutting. Moreover, both ICI and BS had long term contracts with the major buyers. In addition these two firms owned the major mineral rights and planning permission might have been refused to new firms. Finally there were considerable economies of scale in the industry so that any new, small firm would have found it difficult to compete. Because these barriers were so substantial the MMC recommended the imposition of price controls to prevent the two firms from exploiting consumers of salt.

Source: Adapted from: 'Barriers to Entry', *Economics*, Autumn 1993.

Question 3

1. What is meant by 'barriers to entry'?
2. Explain why the barriers to entry identified might make it difficult for new firms to compete.

7 Nationalisation and Privatisation

The role of government in the economic life of the country is a topic which occurs in several parts of this book, most obviously in the chapter on markets. This chapter is concerned with a particular aspect of that debate; the activities of government in the production of goods and services. Over recent decades there have been great changes in some industries, from private to public and then back to private ownership. These changes are the consequence, in part, of changes in political control of government, but they also result from changes in the relative power of competing economic arguments.

- On the one hand, some economists are sceptical about the value of market forces and favour public ownership and control of particular industries or firms. Some interventionists and most Marxist economists would be included in this group.
- Opposing this are supply side economists who believe that government run industries are often inefficient and that wherever possible the private sector should take over.

Public ownership and privatisation

This chapter will focus particularly on the nationalised industries, but it should be noted that there are other forms of public ownership. There are, for example, local authority enterprises which are part of the public sector, but which are not nationalised. Thus local authorities run swimming pools and sports centres, and Hull even runs its own telephone service. Those industries which are nationalised are legally public corporations and are run by boards of directors appointed by the Secretary of State. In principle, the government sets out appropriate policies – such as a requirement to charge prices which will cover costs – and then the directors execute these policies.

The idea of publicly owned industries is not limited to Britain. In France, for example, there are a considerable number of nationalised industries, including Renault cars and the match and tobacco industries. The idea of public ownership is an old one and not the preserve of any particular political party. As early as 1912 a nationwide public service of telephones was added to the Post Office and in 1912 a Liberal government passed an act setting up the Port of London Authority, which in many ways provided a model for future public corporations. Between the two World Wars, Conservative governments set up the British Broadcasting Corporation, the London Passenger Transport Board, the British Overseas Airways Corporation (later British Airways) and the Central Electricity Generating Board, which was responsible for the distribution of electricity through a national grid. Although both Liberal and Conservative governments have thus been responsible for setting up publicly owned organisations, the greatest thrust towards nationalisation came with the post-war Labour government. Between 1945 and 1951, the government nationalised coal, steel, railways, the Bank of England and road transport, together with a number of smaller organisations. By the early 1980s, the nationalised industries accounted for approximately 10 per cent of national output, employed 7 per cent of the nation's workers and were responsible for about 17 per cent of total investment. However, in recent years there has been a reversal of policy and a move towards privatisation. 'Privatisation' is a relatively new word and describes the transfer of industrial and other assets from the public sector to the private sector. Previously the transfer of assets from public to private ownership was called 'de-nationalisation' and was carried out on an ad hoc basis; for example, road haulage was partially denationalised in the 1950s.

'Privatisation' can take a number of forms. One view is that of Kay and Silberston (1984) who distinguish three aspects. In the first place it can mean the liberalisation of entry into areas previously dominated by the state; for example, competitors were allowed to compete in certain areas with British Telecom and National Express, even before they were privatised. This is sometimes referred to as deregulation. A second meaning refers to private provision of services, such as hospital cleaning and refuse disposal; activities which were formerly undertaken by publicly employed personnel. The final meaning of privatisation refers to a change in ownership when state owned industries are sold off. This is the most common use of the term and the focus of most of this chapter. Table 7.1 shows the extent of these sales.

***Table 7.1:** Main sales under Conservative governments*

Date	Company	Type of sale
1979	British Petroleum	43.7% of shares*
	ICL	25% holding
1981	Cable and Wireless	94.4% of shares
	British Aerospace	100% of shares*
1982	Britoil	100% of shares*
	Amersham International	100% of shares*
	National Freight Corporation	Management buy-out (MBO)
1983	Associated British Ports	100% of shares
	British Rail Hotels	Trade sale
1984	Enterprise Oil	100% of shares*
	Sealink	Sold to Sea Containers
	Jaguar	100% of shares
	British Telecom	76.1% of shares*
1985	British Shipbuilders	Trade Sales/MBOs
1986	British Gas	100% of shares
	National Bus Company	Trade Sales/MBOs
1987	British Airways	100% of shares
	Rolls Royce	100% of shares
	British Airports Authority	100% of shares
1988	Rover Group	Sold to British Aerospace
	British Steel	100% of shares
1989	Water/sewerage companies	100% of shares
1990	Girobank	Sold to Alliance & Leicester building society
	Regional electricity companies	100% of shares
1991	Generating companies	100% of shares
1992	Trust ports	Trade sales/MBOs
1993	British Rail	Trade sale of some lines

* In tranches: date of first tranche.
Source: 'Guide to the UK privatisation programme', HM Treasury, June 1992.

Key ideas

1. Nationalised industries are just one form of public sector production.
2. In the past, Conservative and Liberal governments have taken firms into the public sector; now this policy is most closely associated with the Labour Party.
3. Privatisation can be defined in various ways. Three aspects are examined here; liberalising entry into areas previously dominated by the state, private provision of services and selling off state owned industries.

The case for public ownership

'Public ownership' has been used in this subheading rather than 'nationalisation' because some economists who favour public ownership do not like the particular form of ownership and control which characterises nationalised industries. They believe that nationalised industries are often cumbersome and bureaucratic; responsive neither to the needs of consumers nor of their workers. Despite this they believe that there are strong arguments for public ownership, but with more democratic forms of control than those currently used for nationalised industries. For example, some writers suggest that the workers in a firm should control it. This line of argument would be supported by Marxists and also by many non-Marxists who support a mixed economy.

The natural monopoly argument

Natural monopolies were discussed in the previous chapter. These are industries where the initial costs are high, but where there are large economies of scale so that the marginal cost of production is very low. A good example of a natural monopoly is the supply of clean water to houses. The start up costs of constructing reservoirs and laying pipes to every house are enormous. However, once constructed, the costs of supplying an extra gallon of water are very low. These characteristics mean that it would be difficult, if not impossible, for a competitor to challenge an existing supplier. Hence there is a 'natural' monopoly. Other examples are the construction of railway or telephone lines. In such cases there is a possibility that a privately owned firm would exploit its position and charge high prices in the knowledge that it is safe from competition. One answer to this problem is to take the industry into public ownership. Then 'fair' prices can be charged and consumers protected from exploitation.

Economists opposed to public ownership recognise the problem, but argue that a better solution is to allow private ownership and then to regulate the monopoly. This is discussed later in the chapter.

Externalities and merit goods

Externalities occur when the actions of a firm or individual spill over on to others. Thus if a firm decides to transport its goods by road there will be an increase in congestion, more pollution and a greater likelihood of accidents. These disadvantages are not borne by the firms, but fall on others. Hence there is a case for keeping open railway lines which would not otherwise be profitable in order to prevent an increase in road traffic.

Merit goods are those which society believes should be provided in greater quantities than would be provided by market forces. For example, closing rural railway lines may mean that local industries close or that people are forced to move homes to be near their work. Similar arguments apply to the provision of telephone and electricity lines and the delivery of mail in rural areas. If these activities are unprofitable they will not be undertaken by privately owned industry. Public ownership can solve the problem because it can take into consideration the social consequences of decisions and not be ruled solely by questions of profitability.

The 'lame duck' argument

Sometimes vitally important industries run into trouble. This happened to Rolls Royce and to British Leyland (now Rover). Some economists believed that the government should not have interfered; that it should have let market forces take their course. This would have meant that both companies would have gone bankrupt. However, the government took both companies into public ownership. The reason for this was that it believed that there would have been considerable negative externalities if the firms had closed down. In the case of British Leyland, a collapse would have affected a large number of the company's suppliers and the result of non-intervention would have been many bankruptcies and a significant rise in unemployment. The Rolls Royce argument was similar, but there was an additional point. Rolls Royce was an important supplier of defence material to the British government, so there were strategic reasons for intervention. Consequently both companies were taken into public ownership, though they were not formally nationalised – the government bought shares and put in money to ensure that the companies survived. This 'lame duck' argument was also one reason for the nationalisation of the coal and rail industries. After the Second World War these industries were extremely run down and needed massive new investment. Public ownership was seen as the best way to achieve their regeneration.

Equity

There are also equity arguments for public ownership. Some of these have already been mentioned. Private industries seeking to maximise profits would not provide services such as electricity to poorer regions; a nationalised industry would have different criteria for decision making and could supply such services.

However, the main equity argument concerns the distribution of wealth and involves people's values. Those economists who would like a more equal society see public ownership as one way in which this goal can be reached. In 1956 Hugh Gaitskell, then leader of the Labour Party, published a pamphlet called *Socialism and Nationalisation* in which he suggested several arguments in favour of public ownership:

'The first is in essence a Marxist argument...The flow of unearned income – of rent, interest and profits – is the root evil of capitalism; it represents the toll laid upon the workers by the owners of capitalism, who therefore deprive them of their rightful earnings...'

Gaitskell's second main argument relates to the working of the capitalist system. Both in the light of experience and on theoretical grounds, he claimed that the free individualist economy led perpetually to the unnatural result of 'poverty in the midst of plenty'.

Thirdly, he argued that the private possession of capital inevitably gave too much power to those who own it. This line of argument develops from a belief in a more equal society. It suggests that private ownership leads to greater inequality, and that one way to combat this is for the state to take over industries so that the benefits accrue to the people as a whole and not to a few owners. Counter arguments are put forward by those who do not share the value of greater equality and also by those who think that this is an inefficient way to achieve the goal. This latter group believes that other measures, such as higher taxes on the rich, would be more successful and that, in any case, if the owners of firms taken into the public sector were paid compensation the effect on the distribution of wealth would be trivial.

Arguments about the equity aspects of public ownership are bound up in the debate about the prices which these firms should charge. Since they are often monopolies, they could charge high prices and make huge profits. This would penalise consumers. On the other hand, it has been suggested that prices should be kept low in order to help poor consumers. However, this may lead to excessive consumption and to a waste of resources. Many economists suggest that public sector firms should adopt 'marginal cost pricing'; that is, they should charge consumers the marginal cost of producing the product. However, this may be difficult to calculate and it can lead to the firms making losses.

Market failure

Another line of argument in favour of public ownership derives from the belief that market systems of allocating resources are likely to fail and that the state should intervene. In particular it is argued that market systems are characterised by unemployment and that, left to themselves, private enterprise firms would not invest enough to ensure a high rate of economic growth. The solution is for the state to take over 'the commanding heights of the economy', i.e. the most important firms in the economy, impose its political will on these, and so ensure high levels of investment. This was one reason why the post-war Labour government nationalised the Bank of England and such industries as coal and steel.

Marxist arguments

Marxists would accept many of the arguments given above in favour of public ownership, but they would add others. Since they believe that crisis and conflict are inevitable in a capitalist economy, they advocate a large scale extension in order to reduce such conflicts. Only in this way can problems such

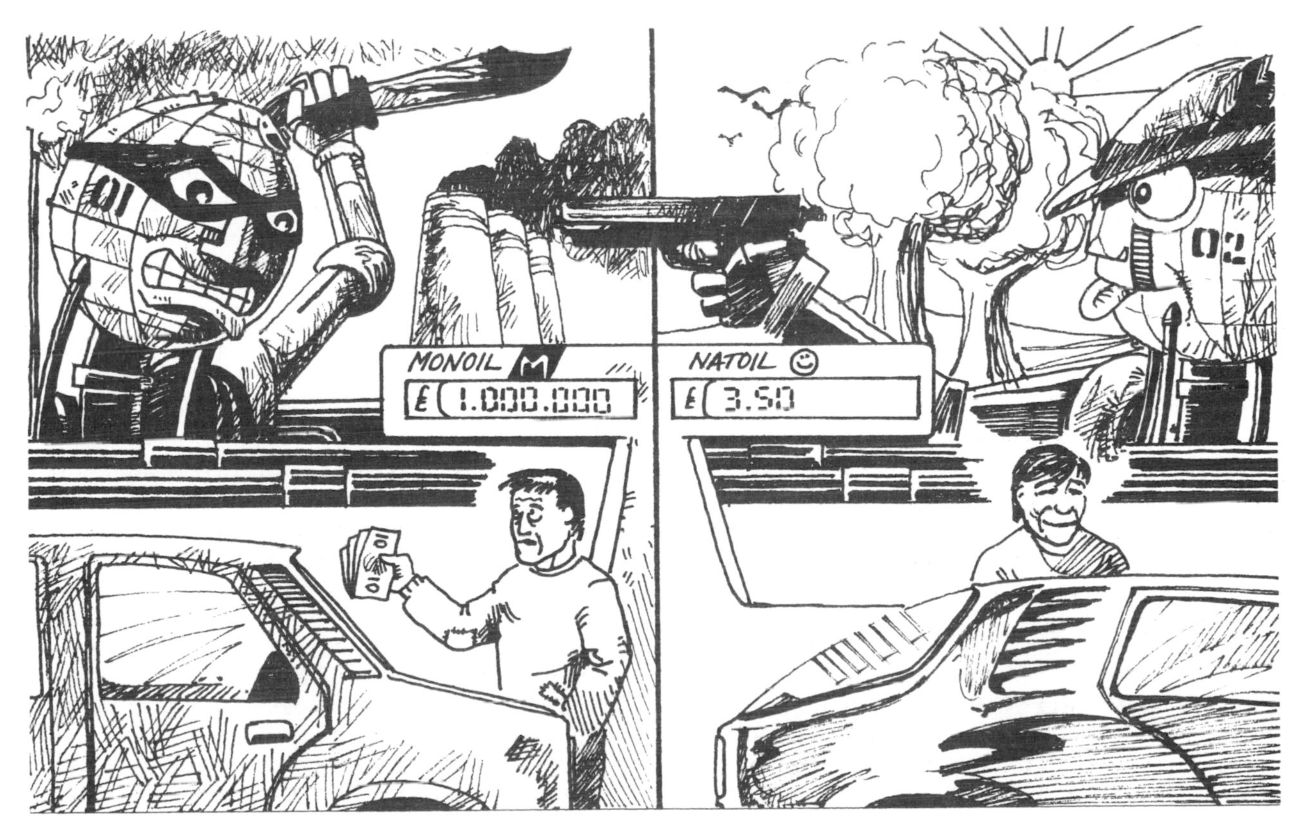

as unemployment be solved, since public sector firms can take on more workers, even though this may lead to a fall in profits.

Key ideas – summary of the argument for public ownership

1. Natural monopolies exist in a number of industries and these should be in the public sector to prevent exploitation of consumers.
2. Since they do not have to be guided by the profit motive, public sector firms can allow for the existence of externalities and supply merit goods.
3. If important industries run into difficulties, the public sector can save these firms, thus maintaining employment and output.
4. Private ownership leads to huge divisions between rich and poor; public ownership can reduce these divisions.
5. The state needs to own and control the 'commanding heights' of the economy in order to ensure full employment and steady growth.
6. Private ownership means that profits go to shareholders who usually take no part in the running of firms. Public ownership allows the workers to receive the full fruits of their labour.
7. Marxists would argue that only a large scale extension of public ownership can solve economic problems such as unemployment.

Policies

In the first place, measures to privatise publicly owned industries should be resisted. Secondly, some firms should be taken into public ownership. For some Marxists, this would be a large number, sufficient to change the nature of capitalist society. Others would only support a much more modest policy of public ownership and many of these would oppose nationalisation because they regard this particular form of public ownership as unnecessarily bureaucratic. Instead they advocate alternative forms of public ownership, for example, workers' co-operatives. These could take many forms, but the essence of such organisations is that the workers in a firm own the company, receive all the profits, and are responsible for decision making.

The case for privatisation

Critics of public ownership frequently begin by arguing that privatisation should take place because publicly owned firms are not efficient. They focus on two forms of efficiency, allocative efficiency and X-efficiency, and they also point out the benefits of wider share ownership.

Allocative efficiency

As its name implies, allocative efficiency is concerned with the allocation of resources. A system is efficient in this sense when it produces the 'best' combination of goods and services – usually this means those desired by consumers – by means of the most efficient combination of inputs. The argument is that privatised firms would be more responsive to consumers' needs. Since profits accrue to the owners – and sometimes to the managers in the form of incentive bonuses – the people who run private sector firms have a direct incentive to provide the goods and services which consumers want. This means that privatised firms would be more innovative in producing new products in response to changes in public taste and be more concerned to ensure the goods which they produced were of a high quality.

X-efficiency

X-efficiency is a rather pompous term used to describe a simple concept. A firm is X-efficient if it produces a given output at the lowest possible cost. The argument is that without the spur of competition, nationalised industries will be able to have a quiet life, content to produce in traditional ways without worrying too much about improving efficiency. On the other hand, privatised industries will face the disciplines imposed by the market. If they are not efficient they may be forced into bankruptcy. Even if that does not occur, poor performance will mean it is difficult to raise money for expansion. Moreover, the price of the shares will fall, penalising not only shareholders, but also those managers who receive financial incentives related either to profits or to the price of shares. To this argument the critics of privatisation retort that profits and share prices depend far more on external factors, such as the state of the economy or changes in the general level of prices, than on a firm's efficiency. Further, they maintain that there is little hard evidence that large companies find it difficult to raise money to finance developments, so that the 'discipline' of the stock market is more myth than reality. A further claim is that privatised industries will be more efficient because they will face competition. However, merely privatising an industry does not increase the amount of competition, which depends on other factors such as the presence or absence of competing firms, rather than the form of ownership of one firm. Hence privatised firms, such as British Gas and British Steel, face little more competition now than they did when nationalised.

Empirical evidence about efficiency

The arguments about efficiency are hard to judge because the empirical evidence is difficult to evaluate. In competitive industries the level of profits is a good measure of efficiency, but in publicly owned industries it would be more likely to measure the extent of price increases. If the Post Office put up its prices, then its profits would also rise; but this would say nothing about its efficiency.

Another difficulty in making comparisons is that public sector firms may have different objectives; for example, they may be required to offer socially desirable but loss making services. The ideal way to make comparisons would be to find firms which are identical except that one is in the public sector and one the private. Such examples are hard to find; even when similar firms can be found, they differ in other important characteristics. For example, in the USA it is possible to compare electricity generating firms in both public and private sectors, but they differ because their markets differ. Thus one may be supplying a concentrated urban area whilst another has to supply electricity to scattered rural communities.

Despite the difficulties, a number of comparisons have been made. For example, Caves and Christensen (1980) compared the publicly owned Canadian National railway with the privately owned Canadian Pacific. These were fairly similar firms, both operating coast to coast freight and passenger services. They concluded that the privately owned firm had a slightly better productivity record, but the difference was not great. A survey of 30 studies in different countries by Yarrow (1985) concluded that privately owned firms tended to be more efficient than publicly owned firms if both operated in competitive markets. When the market was not competitive, there was little difference. However, Millward and Parker (1983) also conducted a wide ranging survey and concluded that 'while the evidence is rather mixed, there is some evidence that competition does reduce the costs of public firms and regulation raises the costs of private firms... there is no general indication that private firms are more cost conscious than public firms'. Similarly, Ferguson (1988) summarised 15 comparisons of public and private sector efficiency and found little difference. For example, in the electricity generating industry, two studies reported no difference between the sectors, three found the public sector to be more efficient, whilst one study found private sector firms to be more efficient.

Hence the research evidence is not conclusive. It may be that the question of ownership is less important than other factors such as the way in which public sector firms are allowed to operate by the government and the way in which private sector firms are regulated.

Wider share ownership

Another argument in favour of privatisation is that selling nationalised industries increases share ownership, and that this is desirable because it gives people a stake in the wealth of the nation. It therefore contributes to political stability. This argument would be attacked by Marxists and others on the grounds that individual rewards from owning a few shares are so trivial that they do not really give people a stake in the wealth of society.

Another argument in this context is that, since the workers in privatised firms often receive shares on a preferential basis, they will have an increased motivation to work hard. Consequently efficiency will improve in privatised firms.

Criticisms of privatisation

Privately owned firms which have some monopoly power, particularly those that are natural monopolies, must be regulated and this is difficult to achieve. Sometimes the regulatory board has too little power and even when it has sufficient power it often fails to use it. This is called 'regulatory capture' and occurs because the firm and those who are supposed to regulate it become very close, so that the regulators become sympathetic to the firm.

Critics of privatisation make a number of other points. Thus the Trades Union Congress makes the following claims:

- People will only buy shares in successful businesses so it is only the profitable public enterprises which are 'sold off'. Hence the government is penalising successful public enterprise.

- Privatised companies have been sold too cheaply. Moreover, the Exchequer loses the income from the profitable nationalised industries which it formerly received and is left to fund unprofitable industries.
- De-nationalisation is likely to break up an industry's network of services and its ability to cross-subsidise loss making activities, such as rural postal deliveries, with the profits made from delivering business mail in the cities. To this argument the supporters of privatisation retort that cross-subsidisation is undesirable – the price which is charged for a good should reflect its cost of production. If rural postal deliveries are thought to be desirable, then the cost should not be borne by other consumers, but by the community as a whole.

The claim is also made that the government is taking a very short-term approach and is selling off the country's assets to finance tax cuts – 'selling off the family silver' as Harold Macmillan, a former Conservative Prime Minister, put it.

Deregulation

So far, this chapter has focused on privatisation in the sense of selling off public sector firms. However, allowing private sector firms to provide services previously restricted to public sector organisations is an important aspect of privatisation. It is argued that this benefits consumers by giving them lower prices. Thus in 1981 a Telecommunications Act was passed which allowed new operators to compete in certain areas with British Telecom, and subsequently a licence was given to Mercury, a recent entry to the telecommunications business. The result was that British Telecom cut prices on its 100 highest density routes – most of which would also be Mercury routes. Those who dislike privatisation point out that this kind of result can be achieved whether or not a firm is in private or public ownership. Moreover, they point out that although British Telecom cut these particular prices, it subsequently raised prices in areas not facing competition from Mercury. Thus domestic users found their British Telecom charges rising faster than large business users.

Private provision

This is the third aspect of privatisation. It has been particularly important for local authorities and the health service because it is concerned with the private provision of services such as hospital catering and cleaning and with refuse collection and vehicle maintenance. It is sometimes called 'contracting out', and can be regarded as a move away from a monopoly position (for example, where a local authority has employed its own refuse collectors) to one of competition where contractors put in bids to operate the service. A number of claims are made for private provision. For example, E.V. Savas (1983), in a pamphlet published by the Adam Smith Institute, claims that:

'Contracting out permits a lesser intrusion of purely political factors into the process (of providing services). It means that there are fewer patronage positions to dispense... I believe that it is politically attractive to be an efficient deliverer of public services, even if it takes contracting out and foregoing patronage positions'.

Contracting out services makes it possible for the government to take advantage of specialised skills which may be lacking in its own workforce. It also permits firms to take advantage of economies of scale which may arise when they specialise in the provision of particular services.

Supporters of the privatisation of services also claim that putting out services for tender increases competition and means that the public gets the service at the lowest possible cost. One reason for this is that it is claimed the public sector unions whose members provide these services have had too much power and have insisted on conditions of service and inefficient work practices which are advantageous to their members, but which penalise the public.

Against this, a number of arguments are put forward. In the first place it is suggested that the only reason privatised services save money is that the firms cut the pay and work conditions of their employees. Since the workers in these services are already often low paid, this is objectionable on the grounds of equity. Furthermore, the quality of service will deteriorate because contractors will have an incentive to cut corners. The less that is spent on the service, the larger will be the profits of the contractor. And finally, although the service may cost less in the short run, as time passes the firms involved will have an incentive to collude to put up prices, so the community will be the loser.

Key ideas – summary of the argument for privatisation

1. Nationalised industry is inefficient because it lacks incentives to cut costs.
2. Privatised industry will have the incentive of private gain to become more efficient. This incentive will encourage people to cut costs and also to introduce new products.
3. The discipline of the market will penalise inefficient private firms, while no such discipline affects nationalised industry.
4. Contracting out services will save public money.
5. Private enterprise is better than public because public ownership brings in political considerations which reduce efficiency.

Policies

In recent years, governments have favoured privatisation and argued that since public ownership is to be deplored, publicly owned firms should be sold off and returned to the private sector. Whilst this may not be possible in the short run because the industry is making losses, it should be done as soon as possible. In the meantime, nationalised industries should be pruned of loss-making activities to facilitate privatisation. Many more services should be contracted out. In addition to refuse collection, hospital cleaning and laundry, many other activities could be privatised. Examples are cleaning schools, running swimming pools, building and running prisons. In addition, schools should be encouraged to opt out of local government control and private medicine should be encouraged.

Regulation

Governments intervene in markets when they fail to allocate resources in a satisfactory way. Regulation is one way that they intervene. For example, governments intervene to stop people practising as doctors unless they have proper qualifications. That is because people lack the information needed to make a good decision about treatment and so have to trust the provider. Similarly the government insists on building regulations because the ordinary consumer is not able to judge the safety of buildings. Governments also intervene by making regulations to preserve attractive countryside.

However, we are concerned here with a special form of intervention. In recent years a number of utilities have been privatised. These include gas, electricity and water supply. These are all natural monopolies, where the fixed costs are very high but the cost of supplying an additional unit is very low. Under these conditions, competition is very unlikely – for example, it would be extremely difficult for a new firm to be able to pay the huge costs which would be involved in connecting a gas pipe to millions of homes so that consumers could have a choice of gas supplier. Hence existing suppliers have an effective monopoly, and without government intervention they would be able to exploit this by charging high prices and providing poor service. Consequently, the government regulates certain aspects of their behaviour.

The major regulatory authorities are the Office of Telecommunications (OFTEL), the Office of Gas Supplies (OFGAS), the Office of Water Services (OFWAT) and the Office of Electricity Regulation (OFFER). These bodies have a total staff of about 500; relatively few to undertake duties which have important effects on every household.

Their duties are laid down by law and differ slightly, but all of them have two major tasks. These are to operate a system of price controls to protect consumers and to facilitate competition wherever this is possible. The system of price control is usually based on that originally laid down for telecommunications. This is the RPI – X formula where RPI is the rise in retail prices and X is changed from time to time; currently it is 7.5 per cent. Hence if the rate of inflation is 5 per cent, BT will have to cut its prices by 2.5 per cent. The formula therefore encourages BT to cut costs since it then benefits from higher profits. The price which BT can charge is lower than the rate of inflation because it is assumed that the telecommunications industry is one where technological advances make it relatively easy to cut costs. In the case of water the formula is RPI + K where K varies between companies. In this case the firms are allowed to increase prices by more than the rate of inflation in order to generate funds for investment to improve water supply and sewerage. The formula for electricity allows electricity distributors to pass on to consumers increases in the prices they pay to electricity generators.

The most aggressive regulator has been OFGAS, which has attempted to bring competition into the industry. For example, it forced British Gas to bid for no more than 90 per cent of all new gas fields in the North Sea. This allows other firms to produce gas. Moreover, OFGAS 'found extensive discrimination by BG in the pricing and supply of gas to contract customers'. According to OFGAS, British Gas was charging some customers higher prices than others; those charged higher prices were those least likely to be able to find an alternative source of supply. OFGAS forced British Gas to charge all customers according to general tariffs.

Regulation is not a perfect solution to the problem of natural monopolies. In the USA there have been many examples of 'regulatory capture'. This is the phrase used when a regulator works so closely with a firm that it becomes sympathetic to its problems, and ceases to be tough. Alternatively, there is a danger that regulation breeds regulation. When a regulation is seen to be inadequate a new one is passed so that eventually the regulator ends up with more power over the industry than the minister had when the industry was nationalised.

How has a privatised British Telecom performed?

For many years the telephone service in the UK was run by the Post Office. Then telecommunications was hived off, but still remained in the public sector. In 1984 the government transformed it into a public limited liability company and sold off over half of the shares. In 1991 a further sale of shares took place, leaving the government with around 22 per cent of the shares.

Consequently British Telecom (BT) is now firmly in the private sector of the economy, and since it is a business where the fixed costs are very high (connecting lines to a house) and the marginal costs low, it is a natural monopoly. Moreover, since about 90 per cent of British households have a phone, the way it operates affects almost every family. Even this underestimates its importance because the telecommunications business is much broader than the domestic phone service. It includes such services as mobile phones, fax and radiopaging, and it is a major purchaser of telecommunications equipment from manufacturers.

When the industry was privatised an attempt was made to encourage competition. Although it was impractical for other companies to connect up millions of households, other companies were allowed to use the BT network. The main competitor was Mercury Communications Ltd., a subsidiary of Cable and Wireless, which has a long distance network made up of digital microwave links and optical fibre cables. However, BT still dominates the market with nearly six million business exchange connections compared with Mercury's 600,000. The dominance is even more marked in residential services where Mercury has 200,000 domestic consumers compared with BT's 20 million, giving BT a 97 per cent share of both markets in total. There may be more competition in future, for example, from various cable companies who intend to operate phone services using the lines used for cable TV.

Because of its importance, the question arises: has the privatisation of British Telecom been beneficial?

However, it is not possible to give a simple answer to the question. In a competitive market the level of profits is a good indicator of efficiency. On this criterion BT has done well. Its shares have outperformed the Financial Times index, and profits have grown well. However, the telecommunications market is not fully competitive, so that profits may merely reflect BT's ability to exploit its monopolistic position.

Price is another criterion which can be used to judge success. Because of the formula which controls pricing, BT's prices have risen by less than the rate of inflation, suggesting that consumers have benefited, but this may have been the position even if the firm had stayed in the public sector.

Increased productivity is another criterion that can be used to measure a company's performance. Here, BT can show considerable improvement. For example, in 1992 it cut its labour force (which exceeded 200,000) by 35,000 whilst output, as measured by the number of calls, was fairly constant. However, critics would argue that in a technological industry, it is relatively easy to increase output per person by cutting staff and replacing them by machines.

Consequently, there is no certain answer to the question of whether or not the community has benefited from the privatisation of BT. It may be that in many industries the extent of competition is more important than the forms of ownership since fierce competition may lead to benefits to consumers whether or not the business is owned by the government or by private investors.

Conclusion

For most of the period since the Second World War the nationalised industries have been an important part of the economy. In 1987 they accounted for 5.5 per cent of UK output and employed 800,000 people. Since that time their importance has declined substantially, so that by 1992 their share of GDP was only 3 per cent.

The public sector has its supporters and its critics. Its supporters are sceptical of the argument that market forces are the best way to allocate resources. Instead they believe that government intervention is necessary to prevent market failure and that public ownership brings positive benefits to society. Its critics believe the public sector is less efficient than the private and for this reason the government should take all possible measures to reduce the size of the public sector. The economic evidence is inconclusive. What is certain is that people's values in this argument affect the way in which they interpret the evidence.

Data questions

A tale of two telephone firms: British Telecom thrives, NTT struggles

BT recently announced pre tax profits of £3.1 billion – no change on the previous year despite the recession. NTT's profits, due to be released shortly, are expected to be just over £1 billion, a drop of a third. BT's return on sales was 23%, NTT's a more normal 7%.

The difference lies in the way the two firms are regulated. Japan and Britain both privatised their telephone monopolies in the 1980s. But BT faces only one competitor, Mercury. Lax rules have allowed it to make fat profits out of its 95% share of the domestic market. Meanwhile NTT's share of the Japanese market has slid to 73% as three bold new competitors have been allowed to snap at its heels. Regulators have also been tough on NTT, refusing to let it increase prices on its loss-making local calls.

To strengthen its position, NTT has doubled its spending on advertising and has introduced new services such as call conferencing and high speed faxing. To no avail; NTT's competitors have introduced similar services.

Source: Adapted from *The Economist*, May 23 1992.

Question 1

1. Explain what is meant by 'return on sales', 'privatised' and regulation'.
2. What difference would you expect competition to make to prices and profits? Are your expectations confirmed by the experience of BT and NTT?
3. What is product differentiation, and what part does it play in oligopoly? Do the activities of the two telecommunications firms confirm theoretical predictions?

Deregulation, privatisation and employment in the port transport industry

In 1989 over 60,000 workers were directly dependent on the port of Rotterdam for their employment. In the same year Britain's ports employed 42,500 workers. Since then employment in Britain's industry has fallen by over 11,000; in contrast it is anticipated that employment in the port of Rotterdam will rise to 83,000 by the year 2010. Why the difference?

In Rotterdam the port is managed by the local municipality and receives government and municipal investment on infrastructure as part of a national transport plan. In the UK the state owned ports have been privatised, and the dock labour scheme, which gave stability of employment, has been abolished. The cost to the government of deregulation has been £244 million; but the benefits have not been passed on to workers or to customers. Instead the benefits of lower operating costs have been pocketed by the port authorities.

Britain is now the only country in the EC with a predominantly private port transport sector; in other countries they are owned by municipalities or by autonomous bodies subject to public control. This allows co-ordinated investment and national planning of port facilities so that they network with road, rail and canal facilities.

Source: Adapted from Turnbull P., *Deregulation, Privatisation and Employment in the Port/Transport Industry* in University of Leeds Centre for Industrial Policy and Performance Bulletin No. 3, Autumn 1993.

Question 2

1. Explain what is meant by 'deregulation' and 'privatisation'.
2. Summarise the arguments which the author gives opposing moves to deregulate and privatise the industry.
3. What counter arguments do you think might be put by someone supporting these changes?

8 Regional Economics

In the nineteenth century certain regions specialised in a limited range of industries which subsequently experienced massive declines in employment. Localised job losses in industries such as coal mining, iron and steel and shipbuilding were responsible for high rates of unemployment in particular areas.

The first significant policy response came in 1928 when the Minister of Labour set up a Board 'for the purpose of facilitating the transfer of workers, and in particular of miners, for whom opportunities of employment in their own district or occupation are no longer available'. Since then the details of regional policy have varied, but the general approach has been remarkably consistent.

- State intervention has attempted to provide incentives for new industries to move to disadvantaged regions by giving grants or loans and by encouraging the retraining and relocation of workers. Behind the specific details of these policies lies the belief that unrestricted market forces will not reduce regional differences.
- This view is opposed by some supply side economists who argue that government intervention to help particular regions leads to a misallocation of resources – for example, inefficient industries are kept in business. This group suggests that policies should focus on encouraging market forces to operate more effectively.

Before we can examine these views, we must first examine the nature and extent of regional differences in Britain.

How serious are regional differences in modern Britain?

Regional differences in Britain are sometimes summarised as 'the North - South divide'. Whilst this is an over-simplification – there are areas of poverty in the South and prosperity in the North – it does focus attention on the geographical dimension. In the South we find prosperous regions; in the North decline and decay are common. Each of these 'regions' has certain characteristics.

Prosperous regions

Prosperous regions tend to be located in the South of the UK, close to the centre of population and the large EC market. It is in these regions that government departments and large companies have their headquarters, so that the most important economic decisions are made here. The head offices of the majority of the leading financial institutions are also found in these regions. Consequently raising money for expansion is easier and so most new investment is found in these parts of the country. These regions typically have a smaller manufacturing base than their northern equivalents; more importantly, there is no excessive concentration on one or two heavy industries. Instead, there is a well-developed service sector. This mixture of economic activity contributes to a higher level of GDP per head. Moreover, GDP is rising more quickly than in other regions. These areas are characterised by an inflow of population and those people who move in tend to be young, healthy and well educated.

Depressed regions

In many ways the depressed regions of the UK are the converse of the prosperous regions. They tend to be on the periphery of the country, have relatively low GDP per head and have unemployment rates above the national average. For many years they were characterised by declining industries, such as coal, steel, shipbuilding and textiles. Few large companies locate their headquarters there. Young, active people often move out, so that the population tends to be older and less skilled. People in these regions have more illnesses and lower life expectancy than those in more prosperous areas.

Another feature of these depressed areas is that they tend to have relatively large numbers of cities which grew rapidly at the time of the Industrial Revolution. Liverpool is a classic example. Such cities face multiple problems; unsatisfactory housing, high rates of crime and unemployment are common features.

However, in recent years the position has changed. The recession of 1990–1993 was different from all previous post-war recessions. When national unemployment rises, the disadvantaged regions suffer most. The most recent recession was different because the most disadvantaged regions had the lowest rise in unemployment; it was the prosperous South which suffered most. One reason for this was that the South had a collapse of consumer spending which hit local businesses hard. Moreover house prices fell, and the fall was largest in formerly prosperous regions where houses were expensive. In the North and North-West of Britain inefficient industries had gone under in previous recessions; those which were left were 'leaner and fitter'.

Despite the relatively great rise in unemployment, the South remains comparatively well off, with incomes considerably above the national average.

***Figure 8.1:** Rates of unemployment in selected UK regions, 1927-39 (June each year)*

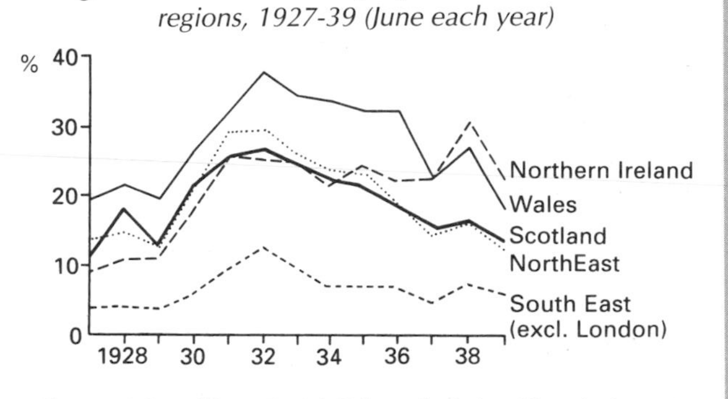

Source: Adapted from *British Labour Statistics, Historical Abstract*, 1886-1968.

***Figure 8.2:** Regional unemployment, percentages, 1992*

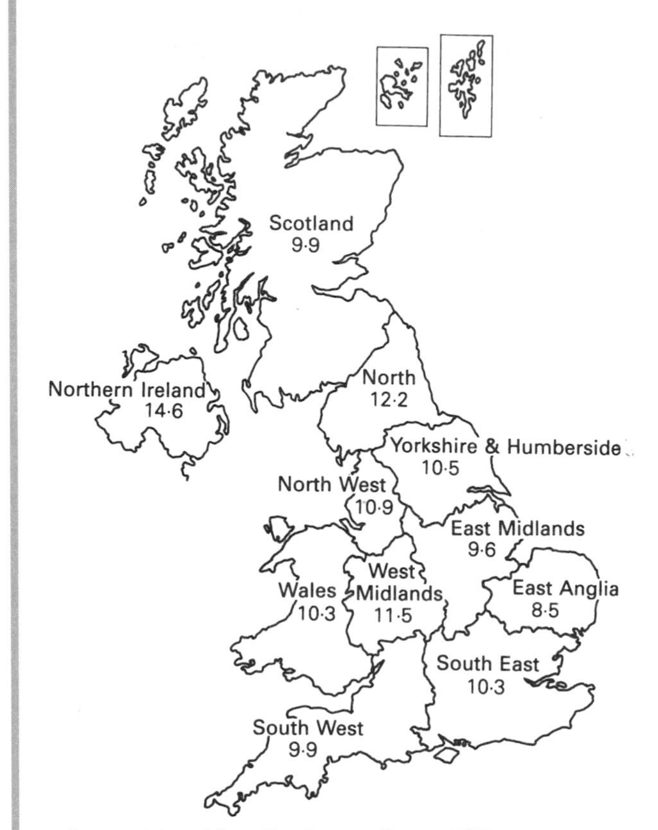

Source: Adapted from *Employment Gazette*, 1993.

Evidence on the UK regions

Unemployment and employment

In considering the relative prosperity of an area, the most easily available evidence, and perhaps also the most telling, is to look at figures for unemployment. Figure 8.1 shows that over half a century ago there were significant regional differences in unemployment. What is also obvious is that the regions which were prosperous then are also those which are doing well today. Those which were depressed then are still characterised by high rates of unemployment, as can be seen from Figure 8.2.

Precise comparisons between the two periods are difficult to make because, over the last half century, there have been changes in the measurement of unemployment as well as in the way the regions are defined. Nevertheless, the pattern is clear. In both periods the highest levels of unemployment are to be found in the North, whilst the South and East have had low levels of unemployment. However, this is not the whole story. In the peripheral regions, not only are people more likely to be unemployed, but they are more likely to have been unemployed for long periods.

Migration

Another indicator of regional inequality is migration. As Figure 8.3 shows, there is a tendency

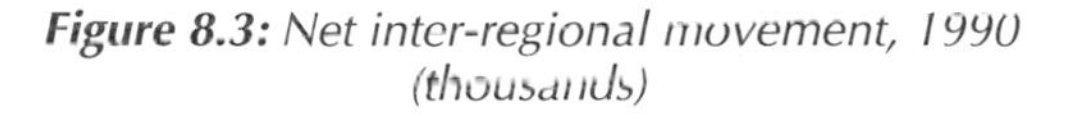

Figure 8.3: *Net inter-regional movement, 1990 (thousands)*

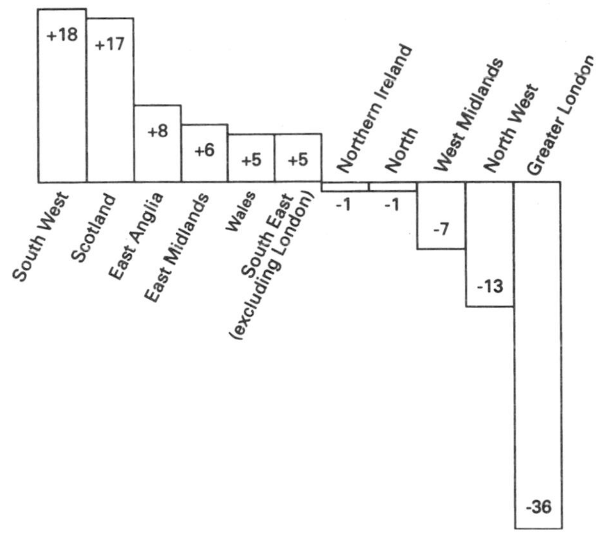

Source: Adapted from *Regional Trends*, 1993.

for people to move out of the Northern and Western regions and into those in the South. There is also a considerable movement of people out of Greater London. The Figure can be misleading, because some people have moved only short distances, for example, out of the cities and into small towns. This may involve crossing regional boundaries and give a false impression. Moreover, some of the movement is of older people moving to retirement homes. This is one explanation of the net migration into Wales, an area of high unemployment. What the Figure does not show is the character of the people who move. Excluding those retiring, most movement is of young, educated and qualified people moving to find work or to obtain better jobs.

Incomes

Regions also differ in their incomes. This can be examined in a number of ways. Figure 8.4 shows the relative position of the regions in their contribution to national output. The greater output per head of the South East is obvious, whilst per head of the population Wales and Northern Ireland produce considerably less than the rest of the country.

These differences in output are reflected in the earnings received by people in the regions. These are shown in Table 8.1. Both men and women in the South East earn considerably more than workers in the rest of the country.

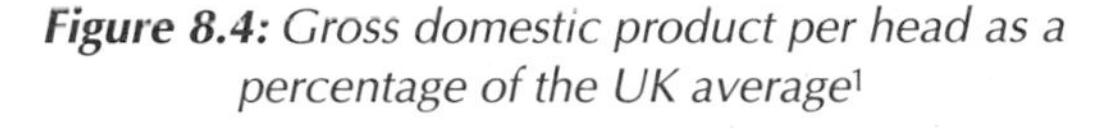

Figure 8.4: *Gross domestic product per head as a percentage of the UK average*[1]

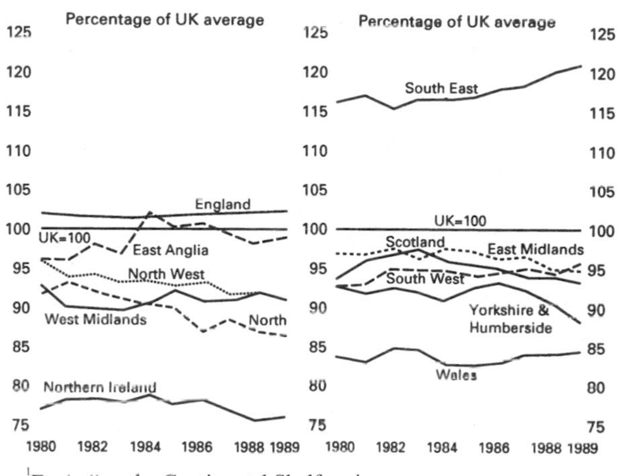

[1]Excluding the Continental Shelf region.
Source: Adapted from *Regional Trends*, 1993.

Table 8.1: *Average weekly earnings in the UK, 1991 (£ per week)*

Region	Males	Females
North	289	196
Yorkshire & Humberside	287	200
East Midlands	293	199
East Anglia	300	203
South East	369	256
South West	297	207
West Midlands	291	202
North West	300	207
Wales	280	199
Scotland	300	207
Northern Ireland	268	198

Source: Adapted from *Regional Trends*, HMSO, 1993.

Education

There are many reasons why some regions are more prosperous than others. One is that the people in some regions have higher standards of education. That is because there is a close link between more education, increased productivity and higher incomes. Table 8.2 shows the educational qualifications in the regions of the UK, as measured by possession of a degree. Again, the difference between the South East and the rest of the country is marked.

These differences in education are associated with differences in occupation. Thus in the South East in 1991, 8.3 per cent of employees were classified as managerial and 5.5 per cent were professional. In the North region only 4.4 per cent were managers and the same proportion were professional.

Table 8.2: *Percentage of the workforce with a degree, 1991*

Region	%
North	6.9
Yorkshire & Humberside	7.7
East Midlands	8.9
East Anglia	8.0
South East	13.6
South West	8.2
West Midlands	7.0
North West	8.3
Wales	7.5
Scotland	7.7
Northern Ireland	8.6

Source: Adapted from *Regional Trends*, 1993.

Thus the evidence is conclusive. Although there are substantial pockets of poverty in the South and of prosperity in the North, people in the North are more likely to be unemployed, and to have lower incomes and educational qualifications and to do different types of job.

The question therefore arises: what should be done to correct these disparities? This debate is examined in the rest of this chapter.

Key ideas

1. Although there are many exceptions, the South of the UK tends to be more prosperous than the North.
2. Depressed regions are characterised by declining manufacturing industries. They have fewer headquarters of large companies.
3. People in depressed regions have lower incomes and higher unemployment rates than people in other areas, and many young people migrate to these prosperous parts of the country.

The free market approach

Economists who favour this approach tend to argue that there is not really a 'regional problem' in the UK. Instead they argue that there is a **national** economic problem which affects all regions but which is particularly acute in some of them. They argue further that this problem arises because market forces have not been allowed to operate freely in the economy.

In considering what is called 'the regional problem', free market economists focus more on the labour market than the goods market. If the labour market functions perfectly, then workers will try to maximise their wages while employers will attempt to hire labour as cheaply as possible. The result will be an equilibrium wage at which there is no shortage or surplus of labour. In other words, the labour market will clear.

In terms of the regions, what should happen when market forces operate freely is that in areas of high unemployment wages will fall, leading to an increase in the demand for labour by firms in the region. Moreover, some firms in places where wages are high because there is little unemployment will be attracted by the possibility of reducing their labour costs; consequently they will move to areas of high unemployment. This will increase demand for labour in the depressed areas and lead to the labour market clearing – no unemployment and no shortage of labour at prevailing wage rates.

One other movement needs to be noted. If the labour market is operating freely, then some people in areas of high unemployment will be attracted by the possibility of earning higher wages elsewhere and will therefore migrate. This will reduce the unemployment problem in areas of high unemployment and increase the supply of labour in places where wages are high, thus pulling down wages in these areas. According to this group of economists, a freely operating market mechanism would eliminate regional differences in unemployment. These differences only persist because markets are unable to operate freely.

Market imperfections

There are three reasons in particular which prevent the labour market from working to remove regional imbalances in unemployment.

Inflexible wages

Wages tend not to fall in areas where unemployment is high. A government White Paper in 1983 claimed:

'Imbalances between areas in employment opportunities should in principle be corrected by the natural adjustment of labour markets. In the first place, this should be through lower wages and unit costs than comparable work commands elsewhere. Wage inflexibility... would increase the attractiveness to industry of areas with high unemployment.'

The White Paper went on to point out:

'There is, however, little evidence that regional wage rates respond readily to variations in regional unemployment.'

This conclusion still applies. In part this is because in many industries wages are negotiated nationally, so that (with the possible exception of a London allowance) workers in an industry doing the same job receive the same wage whatever the local level of unemployment. In the view of supply side economists, this prevents the labour market from cutting unemployment in depressed areas.

Labour immobility

Only a few unemployed workers move out of areas with high unemployment. The reasons for this are well known. In the first place, they may find it difficult to obtain jobs even in areas where unemployment is much lower. This may be because of personal characteristics, such as low levels of education, or because they are ignorant about the jobs on offer in other areas. In addition, the costs of moving may be greater than the prospective benefits obtainable from a new job. The cost of living may also prove to be too high, especially when faced with the prospect of finding accommodation in areas where houses are very expensive. However, the main reasons preventing people from migrating are linked to family responsibilities. Children's education, or the need to care for older relatives, may prevent some people from even attempting to find work in other areas. The need to house families can make moving to other areas impossible. Those living in council houses will find it impossible to get similar accommodation in areas of low unemployment and those who own their own house would be likely to

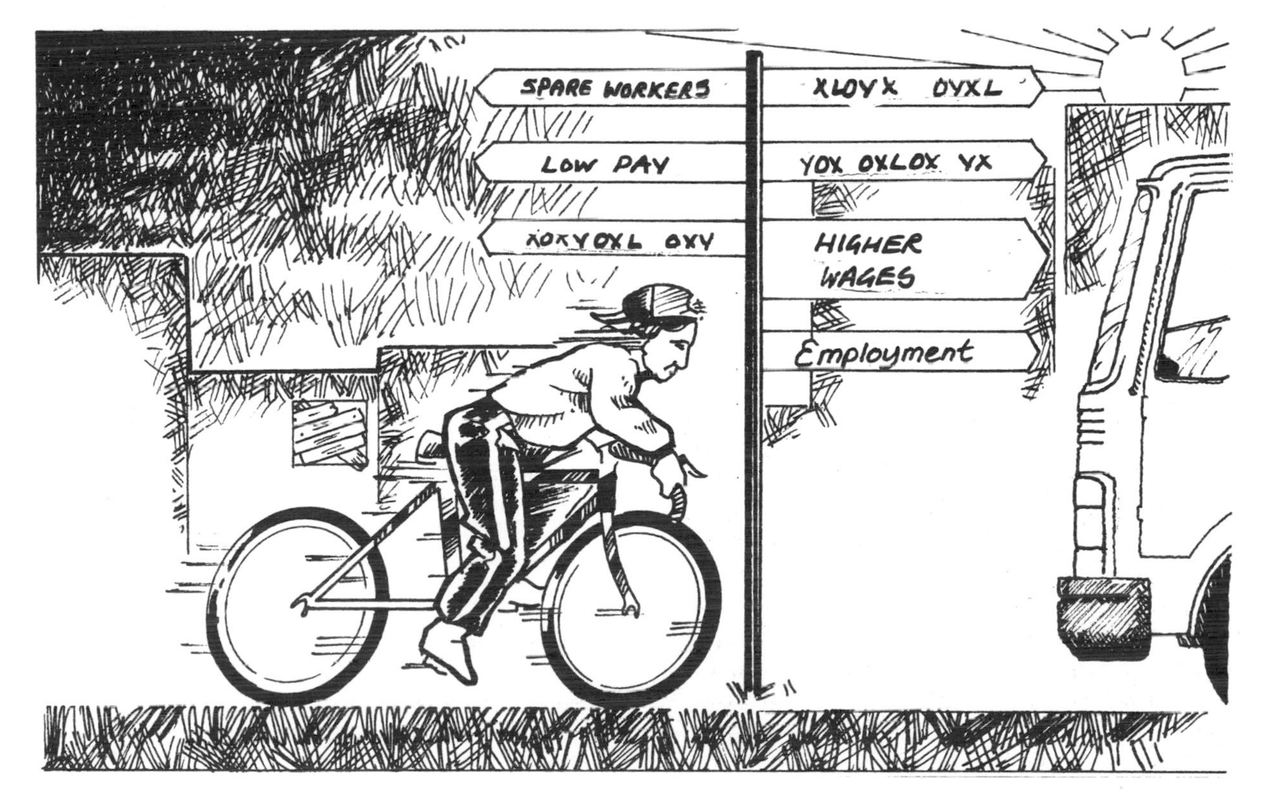

receive a much lower price for the house they sell than for a similar one in a prosperous area. Hence the people who are most likely to move are young people without family responsibilities who are willing to live in bed-sits or similar accommodation for a year or two until they can afford a better place to live.

Firms are immobile

Only a few firms move into areas of high unemployment. This is not surprising. Once settled, most firms stay where they are; there are not many **footloose** firms looking to relocate. If they want to expand into new premises they will be tempted to look at sites close to their present location and will need strong reasons to look further afield. The possibility of taking on workers at lower wage rates may be such an incentive – as will the possibility of cheap premises – but the costs of relocating are high and new labour will need to be trained, which can be expensive.

In the view of supply side economists, these imperfections do not weaken the case for the use of markets to solve regional problems; instead they call for action to remove or reduce these imperfections.

Key ideas – summary of the supply side argument

1. The so-called 'regional problem' is only one aspect of a national problem which occurs because market forces are not allowed to operate as they should.
2. If market forces are allowed to operate, then wages will fall in areas where unemployment is high. This will give workers an incentive to move out of these areas and firms an incentive to move, in order to take advantage of abundant labour at low cost.
3. Governments and trade unions prevent these forces from operating freely.

Free market policies

The points discussed above suggest that market imperfections limit the extent of firms' and workers' mobility. Those economists who support the use of market forces to allocate resources believe that policies should be adopted which would improve the workings of the market mechanism.

Housing

In the first place, they argue that the housing market should be radically reformed – in particular the system of rent controls and guaranteed tenure which keeps down rents so that it does not pay entrepreneurs to build houses to let. If there was no government interference, the market would eliminate the shortage of houses to rent and so facilitate mobility. Without controls, rents would rise, people with empty rooms or houses would make them available for rent and investors would start to build houses, not only for sale, but also to rent. This would increase the supply of places to rent in prosperous areas and, in the long run, might even bring down the level of rents. Arguments such as these led to the 1988 Housing Act, which continued to give protection to existing tenants, but which introduced market rents for new tenants.

Free market economists also argue that mobility would be increased if planning controls on building new houses were relaxed or abandoned. This would also increase the supply of houses to buy. The housing market would be further invigorated if more council houses were sold, since sitting tenants have an asset – their tenure – which makes it difficult to move.

Wages

Supply siders also believe that policies are needed to make wages more responsive to changes in the demand for labour. Although the position is slowly changing, many wages are still decided by national wage negotiations, which ensure that people in different parts of the country receive the same wage for the same job, irrespective of the level of unemployment. If wages were negotiated locally – or, better still, were a matter for individuals to negotiate with their employers – then wages would fall in areas where unemployment was high and perhaps rise in prosperous places. This would increase the incentives for workers to move and encourage firms to locate in low wage areas.

This policy is difficult to implement. A start could be made if the government and the nationalised industries stopped agreeing to common levels of wages across the country. Measures to weaken the power of trade unions would also improve wage flexibility so, for example, the law could be changed to make strikes more difficult and to penalise unions for losses which their actions may cause to employers.

Re-training

One reason for regional unemployment is that many workers in depressed regions have obsolete skills and therefore find it difficult to obtain work. Consequently, one policy which should be adopted is that workers should be encouraged to retrain. This policy would also be supported by interventionists. The difference is that supply siders would limit the role of government to providing incentives to firms and individuals. Interventionists would give a greater role to the government, suggesting, for example, that the government should subsidise or provide training courses.

Planning

Supply siders also argue that planning requirements should be relaxed. The need to get planning permission deters firms from moving because of the time and expense involved. Instead, market forces should determine land use, except where there are substantial spillover effects (such as extensive pollution), when intervention might be needed to correct this distortion. These policies are criticised by those economists who are sceptical of the benefits of unrestricted market forces.

Enterprise zones

One supply side approach to the urban problem is to encourage the formation of enterprise zones. These are areas where there are few planning restrictions and where firms are given exemptions from paying rates for a period. They are one way of reducing government interference in the economic life of cities.

The first enterprise zones were designated in 1981 in areas such as Hartlepool, Clydebank and Belfast. By 1988, twenty nine areas had been designated and the Department of the Environment estimated that there had been an increase of 3,300 in the number of people employed in these areas. Critics of the policy claim that this required a large amount of public spending on the infrastructure, loss of rate income, and that many of the jobs would have been created in any case, or were merely transferred from areas outside enterprise zones.

The case for government intervention

Critique of the free market argument

Supporters of government intervention begin by criticising the market forces argument on a number of grounds. In the first place, cutting wages in areas of high unemployment would be penalising the poorer sections of society and be morally unacceptable. Furthermore, the fall in wages would depress the demand for goods and services in these regions and would therefore make unemployment worse. It would also have a negative effect on worker morale and hence on productivity. Taylor and Armstrong (1988), two economists who have researched the regional problem, give other reasons why the supply side approach is unsatisfactory. They point out that the unemployed are the least likely group to move to other areas because they often cannot afford the costs involved in moving and may also be poorly informed about jobs available in other areas. It is young, highly educated and ambitious people who are most likely to leave, thus depriving depressed areas of their talents. In addition, because of inertia, firms are unlikely to relocate or to start subsidiaries in other areas unless they receive substantial financial incentives, for example, those provided by government grants.

The aims of regional policy

Whilst it is possible to argue about the precise objectives of regional policy, aims that would be supported by some economists include:

- The reduction of unemployment in areas where it is excessively high.
- An increase in the utilisation rate of resources.
- The reduction of population pressure in congested areas.
- The preservation of regional cultures.
- The encouragement of national unity (which may be threatened if some regions are dissatisfied).

Note that these objectives spill over from the purely 'economic' and depend in part on the values of those determining the objectives. Thus it is possible to disagree about which regional cultures should be encouraged – or even to deny that this should be a policy concern at all. The case for government intervention in regional policy rests on the assumption that these objectives are worthwhile and that they will not be achieved by market forces.

Unemployment

Persistent high levels of unemployment in particular regions suggest to economists who favour intervention that market forces can do little to reduce the differences between prosperous and depressed regions. Figure 8.1 showed the rates of unemployment in selected regions of the UK in the 1920s and 1930s. The same pattern persists today. If market forces were going to eliminate such differences, they would have done so in over half a century. Instruments of regional policy have helped to reduce regional differences, but such policies have been inadequate and need strengthening. The main cause of high unemployment in the regions is high unemployment nationally. Therefore policies should be adopted which will bring down the national rate. Most economists who favour an interventionist policy would probably argue that Keynesian policies to stimulate aggregate demand are the best method to achieve this goal. They would also suggest that what is needed is not indiscriminate increases in government spending, but spending which is targeted on depressed areas. This is discussed in more detail in Chapter 17.

One reason why unemployment is concentrated in particular regions is that these regions have a high proportion of declining industries, such as coal, cotton, shipbuilding and steel. Such industries should be helped to adjust, new industries should be given financial inducements to locate in these areas and workers in declining industries should benefit from government-funded training courses.

Utilisation rate

Regional policy can also help to achieve the second objective listed above – an increase in the utilisation rate of resources. Indeed, this is closely linked to the reduction of unemployment. But land, capital and entrepreneurship can also be under-utilised in depressed areas. (This is not to suggest that all resources should be fully used all the time. Workers need time for leisure and it is inefficient to try to make full use of all resources. Farming in the Arctic and the Sahara would be a waste of time and effort and, even in countries such as the UK, some land is not worth exploiting.) Nevertheless, many resources are underused and intervention offers the possibility of obtaining a better use of scarce resources, for example, by enabling unemployed workers to produce goods for which there is a demand and by making use of empty buildings.

Population density

Population densities vary considerably throughout the country and there is often good reason for this – people like to live near their work and it would be idiotic to try to resettle millions of people in the Highlands of Scotland. However, regional imbalance can lead to excessive concentration of economic activity in some urban areas and can cause costs to society in the form of congestion, pollution and noise. This is particularly apparent in developing countries, where some urban areas may be growing exceptionally quickly, but it can also affect industrialised countries, for example, in the form of traffic congestion, especially in large cities such as London. People driving cars or lorries in urban areas cause disagreeable external effects which reduce the welfare of other people. The existence of these externalities leads to a misallocation of resources which can only be reduced by government intervention. This can take the form of regional policy, though it is doubtful if regional policy on its own can solve this problem.

Culture and unity

The goals of encouraging regional culture and preserving national unity are also beyond the scope of regional policy on its own. People in depressed areas, such as Northern Ireland, are more likely to threaten national unity than those in prosperous places. If regional policy is successful it will offer opportunities to the dissatisfied and reduce discontent. But more than economic policy is needed to achieve unity. Similarly, regional policy can stimulate cultural activities in the regions, but cannot ensure that these reach a high standard.

There is another point which needs to be considered when deciding whether governments should intervene in economic life in order to help particular regions. The expansion and development of the European Community and the construction of a tunnel between Britain and the Continent will encourage footloose industries to locate in the south east corner of England. Industries in this location will be close to a rich and rapidly growing market and will have an advantage over industries in other parts of the country. Unless the government intervenes, regional differences in employment and income will grow.

Free market critique of the interventionist approach

Those who oppose government intervention make both theoretical and operational criticisms of the interventionist approach. The theoretical case for the use of markets was discussed in Chapters 2 and 3. Underlying this argument is the belief that intervention by governments leads to a misallocation of resources unless the intervention can be justified on specific grounds, such as the existence of public goods. In the case of the regions, the argument is that these reasons do not arise and that the government should leave economic decision-making to the markets. If, for example, governments intervene by giving grants to industry, the result will be greater inefficiency. This is because the best people to decide the location of a factory are the entrepreneurs whose money is at risk from the decision. If the government offers them money to locate in a place other than that which they would have chosen, the result will be a factory in a less than optimum situation, resulting in higher costs for the firm. Thus Lord Stokes, when in charge of the British Leyland Motor Corporation (later the Rover Group), argued that government intervention in regional policy increased business risk:

'You have cost us a fortune by making us set up factories in places which are quite unsuitable to have factories. You ruin our business; we try to make it survive.'

Moreover, the grants given to firms have not always been cost-effective. Sometimes they have been given to firms which would have located in depressed areas even without a grant, and the cost has been high – figures of £35,000 cost to public funds per job created have been quoted in a few extreme cases. In 1988 the government announced that, in future, grants would no longer be automatic but would be subject to prior investigation, to try to ensure value for money. Instead, they introduced 'Regional Selective Assistance'. This is a discretionary grant towards capital and training costs for projects which would benefit the local community, create jobs and eventually pay their

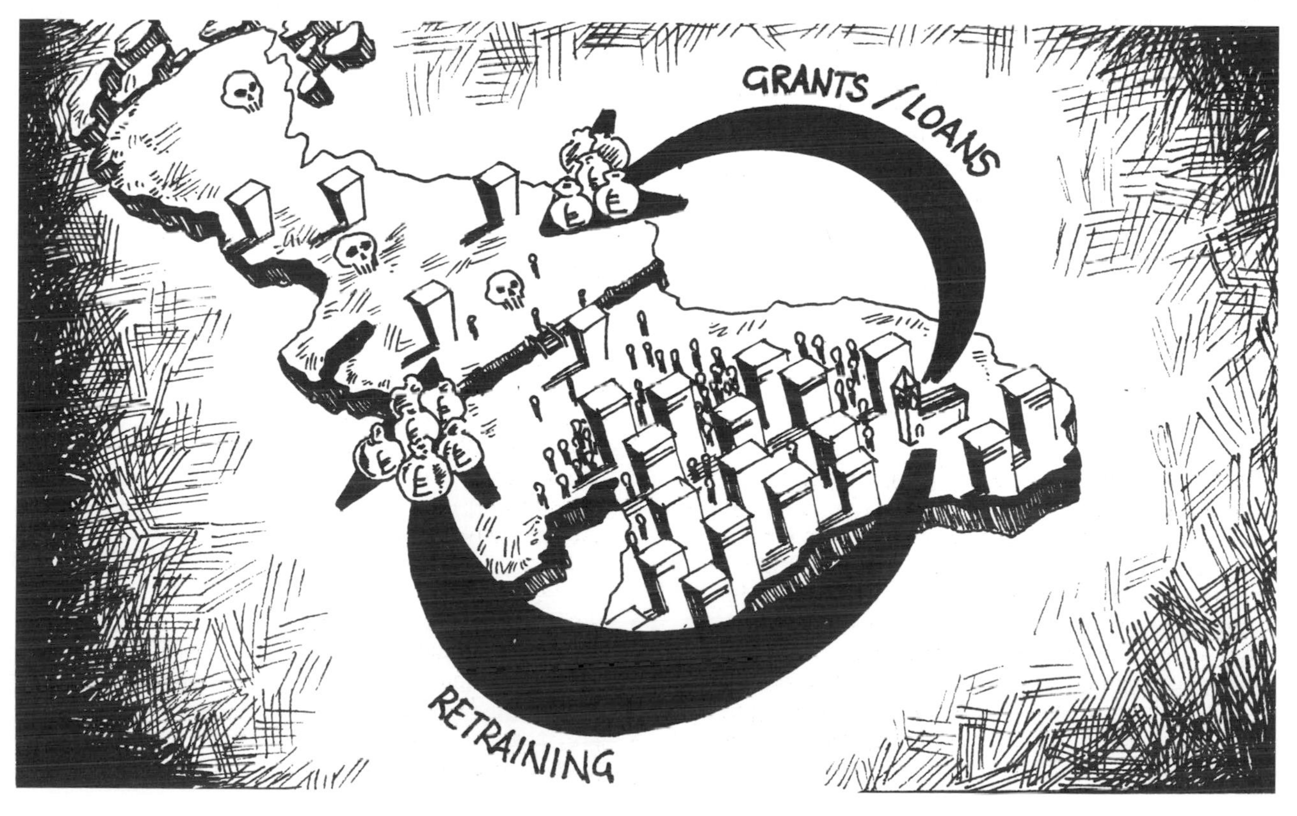

way but which are unable to proceed without the injection of some government money. The government spent £230 million on these grants in 1993.

Key ideas – summary of the argument for government intervention

1. Market forces do not work towards the elimination of regional inequalities.
2. Without government intervention companies would tend to locate in the prosperous areas, thus reinforcing regional differences.
3. Depressed regions suffer from a number of disadvantages – low levels of investment, less education and poorer health, for example.
4. Government intervention is therefore required in order to help achieve the objectives of regional policy.

Interventionist policies

The alternative to a free market is intervention by central and local government. Figure 8.5 shows the assisted areas in 1993. Taylor and Armstrong (1988) suggest a number of improvements to the present policy. In the first place, there needs to be a substantial increase in the level of investment grants to stimulate the development of new products and new techniques in depressed areas. More spending is also needed on the infrastructure of the less prosperous areas. If these areas had good communications, excellent training facilities and attractive environments, companies would be encouraged to locate there.

Agencies with a wide range of powers need to be set up in the regions to stimulate development. Initiatives by local authorities have been on a limited scale and could be extended if the central government introduced a regionally-discriminating policy towards new and small firms.

Similarly, a more active policy needs to be taken to encourage a more equitable distribution of venture capital. Since most large firms have their headquarters in the South, locations in other areas tend to be neglected when new initiatives are being developed. Another policy which would help the regions would be for the government to relocate more of its own activities in the regions.

Figure 8.5: *GB assisted areas as at 1.8.1993*

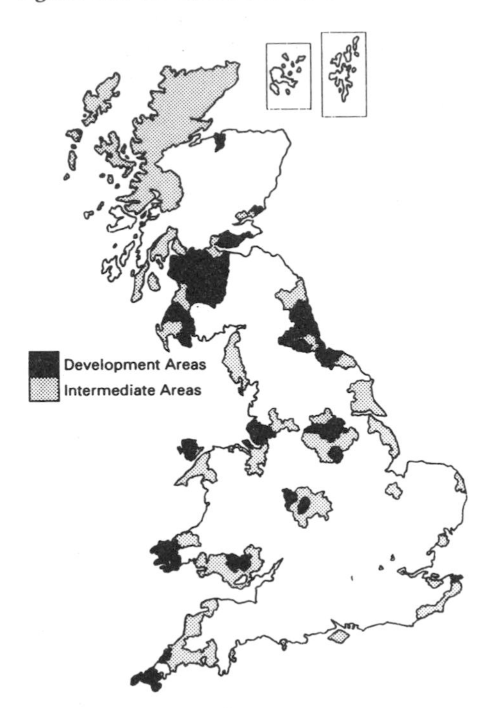

Source: Adapted from the DTI.

Do Enterprise zones work?

The creation of Enterprise zones was an example of supply side policies in action. They rest on the assumption that government intervention harms business initiative and that if firms were given more freedom then businesses would respond by creating jobs.

But it is very difficult to judge whether or not they have been effective. The North East Lancashire Enterprise Zone was set up in 1983 with a total area of 115 hectares in several sites. The cost to the public of one of these sites was £1.4 million by 1988, spent largely on infrastructure and rate relief. Some 437 people now work on the site, so that the cost per job is £3,200. Supporters of the scheme argue that this is a small price to pay for permanent jobs; in addition to the benefits to the people who get jobs, the government saves because it will now have to pay less on social security and will receive more in taxes.

However, critics point out that many of the jobs would have been created anyway – firms were just taking the money to do what they were going to do even without government help. Moreover they argue that areas just outside the enterprise zone have been adversely affected because firms have transferred from these areas to the zone to receive the benefits. Neither of these arguments is conclusive, and consequently it is not possible to come to a definite answer to the question 'Do enterprise zones work?'.

The impact of the EU

In recent years there has been a huge growth in the European Union's regional policy. One reason has been that the EU has increased in importance as a result of the Single European Act, which was designed to sweep away barriers to trade. As trade increases, measures need to be taken to help those regions that are less developed. Three structural funds play the principal role in the EU's regional policy. The European Regional Development Fund (ERDF) was set up in 1973 to help depressed regions; its work is complemented by the European Social Fund, which finances training and other social policies. The European Agriculture Guidance and Guarantee Fund provides job opportunities in rural areas.

The EU doubled its spending in real terms on these funds between 1989 and 1993. They are designed to contribute to the attainment of the following five priority objectives:

- Promoting the development of regions whose development is lagging behind. In practice this means Spain, Portugal, Ireland, Southern Italy and Greece.
- Converting regions affected by industrial decline. These so called 'Objective 2 regions' in the UK are shown in Figure 8.6.
- Combatting long term unemployment.
- Facilitating the integration of young people.
- Promoting the development of rural areas.

EU regional help is usually channelled through support channels. These are carefully planned initiatives where the EU, the government and other local and regional authorities work together to ensure coherent policies; partnership is preferred to unco-ordinated efforts.

Conclusion

The evidence is clear; there are substantial differences between regions in the UK and these differences persist over long periods of time. People who live in regions that have high levels of unemployment also tend to have lower incomes, lower educational levels, higher rates of infant mortality and are more likely to live in decaying towns.

However, arguments develop about what should be done to rectify this position. One school of economists favours more emphasis on market forces, believing these will encourage labour mobility and also persuade firms to move into depressed regions in order to benefit from lower wage rates. This group favours policies which will weaken trade unions and encourage local wage negotiations. They also advocate the removal of many planning restrictions and the removal of government controls on housing.

Their opponents believe market forces would exacerbate the problem; that firms which were mobile would tend to locate in the richer areas of the country. Hence the government needs to intervene in order to give firms incentives to locate in the depressed areas. There is no universal agreement about the precise nature of such incentives, but the consensus would favour more generous grants, government spending on infrastructure in poor regions and greater concentration of the government's own expenditure in depressed areas.

Figure 8.6: *'Objective 2' regions of the UK*

Source: Adapted from DTI.

Data questions

Some indicators of economic and social disadvantage in Great Britain

(All figures are GB=100)

Region	Disposable income per head	Male earnings	Male mortality rate	Dwellings owner occupied
North	88	90	111	88
Yorks/Humberside	95	89	104	99
East Midlands	97	91	97	106
East Anglia	101	94	88	104
South East	114	116	90	103
South West	101	93	90	110
West Midlands	93	90	102	101
North West	91	94	110	101
Wales	87	86	104	107
Scotland	94	94	115	69

Source: Adapted from *Regional Trends,* HMSO, 1992.

Question 1

1. Draw a chart to illustrate these figures. (Alternatively, calculate correlations between the various statistics). To what extent do your results illustrate the continuing existence of regional disparities?
2. What action, if any, do you think that the government should take to reduce differences between regions?

UK regional policy

Overall, the 1980s have seen important changes to UK regional policy, and three main themes can be identified. Firstly, the regional problem has come to be seen as a problem of the region rather than a national problem, and is to be solved by indigenous development rather than the diversion of activity from elsewhere. Market forces may cause relocations to the assisted areas, but these would be fortuitous rather than planned. Second, there has been a shift away from the direct subsidisation of employment towards employment creation through improved competitiveness. Third, the design of policy has become increasingly dictated by employment cost-effectiveness and there has been a move towards the discretionary assistance of small firms. These changes have led to a reduction in regional policy spending over this decade of approximately one half in real terms.

Source: Colin Wren, *Regional Policy in the 1980s,* National Westminster Bank Quarterly Review, November 1990.

Question 2

1. What is 'the regional problem'?
2. How might market forces cause relocations of activity?
3. Comment on the effect of a reduction in regional spending on:
   (i) taxpayers
   (ii) people living in depressed areas.

9 The Theory of Distribution

Why does Paul McCartney earn more than the Prime Minister? Why do some people who work hard earn very little money? How do firms decide how many workers to employ? Questions such as these are the province of distribution theory, which analyses how the factors of production (land, labour, capital and entrepreneurship) are rewarded. This chapter will focus on the labour market, though the method of analysis is applicable to the other factors.

Two questions dominate the chapter. The first is the debate concerning what determines the rewards received by the factors of production. One group emphasises demand and supply; another suggests that the labour market may often not reach equilibrium. The other question discussed in this chapter concerns the extent to which government intervention in the labour market is necessary.

- One approach to such questions is to say that these markets are like any other market and that the forces of demand and supply should determine issues such as the number of people to be employed and how much they should earn. Just as these forces allocate resources efficiently in markets for goods and services, so it is argued that demand and supply will lead to an efficient allocation of resources in factor markets.
- On the other hand, some economists believe that factor markets are different to other markets. Take labour as an example. People are less mobile than goods such as potatoes or pins, and therefore what might be a satisfactory system for allocating other resources will not be so for labour. Moreover, people are not inanimate objects and so the assumptions made about goods cannot be made about labour. Consequently problems such as poverty would result if the market was left to its own devices.

How are the rewards to the factors of production determined?

One approach to the economic analysis of factors of production is to analyse these markets as we would any other. Supply siders would tend to take this approach. Their emphasis focuses on the way that the forces of demand and supply determine the quantity of a factor which is employed, and the rewards that factor will receive. Other economists accept that demand and supply analysis can explain a great deal, but they emphasise the limitations of markets; for example, some economists would argue that labour markets may never reach equilibrium because labour is immobile and slow to respond to change.

The supply of labour

Not everyone participates in the labour market. In 1992, 27,923,000 people in the UK were classed as economically active, mostly as employees. This figure also includes the unemployed. However, there were also 16,156,000 people aged 16 or over who were classed as economically inactive. Those who are inactive include the young, the old and women with young children – which explains the much lower participation rates for women shown in Figure 9.1.

There are other influences on the participation rate. As with the market for goods, the prime determinant of supply is the price which will be received for the product. A rise in price will usually lead to an extension in supply, i.e. a move up the supply curve, and a fall in price will lead to a reduction in the quantity supplied. In the labour market, the 'price' is the amount which will be earned in wages, and it seems reasonable to assume that an increase in this price will encourage people to supply more labour. To take an absurd example, at a wage of £10 a week not many people would wish to work; at £10,000 a week there would be no lack of applicants.

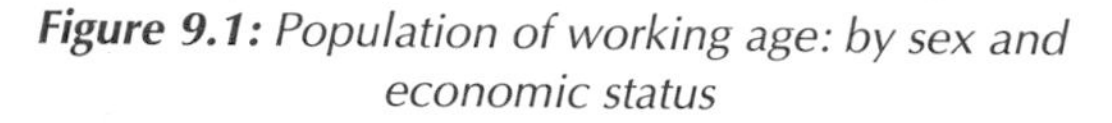

Figure 9.1: *Population of working age: by sex and economic status*

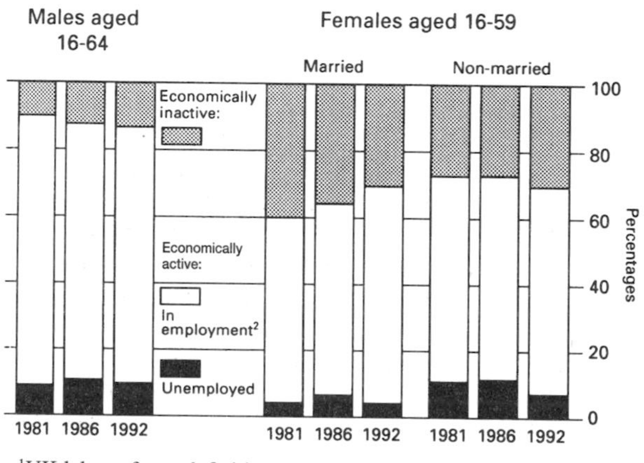

[1]UK labour force definitions for 1981, ILO/OECD definitions for 1986 and 1992.
[2]Includes those on government schemes for 1986 and 1992. In 1992. Unpaid family workers are also included.

Source: Adapted from *Social Trends*, HMSO, 1993.

However, the labour market is rather different from other markets because people can analyse their position, whilst goods such as carrots or lipsticks cannot. Even at a high wage some people may be reluctant to take a particular job because they do not like it. Some nurses would not like to work in an abortion clinic whatever the pay, and many of us would be reluctant to work as a steeplejack or boxer. Hence high rates of pay may not necessarily be associated with a high supply of labour.

In some cases rises in pay may actually lead to a fall in the supply of labour. A rational person will want to work so long as the marginal utility produced by an extra hour's work exceeds the utility obtained from an hour's leisure. A higher real wage increases the quantity of goods which can be bought for an extra hour's work and therefore induces the individual to work longer. On the other hand, a higher real wage would permit people to maintain their income and at the same time enjoy more leisure. Hence when pay increases, some people would choose not to work longer hours and indeed may choose to work less whilst maintaining their level of income. This means that the supply curve of labour may slope backwards, as shown in Figure 9.2. In this Figure an increase in wages causes the quantity of labour supplied to increase until the wage reaches W_2. Then as the wage rises further the quantity of labour supplied will fall, and at wage W_3 the quantity of labour will only be q_3.

Figure 9.2: *A backward sloping supply curve for labour*

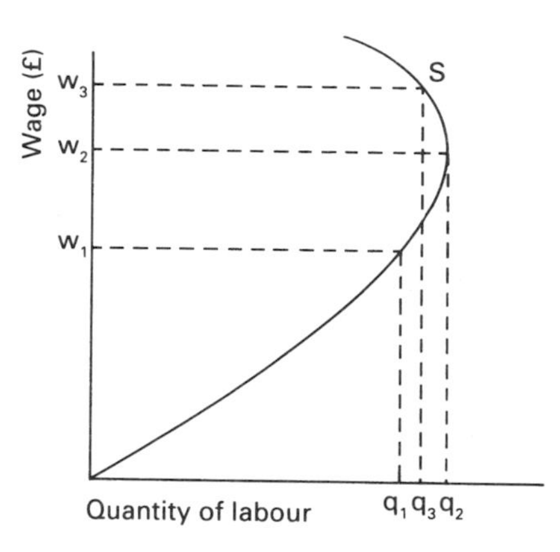

The demand for labour

A firm's demand for labour is a **derived** demand. Firms employ workers not for the pleasure of employing them, but because they want people to produce goods and services. If demand for a product rises, then demand for the labour making the product will also tend to rise. However, this does not explain what factors determine the demand for labour in the first place.

Just as the rational worker considers the wage that is offered and then decides whether to work, so the rational employer considers whether an additional worker will bring in more money than the increased cost in wages. The argument is shown in Table 9.1. As this shows, the eleventh worker increased output by nine items (to use the jargon, the **marginal physical productivity** of the eleventh worker is nine). If these items sell for £10 each, then the firm's income will rise by £90 as a result of employing this person. (To use the jargon again, the **marginal revenue product** of this worker is £90).

Since the wage of this worker is £60, it will pay the firm to employ this eleventh worker (for simplicity we are ignoring other costs, such as raw materials). However, as the number of workers rises the marginal revenue product falls (because diminishing returns occur, as discussed in Chapter 5). If the thirteenth worker was employed revenue would rise by only £40 while the cost in wages would be £60. It would be unprofitable to employ this worker.

Table 9.1: *Marginal revenue product and wage rate*

Number of workers	Total output per week	Marginal physical product	Marginal revenue product (£10 per item)	Wage rate per week (£)
10	100	–	–	–
11	109	9	90	60
12	116	7	70	60
13	120	4	40	60

The approach illustrated in this example is called the marginal productivity theory and represents a neo-classical approach to the labour market. It suggests that a firm seeking to maximise profits will employ extra units of a factor of production, such as labour, until the cost of employing that factor equals the extra income it generates. The theory thus predicts that, other things remaining unchanged, a rise in wages will lead to a fall in the number of workers employed whilst a rise in labour productivity will have the opposite effect and lead to firms taking on extra workers.

Criticisms of this approach

Critics argue that the labour market frequently fails to clear. This is because the number of workers, the hours they work and the wages they receive are often determined more by negotiation and by custom and practice than by the results of marginal analysis. Hence changes in wages and employment levels are unlikely to bring the market into equilibrium. If this is so, then the neo-classical theory of wage determination is unrealistic.

Even if the overall approach is accepted, there are complications in practice. Firms may not try to **maximise** profits and instead may be satisfied with **reasonable** profits.

If this is the case, then firms may not cut the number of workers as wages rise. This will be the result if the firm takes a paternalist attitude to its workers and is reluctant to make them redundant. Above all, if the firm is not operating in a competitive market for its goods, it may respond to a rise in wage costs by exploiting its monopolistic position and putting up the price of its products.

The neo-classical theory predicts that people with scarce skills which are needed to produce desirable products will earn more than those without such skills. Figure 9.3 gives some figures for incomes in Britain. Non-manual workers tend to earn more than manual workers and one explanation for this is that they have more educational qualifications and are more productive than manual workers. However, an alternative explanation also fits this data – that non-manual workers earn more money because they are more likely to be promoted even though they are no more productive.

Similarly, one explanation of men earning more than women is that men are more productive – they are more mobile, more likely to go on training courses and to work overtime than women and hence produce more goods than their female colleagues. This would cause men to have a higher marginal revenue product than women and so earn more. An alternative explanation is that women earn less because of discrimination at work which limits their choice of jobs and chances of promotion.

Figure 9.3: *Earnings in Great Britain (£ per week)*

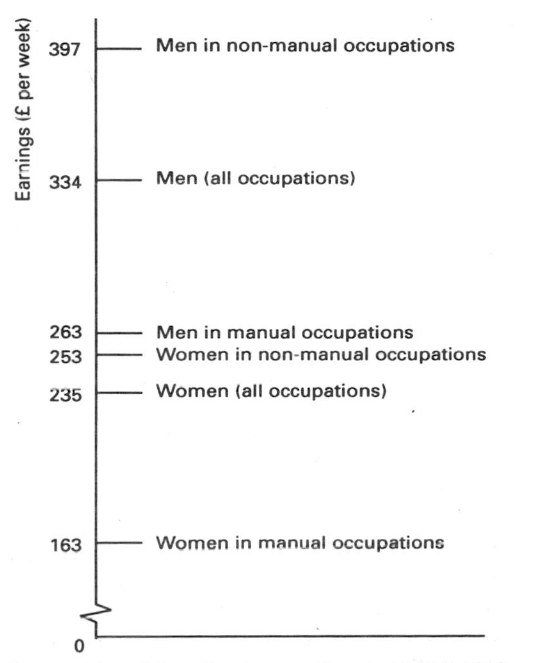

Source: Adapted from *Employment Gazette*, HMSO, 1993.

Economic rent

The concept of economic rent is an important part of the neo-classical theory of distribution. The analysis begins by dividing the total earnings of a factor of production, such as labour, into two. One part, called **transfer earnings**, is the amount that a factor must earn in order to stop it transferring to another use. Transfer earnings are the opportunity cost of employing a factor. The other part of a factor's earnings is called **economic rent** and is the excess which a factor earns over what is needed to keep that factor in a particular employment. Note that this is a different definition of rent to the one used by the 'man or woman in the street' who associates the word rent with payment for the use of a house or flat. Economic rent can be illustrated by taking the example of a professional footballer who may earn £200,000 a year, but who in any other occupation could only earn £10,000. This £10,000 is his transfer earnings and the other £190,000 he earns is economic rent:

Total earnings = Transfer earnings + Economic rent

Economic rent arises when the demand for a factor of production is greater than its supply, which is relatively scarce.

Figure 9.4 illustrates the concept. The curve 0S shows the supply of labour – how much each worker needs to be paid to stay in a particular employment. In this case equilibrium occurs when three workers are employed at a wage of w_3. However, the first worker would have been willing to work at a wage of only w_1. Hence this worker's transfer earnings are $0w_1$ and the rest of the wage, $w_3 - w_1$, is economic rent. At the other extreme the third worker does need to be paid a wage of w_3

Figure 9.4: *Economic rent*

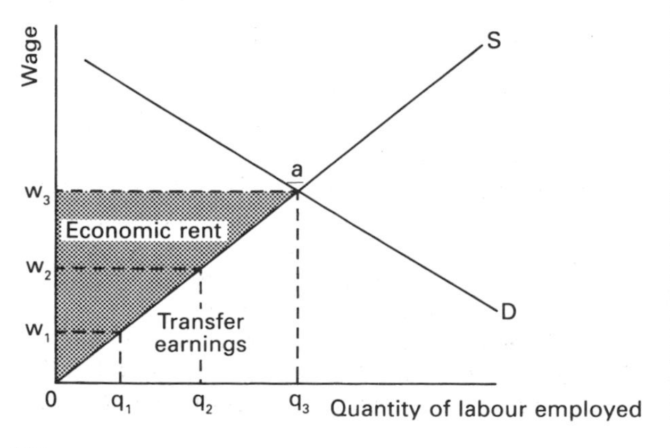

in order to work in this occupation. Hence all this worker's earnings are transfer earnings.

Looking at all three workers, total factor earnings are $0w_3$, aq_3. Transfer earnings are the area under the supply curve $0aq_3$. Economic rent is $0aw_3$, the area between the supply curve and the actual wage.

Economic rent and the price of land

The notion of economic rent was developed by the British economist David Ricardo, who used it to analyse a particular question. In the Napoleonic wars there were large rises in corn and land prices. Did the rise in land prices force up the price of corn, or did the high price of corn increase the demand for land and so push up land prices?

Figure 9.5: *Earnings of a factor in fixed supply*

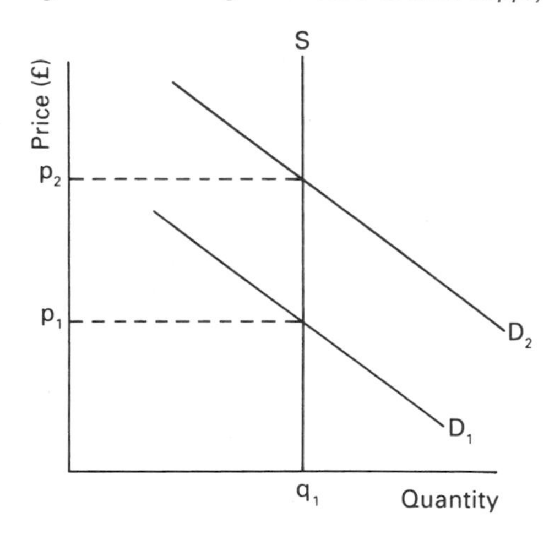

Ricardo assumed that land had only one use, to grow corn. This meant that its supply was fixed, as shown in Figure 9.5. Hence the price of land was totally determined by the demand for land. In other words, all the price of a factor of production in perfectly inelastic supply is economic rent – it has no transfer earnings. Thus it was the high price of corn which caused an increase in the demand for land and a rise in its price, rather than the price of land pushing up the price of corn. Note that this analysis depends on the assumption that land has only one use. In the real world a particular piece of land can be put to many different uses. This means its supply for any one use is elastic, so that it has transfer earnings.

In principle it would be a good idea to tax economic rent since this would not reduce the supply of the factor. In practice, however, this has proved impossible because it is too complicated to differentiate economic rent from transfer earnings. Thus it would not be possible to find out how much every professional footballer could earn in another occupation and then impose a tax on any earnings above this.

Key ideas

1. Distribution theory analyses how much of a factor of production will be employed and the rewards it will receive.
2. The supply of labour will depend on factors such as the level of wages, but increases in wages will not always cause an increase in the supply of labour.
3. Marginal productivity theory suggests that more of a factor of production will be employed until its marginal revenue product equals its price.
4. Marginal productivity theory is criticised on a number of grounds. Markets may not clear, for example, if firms are paternalistic and do not reduce the quality of labour employed when wages rise.
5. Economic rent is the excess which a factor earns, which is more than is needed to keep the factor in a particular employment.

The market forces approach

In *1980s Unemployment and the Unions* (1984), the Nobel Prize winner F.A. Hayek claims:

'Nobody is morally entitled to claim a share in the wealth which such a society produces unless he is prepared to obey the discipline of other people's wants or other countries' production methods that are ultimately the sources of our wealth... the size of the national product will depend not on individuals "working hard" but on making the "right" (desired) things in the "right" (most economic) manner and at the "right" time (required by the consumer in the market).'

Hayek goes on to argue that it is only through the prices that people find in the market that they can learn what to do and how to do it. High standards of living depend on the division of labour, and the specialisation which this implies is only made possible by the flow of information provided by the price system.

Another key feature of the price system is that it provides incentives to people to become more productive, for example, by changing jobs or by undertaking training. In this way the economy benefits from higher levels of production. For this group of economists, profit – the difference between costs and returns – is the true measure of the social usefulness of people's efforts, and production at a loss is an offence against the best use of resources. The market thus induces firms to obtain, from a given input of resources, as large a profit as possible.

This efficient use of resources depends on competition, and anything which restricts competition is to be deplored. Some of these restrictions were discussed in the last chapter. If people cannot move to alternative employment because housing is short, then the labour market will not be able to operate efficiently. Similarly, if the government, the largest employer in the country, does not respond to the signals given by the price system, then the whole labour market will be affected. For example, the approach suggests that in areas where the price of labour is low, the government should pay lower wages than it does where labour is in short supply. If it does not do this, the labour market will be distorted.

Trade unions

However, for these supply side economists, the prime reason why labour markets do not work efficiently is because of the actions of trade unions. They see trade unions as a monopolistic element in the market which distorts the efficient allocation of resources. They do this by restricting the supply of labour, as shown in Figure 9.6. In a market without trade unions equilibrium would be at A, where the demand for labour equals the supply. The wage rate would be w_1 with q_1 units of labour employed. If a trade union could restrict the supply of labour (for instance by insisting on a 'closed shop' where everyone has to join a union) then the new equilibrium would be at B; the union has succeeded in pushing up wages, but at the cost of reducing employment from q_1 to q_2.

This line of argument is criticised by supporters of unions, who argue that few unions have the strength to move the equilibrium wage far from the level that would be obtained by market forces, and that in most cases the demand for labour is inelastic; in other words the demand curve in Figure 9.6 should be drawn much more vertically because the firm's demand for labour is not much affected by changes in wage rates. If a union negotiates a 5 per cent increase in wages, few firms are going to reduce their labour force significantly. If this is so, then the movement from q_1 to q_2 would be much smaller than is shown in the Figure. Moreover, critics of the supply side approach argue that the market for the products made by most firms is not perfectly competitive. This means that it is possible to put up prices for the firm's products and so increase the demand for labour to make the product. In the diagram this is shown by the second

Figure 9.6

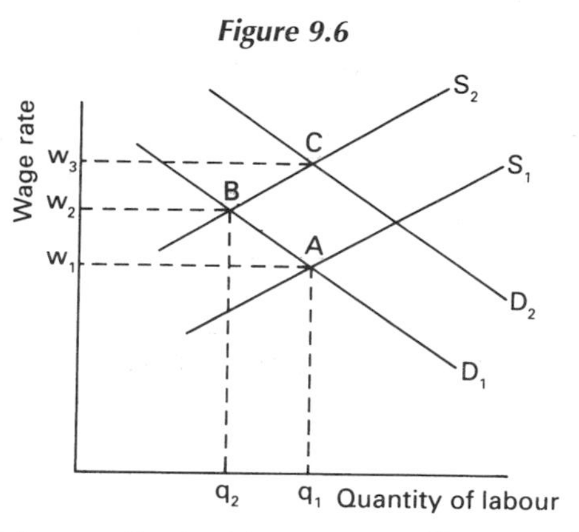

demand curve D_2. In this case, equilibrium will be at C – the actions of the unions have had little effect on the quantity of labour employed, but have succeeded in obtaining higher wages for their members.

Empirical evidence

There has been a good deal of empirical research into the activities of unions. Some of this is concerned with their effect on employment and is presented in Chapter 17. As that chapter shows, there is considerable disagreement amongst those who have undertaken research; some economists, such as Patrick Minford, Professor of Economics at Liverpool University, believe that unions are a prime cause of unemployment, whilst others believe their effect on employment is minimal.

There is also disagreement about their effect on wages. This is not surprising, because the research usually involves comparing what has happened in unionised industries with what would have happened if there had been no unions – something that is very difficult to do. Most research suggests that unions do succeed in obtaining higher wages for their members, but that their success varies over time and between occupations. Stewart (1991), for example, finds that the union mark up averages 9 per cent but that their success varied from 18 per cent in shipbuilding to only 2 per cent in electrical engineering. Other researchers, such as Blackaby (1991), estimate that unions have a bigger effect, increasing the wages of their members by 22 per cent compared to those of non-union workers. One reason for union success may be that they have reduced the supply of labour, but an alternative explanation is that unions co-operate with management to increase productivity so both employers and workers benefit.

Key ideas – summary of the market forces approach

1. Whilst the labour market has certain characteristics which make it unique, the most efficient way of allocating resources in this market, as in others, is through the forces of demand and supply. Anything which distorts market forces reduces efficiency.
2. When the market works well, those with scarce, desirable skills will earn high wages, those without will have an incentive to re-train. Similarly, firms will move to locations where labour is relatively cheap.
3. The government distorts the labour market by paying similar salaries to people across the country irrespective of the scarcity of labour.
4. The trade unions distort the labour market by forcing up wages and causing rigidities in the market.

Supply side policies

Supply side policies are designed to make the labour market work more effectively. Since the government is the largest employer it can do most to improve the position. In the first place, some of its activities can be privatised so that firms can compete to supply goods and services, such as cleaning services to schools and hospitals. Where services cannot be privatised, the government should take greater account of the labour market. It should consider moving some of its activities to areas where labour is cheap and it should pay the 'going rate' for labour. This means that in areas of high unemployment wages should be lower than they are elsewhere. This implies an end to national wage bargaining.

Similarly, the position of trade unions should be

weakened. There are various suggestions for achieving this, but they tend to concentrate on weakening the legal status of unions, for example, by making them liable for any losses suffered by firms where unions have called strikes. There are also suggestions for making it more difficult to call strikes or to instigate other industrial action.

The interventionist approach

Markets may sometimes be marvellous, but they are not without fault. This is the central argument of those who dispute the supply side approach. In particular they argue that without government intervention there will be undesirable inequalities. These are manifested in several ways, but particularly in the form of low pay, inequality for women and discrimination against ethnic minorities.

Low pay

The arguments against trade union intervention in the labour market have been given in the section above, but there are strong arguments in their favour. In the markets for goods and services both buyers and sellers usually have more or less equal power. If a customer does not like a particular product, an alternative can be bought. Similarly, a producer will usually find it easy to find a substitute customer. The position in the labour market is very different. In the first place, a person with particular skills may find it difficult to find an alternative purchaser for specialised skills. A firefighter will not easily find employment outside the fire service and most social workers are forced to find employment within local government. Hence employers are in a much stronger position than workers, because workers often find it difficult to sell their specialist skills to alternative employers.

Moreover, in any dispute the employer can usually call upon the services of many lawyers and has the financial resources to withstand a dispute much better than could an individual worker. Trade unions can help to redress this balance. If the workers are united they can put pressure on the employer to provide higher wages, better working conditions (such as longer holidays and shorter hours) and greater safety at work than would be offered without union power. Moreover, unions help to mitigate the extent of low pay. If market forces are allowed to operate without any government intervention, then people with certain characteristics will tend to earn much less than others.

Factors associated with low pay are:

- Low levels of education and training. For various reasons some children do badly at school. Low levels of intelligence, poor teaching, parents having low educational qualifications, low social class, poor health – all these factors are associated with low educational achievement. In turn there is a close link between the level of education and the subsequent level of earnings. Those people with high educational qualifications tend to earn more than those with poor qualifications. The position is exacerbated because, once at work, those people with a good education tend to be selected for further training and this leads on to higher incomes. Of course, there are many exceptions to this generalisation. Teachers are an example of a group with high qualifications but relatively low levels of pay, and there are many examples pop singers and sportsmen are notable – who have high incomes despite low qualifications.
- Particular occupations or industries. Some jobs and some industries are associated with low pay. Cleaners, shop assistants and hairdressers are examples. Such workers are often employed by small employers and are not in trade unions. Left to the mercy of market forces, it is argued that their position will deteriorate.

Women workers

As Figure 9.7 shows, women earn less than men. One reason for this is that women are concentrated in the 'caring occupations', such as nursing, which are traditionally low paid. However, even within the same occupation women earn less on average than men. Teaching is an example. Occasionally, lower pay for women may be due to prejudice; but probably other reasons are more important. Until recently women on average have had lower educational qualifications than men. Now the achievements of both sexes are about equal at GCE A level, and girls do better than boys at GCSE.

It remains true that women undergo less training than men once they are employed and are less likely to be promoted. This reflects a deep-seated view in society about the role of women; that it is the role of women to look after the children. Hence once children are born it will usually be the job of women to look after them and this career break reduces the likelihood of promotion. Similarly, when children are ill it is usually the women who have to stay off work to care for them. This makes employers more reluctant to employ women in responsible posts. Moreover, women frequently

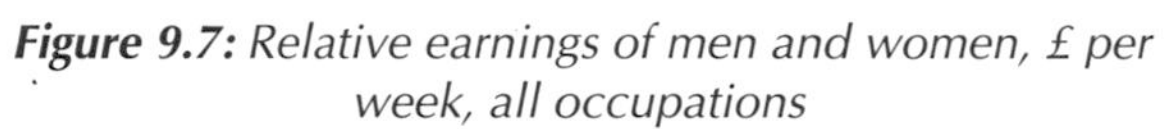

Figure 9.7: *Relative earnings of men and women, £ per week, all occupations*

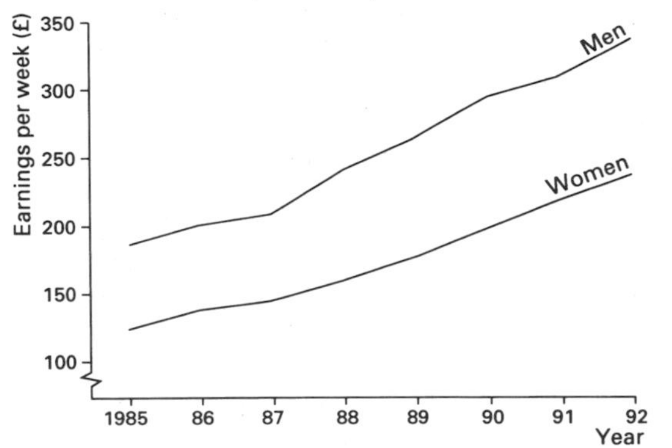

follow their husband's careers. If the man is offered promotion in another area, his wife may feel obliged to give up her job and follow. All this means that, left to market forces, employers will prefer to take on men rather than women and hence men will earn more than women. Consequently interventionists argue that this is unfair and that it devalues the contribution which women could make to the economy. Hence they advocate state intervention in order to remedy the position.

Ethnic status

People from ethnic minorities tend to earn less than those from the majority culture. In part this is because they may have many of the characteristics discussed above which are linked to low pay. Thus, while there are many exceptions, people from ethnic minorities in the UK tend to have lower levels of education, receive less training and, when in work, to be employed in jobs associated with low pay. Moreover, as Figure 9.8 shows, they are more likely to be unemployed. The reasons for this are too complex to be explored here, but there is no doubt that prejudice also plays a part. Sometimes this is overt – employers refuse to consider black applicants or are reluctant to promote them. More often the discrimination is hidden – employers fail to select suitable black applicants because subconsciously they think they are inferior, or because they think white workers will be reluctant to work for a black boss. Hence interventionists argue that, without government intervention, this discrimination will continue.

Figure 9.8: *Unemployment rates[1]: by ethnic origin, Spring 1992*

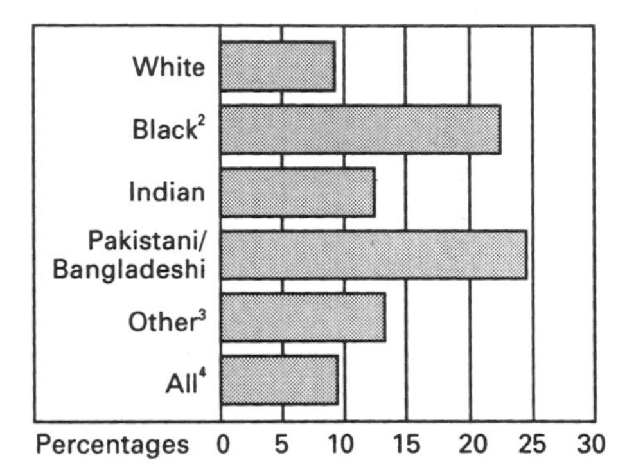

1. Unemployed based on the ILO definition as a percentage of all economically active.
2. Includes Caribbean, Africa and other black people of non-mixed origin.
3. Includes Chinese, other ethnic minority groups of non-mixed origin and people of mixed origin.
4. Includes ethnic group not stated.

Source: Adapted from *Labour Force Survey*, Employment Department, 1993.

Key ideas – summary of the interventionist approach

1. Unrestricted market forces lead to an unsatisfactory allocation of resources in the labour market.
2. Employers are much more powerful than individual workers; left to themselves workers would be exploited. Trade unions and government action can protect workers' rights.
3. Those who do badly in such a system include women, ethnic minorities and those with low educational qualifications or in particular occupations.
4. The state needs to intervene in order to achieve a more equitable distribution of income and also to improve the allocation of resources – if women and black people are not allowed to make a full contribution to the economy, then the country will be poorer.

Interventionist policies

Where specific groups can be identified which suffer from discrimination, this approach suggests that statutory bodies, such as the Equal Opportunities Commission, should be set up to help remedy the position. These can help employers establish procedures which reduce the likelihood of indirect discrimination and can take legal action when the laws against discrimination are broken, so helping workers who feel that they are not receiving their due. For example, the law says that women should receive equal pay when they undertake work of equal value to that of men, but this can be difficult to prove. The Commission can offer help to people in this position. In the case of disabled people, employers are supposed to employ a quota, but this requirement is often ignored. It is therefore suggested that the law should be tightened.

An important proposal made by this group of economists is that a law should be passed which lays down a legal minimum rate of pay. This was discussed in Chapter 3. Such a law would say that all adults working above a certain number of hours a week would be legally entitled to receive a wage of, say, £150 a week. Its proponents say that this is the only way in which the low paid can be guaranteed a reasonable income. Its opponents argue that this would cause employers to employ fewer workers, causing a rise in unemployment. This is accepted by many supporters of the proposal, but they suggest that the rise would be very small and that, in any case, the level of employment can be increased by government intervention to stimulate the economy.

Wages Councils

Wages Councils were independent statutory organisations that set minimum rates of pay for 2.5 million workers in four main sectors of the economy – hotels and catering, the retail trade, clothing and hairdressing. The minimum rates of pay in 1992 ranged between £2.59 and £3.10 per hour. Once set, these rates were legally enforceable. Wages Councils therefore represented a strong interventionist policy and were opposed by those favouring market forces. Consequently, under the 1993 Trade Union Reform and Employment Rights Act, these Councils were abolished.

Gillian Shepard, the Secretary of State for Employment said, 'The Wages Councils were established when there were no employment rights and little social security provision. They have no role to play in the Nineties.' Moreover, 'Where Wages Councils force companies to pay more than they can afford, they destroy jobs.' This view was rejected by Chris Pond of the Low Pay Unit: 'The gap between those on the national median wage and those on the bottom of the scale is greater now than it was when the Councils were first introduced. In the EC, only the UK and Ireland failed to provide minimum wage legislation in some form'. Interventionists also argue that low wages encourage firms to be inefficient because employers have no incentive to invest in training or in modern plant or equipment. Without a minimum wage the good employer will be undercut by the bad.

So, what does the evidence suggest? Wages Councils were researched by a group of economists (Dickens et al 1993). They investigated three criticisms of the Councils:

- That minimum wages do little to alleviate poverty since most workers covered by these Councils do not live in poor households. The researchers discovered that 50 per cent of families with at least one earner being paid Wages Council rates come from the poorest 20 per cent of families.
- That minimum wages legislation reduces employment since it prices workers out of jobs. Here the researchers found that the empirical evidence was mixed; some previous investigations finding that jobs had been lost, whilst others found that minimum wages has not reduced jobs. They point out that the 1970 Equal Pay Act raised women's wages by 10 per cent but there is little evidence that this reduced jobs for women. They therefore conclude that 'the belief that abolition (of Wages Councils) will increase unemployment is based more on ideology than on hard evidence'.
- That the problem of poverty which Wages Councils were set up to alleviate are not relevant today. The researchers conclude that the widening earnings distribution in the UK means that low pay is an increasingly important determinant of poverty.

Consequently they concluded that there is an increasing need for minimum wage legislation in the UK.

Conclusion

Most economists would probably agree that the forces of demand and supply should play an important part in the labour market. When the market works well it provides incentives for individuals and firms to change their behaviour – for instance, to learn new or scarce skills – in ways which will improve the allocation of resources. However, there is considerable disagreement about the extent to which the market has limitations and hence about the extent to which government intervention is necessary to remedy any defects. Supply siders believe very little intervention is needed and that the government should be primarily concerned with improving the working of the market, for example, by paying different wage rates in different regions of the country and restricting the powers of trade unions. This line of argument is strongly opposed by economists who believe that unrestricted markets will lead to an unsatisfactory position which will penalise many of the weaker elements in society, and that the government should therefore intervene in order to protect groups against discrimination and to help the low paid.

Data questions

Household income in the United Kingdom (%)

Source of income	1971	1981	1991
Wages and salaries	68	63	58
Self employment	9	8	10
Rent, dividends, interest	6	7	9
Private pensions	5	6	9
Social security	10	13	12
Other	2	2	2
Direct taxes	18	19	19
Real disposal income per head (1985=100)	73	89	126

Source: Adapted from *Social Trends*, HMSO, 1993.

Question 1

1. Describe the trends in this Table.
2. What reasons do you think might explain these changes?
3. To what extent might a free market approach see these changes as favourable?

Unions and industrial productivity

The 1992 Trade Union and Employment Rights legislation contained new provisions to further limit the scope for unions to engage in lawful strike action. In the past unions arc said to have inhibited cost cutting and damaged the competitive performance of domestic industry. Is this claim supported by empirical evidence?

Studies in the early 1980s suggested that there was a spurt in labour productivity in manufacturing in the early 1980s resulting from Thatcher's industrial relations reform. However, the most recent research by Nickell, Wadhwani and Wall contradicts this research. Using data from the accounts of 127 manufacturing companies between 1972 and 1986 they found that the unions did not discourage investment or inhibit productivity growth; indeed, unionised firms experienced faster productivity growth than their non-union counterparts.

Yet unions may have failed in another way. They have been unable to prevent low wage, labour intensive routes to profitability and have failed to promote the alternative – a high wage, high productivity virtuous circle. Consequently, the gap between productivity levels in Britain and other European economies is still as high as 30 per cent.

Source: Adapted from Nolan P., *Unions and industrial productivity*, University of Leeds Centre for Industrial Policy and Performance Bulletin No.1, 1993.

Question 2

1. Explain the phrases 'labour productivity' and 'low wage, labour intensive routes to profitability'.
2. Why might it be argued (i) that unions inhibit productivity growth, (ii) that unions encourage it?
3. Why might it be difficult to come to a definite conclusion about the effects of unions?

10 Cost-Benefit Analysis

Firms and governments need to have some way of deciding whether a particular investment would be a good idea. Would it pay a firm to build a particular factory or should the resources be used in another way? Should the government build a new road? Cost-benefit analysis is a sophisticated way of answering such questions. In essence it involves adding together all the costs and then comparing these with all the benefits which would follow if an investment went ahead. If the expected benefits are greater than the costs, the investment should proceed. The debate centres around the following arguments.

- Supporters of the technique argue that it provides the best way of appraising potential investments and should be used extensively in both private and public sectors.
- Critics suggest that it gives a spurious accuracy. They argue that it ignores political and social factors, which are particularly important in the public sector and which are the focus of this chapter.

How accurate is the technique of cost-benefit analysis?

Three decades ago Prest and Turvey (1965) defined cost-benefit analysis as:

'a practical way of assessing the desirability of projects where it is important to take a long view (in the sense of looking at repercussions in the further, as well as the nearer, future) and a wide view (in the sense of allowing for side effects of many kinds on many persons, industries, regions etc.), i.e. it implies the enumeration and evaluation of all the relevant costs and benefits'.

Hence the basic idea is simple. A firm wondering whether or not to invest in a new factory will add up all the costs – land, building, machinery and so on – and then try to estimate all the benefits, chiefly the extra output multiplied by the expected price of the product. If the benefits exceed the costs, then the project should go ahead. Similarly, a government deciding whether or not to build a new road or an airport will also enumerate (place a money value on) all the costs and benefits which would accrue to society if the project proceeded.

However, there are a number of complications and these will be considered in turn.

Discounting the future

'A bird in the hand is worth two in the bush.' Put another way, a certain sum of money now is worth more than the same sum in the future.

There are several reasons for this, one being inflation. Money loses its value over time, so waiting means that the recipient will receive less in real terms if forced to accept money at a later date. Even with zero inflation, money in the future is worth less because money received now can provide interest.

Secondly, having the money now gives a choice – the recipient can spend the money immediately or wait. If the money is received now, it can be invested and interest received. Finally, there is a risk involved in waiting. The giver or the recipient may die, or the giver may go bankrupt and be unable to pay any money owed.

For all these reasons, people prefer money now to money in the future and so **discount** future earnings. The amount of the discount depends on the circumstances. If a ninety-year-old offers to pay a debt in a year's time, the wise person asks for earlier payment! If the government issues a National Savings Certificate, the owner is sure of payment in the future, but will require some interest to compensate for losing the use of the money in the meantime.

All this is relevant to investment appraisal because investments involve costs in the near future, whilst the benefits are often spread over a much longer period of time. Since the investor has to wait for the benefits, these have to be discounted. This is shown in Table 10.1, which assumes that prices remain constant.

Table 10.1: *Net present value at discount rate of 10%*

Year	Actual cost	Net present value of costs	Actual benefits	Net present value of benefits
0	500	500	0	0
1			100	90
2			100	81
3			100	72.9
4			100	65.6
5			100	59.1
6			100	53.1
7			100	47.8
8			100	43.0
9			100	38.7
10			100	34.9
Total	500	500	1000	586.1

Net present value

Table 10.1 shows a hypothetical example of a cost-benefit analysis using a technique called **net present value**. In this example a person makes an investment of £500 in year 0. The returns start one year later and amount to £100 a year for ten years. These are discounted at a rate of 10 per cent a year; the £100 which is due to be received after one year is discounted so that it is only worth £90 today. Returns which are not expected for two years have to be discounted twice, so that they are worth only £81. As all the costs in this example are incurred during the present year they do not need to be discounted.

In the example, the net present value of the costs is £500 and the net present value of the benefits is £586. Since the benefits exceed the costs, the project should succeed.

Internal rate of return

A variation of this technique involves calculating the internal rate of return. In the example given in Table 10.1 the discount rate was 10 per cent. If the discount rate was higher, say 15 per cent, then the net present value of the benefits would have been lower since £100 discounted at 15 per cent would give rise to a lower stream of net present values – £85, £72, £61 etc. The total net present value would be only £455, which is less than the value of the costs and therefore the project should not proceed.

At a discount rate of 10 per cent the benefits exceed the costs and at a rate of 15 per cent the costs exceed the benefits. It therefore follows that at some rate between 10 per cent and 15 per cent the benefits will equal the costs. This rate (just under 13 per cent in this example) is called the **internal rate of return**. The project should proceed if this internal rate of return exceeds the desired discount rate.

These two techniques – comparing net present value of costs with net present value of benefits and calculating the internal rate of return – will give the same results in almost all cases. Purists seem to prefer the net present value method, but to most people it is more meaningful to talk about an internal rate of return of 13 per cent than to imagine a figure for net present value.

What rate of discount?

A crucial element in cost-benefit analysis is the choice of discount rate. High discount rates will greatly reduce the number of projects given approval. Private firms will vary their chosen discount rate according to the rate of interest and the amount of risk involved in the project. Risky projects financed by money borrowed at high interest rates will have their expected returns discounted at a high rate, while safe ones undertaken when interest rates are low will be discounted at lower rates.

The choice of discount rate for public sector projects is controversial. Some writers believe that the correct rate for public sector projects is the rate of interest that the government has to pay when it borrows money. Others suggest that this is too low a rate because lending to the government is safe and that the public sector should evaluate its projects at the higher rate used by private sector firms. The argument is important because a higher rate of discount would reduce the number of public sector projects.

Correcting for externalities

In some cases, people can push part of the costs on to other people. If a firm dumps its rubbish into a river it will reduce its costs, but these will fall on to other people in the form of pollution. In this example the private costs to the individual are less than the social costs to the community as a whole. Pollution is one example of an **externality** or **spillover**. When external costs, such as pollution, are added to private costs we obtain social cost – the real cost to society as a whole. In some cases, externalities can be beneficial. It is argued that educating an individual not only benefits that person but also benefits others in various ways, such as improved behaviour from the person who has been educated. In this case, private benefits plus externalities gives us social benefit – the real benefit to society. 'Social' cost-benefit analysis means an analysis considered from the viewpoint of society as a whole, as opposed to a private analysis which considers only the costs and benefits accruing to some participant, such as a firm. Indeed, one difference between cost-benefit analysis undertaken by firms and by government is that private firms usually ignore all externalities and just consider their own private costs and benefits, whilst public sector investments should take account of externalities.

Whilst, in principle, social cost-benefit analysis should take into account all the costs and benefits of a decision, including the externalities, this is often difficult in practice, as is shown later in the chapter.

Key ideas

1. Cost-benefit analysis involves a comparison of all the costs and benefits of a proposed investment.
2. Costs and benefits arising in the future need to be discounted.
3. Cost-benefit analysis can be undertaken by calculating the net present value of costs and benefits or else by finding the internal rate of return.
4. Many external costs and benefits are difficult to translate into monetary values.

The case for cost-benefit analysis

Essentially the case for using cost-benefit analysis is that, although it has problems, it is better than any of the alternatives. Since governments have to use some criteria in order to decide whether to proceed with a project, it is better to use this technique rather than to leave it to personal prejudice on the part of civil servants or politicians or to even less satisfactory methods of evaluation, such as guesswork.

The great advantage of cost-benefit analysis is that it forces people to take account of all the costs, including those not easily translated into money terms. This forces decision makers to face up to the value judgements that arise in many proposals. For example, one argument in favour of building new roads is that it removes traffic from town centres. It is, however, impossible to put an agreed value on quietness. What is possible in cost-benefit analysis is to undertake **sensitivity analysis**. This can be done by first putting a low value on quietness, then running the calculation again with a high value. If this makes little difference to the rate of return, the value put on quietness does not matter. If there is a large difference in the two rates of return, the decision makers are forced to discuss and debate the value of quietness. The problem cannot be evaded. Instead people are forced to discuss the issue. They cannot ignore it, as would happen without such a rigorous investigation.

Many supporters of the technique would claim another advantage. They suggest that even when projects with high returns are passed over in favour of others with lower returns, the technique can still have been useful. This can happen when political considerations are important. For example, it may be better to locate a new project in Northern Ireland than in the South East of England because not only would it help to reduce unemployment in the province, but it would also strengthen the unity of a disaffected part of the UK. This may be the best decision even if the Northern Ireland project has a lower rate of return. Cost-benefit analysis would force decision makers to realise the extra costs they were incurring in order to obtain the political benefit.

Key ideas – summary of the case for cost-benefit analysis

1. It takes a structured approach to the evaluation of proposed developments.
2. It takes into account all the costs and benefits, including those cases where social costs and benefits differ from private ones.
3. Sensitivity analysis can show the importance or otherwise of value judgements.

Arguments against the use of cost-benefit analysis

A major criticism of the technique is that it is inaccurate and yet gives a spurious impression of accuracy. The computer takes in all of the figures and gives out a precise rate of return. Yet many of the figures which go into the computer are extremely imprecise, rendering the results almost worthless.

Moreover, it is so difficult to quantify many of the variables that the figures entered into the computer frequently represent the prejudices of the investigators rather than any objective reality. Hence the results obtained are those which the investigator wants; they merely confirm the original intention. A specific example will illustrate the point. Cost-benefit analysis is often used to investigate the desirability of governments investing in education, yet many of the benefits are not quantifiable. Education plays a part in the creation and maintenance of civilised society; this is a factor which cannot be represented in money terms and so is either ignored, or an entirely arbitrary figure is entered as a benefit. If the government wants the project to go ahead, a high figure can be entered for such a benefit. If the government is opposed to the project, such a benefit can be ignored or its value cut. Thus one benefit of building new roads is that they reduce accidents and deaths. Because these are difficult to measure, a government wishing to build more roads can give a high figure for the benefits arising from fewer accidents and deaths. A government opposing extensive road building would insert a low figure.

Key ideas – summary of the case against cost-benefit analysis

1. The results are inaccurate, yet give the impression of accuracy.
2. If you put garbage into a computer, garbage comes out. Many of the figures that go into cost-benefit calculations are garbage.
3. Many of the costs and benefits are impossible to quantify.
4. There is no agreed way to choose a discount rate, yet this can be the crucial factor in deciding whether an investment should proceed.

Cost-benefit analysis of building a new road

Before building a new road the government calculates the costs and benefits. Some of the costs are obvious and relatively easy to calculate. For example, the money to be paid to the contractor will be known when firms put in estimates for building the road. What is harder to calculate are the costs which fall on to others, for example, those who suffer from noise and dirt during construction. These are real costs, but they do not come in the form of bills and so their size is difficult to estimate.

The benefits are even more difficult to estimate. One benefit is the time saved by people using the new road. This is hard to calculate because it depends on accurate estimates of the amount of traffic which will use the road and then also on calculations of the value of the time saved. A further benefit accrues to people using other roads who will face less traffic in the future. This is an external effect and, again, its value is difficult to calculate.

Another externality is even more difficult to translate into money terms. New roads are safer than old ones, so one benefit of roadbuilding is that lives are saved and fewer people are injured. What value should we put on a life? One solution is to calculate the value of the output the individual would produce if he or she had lived. This is obviously unsatisfactory, but it is the procedure often adopted. Consequently, there are large differences in estimates from different people. In 1989 the Public Accounts Committee of the House of Commons calculated the true cost of a fatal accident at £500,000. This was far higher than the £238,000 which was used by the government in its investigations. If the higher figure was accepted, cost-benefit analysis would cause the government to invest far more in road building that is designed to reduce accidents.

Cost-benefit analysis of education

Investment in education involves both costs and benefits. If we take the example of a government considering whether or not to expand higher education, some costs will be direct (lecturers' salaries and other wage costs, spending on books and other materials, cost of premises etc.) and others will be indirect (the opportunity cost of the goods and services which would have been produced by students if they had not been studying).

The main economic benefit to society is that education makes people more productive. Cost-benefit analysis of education usually assumes that this extra productivity can be measured by the higher salaries received by educated people; that employers pay educated people more because they are more productive. Because these extra earnings arise in the future, they must be discounted. In addition, there are external benefits arising from education, such as a more civilised society.

However, many of these costs and benefits are difficult to measure. How do you measure the

Figure 10.1: *Should society invest in higher education?*

COSTS
(£ per student)

Direct, e.g. salaries	£7,000
Loss of production (measured by salary forgone)	£7,000
Total costs each year	£14,000
Total costs for 3 years	£42,000

BENEFITS
(£ per student)

Extra production (measured by higher salary forgone)	£3,000 rising to £10,000
Externalities	£x
Total benefits over perhaps 40 years	£250,000? but must be discounted

benefits of a more civilised society? Do educated people earn more because they are more productive, or because employers use education as a 'screening' device and tend to promote people with higher qualifications whether or not they produce more?

Table 10.2: *The percentage returns to education, various countries*

Country	Secondary education	Higher education
Kenya	19	9
India	14	11
Japan	9	7
USA	11	11
UK	9	7

Source: Adapted from Psacharapolous, G., 'Returns to Education', *Journal of Human Resources* Vol.20, 1985.

Table 10.2 summarises a large number of cost-benefit analyses of education. It shows that returns to education tend to be higher in less-developed countries, partly because in developed countries there are proportionately more graduates and this higher supply tends to bring down their wages. One limitation of these results is that they exclude the extra benefits, which are difficult to quantify. Despite this, they do tend to support government investment in education. Figure 10.1 shows the approach which is used to calculate the results obtained in Table 10.2. The numbers used in the Figure illustrate the position in the UK.

Cost-benefit analysis of road safety

How many millions should be spent on improving the safety of transport systems? Many might argue that life is priceless. But governments must – and do – put monetary values on life and limb. If governments were to try to eradicate all risks, transport would be prohibitively expensive and slow.

Most rich countries' transport departments have tried to estimate the price of a life. For example, in the USA the cost of a road accident death is $2,600,000; in Britain it is $1,100,000, in Holland $130,000 and in Portugal only $20,000. One method of measuring the value of life is the human capital approach. This prices the value of life as the lost earnings potential of a victim. For those whose output is not marketed, such as housewives, a guess has to be made. But this method has a problem; people are worth more than what they produce. Consequently, governments that use this approach may spend too little on safety.

The other approach values human life using estimates of people's willingness to pay (WTP) for improved safety. This can be done directly by asking people what they would be willing to pay to avoid danger or harm. A less direct alternative looks at prices where risk seems to play a part. Wages are an example: in theory, workers in dangerous jobs should be paid a premium to compensate them for the greater chance of death and injury.

The importance of such methods is that they have a major impact on investment decisions. Whether a road improvement goes ahead depends on some calculation on whether or not it is worthwhile. A low value placed on human life will mean that life saving schemes do not go ahead. Too high a price may mean that resources are wasted which could be better used elsewhere.

Conclusion

Cost-benefit analysis is a method of investigating proposed developments which takes into account all the costs and benefits. If the present value of the benefits exceeds the present value of the costs then the development should go ahead. Alternatively, if the internal rate of return method is used, developments should proceed if the internal rate of return exceeds the chosen discount rate. Supporters of the technique argue that it is a rational way to evaluate proposals. Critics say that it is inaccurate and reflects the value judgements of the researcher.

Data questions

Summary of Channel Tunnel costs and benefits

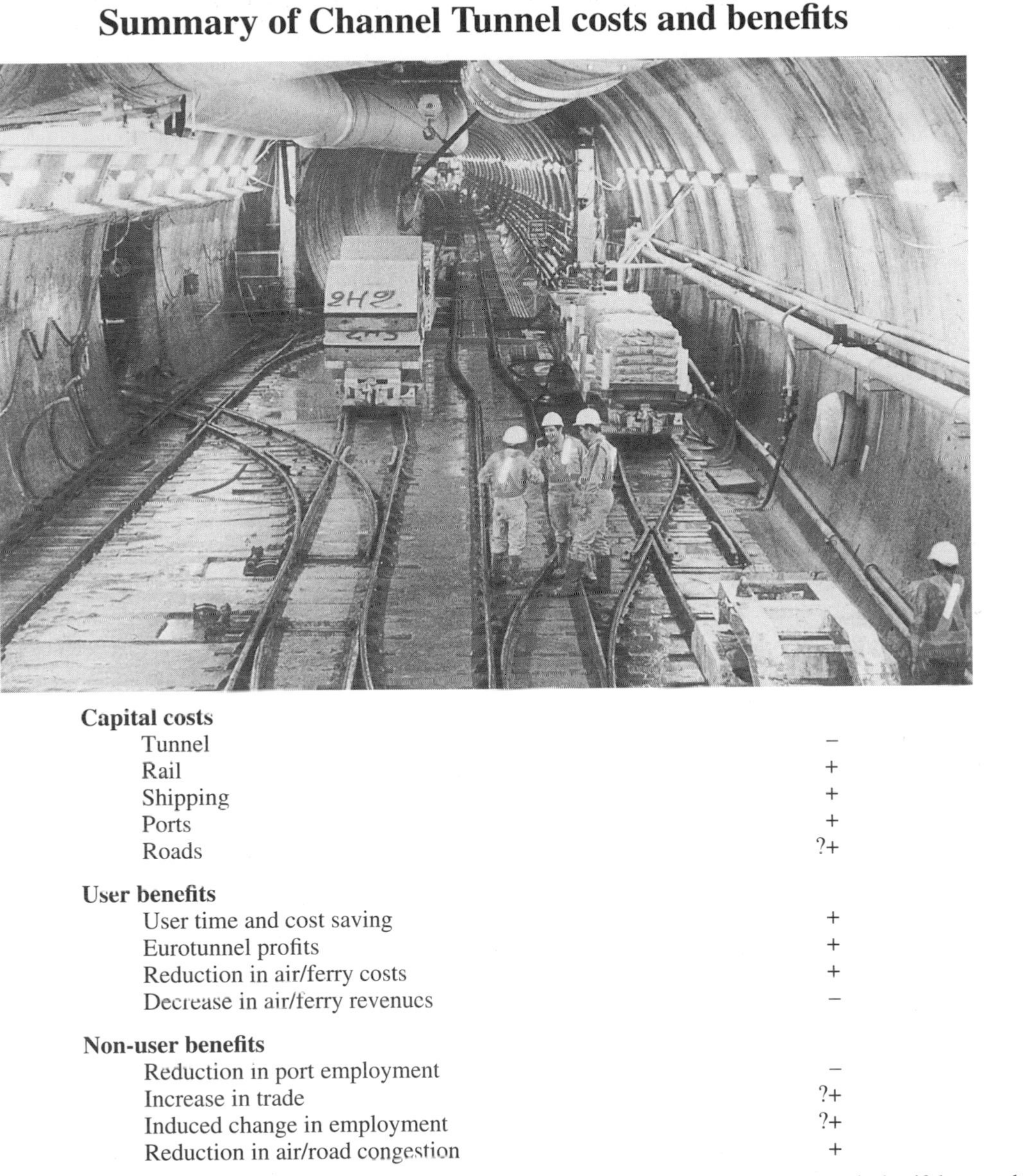

Capital costs	
Tunnel	–
Rail	+
Shipping	+
Ports	+
Roads	?+
User benefits	
User time and cost saving	+
Eurotunnel profits	+
Reduction in air/ferry costs	+
Decrease in air/ferry revenues	–
Non-user benefits	
Reduction in port employment	–
Increase in trade	?+
Induced change in employment	?+
Reduction in air/road congestion	+

Note: In this table + denotes a benefit and – a cost, ? indicates that the effect is uncertain. For roads, the argument is that if the tunnel leads to a switch to rail then fewer roads may be needed than if we relied on lorries. The uncertainty surrounding trade and employment effects depends on the relative impact on the UK and regions on the continent.

Source: Adapted from Vickerman, Roger W., 'Cost-benefit analysis and the Channel Tunnel', *Developments in Economics,* Vol 6, Causeway 1990.

Question 1

1. Explain what is meant by cost benefit analysis. When is this technique useful?
2. Which of these costs and benefits will occur now and which in the future? What procedure should be adopted to make future costs and benefits comparable to current ones?
3. Which of these costs would be particularly important to: (i) environmentalists; (ii) government?

11 Environmental Economics

In recent years people have become increasingly concerned about the environment. This concern takes many forms – saving endangered species, cleaning up pollution, ending global warming – the list is almost endless. Economic analyses can contribute to this debate, but there is controversy among economists about the most effective solution to environmental problems.

- 'Market' economists argue that in many cases environmental improvement can be achieved through the use of market forces.
- On the other hand, 'green' supporters suggest that market forces will not solve environmental problems and that government intervention on a national and international scale is required.

The extent of the problem

Table 11.1 summarises some of the environmental problems which are causing concern. The list is not exhaustive; for example, some people would argue that a basic problem is that the earth's population is growing rapidly, so that more resources are being used and so succeeding generations will suffer.

Despite the problems, there are some encouraging signs. Figure 11.1 shows that, although there has been a significant growth in emissions of carbon dioxide and nitrogen in recent years, sulphur emissions have fallen. This suggests that appropriate measures can lead to improvements in the environment.

Table 11.1: *Selected environmental indicators*

Forests	Each year the earth's tree cover diminishes by some 17 million hectares, an area the size of Austria.
Land (estimated)	Annual losses of topsoil from cropland are at 24 billion tons, roughly the amount of Australia's wheatland.
Climate system	The amount of carbon dioxide, the principle greenhouse gas in the atmosphere, is now rising by 0.4% per year from fossil fuel burning and deforestation.
Plant and animal life	The number of plant and animal species is dropping. Habitat destruction and pollution are reducing the earth's biological diversity.
Air quality	In the 1980s, air pollution reached record levels in hundreds of cities and crop damaging levels in scores of countries.

Source: Adapted from Brown, R. et al, *State of the World 1991*, Earthscan Publications 1992.

Economics and the environment

People from many disciplines study the environment, and the interest of economists is relatively new. Nevertheless, economic analysis can offer valuable insights because economists are concerned with resource allocation, and our environment is our most valuable resource.

Much economic analysis assumes that the economy is a 'closed system' – that it is able to function indefinitely, cut off from the environment. In reality the economy is an open system which must extract, process and discard large amounts of materials. That means it is subject to physical constraints. The way that humans manage their economies has a significant impact on the environment. What is often not realised is that environmental quality impacts on the efficient working of the economy.

Air pollution

Figure 11.1: *Emissions of greenhouse gases*

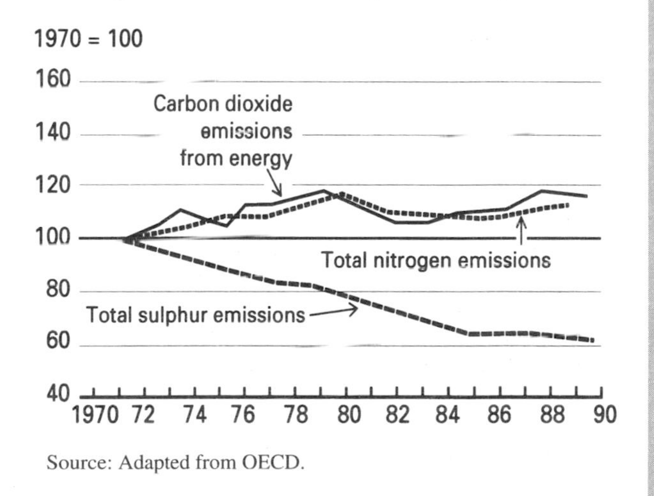

Source: Adapted from OECD.

Sustainable development

One concern of environmentalists is that if we continue to use resources entering the system at the current rate, future generations will suffer and have lower living standards. The concept of **sustainable development** is often used when analysing the environment. Supporters of this concept argue that we should aim for economic development that meets the needs of the present without compromising the needs of future generations. They suggest that we should not strive to increase our own living standards if that means that future generations will be denied.

Concern about sustainable development leads to policies which affect the current distribution of resources. Since poverty leads to the destruction of environmental resources, for example, by cutting down tropical forests or by using oil which cannot be replaced, supporters of sustainable development suggest that richer countries should assist poorer ones. One way in which this can be done is by transferring appropriate technology in return for promises to conserve some particularly valuable environmental asset such as a tropical forest.

The general issue raised by the idea of sustainable development is 'How should we treat natural environments in order that they can play their part in sustaining the economy as a source of improved standards of living?' (Pearce & Turner, 1990). Two rules follow:

- Always use renewable resources, such as forests, in such a way that the rate of use is not greater than the natural re-generation rate.

- Always keep flows of waste material at or below the capacity of the environment to assimilate them.

However, in practice these rules can be modified. Since exhaustible resources, such as oil, will run out at some time in the future, the rules suggest that there can be **substitutability** between exhaustible and renewable resources. For example, as exhaustible resources decline they can be replaced by other resources that are renewable. Hence fossil fuels such as oil can be replaced by wind, solar or tidal sources. In addition the rules can be modified to allow for the fact that a given standard of living can be secured from a reducing stock of resources. This is because resources can be used more efficiently, and there is strong evidence to suggest that this is happening. For example, most advanced economies now use less energy to produce a unit of output than they did a generation ago.

Key ideas

1. There is concern that we are using up the earth's resources.
2. Sustainable development suggests that we should meet the needs of the present without compromising the needs of future generations.

Cost benefit analysis in action

One way to put these rules into operation is to use cost benefit analysis, the technique described in the last chapter. Cost benefit analysis provides information on environmental quality as measured in terms of money. For example, one way in which the environment can be improved is to fit pollution control equipment to coal powered electricity generating stations in order to reduce emissions of gasses such as sulphur which cause acid rain. This has severe environmental effects, such as killing trees and making rivers and lakes acid so that marine life dies. In cost benefit analysis, the costs of the control equipment can be compared to the benefits which would result from such control; if the benefits exceed the costs, the project is worthwhile. That is why monetary units should be used, because if benefits and costs are measured using different units, no real comparisons can be made.

Environmental economists suggest that the total economic value of any asset or resource has three components: 'actual use value', 'option value' and 'existence value'. That is:

Total economic value
= actual use value + option value + existence value

Actual use value is the price which people are willing to pay for the use of some resource. Hence the actual use value of a forest is the amount of money someone is willing to pay for the forest in order to use the wood. **Option value** is the way in which we can value people's willingness to pay for the preservation of an environment against some possibility that the individual will make use of the asset in future. This future use can include exploiting the asset, for example, by cutting down the trees, but it also includes willingness to pay so that future generations can benefit from the preservation of the asset. **Existence values** are intrinsic and are not necessarily associated with actual use or even the option to use the asset. People may value certain things which cannot be bought, such as a beautiful view or the life of a beautiful creature such as a whale.

The difficulty with this approach is that option and existence values are not easy to calculate. Use values can be obtained from the amount of money which people actually pay to use an asset; but how do we value things which are not actually bought or sold? One response to this problem is to make use of 'contingent valuation'. This involves taking a survey to find out people's willingness to pay for some improvement, such as purer water or the conservation of a rural area threatened with a new road scheme.

Two examples will clarify this approach. A study at Middlesex Polytechnic estimated that people who used beaches were willing to pay £14 to £18 a year in order to protect recreational beaches from erosion. This is an estimate of use value. The study also sampled people who did not use beaches and obtained an existence value of about £21 a year.

Another example comes from Germany. Berlin citizens were asked how much in DM an improvement in clean air was worth to them. The results were then extrapolated to the whole of the Federal Republic. The result shows that young people were much more concerned with air quality than old people. Overall the results suggested that the benefit for air nationwide to be improved to the quality found in small towns was approximately 10 billion DM. The benefit of air improved to resort quality was about 20 billion DM. This kind of procedure gives some kind of yardstick against which the costs of procedures to improve air quality can be measured.

Such procedures can easily be criticised. The obvious problem is that such valuations are hypothetical; the people involved do not actually have to hand over any money, so the values they suggest may differ considerably from that which they would actually be willing to pay in practice.

Moreover, as we saw in the last chapter future costs and benefits need to be discounted. This presents particular difficulties in environmental economics since many of the benefits, such as the continuance of a beautiful view, stretch far into the future. Conventional discounting techniques would mean that these benefits in the distant future would be discounted almost to extinction. In other words, discounting contains an inbuilt bias against future generations. Consequently, it is not surprising that in the context of the environment there are a number of objections to discounting. One is that discounting relates to individual time preference; it is quite rational to override individual preferences (which are conditioned by uncertainty about the future) with those of society. Individuals will die but society will continue, and it is therefore plausible to put greater emphasis on the future. If equal priority is given to future and present generations, then it is acceptable to reduce the impact of discounting. One way in which this can be done is to integrate a **sustainability requirement** into the analysis. That is to say that, whatever the other costs and benefits associated with any decision, the stock of environmental capital should be kept constant. Thus projects which failed this test should not proceed, even though the potential benefits exceed the potential costs.

Key ideas

1. Cost benefit analysis can be used to evaluate environmental proposals.
2. Total economic value has three components: actual use value, option value and existence value.
3. Difficulties in using cost benefit analysis include how to value benefits and how to discount the future.

The free market approach

Economic analysis focuses on the allocation of resources; and supporters of markets argue that they offer the most desirable way to allocate resources. It is therefore not surprising that in matters concerning the environment – the greatest resource of all – they put forward a strong case to the effect that market forces are the best way to approach the problem. At the heart of this approach is the individual and a belief that individuals respond to incentives, particularly material incentives.

Pricing

One of the concerns of environmentalists is that modern societies use up too many resources which cannot be replaced. A prime example is oil, laid down over countless ages but being used up at a rapid rate by people who take little thought for the needs of the future.

Markets offer a solution. As a resource such as oil is used up – becoming scarce – its price will rise as demand exceeds supply. That will cause less to be demanded as consumers buy cheaper alternatives or simply use less of the resource. For example, when the price of oil rose in the 1970s, people bought cars which used less oil, and also switched to gas central heating. The rise in price will also encourage more oil exploration, and companies will develop oil fields which were not competitive at a lower price. Moreover, the high price of oil will cause manufacturers of competing products to develop alternatives. For example, oil is used in plastics; if plastic products rise in price then wood or metal alternatives will become competitive, so decreasing the use of oil. In this way the scarcer oil becomes, the more alternatives will develop, all without any government intervention.

Property rights

Supporters of free markets argue that one reason environmental problems arise is that no one owns the environment; it is seen as a free good. Since no one owns it, no one takes care of it. Hence the solution to problems such as pollution is to give people property rights. They argue that in an economy with well defined property rights, individuals and firms would have every incentive to use natural resources as efficiently as possible. For example, if the right to discharge smoke into the environment could be bought, then firms who discharged smoke would have to buy this right. This would make their products more expensive than those produced by competitors who had installed control equipment. It would therefore give them an incentive to discharge less smoke.

Another advantage is that the existence of property rights could also compensate those who suffer from the pollution. Negotiations between polluters and sufferers could lead to a position where sufferers are compensated and polluters have incentives to pollute less. This would occur through the workings of the markets, without any government intervention except the creation of markets in this area.

Market policies

Incentives

Supporters of markets argue that policies should rest on two principles:

- there should be incentives to behave in environmentally desirable ways;
- policies should increase economic efficiency.

The most direct way to reduce environmental waste is to introduce incentives. If it costs people more to dump rubbish, they will have an incentive to cut back on the rubbish they create. Yet at present it usually costs the individual household no more if they put out additional rubbish. This can be changed by the introduction of 'pay to throw' schemes. These are common in the USA, where households are charged a basic fee but have to pay a supplementary fee for every bit of additional rubbish.

The problem with such schemes is that they create an undesirable incentive – to throw away this additional rubbish; exactly the opposite of what is desirable. Consequently market supporters suggest that the logical policy is to tax *consumption* at a rate which reflects the costs which would be imposed on society if it was illegally dumped. The proceeds of this tax could then be returned as a subsidy on recycling and rubbish disposal. This kind of idea is an example of a **market based instrument**; these lie at the heart of the market approach.

Another example is that of refundable deposits. In these schemes, individuals have an incentive to return their cans to the shop so that they can be recycled. However, this may clash with the other principle of market schemes, that they should be efficient. It is quite possible that the costs to the consumer in time and perhaps petrol, added to the costs to the manufacturer of collecting and then processing such bottles and cans, may actually use up more resources than they save.

There is an international dimension to waste disposal. Rich countries should recognise that they do not have the facilities to recycle more than a fraction of the rubbish they create, so they could offer to pay other countries handsomely to take their rubbish. This might relieve the problem in the richer countries, and would also generate incomes in poorer countries.

Another example of how incentives can be used to solve environmental problems concerns city centre traffic. This causes temporary problems such as congestion, but it also has long term implications since car emissions damage buildings and cause ill health in humans. One approach to this problem is to make people pay to use the city centre. At present this is administratively difficult, but modern technology – such as machines which read licence plates – has the potential to solve this difficulty. Making people pay to drive in city centres would give them an incentive to use alternatives such as public transport.

Finally, supporters of markets would argue that, given appropriate information, consumers are the best judges of their own best interests. Consequently if they decide that green products, such as green washing powders, are in their best

interest, they will buy them. Producers of such products will then make good profits and expand. Producers of less environmentally friendly products will face declining sales, and will be forced to change. If consumers do not want green products, then it is unacceptable for governments to force manufacturers to produce them, so government intervention is undesirable.

The British government's policy was set out in *This Common Inheritance: Britain's Environmental Strategy* (1990). This argued that the government was seeking to solve environmental problems by

'working with the grain of the market. The ideas include various forms of pollution tax and other economic instruments, all designed to encourage consumers and producers to behave in ways which benefit the environment... In the government's view market mechanisms offer the prospect of a more efficient and flexible response to environmental issues... the right price signals should be able to cause very significant environmental improvements.'

The government then suggests as an example that increases in the price of energy will force people to be more efficient in its use.

Key ideas

1. Individuals respond to incentives.
2. As resources are used up their price will rise, demand will fall and alternatives become profitable.
3. Property rights over the environment will give incentives to people to use resources efficiently.

The interventionist approach

Interventionists criticise the market forces approach. They suggest that in some cases governments can indeed make use of market forces, for example by creating incentives for individuals and firms to act in certain ways. Overall, however, interventionists suggest that these measures will be inadequate and that direct government is required.

They argue that regulation has proved effective in the past and is needed for the future. For example, many British cities used to be wreathed in dense fogs in winter, causing thousands of deaths from respiratory diseases, particularly among old people. Then Clean Air Acts were passed in 1956 and 1968 which stopped people burning coal in many areas. The result was that such fogs have now disappeared. Similarly, the MOT test for cars was extended so that it restricted emissions of gasses. Examples such as these show that regulation can achieve improvements that would not occur just by using market forces – it does not pay individuals to expel less gas from their cars, neither is it necessarily in their interest to stop burning coal in their houses.

Interventionists argue that government action is now needed in many areas. For example, it is possible that technological improvements can have significant beneficial effects, but it may not pay entrepreneurs to invest in research in this area. Thus solar and wind power offer the possibility of providing energy without many of the undesirable effects of present methods of energy production, but private sector firms may not think it in their interest to investigate such possibilities. Hence government sponsored research is needed. Similarly, whilst it might pay people to insulate their houses, more could be done if the government imposed regulations to ensure that all new houses have high levels of insulation.

Government intervention is also needed to increase recycling. Individuals can help by taking empty bottles to a bottle bank, but much more could be achieved if government intervened by imposing regulations. For example, in Germany householders have to separate out much of their rubbish so that it is easy to recycle. Specified bags are provided to help this separation. Such measures could be made more effective if firms were forced by law to recycle a certain proportion of their output.

Many kinds of industry harm the environment. Energy creation, whether from fossil fuels or from nuclear sources, is an obvious example. Almost all manufacturing requires the disposal of waste products. Regulations could play a significant part in reducing waste disposal and encouraging more environmentally sympathetic designs.

One of the main causes of environmental degradation is the rapid rise in population. More people means that more energy is needed, more resources are used and more waste is created. Consequently, governments should act in order to encourage smaller families. They can do this, for example, by making contraceptives easily available and by subsidising birth control information centres. Indirect measures also affect population growth. Improving the education of girls is likely to

lead to their getting better jobs and then choosing to have fewer children.

An example of intervention on an international level was the Earth Summit held in Rio in 1992. Over a hundred countries were represented and signed a World Climate Convention which pledged governments to reduce greenhouse gas emissions. They also signed an action plan called 'Agenda 21'. This contained twenty six principles, such as 'In order to achieve sustainable development, environmental protection shall constitute an integral part of the development process and cannot be considered in isolation from it'. However, the policies which were needed to achieve the goals were left to national governments, and it is likely that in many cases the principles are so vague that there will be few results. If governments do take the action plan seriously they will have to intervene in the economy to ensure that goals are achieved.

Market critique of intervention

Supporters of markets make a number of criticisms of this approach. For example, interventionists would regulate pollution by setting standards, but there is no way of deciding that the standards are set at the correct level. Moreover, the costs of complying with these standards may leave domestic producers at a disadvantage compared with their overseas competitors. Even if the regulations do improve the environment, they may be inefficient in the sense that the costs of complying are greater than the benefits obtained.

Similar arguments apply to recycling. The costs of collecting, cleaning and then processing waste material may exceed the benefits obtained by recycling. Consequently, market economists argue that it would be better to emphasise market forces

Key ideas

1. Market forces are not enough – government intervention is needed.
2. Regulation can increase recycling and impose standards of allowable pollution.
3. Government action can reduce population growth.

Energy

Energy use is a crucial part of the economics of the environment. It is important partly because many ways of producing energy use up exhaustible resources such as oil, or else they have undesirable side effects, as when nuclear fuels are used. In addition the production of energy can produce acid rain as well as global warming.

One concern in this area is the fear that as economic growth occurs, more energy will be needed. However, the facts seem to suggest otherwise. In 1989 Britain produced 25 per cent more GDP than in 1979 without using any more energy. How was this achieved?

Supporters of intervention would suggest that it was not through the use of market forces since in real terms the price of energy fell. Instead they would point to government action such as the money spent by the Energy Efficiency Office, the use of building regulations to promote better insulation of buildings and the use of grants to improve energy use. Market supporters would argue that many of the government's actions – such as the use of subsidies – made use of financial incentives, a crucial part of the market forces approach. So here we have an example where a combination of the two approaches has been successful.

Conclusion

As living standards in the West have risen, concern about the environment has increased, suggesting that perhaps environmentalism only becomes a major political concern when the material quality of life is satisfactory. The two approaches to the environment discussed here are not entirely opposites. Most environmental economists would suggest that a mixture of market and interventionist approaches is needed. Indeed, in some cases the two approaches overlap. For example, a government which wished to reduce the use of oil could impose taxes. This could be regarded as intervention, since it would be an intervention in the market; but taxes rely on incentives – that a higher price will be an incentive to people to reduce consumption. Hence it could be regarded as a market forces approach.

The approach adopted depends as much on the individual's values as much as it does on economic analysis. Those economists who favour economic growth as a main aim of government policy tend to emphasis market forces. 'Green' economists place less emphasis on growth and more on conservation, and tend to stress the need for government intervention.

Data questions

How to rescue the rhino

Environmentalists seem to combine the dottiness of the old lentil consuming beard and sandals brigade with the authoritarian urges of born again socialists. The latest campaign of these busybodies is directed at the trade in rhino horn, which is bought by Chinese in Taiwan who labour under the delusion that when powdered and swallowed it will stimulate their sexual drive. As a result, rhino horn is now more expensive per pound than gold. So a body describing itself as the Task Force seeks a British boycott of Taiwanese goods as a way of compelling them to desist from taking a powder and thus helping to keep the rhino alive.

In fact it would be hard to think of a policy better calculated to eliminate the rhino in short order. The one way to preserve these splendid beasts is to create property rights in them. There is no threat of cats, dogs or cattle dying out because they are privately owned. The elephant herds in Zimbabwe are increasing because they are farmed and the local tribesmen receive a portion of the profits. In Kenya, where there has been a total ban on ivory sales, many elephants are being killed by poachers and the herds are diminishing.

Source: 'Homo oeconomicus' in *Economic Affairs*, February 1993.

Question 1

1. Explain what is meant by 'property rights' and show how these might protect the rhino.
2. What criticisms would interventionists make of this approach? What measures might they suggest?

The Bruntland Report

Our Common Future, usually referred to as the Bruntland Report, is a report of the World Commission on Environment and Development set up by the United Nations and chaired by the ex-Prime Minister of Norway. The Report points out that 'It is impossible to separate economic development issues from environmental issues; many forms of development erode the environmental resources upon which they must be based... What is needed now is a new era of growth – growth that is... socially and environmentally sustainable... Sustainable development is development that meets the needs of the present without compromising the ability of future generations to meet their own needs'.

Source: Anderson, V., *Alternative Economic Indicators,* Routledge 1991.

Question 2

1. Explain what is meant by 'sustainable development'.
2. How would (i) supporters of markets and (ii) interventionists try to achieve sustainable development?

Trying to keep the lid on the recycling boom

Every Saturday, millions of shoppers return from the nation's supermarkets to unload their groceries and dump tonnes of waste packaging in their rubbish bins, most of which is then buried by local authorities in landfill sites. This added up to 3.6 million tonnes last year and the weight of household garbage is expected to grow to 4.2 million tonnes by the end of the decade.

At the moment only about an eighth of this is recycled, with plastics having by far the lowest recycling rate. Britain lags behind most of Europe in its recycling endeavours, but the government has insisted on a voluntary approach. An alternative approach has been adopted by Germany, which has imposed regulations resulting in a flood of waste material which has undermined the economics of the developing recycling industries in other countries. This is because Germany's reprocessing capability is 250,000 tonnes, whilst 450,000 tonnes has built up, forcing Germany to export its waste to other European countries. Britain wants Germany either to collect less waste plastic or to burn it – a solution not favoured in Germany. The crisis has illustrated the European dimension of the issue and emphasised the need for a European Packaging Directive which has been stuck in the Euro system for years.

Source: Adapted from *The Guardian*, 30 October 1993.

Question 3

1. How do you think that German exports have 'undermined the economics of the developing recycling industries in other countries'?
2. Do you think that the events discussed here give support to the interventionist or the market forces approach?
3. What do you think are the costs and the benefits of recycling waste material?

12 Measuring National Income

How is the economy doing? National income accounting attempts to answer this question. It does so by measuring the performance of the economy in various ways, for example, by calculating the output produced in the country during a year. There is some disagreement about the accuracy and usefulness of the figures which are produced.

- Some economists think that, although not perfect, they are a reliable indicator of what is happening in the economy.
- Others feel that the figures have considerable limitations. The debate is important because national income statistics are used in many areas of economics, for example, in measuring living standards and in examining economic trends.

Constructing the accounts

Before considering the uses and limitations of national income statistics, we must first examine how the figures are obtained and evaluate their accuracy.

Figure 12.1: *GDP factor cost, 1985 prices (1985=100)*

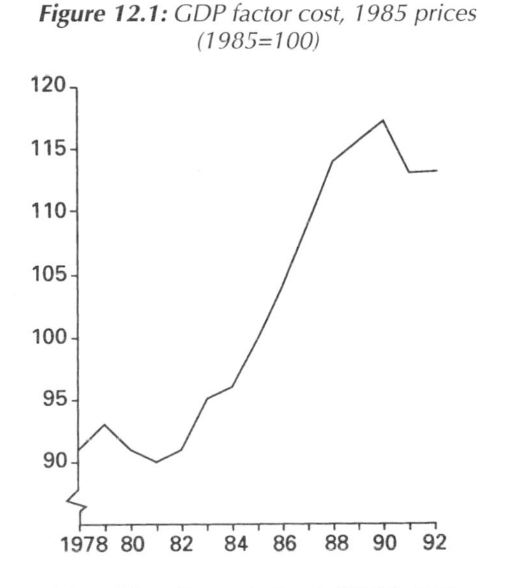

Source: Adapted from *Economic Trends*, HMSO, 1993.

National income can be defined as the total money value of all the goods and services produced by a country during a year. Hence the rate of growth of national income is probably the most important indicator of a country's economic performance. Governments of all political parties boast of the rise when it is high and find excuses when the growth rate is low.

Figure 12.1 shows the growth rate of the UK economy in real terms (that is corrected to eliminate the effects of inflation) between 1978 and 1992. Over this period the economy has grown by about a quarter, i.e. at an average rate of just over 1.7 per cent a year. However, there have been large variations in this rate and in some years national income has actually fallen.

Three ways to measure national income

National income can be measured in three ways. By definition these must be equal because they are different ways of measuring the same thing – the growth in output of the economy. The three different methods are shown in Figure 12.2. This is a simplified explanation and is developed further in Chapter 13.

One way to measure national income is to calculate the value of all goods and services produced by the people of a particular country. This is called Gross Domestic Product (GDP) by the output method. Unless people from outer space come to earth and steal some of these goods, GDP calculated by the **output method** must equal the amount of goods and services which is either bought, or not purchased and put into store. When GDP is calculated in this way it is called the **expenditure method**.

When something is produced it gives rise to incomes. These can accrue to several people – the workers who make it, the people who sell it, or as profits to the owners. The income generated must equal the amount spent on the product; if a table is sold for £100, then this £100 must go to one or more people as income. Hence GDP calculated by this **income method** equals that calculated by the expenditure method.

We will now consider each of these methods in turn.

Figure 12.2: *The national income accounts – three ways of measuring economic activity (1992)*

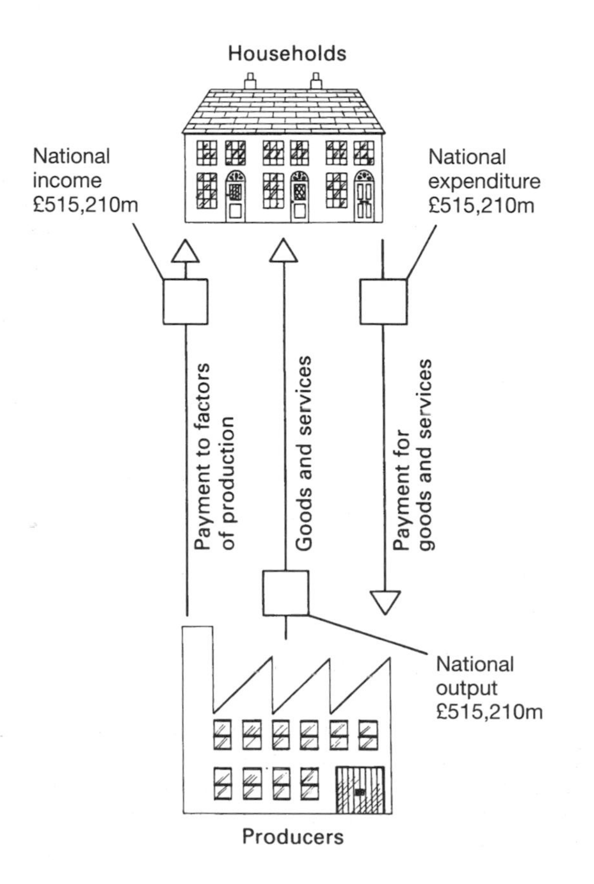

The output method

This involves adding together the final output of all the producers in the economy. **Final** output is stressed in order to avoid double counting. Assume that the chair on which you are sitting was bought for £20; that is the value of the chair. However, this output came from several industries. The forestry industry contributed the wood, the furniture industry manufactured the chair and the distribution industry sold it. In order to avoid double counting we need to add together the **value added** by each of these industries. An over-simplified example will show the procedure:

Forestry: value of inputs £0, value of output £5, value added £5.

Furniture: inputs from forestry £5, value of output £15, value added £10.

Distribution: inputs from furniture industry £15, value of output £20, value added £5.

Hence in constructing the national output table the contribution of each industry can be shown by its value added, in this case £5 + £10 + £5 = £20. The sum of values added by all the firms in the economy becomes the nation's national output.

Figure 12.3: *Share of national output*

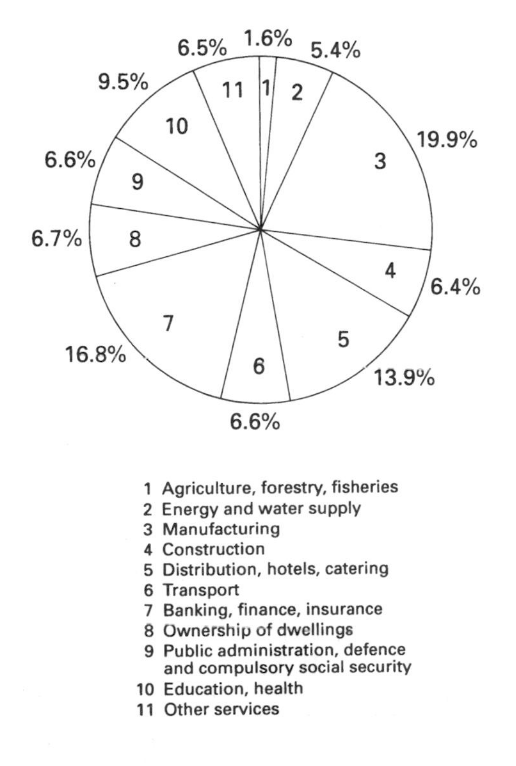

Source: Adapted from *UK National Accounts*, HMSO, 1993.

Figure 12.3 shows the relative importance of the various industries in the UK economy. As can be seen, manufacturing contributes less than a quarter of the nation's output – far short of what services provide. Table 12.1 contains similar information, but in the form of a table. In this Table a figure for financial services is deducted. This is to prevent double counting, since the services of banks and other financial institutions contribute to the output of individual industries and are therefore also included separately. Hence a deduction is made here.

Table 12.1: *National income statistics, UK 1992 - Output method*

	£ million
Agriculture, fishing and forestry	9,309
Energy and water supply	13,717
Manufacturing	114,698
Construction	32,002
Distribution, hotels and catering	72,549
Transport	41,613
Banking, finance and insurance	121,704
Public admin., defence, social security	36,606
Education and health services	52,509
Other	42,734
Total	537,440
Less adjustment for financial services	-2,216
Statistical discrepancy	-20,014
Gross domestic product at factor cost	515,210
Net property income from abroad	5,777
Gross national product	520,987
(Less) Capital consumption	-63,984
National income	457,003

Source: *UK National Accounts*, HMSO, 1993.

The expenditure method

As Table 12.2 shows, by far the largest item of expenditure is that undertaken by consumers on durable consumer goods, such as video recorders or washing machines, on non-durable goods, such as bread or gas and on services, such as hairdressing or bank charges. The difference between durable and non-durable goods is taken, rather arbitrarily, to be whether or not they last longer than one year.

Government expenditure is another major item. Note that this excludes transfer payments, such as student grants or pensions, because these are transfers from one part of the population to another and do not represent final consumption. Investment (called 'gross domestic fixed capital formation' in the Table) is another important item. This tends to be difficult to forecast in advance because it fluctuates quite considerably. This means that the share of investment in national income also fluctuates. Finally, to get a full measure of expenditure we need to add exports (which are bought by foreigners) and subtract imports (because the money spent on these goes abroad).

Table 12.2: *National income statistics, UK, 1992- Expenditure method*

	£ million
Consumers' expenditure	386,201
Central government	79,176
Local authorities	50,693
Gross domestic fixed capital formation	91,800
Value of physical increase in stocks and work in progress	-2,041
Exports	139,523
(Less) Imports	-149,594
Statistical discrepancy	-800
Gross domestic product at market prices	594,592
(Less) Taxes on expenditure	-83,394
Subsidies	6,342
Gross domestic product at factor cost	515,210
Net property income from abroad	5,777
Gross national product	520,987
(Less) Capital consumption	-63,984
National income	457,003

Source: *Economic Trends*. Annual Supplement, HMSO, 1993.

We can represent the economy's total expenditure on goods and services by the equation:

Expenditure = C+I+G+X-M

where C = consumption, I = investment, G = government spending, X = exports and M = imports. We will meet this equation again when we discuss aggregate demand in Chapter 13 and it is worth remembering.

The income method

The data required to complete the figures for 'incomes' in the national income statistics are obtained by the Inland Revenue. These figures are shown in Table 12.3. As you can see, by far the largest item is income from employment, which accounts for about two-thirds of total incomes. The share of profits varies from year to year, rising when the economy is expanding, but falling in years of depression. Transfer incomes, such as student grants and pensions, are not included. This is because the figures only measure incomes arising from the production of goods and services (and students are assumed not to produce anything!).

During the year, some people will have become 'richer' because they own stocks of goods which have become more valuable. Since GDP is concerned with items which are produced during a given year, changes in the value of existing stocks should not count, so a figure for stock appreciation is deducted when the income method is calculated.

Table 12.3: *National income statistics, UK, 1992- Income method*

	£ million
Income from employment and self-employment	342,384
Gross trading profits of companies	63,532
Gross trading profits of public corporations	2,808
Gross trading surplus of general government enterprises	119
Other income, e.g. rent	107,605
(Less) Stock appreciation	-2,664
Residual error	1,222
Gross domestic product at factor cost	515,210
Net property income from abroad	5,777
Gross national product	520,987
(Less) Capital consumption	-63,984
National income	457,003

Source: Adapted from *Economic Trends.* Annual Supplement, HMSO, 1993.

Some complications

Measuring the output of an entire economy is clearly a complex process and a number of complications arise which need to be discussed:

- Market prices or factor cost? The value of a product, so far as consumers are concerned, is the price paid for it in the shop – the market price. This often includes tax, so if the retail price was used to calculate national output, it would lead to the ridiculous result that the nation's output would rise if the Chancellor put up VAT. Similarly, a government subsidy to an industry would lead to a fall in national income. Hence the figures are sometimes shown at market prices, but more often at factor cost. This means that the market price has been adjusted to remove the effect of any tax on the goods and also any subsidy. Taxes are removed and subsidies are added to GDP at market prices in order to change the figure to one at factor cost.
- Transfers. If I sell you a book I have read, no current production is involved. Consequently such transfers are excluded from the accounts. However, the same book bought from a second-hand bookshop would involve a payment for the seller's service and would be included in the accounts.
- Non-marketed goods. The national accounts only include goods which are bought. Hence DIY activities are not counted. Neither are the activities of 'housewives'. Cooking a meal in a cafe where it is bought adds to GNP; cooking at home does not. This omission is criticised by some people, and is discussed later in this chapter.
- The public sector. What is the value of the output of your school or college? Something is being produced – at least occasionally – but how can it be measured? In the private sector the value of a product is what the purchaser is willing to pay, but this method cannot be used in state schools or for defence, the services of the police or the health service. The unsatisfactory solution used in the national accounts is to use the cost of the service as a measure of its output. Hence we can have the position where if there is an increase in efficiency, so that a service is produced at less cost, this then shows as a fall in output.
- Residual error. The three approaches to measuring the national income must come to the same total. However, the complexities of collecting the statistics are such that in practice they do not agree. To solve this dilemma a figure for residual error is added to make the figures agree. Note that this figure for residual error is not an accurate measure of the actual error, since this is not known. It is merely a

statistical device to make the three totals agree. This leads to questions about the validity of using the figures in economic analysis.

Which measure of national income?

So far we have been discussing Gross **Domestic** Product (GDP). However, if you happen to own an oil well in Alaska, or a tea estate in Malawi, you will realise that some people receive incomes from property they own in other countries. Similarly, some foreigners own property in this country. When these flows of money into and out of the country are taken into account, we obtain a figure for Gross **National** Product (GNP). For the UK this has always been a positive item because British people own more overseas assets than foreigners own assets in this country. Hence GNP is greater than GDP in the UK.

The relationship is shown by the equation:

$$\text{GDP} \pm \text{net property income from abroad} = \text{GNP}$$

Capital consumption

Another complication takes account of the fact that, during any one year, machines and buildings deteriorate. In the official statistics this is called capital consumption or depreciation and is shown by a move from **Gross** National Product to **Net** National Product (NNP).

An increase in NNP is the best measure we have of the real change in living standards and NNP is the official measure of national income (though the term is often used more vaguely to include other measures such as GDP or GNP). One problem which arises is that any precise measure of depreciation is impossible; imagine the difficulty in trying to list all the cars in the country and then estimating the fall in their value during the year. Hence it is estimated by using a series of accounting conventions and does not vary much from year to year.

The relationship between GNP and NNP is shown by the equation:

$$\text{GNP} - \text{capital consumption} = \text{NNP}$$

Figure 12.4 illustrates the two above formulae in the form of a diagram.

Figure 12.4

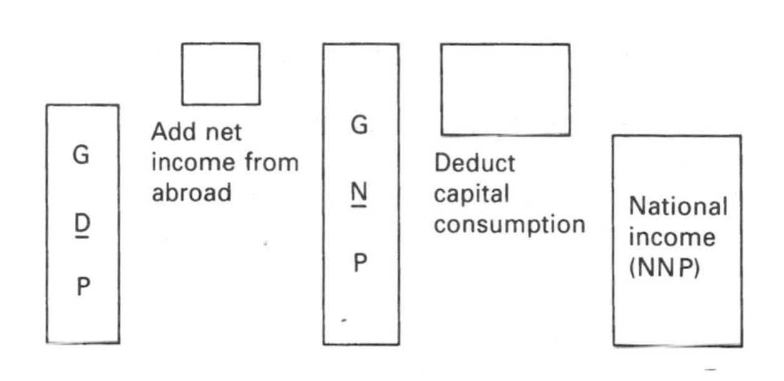

Key ideas

1. National income is the money value of all the goods and services produced in a country during a year.
2. It can be measured in three ways: by counting output, expenditure and income. In theory, all three should give the same result.
3. The figures can be expressed at market prices or at factor cost. The statistics exclude transfers and non-marketed goods. The output of government services, such as education, is measured at the cost of producing the service.
4. GDP measures what is produced in the domestic economy. GNP adds to this property income from abroad. When capital consumption is deducted from GNP, the result is national income.

Uses of the national income statistics

The previous sections dealt with the problems of obtaining an accurate figure for the national income of a country. Despite the difficulties, most economists would argue that the national income statistics have important uses for economists both inside and outside the government.

The prime purpose of the national income statistics is to facilitate government planning. If the Chancellor is considering cutting the rate of income tax, the statistics make it possible to forecast the effect that this would have on such things as economic growth and the balance of payments. This can be done by feeding the figures into a computer model of the economy.

National income statistics are the usual way to measure the rate of economic growth. They are also used to compare the current rate of economic

growth with the rate in the past and with the rate of growth and standard of living in other countries. That is because most countries use similar methods to construct the national income statistics, so comparisons are possible.

Economists in industry make considerable use of the statistics to analyse economic developments and their effect on individual firms. For example, they can make predictions about the future growth of the economy and how this will affect particular industries. Similarly, academic economists use the accounts to comment on matters as diverse as the share of wages in the national income or to compare the relative importance of manufacturing in one country with another.

Key ideas - uses of national income statistics

1. National income statistics are essential for governments when planning their budgets.
2. The figures are used to make comparisons with the past and with other countries.
3. Economists use the statistics to analyse particular sectors of the economy.

Criticisms of the national income accounts

Economists generally agree that the national income accounts have their uses, but there is substantial argument about these uses in any particular situation. This is because the accounts have considerable limitations and are sometimes used for inappropriate purposes.

Limitations of the figures

- They are not accurate. This is inevitable because measuring the economic activity of an entire country can never be done precisely. People sometimes fail to fill in forms or they complete them inaccurately.
- The 'black economy' distorts the figures. This is the name given to work that is not reported to the authorities. Teachers giving private lessons have been known to 'forget' to inform the tax authorities about the income they have received. The black economy is probably most prevalent in the area of domestic repairs, where discounts are often given for cash payment. This means that the statistics for this and similar areas of the economy are inaccurate. However, they do not distort the comparisons between total

GNP in one year and the next because the size of the black economy does not vary much over one year, so that the error is similar in both years. Comparisons over a longer period will be affected by changes in the size of the black economy.

- A rise in national income may not mean a rise in living standards. This is because the rise may occur as a result of increased spending on items such as defence, which do not improving living standards. Similarly, an increase in national income may be accompanied by a rise in undesirable externalities, such as pollution, or a fall in the quality of goods.
- The accounts only measure **paid** activities. They therefore exclude DIY activities and the work of housewives. If over a period of years there is a rise in DIY activities, then this will not be shown in the official figures and comparisons over several years will be inaccurate. These omissions are a severe problem in some countries where many economic activities are unpaid. In large parts of Africa and Asia, women collect water and wood, people build their own houses and live off food that they have grown. If these unpaid activities are not counted, then the figures will greatly under-estimate the level of GNP in these countries. If some attempt is made to estimate their value in order to give a truer picture, then insoluble problems of valuation arise. Imagine trying to estimate the value of all the water collected by all the women in India over a year!
- National income often rises in time of war, or the threat of war, because money is spent on weapons. This will push up GNP, but the people may be acutely short of goods to buy.
- When making comparisons with the past, adjustments have to be made to allow for inflation. If prices have risen by 5 per cent and GNP has also risen by 5 per cent, then the country is no better off. Hence it is important when looking at the figures to see whether they are in **nominal** terms, i.e. the actual figures not adjusted to remove the effects of inflation. If GNP rises by a nominal 5 per cent, but inflation is 3 per cent, then the real rise is 2 per cent. The extent of inflation can be calculated fairly accurately over a short period, such as one year, but it is much more difficult to do so over a long period. One reason is that new products appear and existing ones become obsolete, so it is impossible to measure price rises accurately.
- Another adjustment that has to be made when making comparisons with the past is that the figures have to be adjusted to allow for population changes. If national income has risen by 10 per cent, but population has also risen by 10 per cent, the average person is no better off.
- Many factors affect the quality of life but are excluded from GNP. Over the last few decades, people have come to enjoy more leisure, largely because they work fewer days. The national accounts take no note of this. Similarly, the quality of many products has improved – a modern TV is far superior to one made many

Does a rise in GDP mean a rise in living standards?

years ago. On the other hand, economic growth may be accompanied by increased pollution, overcrowded cities and a frenetic lifestyle – factors ignored by statisticians. The national income accounts measure some of the **quantitative** factors affecting life, but they ignore many features of the **quality** of life.

- The figures say nothing about the **distribution** of income within a country. In some countries a small elite has a large share of the economic cake; in such countries figures showing a high average income per head may give the wrong impression of typical living standards.

International comparisons

Table 12.4 illustrates GDP in several areas of the world. It also illustrates some of the difficulties of making such comparisons. The first difficulty is in deciding what constitutes 'low and middle income economies'. Clearly, there are no automatic criteria for allocating countries to a particular category, yet deciding to include or exclude particular countries from this group can change the whole picture.

Comparisons between countries may be misleading for other reasons:

- National income figures are compiled in national currencies. In order to make comparisons, these have to be converted to a common currency, usually US dollars. However, exchange rates vary daily and changes in exchange rates can give a misleading impression of changes in living standards.
- People's needs are not the same in all countries. In warm countries less needs to be spent on heating and clothing, so that even if two countries have identical national incomes, they may have different living standards.
- Countries are not always consistent in the way they prepare the statistics. For example, some countries may exclude or conceal spending on items such as defence.

Table 12.4: *GDP per capita for low and middle income economies, 1991*

Region	GDP (US $ billions)	Population (millions)	GDP per capita (US $)
Subsaharan Africa	178	489	364
East Asia	1059	1668	635
South Asia	335	1153	290
Middle East and North Africa	463	245	1889
Europe and Central Asia	1335	501	2664
Latin America	1176	446	2636

Note that this table is for 'low and middle income economies'. This means that 'Europe', for example, excludes countries such as the UK and Germany, but includes countries such as Greece and Hungary. Similarly, 'East Asia' includes China but not Japan.

Source: Adapted from *World Bank Annual Report,* World Bank, 1993.

Yet these difficulties do not mean that comparisons between countries are meaningless. The Table does make it clear that some parts of the world are much poorer than others. South Asia, including India, Pakistan and Bangladesh, and Africa south of the Sahara are obviously very poor areas compared to, say, the Caribbean. This has policy implications. For example, if the richer countries want to relieve great poverty they will focus their efforts in the areas of greatest need. So *precise* comparisons may be impossible, but *meaningful* ones can be made.

Key ideas - criticisms of national income statistics

1. The national income accounts are inaccurate, for example, they exclude the 'black economy' and ignore unpaid activity such as DIY.
2. They also ignore many factors affecting the quality of life, such as the existence of pollution.
3. Comparisons with the past are difficult because the composition and the quality of goods change over time.
4. Comparing living standards between countries is particularly inaccurate because the statistics are compiled in different currencies and because people in different countries have different needs.

Conclusion

The national income accounts are essential for the modern economist. They provide a wealth of detail about the economy and, considering the problems involved in compiling them, they can provide a reasonably accurate picture provided they are used sensibly. However, they can be put to uses for which they are inappropriate or used to support precise conclusions when they can give only approximate indications, such as when they are used to compare living standards in different countries.

Data questions

UK gross domestic product by category of expenditure

(£ million, current prices)

	1981	1982	1983	1984	1985	1986	1987	1988	1989	1990	1991
Consumers' expenditure	155,412	170,650	187,028	200,261	218,947	243,030	267,523	302,057	330,532	350,411	367,853
Gross domestic fixed capital formation	41,304	44,824	48,615	54,967	60,353	64,514	74,077	89,857	103,262	106,028	95,442
General government final consumption	55,374	60,363	65,787	69,760	73,805	79,381	85,349	91,729	99,029	109,878	121,899
Value of physical increase in stocks and works in progress	-2,768	-1,188	1,465	1,296	821	716	1,388	4,782	3,138	-1,462	-5,303
Export of goods and services	67,432	72,694	80,056	91,852	102,208	98,319	107,031	107,705	122,049	133,500	135,115
less imports of goods and services	60,388	67,762	77,529	92,669	98,866	101,070	111,868	124,788	142,693	147,728	140,415
Statistical discrepancy	-1,515	-694	-1,108	330	–	–	–	–	–	-277	-445
Gross domestic product at market prices	254,851	278,887	304,314	325,797	357,268	384,890	423,500	471,342	515,317	550,350	574,146
less Taxes on expenditure	42,465	46,467	49,500	52,576	56,592	62,947	69,074	76,133	79,967	76,967	83,023
Subsidies	6,369	5,811	6,269	7,537	7,225	6,187	6,173	5,918	5,782	6,069	5,878
Gross domestic product at factor cost	218,755	238,231	261,083	280,758	307,901	328,130	360,599	401,127	441,136	479,452	497,001

Source: Adapted from *Economic Trends*, HMSO, 1993.

Question 1

1. Explain what is meant by:
   (i) statistical discrepancy
   (ii) market prices
   (iii) factor cost.
2. Draw graphs to find out which categories of expenditure have grown most rapidly over the decade.
3. Which categories fluctuate the most?
4. To what extent do the figures show that the standard of living rose over the decade?

What GDP figures overlook

As far as the environment is concerned, the main areas of measurement error in the traditional national accounts are:
i) monies spent in correcting environmental damage;
ii) decline in the stock of natural resources;
iii) pollution damage.

It could easily be argued that the expenditures incurred by households trying to protect themselves against the adverse consequences of the production process should be excluded from the GDP figures – especially if these costs do not improve welfare. For example, if I double glaze my house because there is an increase in noise from road traffic in the street, the expenditure incurred as a result does not raise my welfare but only helps me return to he low noise level I enjoyed prior to the traffic increase. Conventional national accounts, however, would show an increase.

Similarly, if a forest is chopped down to get wood, the monetary value of the wood is included in GDP statistics, but nothing is subtracted to reflect the loss of the forest. The same applies when coal and oil are extracted from the nation's reserves.

The third environmental factor that needs to be accounted for is the propensity of modern industry to pollute. For example, if the public water supply is contaminated, people buy bottles of water instead. As a consequence GDP increases because bottled water involves greater expenditure than tap water. Again, economic statistics show an increase whilst the quality of the environment has depreciated.

Source: Myers, D., 'GDP and the environment', *Developments in Economics* Vol 9, 1993.

Question 2

1. Explain what is meant by 'GDP'. How does this differ from 'national income'?
2. Suggest an example to illustrate each of three possible areas of 'error' in the national accounts.
3. What other limitations of national income statistics exist? Do these invalidate the use of the statistics for measuring economic welfare?

13 Determinants of National Income

This chapter and the next could well be regarded as one because they each emphasise a particular approach to macro-economics – the study of the economy as a whole. In that sense they are crucial because many of the chapters that follow elaborate and develop the ideas found here.

- This chapter is largely, though not entirely, concerned to elaborate the Keynesian approach – a prime example of interventionism – to the problem of analysing the factors that determine the level of national income. It will set up a theoretical model of the economy as a whole, and then look in some detail at two of the most important variables – consumption and investment.
- The next chapter will give more emphasis to the supply side approach to macro-economics.

The circular flow of income model

There are a number of ways in which the basic Keynesian model can be developed, but a relatively easy way is to build up a model of the circular flow of income in the economy. A simplified version of this model was presented in the last chapter in Figure 12.2.

Figure 13.1: *The circular flow of income*

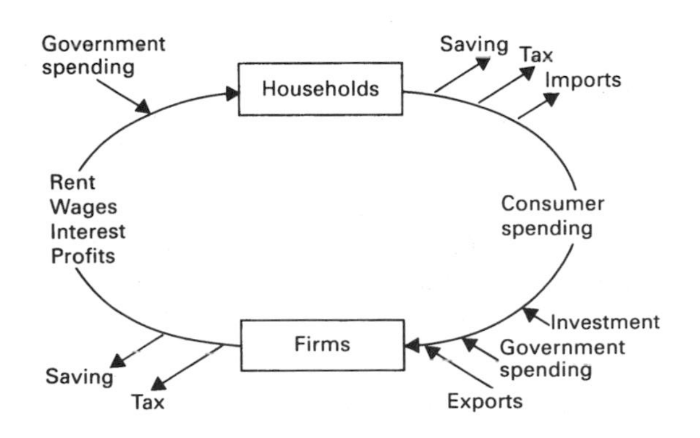

As Figure 13.1 shows, income flows from households to firms in the form of consumption spending by households on goods and services produced by firms. Similarly, income flows from firms to households in the form of wages, rent, interest and profits (remember the income approach to measuring national income in the last chapter?). These flows are disturbed by various **injections** into the system and by **withdrawals** from the system. Injections and withdrawals change the level of the flow, just as the level of water in a bath varies according to the amount of water coming in from the tap and the quantity escaping from the plug hole.

Withdrawals

Withdrawals, which remove income from the circular flow, come in three ways. Both firms and individuals save money in the sense that they do not pass it on. Later in this chapter we will explore in some detail the determinants of an individual's saving and consumption. For the present, it is enough to note that an increase in savings will lead to a fall in the level of the circular flow of income. Another withdrawal from the flow comes in the form of spending on imports; in this case the money is leaked to firms in other countries. The final withdrawal arises when the government takes money from firms and families in tax. Note that the prime determinant of all these withdrawals is the level of income. People with high incomes will tend to save more, buy more imported goods and pay more in tax.

Injections

There are also three injections into the system. These raise the level of incomes in the circular flow. Some firms receive money from other firms when they sell investment goods, such as factories or machines. A firm such as ICI receives most of its income not from selling consumer goods to families, but by selling chemicals to other firms. A second injection arises when firms export goods to other countries. In this case they receive money from foreign families and firms.

The final injection comes from government spending. This takes many forms. For example, households obtain money from the government when they work in the public sector, whether they are typists, teachers or tank drivers. Some households also receive income from the government, for example, when they receive transfer payments such as pensions or student grants. Similarly, firms obtain money from the government when they receive grants or sell goods as varied as chalk or aeroplanes to the public sector. All these injections into the system increase the circular flow of income.

To summarise:

Injections	**Withdrawals**
Investment	Saving
Exports	Imports
Government spending	Tax

Figure 13.2: *Injections, withdrawals and the level of income*

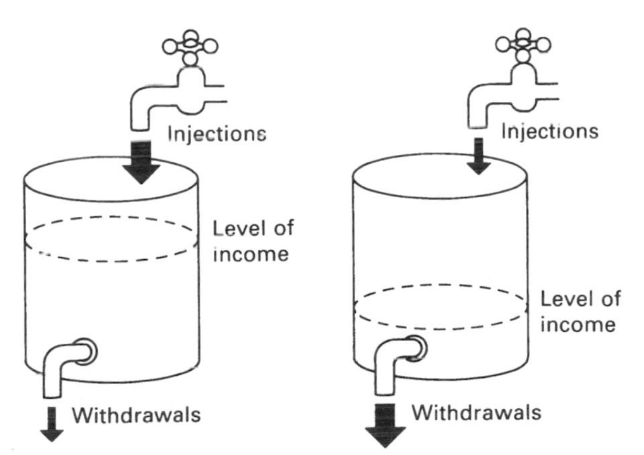

The size of withdrawals is largely determined by the level of incomes; for example, as incomes rise people save more. The level of injections is determined by other factors and is discussed in later chapters. Injections are said to be 'autonomous' of income.

Policy implications

An increase in injections will raise the circular flow of income, while a fall will lower the level of incomes. On the other hand, a rise in withdrawals will lead to a fall in the circular flow, while a fall in withdrawals will lead to a rise in incomes. Although this circular flow model of the economy is rather simplistic, it can be a powerful tool of analysis and it does suggest policies. For example, if the government wishes to stimulate the economy (in order to increase the rate of growth or create more jobs) then it should either increase injections by spending more, or reduce withdrawals by cutting taxes.

Real life is more complex than this and in the next few chapters we will explore the implications and limitations of this model in some detail. In the meantime we need to give a more formal exposition.

Equilibrium

'Equilibrium national income' means that the level of national income shows no tendency to change.

National income will be in equilibrium when injections equal withdrawals. We can deduce this because, as the last chapter made clear, national income calculated by the income method equals national expenditure.

Now:

National Income (Y) = Consumption (C) + Tax (T) + Savings (S) + Imports (M)

that is, income is either spent, taxed, saved or spent on imports.

Similarly:

National expenditure = Consumption (C) + Government spending (G) + Investment (I) + Exports (X)

that is, national expenditure on economic activity arises from consumption, government spending, investment spending and exports.

Since National income = National expenditure then:

$$C + T + S + M = C + G + I + X$$

Subtracting C from both sides gives:

$$T + S + M = G + I + X$$

or Withdrawals = Injections.

Since withdrawals equal injections, we need to discover how this comes about. How does the

Figure 13.3: *Equilibrium level of national income*

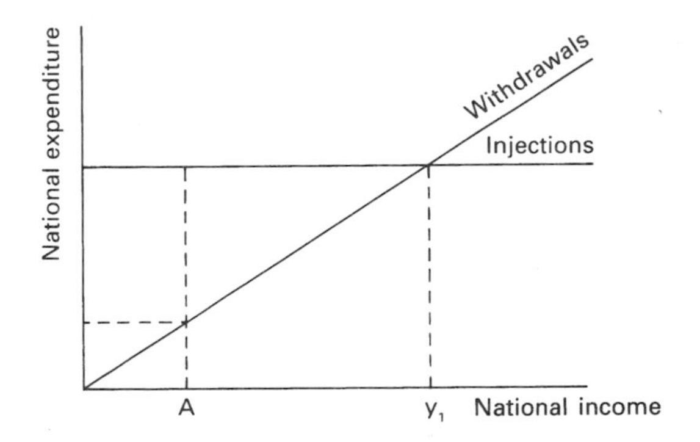

economy operate to maintain this equality? In Figure 13.3 the vertical axis measures national expenditure; the horizontal axis measures national income. In this model the level of injections is taken as given – or at least injections do not vary with the level of income, whereas withdrawals do rise as incomes increase. The equilibrium level of national income occurs where injections equal withdrawals at y_1. At any other position the economy would not be in equilibrium and changes would take place which would move the economy towards equilibrium. For example, if the economy was at point A, injections would be higher than withdrawals. This would lead to a rise in the circular flow of income – shown on this diagram by a movement to the right – until injections equal withdrawals at y_1.

The effect of changes

Figure 13.4 shows the effect of changes. A rise in government spending leads injections to rise from z_1 to z_2. This leads to an increase in national

Figure 13.4: *A rise in injections*

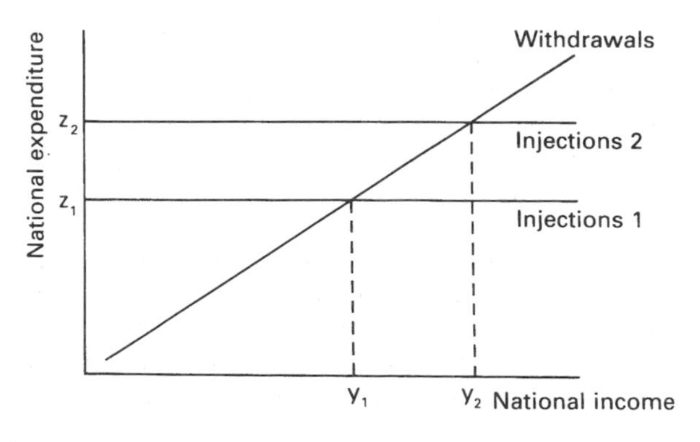

income, which rises until injections equal withdrawals at y_2. A fall in injections, for example from z_2 to z_1, has the opposite effect.

Figure 13.5 shows the effect of a fall in withdrawals. The slip of the withdrawals line measures the rate at which withdrawals rise as incomes rise (the top part of the Figure shows that as incomes rise by 10 withdrawals rise by 6). If there is a fall in withdrawals, caused, for example, by a cut in income tax, then the rate of withdrawals would fall, in this case to 4 in 10. The effect would be a rise in national income from y_1 to y_2.

Figure 13.5: *A fall in withdrawals*

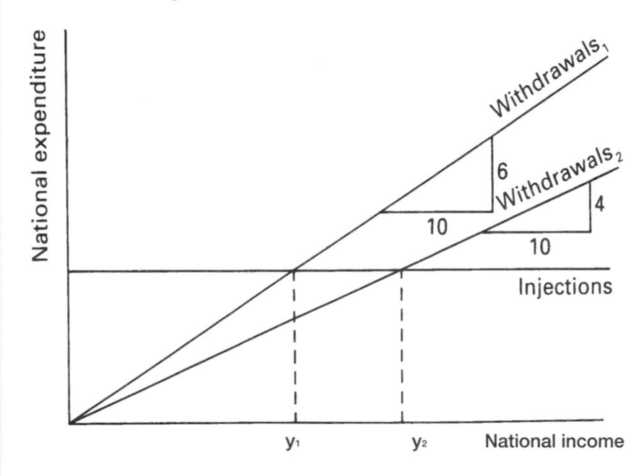

The paradox of thrift

The paradox of thrift arises because the result of people wishing to save more may lead to a fall in the level of savings. This may occur in the following way.

If people desire to save more, this will lead to a rise in the level of savings in the short run. However, in the longer run, this rise in savings means an increase in withdrawals and so a fall in incomes. Now the prime determinant of how much is saved is the level of income. A fall in incomes will cause people to save less. Hence the paradox; a desire to save more may lead to a fall in savings.

The multiplier

Look back at Figure 13.4 and compare the extent of the original rise in injections with the resulting rise in national income. It is clear that the rise in income is larger than the rise in injections. Why?

Let us begin with a simple explanation. If I were to win a million pounds on the pools and invest it by building a diamond mine in Birmingham, there would be a rise in injections of a million pounds. That is stage one.

The people who received this money – landowners, workers etc., would then spend some of the money on extra goods, such as cars, leading to a rise in national income, its size depending on the extent to which the withdrawals took money out of circulation. That is stage two.

In turn, people in the car industry would spend more money, say on furniture. Again there would be a rise in national income. The process would continue, with each successive rise in income becoming smaller because at each stage some money would be withdrawn.

This relationship between a change in injections and a resulting change in income is called **the multiplier**. It is defined as the amount by which a change in injections will lead to a multiplied change in income. We can show the effect numerically. If we assume that £6 in every £10 is consumed, then £4 will be withdrawn (because income must be either consumed or withdrawn – see the circular flow diagram to confirm this).

Original injection	£1,000,000
Extra income stage 2	£600,000 (60% of 1,000,000)
Extra income stage 3	£360,000 (60% of 600,000)
Extra income stage 4	£216,000 (60% of 360,000)
etc.	

A quicker way to calculate the full effect is to use the multiplier formula:

$$\text{The multiplier (k)} = \frac{1}{\text{MPW}}$$

where MPW is the marginal propensity to withdraw. This is the proportion of any increase in income which is withdrawn. In the example above this was 0.4, so that the multiplier was 2.5. Hence the total effect of an increase in injections of £1,000,000 would be to raise national income by £2,500,000. If more is withdrawn, then the multiplier will be smaller. If the marginal propensity to withdraw was 0.5, then the multiplier would only be 2.

The extent of any change in income can be found by using the formula:

$$\Delta \text{ Income} = \text{k} \times \Delta \text{ Injections}$$

so that if $k = 1 \div 0.5$, an increase in injections of £1,000,000 would cause incomes to rise by £2,000,000.

In the formulation of the multiplier given here, the determinant of the size of the multiplier is the marginal propensity to withdraw. In some formulations this is split up into its components of savings, taxes and imports, so that the multiplier is shown as:

$$\text{(k)} = \frac{1}{\text{MPS+MPT+MPM}}$$

where MPS = marginal propensity to save, MPT = marginal propensity to pay tax and MPM = marginal propensity to import.

Key ideas

1. Income flows from households to firms and back to households.
2. This flow is altered by injections (investment, exports and government spending) and by withdrawals (savings, imports and taxes).
3. A rise in injections will increase national income; a rise in withdrawals will lower it.
4. The paradox of thrift suggests that if people decide to save more, national income will fall, and hence the level of savings will also fall.
5. Changes in injections have a multiplied effect on income, the extent depending on the marginal propensity to withdraw.

An alternative approach

So far we have analysed the determination of national income by using an approach using injections and withdrawals. An alternative way to look at this problem is to use an approach focusing on income and expenditure.

In the last chapter, we saw that national income calculated by the output and income methods equalled that calculated by the expenditure method, and that national expenditure was composed of C + I + G + X - M (consumption + investment + government spending + exports - imports). The approach to the determination of national income discussed in this section builds on this relationship and is illustrated in Figure 13.6.

The equilibrium level of national income occurs where aggregate planned expenditure equals total output. In the Figure this is shown by a line drawn at 45°. At every point along this line, planned expenditure equals total income. E_1 shows planned expenditure. This line slopes upwards because the largest item in national expenditure – consumption – rises as income rises.

Original equilibrium is at A where planned expenditure equals national income y_1. If there is then a planned rise in some part of national expenditure, such as investment or government spending, the result is a new equilibrium at B, with national income rising to y_2. A cut in planned expenditure would have the opposite effect, leading to a fall in national income.

Figure 13.6: *The income-expenditure approach*

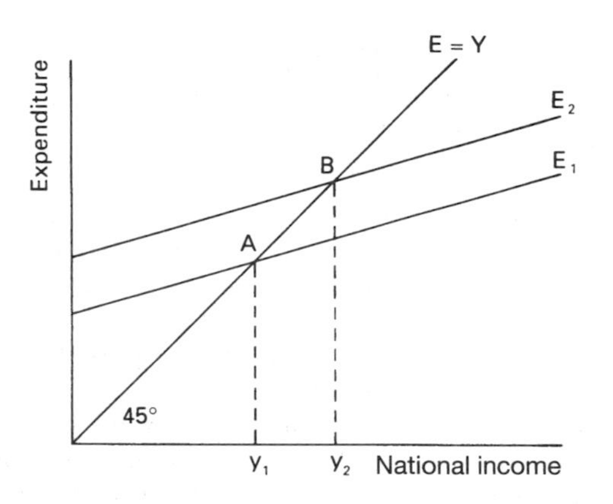

Inflationary and deflationary gaps

This model suggests that the economy can be in equilibrium at less than the full employment level of output. This has clear policy implications since it suggests that the government should intervene to change the equilibrium.

Keynes developed the model in order to reduce the level of unemployment. His ideas are developed in detail in the chapter on unemployment, but in brief he argued that the level of employment depended on the level of aggregate demand. If demand for furniture rises, then employment in this industry will also rise. If demand for cars increases, then the number of jobs in car manufacturing will also rise. By increasing aggregate demand – that is, demand for all goods and services – the government can increase the number of jobs. If the government goes too far, so that the demand for goods outstrips the economy's capacity to supply them, the result will be a rise in prices. These two possibilities are usually called deflationary and inflationary gaps (though other terms such as expansionary and output gaps are also used).

The deflationary gap is the amount by which desired aggregate expenditure is less than the level of national income needed to ensure full employment. If it is estimated that at full employment the country could produce goods to the value of £550,000 million, but the economy is only producing goods worth £500,000 million, then there is a deflationary gap of £50 million. In order to secure full employment, national expenditure would have to be increased by this amount. The position is shown in Figure 13.7 (i).

In this Figure, E shows total expenditure and yf is the full employment level of national income. However, the actual level of national income is y_1 which is less than yf; hence there is a deflationary gap which is shown as AB. This is the amount by which expenditure needs to rise in order to reach the full employment level of output. Note that the economy is in equilibrium, but not at a full employment level. The rise in expenditure needed to bring equilibrium at the full employment level can be brought about in a number of ways; for Keynesians, the most usual policy prescription would be for the government to increase its spending.

Figure 13.7: *(i) Deflationary gap*

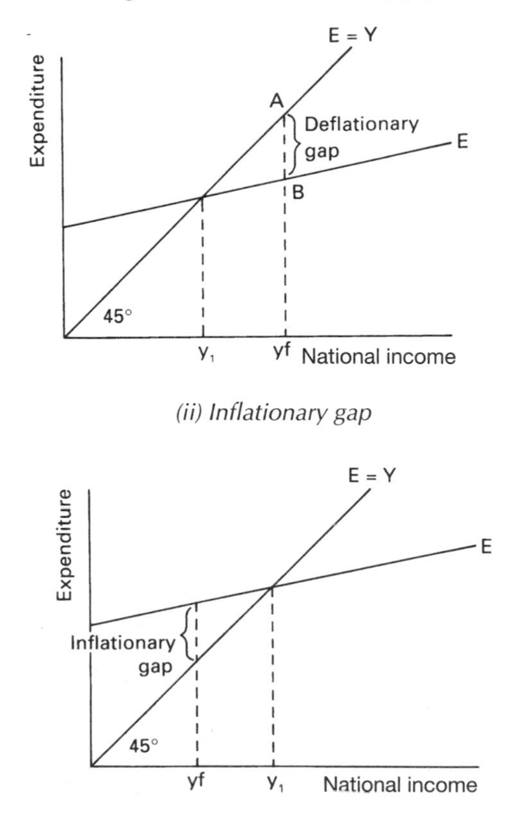

An inflationary gap exists when the equilibrium level of national income is greater than the level of output which can be produced at full employment.

Figure 13.8

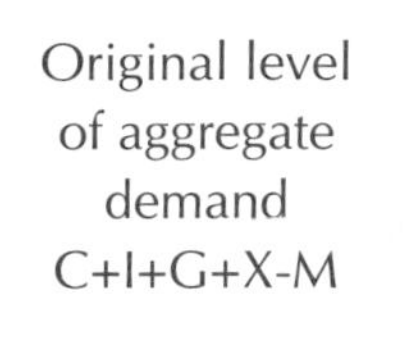

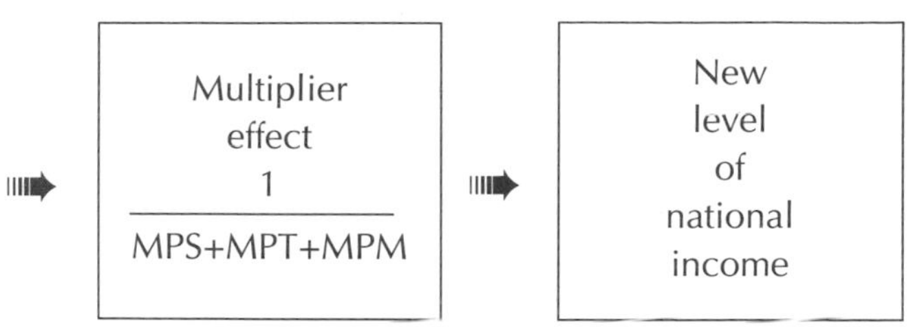

Since the demand for goods is greater than the supply, prices will rise. This is shown in Figure 13.7 (ii), where the economy is in equilibrium at y_1. However, the economy can only produce yf goods and services. Since this is less than y_1 there is an inflationary gap, AB. This is the amount by which aggregate expenditure would have to fall if there was to be equilibrium at the full employment level of output. This situation is sometimes called **demand pull inflation** because it illustrates the position when prices rise due to excess demand. This is discussed in more detail in Chapter 18.

Supply side critique of this model

This account of the determinants of national income is essentially that presented by Keynes. Supply side economists do not accept all the features of this model. In particular they reject the conclusion that the government can increase national income and employment by spending more. They suggest this would merely lead to a rise in inflation. The reasons which lie behind this conclusion are presented in detail in the next chapter.

Key ideas

1. One approach to the determination of national income is to use a model focusing on planned expenditure and income.
2. The equilibrium level of national income occurs when planned expenditure equals total output. A change in planned expenditure will lead to a change in national income.
3. A deflationary gap is one where desired aggregate expenditure is less than the full employment level of output. An inflationary gap exists when the equilibrium level of national income exceeds the full employment level of output.

The components of aggregate demand - consumption

So far in this chapter we have set up a model of how the economy as a whole operates. Now we need to flesh out the model by looking at some of the components of aggregate demand. In later chapters we will look at government spending and tax, and at imports and exports. Here we will focus on consumption and investment. Consumption is the largest item in aggregate expenditure. Therefore in order to predict future levels of expenditure we need to be able to understand what factors affect the level of consumption.

One obvious influence is the level of income. This can be deduced from Figure 13.1, which shows that income affects the level of saving. Indeed after taxes have been deducted, consumers have the choice of saving or spending their money, so we can write:

Disposable income = Consumption + Saving

This makes it clear that in this approach 'saving' can be defined as 'not spending'.

Determinants of consumption

It is quite easy to draw up a list of the factors which influence families to consume:

- Level of income. We would expect people with higher incomes to spend more than those with low incomes.
- Level of wealth. Millionaires spend more than paupers. More generally, changes in the level of wealth will cause people to adjust their spending patterns. Thus a rise in house prices may make people feel richer and induce them to spend more.

- Rate of interest. High rates of interest may encourage some people to save more and spend less. They may also discourage people from borrowing to buy durable goods. Moreover, if people are paying high interest rates on their mortgages, they will have less to spend on other goods.
- Credit terms. If it is easy to obtain credit and repayment terms are attractive, then people may borrow more to buy goods. On the other hand, if they have to make large deposits and pay back the money quickly, then less will be borrowed and spent.
- Expectations. If people expect prices to rise in the future, they may decide to buy now. Similarly, if they expect their incomes or wealth to rise in the future, they may spend more now. If you are the only relative of a 90 year old millionaire there may seem little point in saving.

The consumption function

The phrase 'consumption function' describes the relationship between what households plan to spend on consumption and all the other factors which influence this amount. In order to develop a theory, we will adopt a typical economist's practice and assume all the variables except one are constant and then see what happens when that one variable is changed. In this case the variable to be considered is income.
Figure 13.9 illustrates the relationship between planned consumption and disposable income. The 45° line shows the points at which consumption equals income – that is, where people spend all their income. At low levels of income people's spending is higher than their income – they 'dis-

Figure 13.9: *The consumption function*

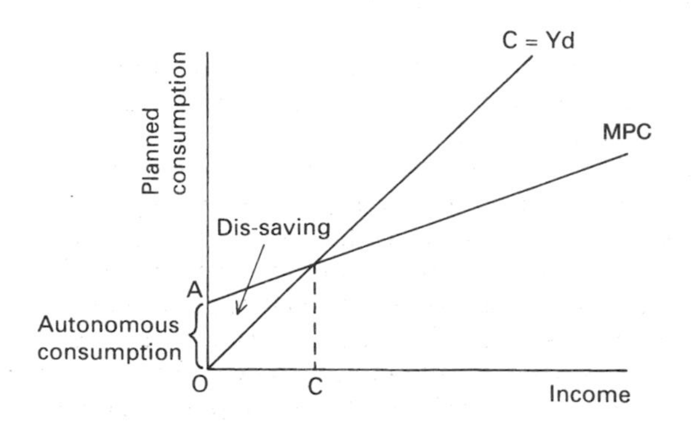

save'. Even when their income is zero, people will still spend something on consumption. In the diagram this is labelled OA and is called 'autonomous consumption'. At point C all income is spent. At higher income levels than this people save – their income is higher than their spending.

Propensities to consume

Two terms need to be understood. The **average propensity to consume** (apc) is the total spending on consumption, C, divided by total income, Y:

$$APC = \frac{C}{Y}$$

The **marginal propensity to consume** (mpc) is the change in consumption divided by the change in income:

$$MPC = \frac{\Delta C}{\Delta Y}$$

(The Greek letter Δ in this equation stands for 'change in'. For example, if income rose by £10 and consumption rose by £8, the mpc would be 0.8.)

Look back at Figure 13.9. The slope of that line shows the mpc. A steep slope would show a high mpc – consumption rising quickly with rises in income. A gentle slope shows a low mpc – a large rise in income leads to only a small rise in consumption.

Saving and consumption

Saving and consumption are tightly linked. If we ignore taxes and foreign trade, then income must be either spent on domestic goods or saved. Hence saving can be defined as 'not spending'. Consequently any rise in income must lead to a rise in either consumption or saving or in both these variables. Similarly, where mpc is the marginal propensity to consume and mps is the marginal propensity to save we can write:

$$MPC + MPS = 1$$

The Keynesian theory of the consumption function

Keynes developed a theory of the consumption function in his book *The General Theory of*

Employment, Interest and Money (1936).
He wrote:

'The fundamental psychological law, upon which we are entitled to depend with great confidence...is that men are disposed, as a rule and on the average, to increase their consumption as their income increases, but not by as much as their increase in income.'

Figure 13.10: *The Keynesian consumption function*

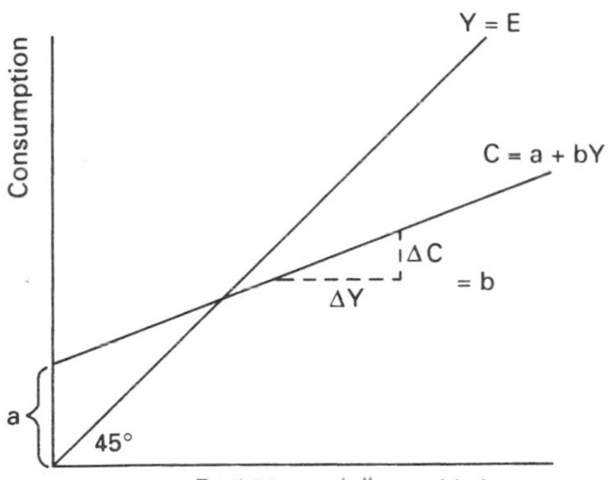

This line of argument leads to the Keynesian consumption function which is usually expressed as:

$$C = a + bY$$

where a is the autonomous consumption shown in Figure 13.10, and b is the marginal propensity to consume.

The Keynesian view is that when income rises, so does consumption, but by a smaller amount. In other words the mpc is less than one. Keynes also argued that the rich would spend more than the poor, but their consumption would be a smaller proportion of their income than that of poorer people. For example, students often spend all of their income, whilst millionaires spend much more in total, but this large total represents only a small part of their total income. Put formally, this means that the average propensity to consume falls as income rises. There is some evidence to support this argument. If data on real personal disposable income and consumption for the last thirty years are plotted on a graph the result is that shown in Figure 13.11.

As the diagram shows, autonomous expenditure is about £14 billion (at 1980 prices) and the mpc is about 0.8. This result is obtained by using time series data – that is, data generated over a long period of time. However, more detailed analysis suggested that if cross section data is used, i.e. data for different groups of people at one particular point in time, then a much flatter consumption function results. Moreover, subsequent investigation showed that Keynes' formula did not always allow accurate predictions to be made of future levels of consumption. Thus if economists entered actual data into the Keynesian consumption function, and then attempted to predict future levels of consumption, the results were not entirely satisfactory.

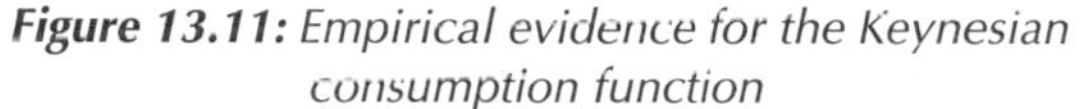

Figure 13.11: *Empirical evidence for the Keynesian consumption function*

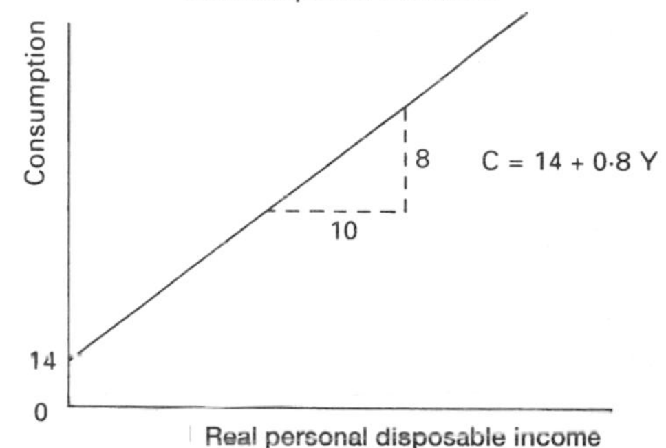

> **Key ideas - summary of the Keynesian consumption function**
>
> **1. Consumption depends on current disposable income.**
> **2. The marginal propensity to consume is positive but less than one.**
> **3. Average propensity to consume falls as income rises.**

Friedman's Permanent Income Hypothesis (PIH)

Since Keynes put forward his theory a number of refinements have been suggested and a number of alternative theories expounded. One, put forward by Milton Friedman, is called the Permanent Income Hypothesis (PIH). As its name implies, the essence of this theory is that people's spending depends less on their current income than on the basis of their long-term expectations. Current spending is determined by 'permanent income', which is what an individual expects to receive over a lifetime. Hence students may be poor, but have expectations of higher income in the future and so are willing to spend virtually all of their income. In contrast, middle-aged people will expect their incomes to fall on retirement and therefore save a relatively large part of their income. In general, this theory suggests that people's level of consumption will be fairly constant over time, since temporary fluctuations in income, such as an unexpected bonus, will not have much influence on the individual's expectations of permanent income. The theory also implies that periods of boom will have little effect on spending plans unless they last long enough to change expectations about permanent income. Friedman also suggested that the proportion of future income that is spent would depend on a number of other factors, such as the interest rate, education, age and tastes.

Its supporters claim that the PIH can explain much of the data about consumption, but one difficulty in testing the theory is that it is difficult to measure people's expectations about the future and consequently to match these with spending patterns.

Key ideas - the PIH

1. Current spending is determined by permanent income.
2. Permanent income is determined by expectations about the future.
3. Temporary fluctuations in income have little effect on current spending.

The components of aggregate demand - investment

The importance of investment

Understanding investment is important to economists for two reasons. In the first place, investment is an important part of aggregate demand, so that if we are to understand and predict aggregate demand we need to be able to predict future investment. This is difficult because the level of investment tends to fluctuate quite considerably. Secondly, the amount of investment will affect future standards of living. More investment today will tend to mean higher standards of living in the future, though the relationship is not automatic.

What is investment?

Investment can be defined as expenditure on productive physical assets, such as factories, machines and raw materials. It can be defined in gross terms, which is the total amount of money spent, or net of depreciation of assets which have become obsolete or worn out. Investment can also be divided into various categories. 'Fixed capital formation' is concerned with expenditure on fixed assets (which includes vehicles!) whereas the other prime component of investment is inventories or stocks of goods. Whatever the category, investment usually involves giving up present consumption in order to produce more in the future. Investment is undertaken by different groups of people as Table 13.1 shows. The relative importance of each sector varies over time. One reason for this is political; the number of public corporations has fallen in recent years because of privatisation and consequently the level of investment undertaken in this sector has also fallen.

Alternative explanations

Because investment is so diverse, both in its type and in its origins, it is not surprising that no one theory gives a fully satisfactory explanation. In this section we will consider what determines the level of fixed capital formation.

The acclerator

This suggests that the **level** of investment depends on the **rate of change** in the level of GDP. In other words, an increase in GDP from £100 billion to £105 billion will lead to a rise in investment, but if GDP stays at this high level no new investment will be undertaken.

A simplified example will clarify the idea. Assume consumers usually buy 20,000 radios a year. These radios are produced on ten machines, each of which produces 2,000 radios a year. Each machine lasts ten years so that the producers replace one machine each year. In this case gross investment is one machine, net investment is zero.

What will happen if GDP rises by 10 per cent and spending on radios also rises by 10 per cent?

Table 13.1: *Gross domestic fixed capital formation (£ million, 1990 prices)*

	Private Sector	General government	Public corporations	Total
1985	65,820	8,441	7,277	81,575
1986	67,877	9,163	6,645	83,685
1987	78,013	9,027	5,220	92,260
1988	92,043	7,579	5,104	104,726
1989	94,778	10,054	5,671	110,503
1990	89,162	12,659	4,955	106,776
1991	79,697	12,688	3,880	96,265
1992	76,530	13,760	4,424	94,714
1993	76,976	13,504	4,972	95,452

Note: Due to rounding, totals do not always add up to the sum of the parts.

Source: Adapted from *Economic Trends*, HMSO, March 1989.

Consumers will wish to buy 22,000 radios. In order to produce this quantity, producers will need to buy two new machines; one to replace the worn out machine and one to satisfy the extra demand. In this hypothetical example, a 10 per cent rise in GDP has led to a 100 per cent rise in investment in machines. However, if GDP – and demand for radios – remains constant at the new higher level, then only one new machine is needed in the next year to replace the machine which will have worn out. This means a fall in investment from two machines to one, despite the fact that GDP remains at a high level.

The accelerator principle can be expressed as:

$$\text{Net } I_t = v(Y_{t2} - Y_{t1})$$

Where I_t is investment in year t, $Y_{t2} - Y_{t1}$ is the change in income or GDP between one year and the next and v in the equation is the accelerator coefficient, or 'capital-output ratio'. This is the relationship between the amount of capital in the economy and the quantity of goods that this produces. If £6 of capital was needed to produce £1 of goods, then the capital-output ratio would be 6. This means that if GDP rises by £10 million, then £60 million of new investment will be needed to satisfy this rise.

Complications and criticisms

The outline of the accelerator principle so far given would account for large fluctuations in the level of investment, but it is too simplistic. In the first place there may be excess capacity in the economy so that firms can produce extra output without buying any more machines. Secondly, the capital-output ratio will vary over time. One reason for this is that **expectations** vary. Sometimes entrepreneurs will be confident and buy new machines even though they have some spare capacity. At other times they will be cautious and not invest, even though demand for their product is rising.

Finally, firms may be unable to invest even if they want to, because companies making capital goods may be unable to increase output as they are already working at full capacity.

One complication which this account has so far ignored is that there are time lags in the process; firms do not adjust their investment plans immediately. This makes the theory difficult to test because different lags may give different results. Research does give some support to the theory and the accelerator principle is used to predict the level of investment in many economic models, but it cannot give a full explanation of changes in the level of investment.

The rate of interest

It seems plausible to suggest that the rate of interest will affect the level of investment. If a firm expects an investment to give a return of 10 per cent but it has to borrow the money at 11 per cent, it will not go ahead. If it could borrow the money at 5 per cent, the firm would undertake the investment. Figure 13.12 shows the demand for investment as a typical demand schedule, sloping down to show an increase in the demand for investment as the price (in this case the rate of interest) falls.

Unfortunately the common sense implicit in this line of argument is not given much support by the evidence. Almost every investigation shows there is little relationship between the rate of interest and the level of investment. One reason is that the other factors discussed here are more important. Another is that small changes in the rate of interest will not have much effect if the firm believes the investment will be very profitable or that it will pay off very quickly. Hence the evidence suggests that the demand for investment schedule shown in Figure 13.12 is very inelastic.

Figure 13.12: *An investment demand schedule*

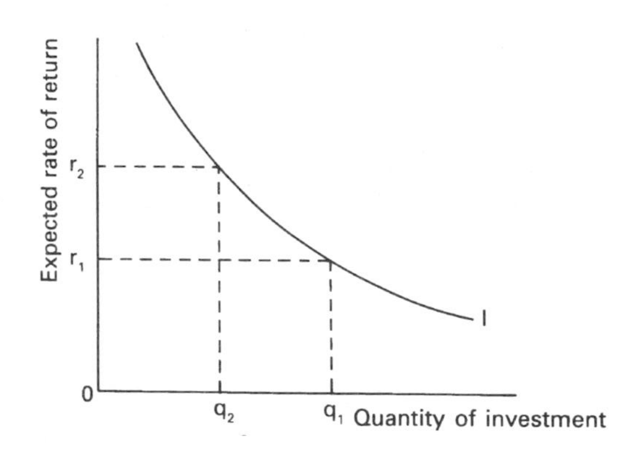

Profitability

Firms invest in order to make profits. Hence we should expect the level of investment to be linked to the level of profits. Moreover, when profits rise entrepreneurs may become more optimistic and so be more inclined to increase investment. Another reason is that firms making high levels of profit can use some of their profit to finance investment, and they also find it easier to borrow money. Research evidence does suggest a link between profits and investment. For example, profitability and the level of investment have both been lower in the UK than in competing nations. However, this link does not take us much further in the job of constructing a full theory of investment, because if we adopt this approach we then need to construct a theory of profits. There is no generally accepted theory of profits, but one influence is the level of incomes; as incomes rise so do profits.

Other influences on investment

New discoveries affect investment. Historically, the invention of the railway and the car led to a huge amount of investment. More recently, the discovery of oil in the North Sea caused some firms to spend large sums of money on new investment. The availability of finance may also affect the decision to invest. If firms find it easy to obtain money from financial institutions they will be more likely to invest. Small businesses often complain that it is difficult to obtain long-term finance, but this is disputed by the banks and by some independent commentators. In any case the availability of finance does not vary much from year to year, yet the level of investment does fluctuate. Hence it appears that while this may influence the total amount of investment it does not explain the fluctuations.

Government policy also affects investment in a number of ways. If entrepreneurs approve government actions they will become more optimistic and invest more. Governments can also influence some of the variables, for example, by making finance available to small firms, or by bringing down the rate of interest. Finally, much investment is undertaken either directly by government – roads are a good example – or indirectly by public corporations, such as the Post Office. In this case commercial considerations, such as profitability, will influence the decision to invest, but government intervention can force nationalised industries to invest more than they would wish. Similarly, government can constrain investment in these public sector industries. Finally, an entrepreneur's decision to invest will depend on the methods used to analyse possible projects. These were discussed in Chapter 10.

Key ideas - the factors influencing investment

1. The accelerator principle suggests that investment is largely determined by changes in the level of national income.
2. High rates of interest may deter investment; low rates encourage it.
3. Expectations, for example about future profitability, will also have an effect.
4. Other factors, such as the availability of finance and government policy, influence the level of investment.
5. There is no completely satisfactory theory of investment.

Investment and GDP

The complex relationship between investment and GDP is illustrated in Figure 13.13. A simplistic explanation of the relationship might suggest that the countries which invest most would have the fastest growth in GDP. The figure suggests that there is a positive relationship between these variables, but that the relationship is complex.

There are several reasons for this. One is that some countries may make more efficient investments than others; for example, in one country a given investment may give rise to a high increase in GDP whereas in another country investments may be badly chosen, or may not give much benefit because of other factors such as poor management or labour relations. Moreover, the Figure may be misleading because there is data for only five countries and for a dozen years; a bigger selection of countries or different time periods may give different results. Despite these limitations, economists would argue that countries which would like high rates of economic growth should invest a high proportion of their GDP.

Figure 13.13: *% change in investment and GDP, 1979-1991*

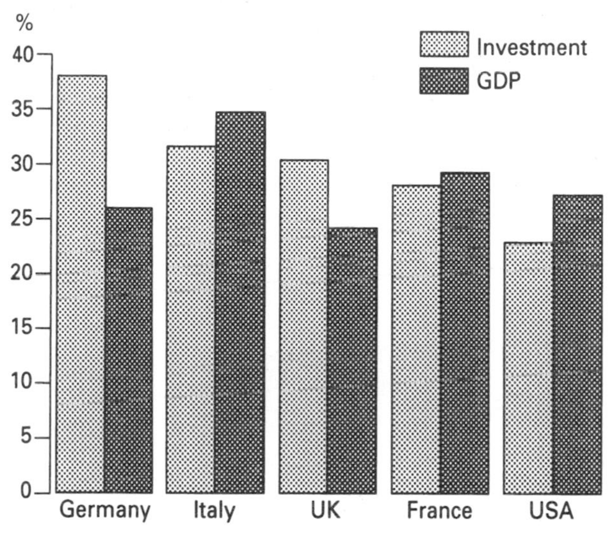

Source: Adapted from *Economic Survey of Europe 1991/92*, U.N., 1992.

Conclusion

This chapter began by attempting to explain the Keynesian theory of the determinants of national income. This was approached in several ways. The circular flow of income with various injections and withdrawals provided a simplified way. This was then developed more formally.

Two of the variables were then analysed in more detail – consumption and investment. In both cases a number of explanations were analysed, none of which could give a complete explanation of such complex phenomena.

The Keynesian theory of national income focuses on aggregate demand. As the introduction pointed out, supply siders criticise this approach and instead emphasise aggregate supply, the subject of the next chapter.

Data questions

Treasury model

In the Treasury model, for example, a one per cent increase in manufacturing output results in a 2 per cent increase in investment five quarters later; for private non-manufacturing, the figure is 4.5 per cent. Another important determination of investment is the cost of capital relative to the return on capital. This depends on the relationship between the price of capital goods and the price of industrial equities, together with the rate of interest and the cost of labour compared with that of capital. In this analysis, we concentrate on the effect of output on investment.

This link could be termed a decelerator as much as an accelerator, since the falls in both investment and output, particularly in manufacturing, have been bigger than the rises, notably between 1979 and 1982. The changes in investment have averaged about 2.5 times the changes in output in manufacturing since 1970, measuring between peaks and troughs in the business cycle. Between 1972 and 1979, the usual time lag was six months. In the case of the two-year decline in manufacturing output from the middle of 1979, the fall in investment began at about the same time, but lasted for four years, until the first quarter of 1983.

Source: *Lloyds Bank Review*. January, 1984.

Question 1

1. (i) Describe how changes in output affect investment.

(ii) Why are there time lags in the process?

2. What factors other than output influence the level of investment?

3. What effect will these changes in the level of investment have on national income?

Personal disposable income and consumption

(£ million, 1985 prices)

Year	Personal disposable income	Consumption
1971	171,321	161,582
1972	188,992	171,704
1973	201,020	180,843
1974	199,433	178,216
1975	200,419	177,500
1976	199,699	178,279
1977	195,333	177,483
1978	210,313	187,510
1979	222,300	195,664
1980	225,882	195,825
1981	224,147	196,011
1982	223,044	197,980
1983	228,950	206,932
1984	236,931	210,959
1985	244,818	218,947
1986	254,849	232,996
1987	263,807	245,823
1988	279,686	264,096
1989	292,350	272,917
1990	299,598	274,744
1991	297,419	269,033
1992	304,419	361,446

Source: *Economic Trends,* HMSO, 1993.

Question 2

1. Comment on the relationship between disposable income and consumer spending.
2. What factors other than income might explain the level of consumer spending?
3. Critically discuss any of the theories of the consumption function. Use the figures to illustrate your argument.

14 Aggregate Demand and Aggregate Supply

Until recently interventionist economists have focused largely on the demand side of the economy.

- Hence a typical Keynesian policy for unemployment would be to increase aggregate demand for goods in the belief that this would encourage employers to produce more and take on more workers.
- Supply siders argue that this is a mistaken belief. They emphasise supply and they argue that governments should take measures such as cutting taxes in order to give individuals incentives to produce more. Thus they take what is essentially a micro-economic approach to macro-economics. The argument between these two lines of thought is fundamental to macro-economic policy.

Aggregate demand and aggregate supply

In micro-economics, prices and the level of output of firms are determined by the interaction of the forces of demand and supply. In macro-economics, the interaction of aggregate demand and the aggregate supply determines the level of prices in the economy as a whole and also the level of real national output.

The aggregate demand and supply model (AD/AS for short) presented here has the same basic framework as the large computer models of the economy which are used to predict future economic variables and hence to influence economic policy decisions. The AS/AD model focuses on the short and medium term and assumes a given amount of capital equipment and technical knowledge. Hence it is particularly useful for analysing problems such as inflation, unemployment and the balance of payments, all of which require short and medium-term management of the economy. It is less useful in analysing longer-term problems, such as economic growth.

Aggregate demand

Aggregate demand is the amount of money which people wish to spend in the **domestic** economy. This may not be the same as they actually spend. If aggregate demand exceeds actual national expenditure, then some people will be unsatisfied; they cannot buy the goods they want. If the opposite position applies, so that aggregate demand is less than national expenditure, then some firms end up with unsold goods. This unintended rise in stocks counts as part of national expenditure so far as the national income accounts are concerned.

Because aggregate demand is concerned with domestic expenditure, it includes exports but excludes imports. Aggregate demand can be subdivided into various components: consumption, investment, government expenditure and exports minus imports. That is:

$$AD = C+I+G+X-M$$

Since aggregate demand is the sum of all the individual demand curves in the economy, it slopes down to the right, just like the demand curves used in micro-economics. Thus the aggregate demand curve shows the relationship between the price level and the aggregate quantity of goods and services that are demanded.

Like the demand curve at the micro level, several factors will cause the aggregate demand curve to shift. It will shift to the right when there is an increase in the components of aggregate demand (C,I,G or X) or a fall in M. This can be brought about by several factors such as a cut in taxation, an increase in government spending, cuts in interest rates, or increased optimism causing firms to invest more.

Aggregate supply

The last chapter was largely concerned with the analysis of aggregate demand, and so here we will focus more on the supply side of the economy. The aggregate supply schedule shows the quantity of output which firms wish to supply at each price level. Since the aggregate supply curve is the sum of all the individual supply curves in the economy, it is often drawn rising up to the right, just as individual supply curves are conventionally drawn. However, the actual shape of the aggregate supply curve is a matter of considerable disagreement.

Figure 14.1: *A perfectly elastic aggregate supply curve*

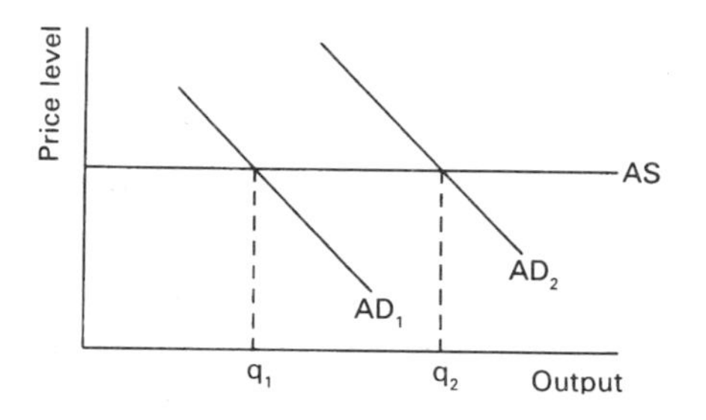

The aggregate supply schedule will be perfectly horizontal as shown in Figure 14.1 if the average costs of firms are constant as output expands. If firms increase output by 10 per cent and total costs rise by 10 per cent, so that unit costs remain the same, then this is the shape of the AS curve. This could occur when firms have excess capacity. In this case, an increase in aggregate demand will lead to an increase in output, not prices. Figure 14.2 shows the opposite extreme. Here total output cannot be increased because the physical capacity to produce more does not exist. Whatever price is offered, firms will not produce more goods. This may be the case when the economy is at full employment. An increase in aggregate demand in this case will only lead to a rise in price and not output.

The actual shape of the curve will depend on two factors:

- The nature of the production function. This is the technical relationship between output and the factors of production. The production function will determine the productivity of labour in the short run. This is because the quantity of capital and state of technology are fixed in this period.
- The behaviour of wages as output changes in the short run. If, to produce 5 per cent more output, firms are forced to pay 20 per cent more in wages, then the supply curve will slope steeply upwards because firms will only be willing to increase output if they can put up prices to cover their higher costs. On the other hand, if firms can increase output without any rise in average costs, then they may be willing to increase output without putting up prices. In this case, the AS curve will be horizontal. Hence the behaviour of the labour market is a crucial determinant of the shape of the AS curve.

Figure 14.1: *A perfectly inelastic aggregate supply curve*

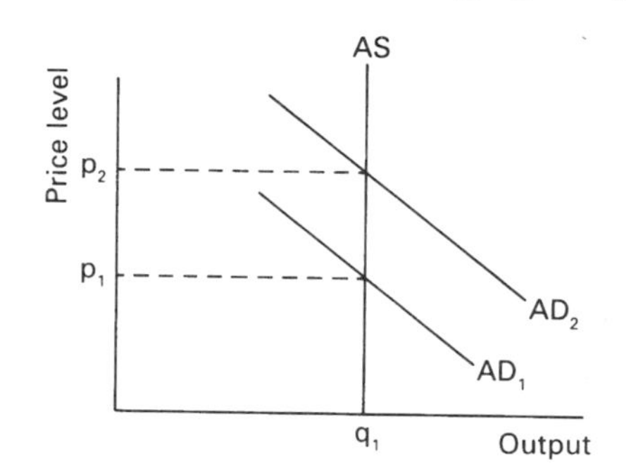

Shifts in the AS curve

If input prices can change in the time period being analysed, then a rise in the price of wages or other inputs will lead to a fall in aggregate supply. This will cause the AS curve to shift to the left, showing that less will be supplied at any given level of prices, or that higher prices would be charged at a given level of output. The same result would occur if workers chose more leisure instead of work. According to some economists this would occur if there was a rise in taxes since this would encourage workers to believe that it was no longer worthwhile to work, or else it would encourage them to work shorter hours.

When these changes are substantial they are called **supply side shocks**. The best example of this is the rise in oil prices in 1973/74 when the price of oil doubled and then doubled again. The result is shown in Figure 14.3. The AS curve moved to the left so that at every level of AD prices were higher and output lower. The reason the curve moved was that firms' costs had risen, so that it was no longer profitable to produce goods at the prevailing price; that is, the supply curves of many firms moved to the left.

The aggregate supply curve sometimes moves to the right, for example, if it becomes more acceptable for women to work or there is a rise in the population of working age. A rise in the stock of capital has the same effect. In both cases the AS curve moves to the right, causing output to rise and prices to fall. Unfortunately changes such as these tend to be long-term and not easy for the government to influence directly, though supply siders believe that lower taxes will encourage more people to choose work and also encourage entrepreneurs to invest. The aggregate supply curve also moved to the right as a result of the fall in raw material prices in the early 1980s.

***Figure 14.3:** A supply side shock*

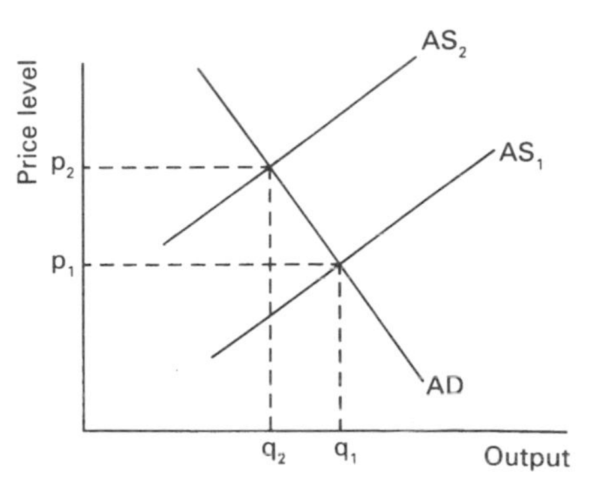

Key ideas

1. **The aggregate demand curve shows the amount of money which people wish to spend in the domestic economy. It is usually expressed in the formula:**

AD = C+I+G+X-M

2. **The aggregate supply curve shows the quantity of goods which firms wish to supply at each price level.**
3. **The shape of the aggregate supply curve depends on the production function and on the behaviour of wages as output changes.**
4. **The aggregate supply curve will shift to the right when the supply of labour increases or there is a cut in raw material prices. It will move to the left if input prices rise.**

The Keynesian approach

There are two Keynesian approaches to the shape of the AS curve. The first is shown in Figure 14.4. This was developed by followers of Keynes in order to illustrate his ideas. When the AS curve is this shape, the AD curve is the major determinant of economic events. The government can increase aggregate demand and the result will be a rise in output without any rise in prices until the full employment level of output is reached at yf. Then any increase in aggregate demand will lead to a rise in prices as shown by AD_3.

***Figure 14.4:** The Keynesian long-run aggregate supply curve (version 1)*

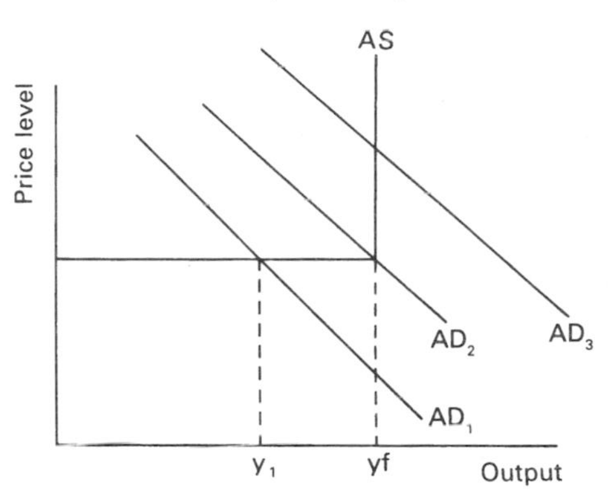

Two assumptions need to be satisfied for the AS curve to be this shape. The first is that the level of money wages must not rise as output rises. This is unlikely to be true; in some cases firms will have to pay overtime rates in order to produce more goods. The second assumption is that firms' marginal product of labour is constant until the full employment level of output is reached. The law of diminishing returns would suggest that this assumption is also untrue since, if more labour is employed, its marginal product will fall if the quantity of capital is held constant, as it is in the short run. Arguments such as these led Keynesian economists to return to the AS curve, which is closer to the original Keynesian formulation. This is shown in Figure 14.5.

This version accepts that the marginal product of labour falls as the level of employment rises and that the demand for labour by firms will fall as real wages rise. However, Keynes argued that although workers would be unwilling to work for a lower **money** wage they would be willing to work for a lower **real** wage than that which currently exists. Thus if money wages do not change when prices rise, some unemployed people will be willing to take jobs and firms will be able to take on more workers at existing wage rates. The same argument applies if money wages rise, but prices rise faster so that the real wage falls – firms will be able to recruit more workers.

This line of argument is shown in Figure 14.5. If the government increases its spending so that aggregate demand rises from AD_1 to AD_2 real output will rise from y_1 to y_2, but there is also a small rise in prices. If there is a further rise in aggregate demand to AD_3, the rise in output is less

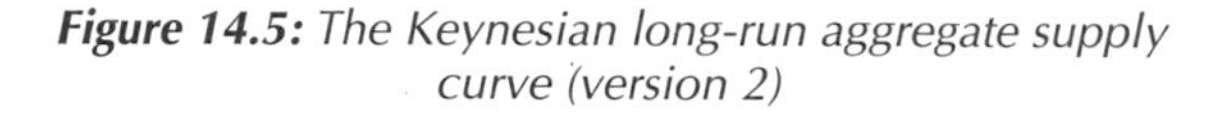

Figure 14.5: *The Keynesian long-run aggregate supply curve (version 2)*

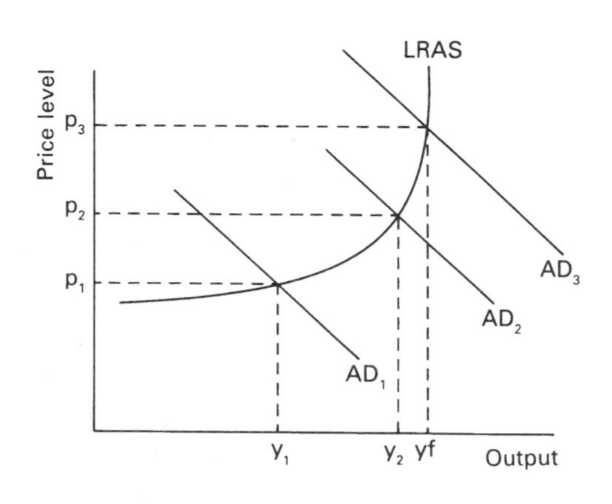

and the rise in prices is greater. Any attempt to increase aggregate demand beyond the full employment level yf will just lead to a rise in prices with no increase in output.

The fundamental belief behind this argument is that some firms can increase output without putting up wages and hence prices; that there are unemployed people who are willing to work at existing or lower wage rates. If this belief is true, then the government can increase its spending in order to push up aggregate demand and this will lead to rises in output and employment. Note, however, that as the economy approaches full employment any given rise in output is accompanied by a proportionally larger rise in prices. In other words, there is a trade-off between output and employment, and the terms of this trade-off worsen as full employment is reached. When full employment is reached, any increase in aggregate demand will lead to a rise in prices without any compensating increase in output.

Behind this discussion lies a key idea. Keynesians argue that markets do not necessarily clear to give full employment. In particular they believe that labour markets are imperfect, so that workers do not rush into and out of the labour market every time there is a change in real wages. Moreover, they argue that in areas of high unemployment, employers can take on more workers at existing wages and so increase output without putting up prices. Therefore there is still room for government to increase aggregate demand in order to achieve full employment.

Key ideas - the Keynesian approach

1. Some unemployed people will be willing to work at existing or lower real wage rates.
2. As a consequence some firms will be able to expand output without putting up wages and prices.
3. The closer the economy moves to full employment, the more firms will have to put up wages to attract more labour and hence prices will rise.
4. The government can expand the economy by increasing aggregate demand. This will lead to a rise in output – and in prices – until the full employment level of output is reached.

Keynesian policies

These are discussed extensively in the chapter on unemployment and need only be outlined here. In essence Keynesian economists suggest that markets do not always solve the problem of allocating resources in a satisfactory way, and that this is particularly true of the labour market. Hence when there is unemployment, the government should intervene to increase national output and employment by increasing aggregate demand. The most convenient way to do this is for the government to increase its own spending.

The supply side approach

At the heart of the supply side approach is the belief that individuals and firms respond to incentives. Lower taxes will stimulate people to work longer and harder, and to be more innovative. Similarly, higher real wages will cause more people to want to work, but will also cause firms to reduce demand for labour. Because of these incentives, the demand for labour will equal the supply, and the labour markets will clear.

Supply siders dismiss the Keynesian arguments and argue that the AS curve is unstable because workers will not accept a cut in their real wages when prices rise. If they cannot push up real wages they will choose to leave the labour market. They

Figure 14.6

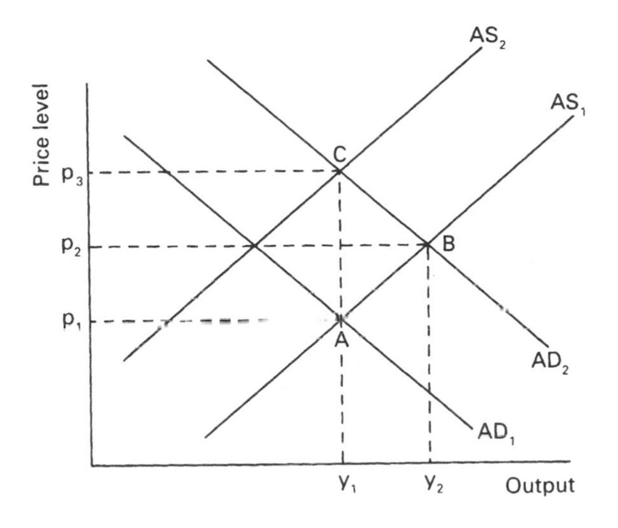

claim that the Keynesian arguments only apply in the short run because markets clear very quickly, and that the short run is so short that they can be disregarded.

The supply side approach is shown in Figure 14.6. This assumes that the supply of labour is positively related to the level of real wages. If prices rise workers will force up money wages until the original level of real wages is restored. Since there is no change in the level of real wages, there will be no change in the demand or the supply of labour. Original equilibrium is at A where AD_1 meets AS_1, the price level is p_1 and output y_1. If the government then increases aggregate demand to AD_2, the short run effect will be a move along the AS_1 curve to B giving a rise in prices to p_2 and a rise in output to y_2.

However, supply siders believe this is only temporary. The rise in prices means that real wages have fallen. Workers do not accept this cut in real wages and force up money wages to their equilibrium level. This rise in real wages cuts firms' demand for labour so that the AS curve shifts to the left leading to a final equilibrium at C, where output is at the original level y_1, but prices are higher at p_3. The government's attempt to stimulate the economy has only resulted in higher prices; output is unchanged in the long run.

(Note that in the Figure the vertical distance between AS_1 and AS_2 is the rise in the money wage rate. This equals the rise in prices p_3 - p_1 showing that the real wage rate is unchanged.)

If this supply side argument is correct it means that the long-run aggregate supply curve is vertical – AC in Figure 14.6. Figure 14.7 reproduces this

Figure 14.7: *Long-run aggregate supply curve*

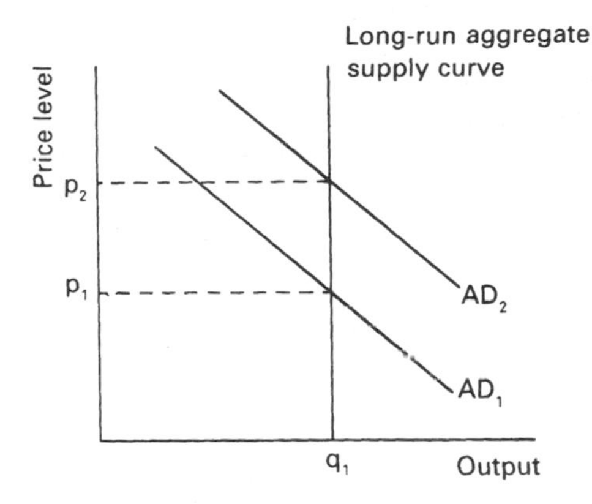

vertical long-run AS curve and shows that the implication of this shape is that demand management policies have no part to play in the management of the economy. Any attempt to increase aggregate demand only results in a rise in price; output is unchanged. This is because output will always be at the full employment level if labour markets are allowed to clear. In this view the level of real national output depends not on aggregate demand, but on supply side factors such as changes in technology, the size of the capital stock and the supply and productivity of labour.

A key point in this approach is 'How long is the long run?'. If it is several years, for example, because wages are slow to respond to changing circumstances or because workers do not respond quickly to changes in real wages, then the move from A to B in Figure 14.6 may lead to a real rise in output which continues for some time. However, if adjustment is swift then this rise may be over before people realise that it has even happened. Supply siders tend to believe that the adjustment is quick because of 'rational expectations'.

Rational expectations

The emphasis on rational expectations in economics rests on two assumptions:

- People are well informed and use all available information so they are as knowledgeable as the government. This means the government cannot fool the people; workers realise that when prices rise their real wage falls and so modify their behaviour, for example, by demanding higher wages or by leaving the labour market.
- That the labour market is very flexible so that demand and supply are in equilibrium in all markets. This means markets clear at all times.

If these assumptions are true, then workers will anticipate the effects of government policy and the labour market will adjust so quickly that any attempt to increase aggregate demand will lead to an almost immediate rise in wages and spending. There will be a move directly up the long-run supply curve without any temporary increase in output. However, these underlying assumptions have been criticised. Many people have little knowledge of economic facts and relationships so that they are unable to predict the results of government action.

The second assumption is also criticised on the grounds that the labour market is slow to react. Once people are in a job they often find it difficult to move to another and are reluctant to leave the labour market even if their wages fall behind the rise in prices. Moreover, shortages of particular skills continue for long periods. For several decades people have said that there is a shortage of physicists in general and of physics teachers in particular, yet the shortage persists. If the labour market adjusted quickly, then wages for physicists would rise quickly, thousands would train to be physicists, and the shortage would disappear. Hence it is argued that the labour market is very slow to adjust. If these criticisms are accepted, then the AS curve is not vertical and there is a place for demand management in running the economy.

Key ideas - summary of the supply side approach

1. Markets are generally the best way to allocate resources and government intervention should be undertaken only in special circumstances.
2. The market is the best way to allocate resources in the labour market. Demand and supply of labour adjust quickly to allocate resources. One reason for this is that people have rational expectations.
3. The long-run AS curve is vertical and, because the labour market clears rapidly, the short-run AS curve hardly exists.
4. Attempts to increase output and employment by raising aggregate demand will only lead to rises in price; output will be unchanged since the labour market will be at full employment if markets are left to clear.

Supply side policies

According to this group of economists, real national output will only be increased when the AS curve moves to the right. Hence policies should be adopted which will encourage such shifts. These policies include tax cuts which will encourage people to enter the labour market. Tax cuts will also provide an incentive for entrepreneurs to innovate and invest in new machinery. Supply siders also favour measures to weaken trade union power, since unions distort the labour market and push up wages. Cuts in some social security benefits will also help to keep down wages, since loss of benefit will force workers to accept jobs at low rates of pay.

Other measures favoured by this group of economists are those which would reduce the extent of government intervention in the economy, such as the privatisation of publicly-owned industries. They also advocate measures in industry and education which would encourage a spirit of enterprise and an increase in investment.

The recession of the early 1990s

At the heart of the Keynesian approach is the belief that recessions are caused by falls in aggregate demand (and that therefore government can mitigate recession by increasing its own spending). In the early 1990s there was a quite severe recession in the UK. Between 1990 and 1992 GDP fell by about three per cent and unemployment nearly doubled from just over one and a half million to three million. Was this caused by a fall in aggregate demand?

Table 14.1: *Consumption and investment in the recession (£million, constant 1985 prices)*

	1990	1992
Consumption	274,744	269,347
Investment	80,464	72,125

Source: Adapted from *UK National Accounts*, 1993.

Table 14.1 focuses on two components of aggregate demand, consumption and investment. It appears to give support to the Keynesian argument, since there was a substantial fall in these two components of aggregate demand, and these would have a magnified effect on GDP because of the multiplier process. Supply siders would accept that there was a fall in these components of aggregate demand, but would argue that instead of the government trying to compensate by increasing its own spending, it should cut interest rates and ease the tight monetary policy which was operating at that time.

Conclusion

Economists' approach to macro-economics often reflects their personal value systems rather than the application of accepted 'proofs'. One reason for this is that the economy is not a laboratory in which one variable can be examined whilst all others are held constant. Hence it is extremely difficult to judge the claims of competing theories. Moreover, an entire economy is too complex for any theory to explain in full and evidence can always be found to support or to criticise a theory.

In essence, Keynesian economists believe there is a greater place for government intervention than do supply siders. They believe that, left to itself, the economy will often be in equilibrium at less than full employment. Government intervention, for example by increasing aggregate demand, can raise the equilibrium level of output and employment, though this may lead to a rise in prices.

This approach is criticised by neo-classical supply siders who argue that the labour market adjusts quickly. If this is so, any attempt by the government to increase aggregate demand will merely lead to a rise in prices with no effect on output. Instead the government should focus its efforts on improving the supply side of the economy.

This chapter has so far given the impression that theses two schools of thought are completely opposed. There is some truth in this impression, but in recent years some Keynesian economists, while maintaining their belief in aggregate demand as a policy variable, have given increasing support to measures which would improve the supply side of the economy. For example, they advocate an extension of education and training to make workers more efficient.

Data questions

The end of government?

I start my call to rebellion from the observed tendency for government to dispose of a growing slice of the community's resources. Precise figuring to several decimal places is hardly necessary. In broad orders of magnitude the total governmental sector has grown in most Western democracies since the war from around 25-35 per cent to nearer 45-55 per cent of national income, and commonly employs between a quarter and a third of the labour force. (These measures do not include the ever increasing 'compliance costs' which government regulation throws on private individuals, families, companies and trade associations.) The obverse is seen in the contraction of the market sector which provides the goods and services consumers are prepared to pay for and so feeds, clothes and shelters the quarter or third of non-producing consumers in what I would prefer to call the 'parasitic' rather than the 'public' sector. (A shrewd wit has said that the private sector is the part of the economy controlled by government and the public sector is the part controlled by nobody!)

Source: Harris, R., *The End of Government?*, Institute of Economic Affairs, 1980.

Question 1

1. Outline the economic theory which lies behind the 'call to rebellion'.
2. What criticisms would Keynesian economists make of this argument?

Britain's economic recovery

Mrs Thatcher's conservative government, which came to power in 1979, was determined to make a complete break with the past in the management of the British economy.

The new strategy effectively abandoned Keynesian short run demand management aimed at full or high employment. Instead, emphasis was placed on improving the long run supply side performance of the economy. Deregulation, the abandonment of control over prices, incomes and capital movements, the return of state owned industries to private ownership and reduction in the power of trade unions were all seen to be necessary. An urgent necessity was to reduce inflation since without price stability the supply side performance of the economy could not be improved. In brief, the new approach seemed to represent a return to classical economics prior to Keynes.

Source: Adapted from Maynard, G., 'Britain's economic recovery', *Economics,* Vol xxv Part 3, Autumn 1989.

Question 2

1. Explain what is meant by 'Keynesian short run demand management'.
2. What effect might the new measures have had on the aggregate supply curve if they had been successful?
3. Why might the policies indicated in the article have been seen as a return to 'classical economics'?

15 Taxation and Public Spending

Governments – and therefore government spending and taxes – are inevitable. However, there is considerable argument between economists about the most desirable level of taxation and government spending.

- Supply siders believe that the role of government should be reduced. They also argue that high levels of taxation discourage work and initiative.
- The opposite point of view is interventionist, often Keynesian. These economists argue that government spending is needed to correct market failure, that high levels of taxation usually do not discourage effort, and that government spending and taxation should be used to redistribute resources from rich to poor.

Fiscal policy is the use of taxation and government spending to influence the level and composition of output, and we will consider each of these in turn before examining how the above perspectives approach fiscal policy.

Taxation

What is a good tax?

One approach to the study of taxation is to consider the characteristics of a good tax. A cynical approach would be to suggest that a good tax is one paid by someone else; that is why total abstainers favour huge taxes on alcohol, non-smokers press for higher taxes on tobacco and the poor shed no tears about taxes on the rich. However, there are certain characteristics to be found in a 'good' tax and many of these were listed by Adam Smith, who suggested four **canons** of taxation:

- The amount of tax should be linked to people's ability to pay.
- The payment of taxes should be clear and certain, both to the taxpayer and the tax collector (so that everyone knows how much is due).
- The way in which taxes are collected should be convenient to the taxpayer.
- The cost of collecting a tax should be small in relation to the amount of money collected.

These canons still apply today. A tax on beards would be a poor tax; it would not be linked to ability to pay and it would be difficult to calculate how much was due. If the beard grew would more tax be payable? Would someone who had forgotten to shave be liable for tax?

However, these original canons need to be augmented by others which are applicable to a modern society:

- The tax collector should be able to assess fairly accurately how much money will be received from the tax.
- Taxes should promote economic efficiency, or at least not significantly worsen the efficient allocation of resources. Thus a tax on pollution may improve the allocation of resources because it would reduce the production of goods with negative externalities (that is, those goods that adversely affect people not directly involved in their production or consumption).
- Taxes should increase equity (fairness); although, of course, it is possible to argue about precisely what is meant by 'equity'.
- Taxes should promote desirable economic goals such as full employment.

Unfortunately no tax has yet been discovered that fulfils all these criteria. Consequently the tax authorities have to consider the **relative** advantages and disadvantages of particular taxes.

Direct or indirect taxes?

A traditional way to classify taxes depends on whether they are paid directly, such as income tax or corporation tax, or indirectly like VAT. Supply siders, who dislike income tax, argue that direct taxes such as this are less desirable than indirect taxes and that the government should shift the burden of taxation away from direct towards indirect taxes. They claim that these have fewer disincentive effects and that to some extent individuals can largely avoid paying such taxes if they choose not to buy highly taxed goods. It was this kind of argument which led the 1979 Conservative government to cut income tax and to raise VAT from 8 per cent to 15 per cent instead. Economists who would like a more equal society tend to see greater merit in direct taxes because they usually take more from the rich than the poor. These arguments are part of the debate about the progressiveness of a tax system.

Progressive, proportional or regressive taxes?

An alternative way of considering taxes is to focus exclusively on their equity aspects – how they affect rich and poor.

There are three possible relationships between taxes and income. Taxes are progressive if they take a larger share of income as incomes rise, proportional if the share of taxes remains constant as incomes rise, and regressive if they take a larger share from those with a low income.

Figure 15.1: *Taxes and income*

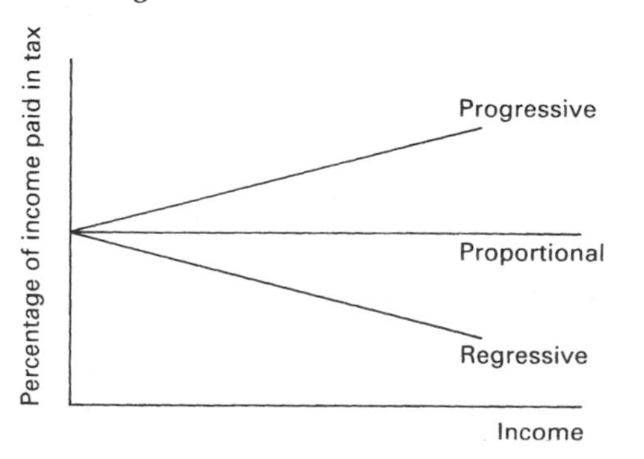

An example will clarify the difference. If A has an income of £10,000 a year and pays £2,000 tax (=20 per cent), whilst B with an income of £5,000 pays £1,500 tax (=30 per cent), the tax is regressive since the tax is taking a larger share of the poor person's income than it does on the rich person's income. If B paid only £1,000 (=20 per cent), the tax would be proportional. If B paid only £500 (=10 per cent), the tax would be progressive. The best example of a progressive tax is income tax, because those with low incomes pay little or no tax and those with high incomes pay at a higher rate. Indirect taxes are often – but not always – regressive. Thus taxes on cigarettes take up a larger share of the income of poor people than of that of the better off.

The council tax

Local taxes have special requirements. The council tax was introduced in 1993-94 to replace the unpopular poll tax. Five principles were laid down in the White Paper introducing the tax. These were:

- accountability;
- fairness;
- ease of collection;
- an equitable distribution of the burden;
- restraint.

'Restraint' refers to a desire to prevent the bills becoming too high. In addition, the government wanted the tax to raise about 14 per cent of local government expenditure. (Local authorities get the rest of their finance from a variety of sources, including government grants and business rates).

The council tax is a combination of a personal and a property tax. The personal element is included through a system of discounts for single households. The property element arises because all domestic properties are valued and placed in bands (for example, band A includes all properties worth up to £40,000). Local authorities then set a tax level for each band.

Supporters of the council tax cite this banding system as evidence that it is a progressive tax. Its critics, however, point out that since households falling within the highest band (which includes properties worth £320,000 or more) pay only four times as much as those within band A, the council tax tends to be regressive.

Taxes and equity

Two principles can be considered when discussing equity and taxation. The first is **horizontal** equity – that people in similar circumstances should be treated similarly. This sounds fair; but if two people are in an aeroplane about to crash and there is only one parachute, what is the equitable solution?

Horizontal equity may suggest that neither should have the parachute. This is clearly stupid. So far as taxation is concerned, horizontal equity breaks down when people can reduce their tax burden either by obtaining specialist advice or by not notifying the tax authorities. Moreover, to some extent every person is unique. Incomes differ but so do needs, so that it could be argued that handicapped people, for example, should pay less tax. **Vertical** equity exists when people in different circumstances are treated unequally. Most people would suggest that those on higher incomes should pay more tax, but there would be considerable disagreement about how much extra tax they should pay.

Tax incidence

Sometimes people can shift the burden of a tax on to others. 'Tax incidence' refers to the eventual distribution of the burden of taxation. Thus the tax on tobacco is paid to the tax authorities by the trader who draws the tobacco from a bonded warehouse. However, the trader will try to pass the burden of the tax on to the customer by putting up the price of cigarettes. Thus the **formal** incidence of the tax falls on those who have the legal liability to pay, but the **effective** liability falls on those who are less well-off as a result of the tax. Traders who say that they have to charge VAT are talking nonsense; they have to pay VAT, but in charging the customer they are seeking to shift the burden.

The effect of the imposition of a tax on price and quantity was discussed in Chapter 3. This showed that a tax on a good raised the price of the good and cut the quantity. The extent of the changes depended on the price elasticity of demand. When demand is inelastic, the price paid by consumers will rise to cover most of the tax, so that producers escape relatively lightly.

Governments usually impose taxes on goods where demand is inelastic. If they put taxes on goods with elastic demand, not only would firms have to bear the brunt of the tax, but the price rise would cause a relatively large fall in the quantity of goods bought, and the result would often be bankruptcy for the firm and very little money for the government.

Poverty and unemployment traps

A poverty trap exists when a low paid worker gains little or nothing from an increase in earnings because this causes benefits to be lost and tax to be paid. The unemployment trap is similar. It exists when jobless people obtain work and find themselves no better off than when they are unemployed because they may lose benefits, have to pay income tax and National Insurance, and have job-related expenses such as travel to work.

In both traps the argument is that the tax and social security system combine to provide substantial disincentive effects. In some cases people are, in effect, paying marginal tax rates of up to and over 100 per cent. In many cases the rate is less than this, but still very high. One solution is to cut tax rates for the low paid, but this is difficult because the government loses large amounts of revenue whilst the effect on any one individual is small. A cut of 1p in the pound in the rate of income tax costs the government over £1,000 million, but would provide little incentive for people to change their way of life. An alternative approach is to cut welfare benefits, but this is opposed on welfare grounds.

Key ideas

1. 'Good' taxes have certain qualities; for example, they are cheap to collect.
2. Taxes can be classed as progressive, proportional or regressive; direct or indirect.
3. Suppliers can sometimes change the incidence of taxation by passing the burden on to other people.
4. The tax system sometimes interacts with the social security system to produce poverty and unemployment traps.

Government spending

Everyone benefits from government spending, but some benefit more than others. As Table 15.1 shows, by far the largest item of public expenditure in the UK is social security, followed by defence, and health and personal social services. The relative importance of these items changes over time. For example, when unemployment rises so will spending on social security. An ageing population will have the same effect whilst a rise in the birth rate will be followed several years later by more spending on education.

Table 15.1: *Public Money 1994-95*

Where it comes from	Pence in every pound	Where it goes	Pence in every pound
Income tax	22	Social security	27
National income	15	Health	11
Corporation tax	6	Defence	8
Value added tax	15	Local government	25
Excise duties	9	Other spending	20
Borrowing	13	Debt interest	9
Other receipts	20		
	100		100

Source: Adapted from *The Budget in Brief*, HMSO, November 1993.

Despite changes in the relative importance of particular items, it is clear that the long-term trend is for public expenditure to rise over time. There are various explanations for this. Economists interested in micro-economics explain the growth by referring to government action to reduce market failure and so provide goods, such as defence, which become more expensive over the years because the technology grows more sophisticated. Moreover, many public services have a high income elasticity of demand, so that as incomes rise over time people want better educational and health services. Structural factors, such as a rise in the number of old people, also lead to more spending.

At the macro level, Keynesian explanations are also used to explain the growth in public spending because this theory suggests that the government should not attempt to balance the budget, but vary its spending and taxation levels according to the state of the economy. And once government spending has been increased it is difficult to bring it down to its former level. Thus the Conservative government elected in 1979 on a promise to cut public spending found itself unable to do this.

Economists interested in the economics of public choice also suggest that politicians obtain popularity by increased spending and that civil service bureaucrats aim to enlarge the size of their individual departments. The result is increased government spending. Supply siders in particular would support this line of argument.

The interaction of government spending and taxation

So far this chapter has considered taxation and public spending separately, but their interaction has a number of important effects.

Effect on the level of national income

Keynesian economists suggest that cuts in taxation and increases in public spending lead to rises in national income and falls in unemployment, assuming there are sufficient unemployed people to make this possible. As was seen in the last two chapters, this line of argument was criticised by supply side economists.

Government spending and taxation can act as **automatic stabilisers** in the economy. Thus when the economy starts to decline government receipts from taxation fall (since fewer people will be paying income tax and government income from VAT may also decline), whilst public spending on unemployment and social security rises. These increases in injections and cuts in withdrawals will both help boost the economy. On the other hand, when the economy is booming, public spending on unemployment falls and government tax receipts rise, thus dampening the expansion.

Effect on the National Debt

The National Debt is mis-named; in reality it is the **government's** debt. Most of the debt is owed by the government to British citizens who own National Savings Certificates, government bonds and so on. Only a tiny proportion is owed to foreigners. The National Debt increases whenever the government spends more than it receives in taxes, which has been the position in most years. In any one year the difference between what the government spends and what it receives is called the Public Sector Borrowing Requirement (PSBR). When the government receives more in taxes than it spends, this is called the Public Sector Debt Repayment (PSDR).

Figure 15.2: *PSBR and PSDR*

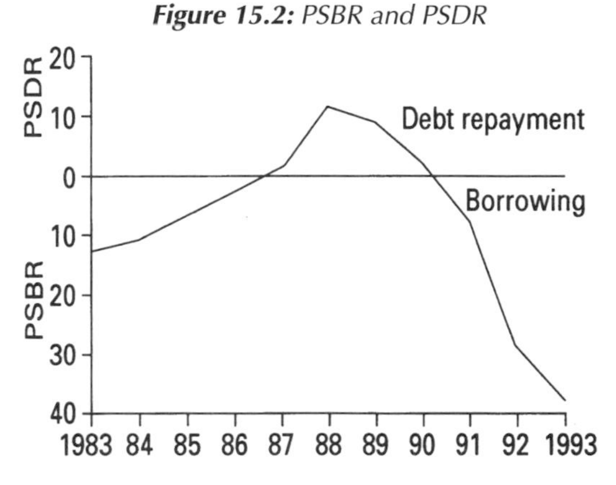

Source: Adapted from *Financial Statistics*, HMSO, 1993.

The National Debt currently amounts to over £180,000 million – a huge sum. Is this a problem? One effect is that the interest on this money forces up taxes. As Table 15.1 shows, 9 per cent of government spending is in the form of interest payments and the government has to raise the money to pay this interest. If instead of increasing taxes the government increases the quantity of money, this may push up inflation. Thus the National Debt may have some undesirable consequences, but it does not mean that the country is in hock to foreigners, nor that future generations will be impoverished – their standard of living will depend on the quantity of goods and services which the country then produces.

An increase in the National Debt does have one undesirable effect. The government has to borrow large sums of money and this pushes up the rate of interest, causing difficulties to borrowers. However, there are many other factors which influence interest rates and increases in the National Debt probably have only a small effect.

Table 15.2: *Redistribution of income through taxes and benefits, 1989 (UK, £ per year)*

	Quintile groups of households ranked by disposable income	
	Bottom fifth	Top fifth
Average per household (£ per year)		
Earnings of main earner	770	19,780
Earnings of others in the household	80	6,640
Occupational pensions, annuities	200	1,290
Investment income	160	1,920
Other income	70	420
Total original income	1,280	30,050
+Benefits in cash		
Contributory	1,710	410
Non-contributory	1,640	250
Gross income	4,630	30,710
-Income tax and NIC	170	6,030
-Domestic rates (gross)	500	710
Disposable income	3,960	23,970
-Indirect taxes	1,120	3,890
Post tax income	2,840	20,080
+Benefits in kind		
Education	920	460
National Health Service	1,230	780
Housing subsidy	110	10
Travel subsidies	40	50
School meals and welfare milk	70	10
Final income	5,200	21,400

Source: Adapted from *Social Trends*, HMSO, 1993.

Effect on Equity

Government spending and taxation interact to redistribute money from some people to others, as Table 15.2 shows. This shows how the people who are a fifth from the bottom and the top of the income range are affected. Both groups benefit from cash repayments, such as child benefit, but the poorer group gain much more from social security. They also lose less because of income taxes and National Insurance payments and from indirect taxes, such as VAT. The poor also gain from 'benefits in kind', such as education and health care, but the difference is very small. Indeed, for some benefits such as education, the better-off gain more than the poor. This is because the children of the better-off are more likely to stay on at school beyond the age of 16 and then go on into higher education. As these are the most expensive parts of the education system they receive most benefit.

Key ideas

1. Government spending has tended to rise over time, partly because many government services have a high income elasticity of demand. Also politicians may favour increased spending in order to gain popularity.
2. Taxes and public spending act as stabilisers in the economy.
3.The National Debt is really the government's debt. It may have some undesirable consequences, but it does not impoverish future generations.

The supply side perspective

The argument about fiscal policy is often just a special case of the general disagreement among economists about the role of markets. Supply side economists tend to suggest that markets are the most efficient way to allocate resources and therefore the role of government should be limited. They argue that government activity impedes the working of the market and so reduces choice and efficiency. For example, if the state provides goods that would not be provided by the market, this means fewer resources are available to produce those goods that people would actually choose to buy. Supply siders argue that the state should

resources in a satisfactory manner. This was discussed in some detail in Chapter 2. Markets are not very good at providing public goods, such as defence, nor allowing for externalities, such as pollution, where the social cost to the society as a whole may be different from the private cost to the producer. Hence government needs to intervene to correct these failures. Interventionist economists also argue that the labour market can be in equilibrium at a high level of unemployment and that governments should make active use of fiscal policy to reduce the level of unemployment. They suggest that government spending should be increased, and possibly taxes cut, in order to obtain a desirable level of aggregate demand and employment. In order to do this the government may have to borrow money. This may have some undesirable consequences, such as pushing up interest rates, but these are outweighed by the benefits. This is a fundamental difference between Keynesian and supply side economists and is discussed in detail in Chapters 13, 14 and 17. Moreover, the interventionists would attack the assumption behind the supply side approach that taxes are too high in the UK. They point out that UK tax rates are typical of those in advanced industrial countries as Table 15.3 shows. Therefore the sometimes unsatisfactory performance of the economy cannot be blamed on high tax rates.

Table 15.3: *Tax burdens as percentage of GDP, 1991*

	Personal	Goods and services	Other	Total
Sweden	31	14	5	30
France	25	12	7	44
Germany	23	11	3	37
UK	17	11	9	36
Japan	18	4	9	31
USA	20	5	5	30

Source: Adapted from Lloyds Bank *Economic Bulletin*, No. 171, 1993.

Merit goods

Merit goods are those which society believes are intrinsically desirable. When this is the case markets would provide too few of these goods because the benefits to society are greater than those accruing to the individual who might buy such goods on the open market. Hence if the provision of swimming pools were left to the market, entry would be very expensive and there would be far fewer pools. Society, through the actions of local councils, has decided that swimming is a desirable activity and, consequently, provides pools even though they usually run at a loss. Sports centres and playing fields are other examples. Left to market forces they would be comparatively rare.

Education and housing are other examples of merit goods. People sometimes talk about the right to education and health care. Whilst many economists would be cautious about using terms such as 'right', a statement such as this does represent a consensus among many people in society that access to education and health should not be dependent on the ability to pay the market price of such services. Hence the state must provide, or at least finance, such services and provide a greater quantity than would market forces.

Individualism

The supply side/market forces argument rests on the assumption that individuals know what is best for themselves and are competent to make utility maximising choices. Interventionists accept that in many cases, perhaps most, this assumption is valid; but they believe that in some cases it is not. Left to themselves, some people would not insure their health, or provide for their old age. So society steps in and forces people in work to contribute so that old age pensions are provided to all and that social security benefits are available to those in need. A strict individualistic approach would suggest this reduces the freedom of the individual to choose whether to insure against these possibilities. Hence some supply siders would abolish state provision in these areas, leaving it to the market. Interventionists believe that state intervention is needed to prevent or reduce poverty. Therefore spending on social security should be a major part of the state's economic responsibility.

Equity

Values influence the way people approach economic policies. Economists who believe in greater equality contend that without state intervention, market forces would lead to a society with great differences between rich and poor. Those who start life with substantial assets will find it relatively easy to increase them. Similarly, people with scarce skills that are valued in the labour market will also grow rich. On the other hand those with few such assets, or who have poor health, suffer accidents, or have to care for children or the old, will find that the market gives few rewards and that the result is poverty. Hence they suggest that state intervention is necessary, not only to help the poor, but also to reduce the gap between rich and poor because they believe that a society without great differences of wealth and income is desirable.

Key ideas – summary of the interventionist approach

1. Markets fail so government spending is needed to correct these failures.
2. The level of government spending and taxes should be adjusted so that the level of aggregate demand is sufficient to reduce the level of unemployment.
3. Merit goods, such as education, health and recreational facilities, would only be provided in small quantities by the market; government spending is needed to provide a desirable supply of these services.
4. Government spending is needed to alleviate poverty. Fiscal policy should be used to reduce inequalities in society.

Interventionist policies

At the heart of the interventionist approach is the belief that positive government action is needed to prevent or mitigate the undesirable consequences of unregulated market forces. The work of Keynes has had a profound effect on many economists and suggests that government spending and taxation should be varied in order to maintain an appropriate level of aggregate demand. ('Appropriate' in this context means a level which would reduce unemployment without generating much inflation.)

Moreover, government should spend money on social services in order to improve the lives of the citizens. One problem is that although this is generally agreed, it is open to argument exactly how much should be spent on these services and how to provide the money in ways which would be most efficient.

Similarly, there is agreement among this group of economists that the fiscal system should be used to create a more equal society. This means that government spending should focus on the needs of the poor and that the taxation system should be progressive. However, there is some disagreement about how progressive the system should be. Some economists favour a wealth tax which exists in many other countries and which compels rich people (for example, those with assets over £250,000) to pay a special tax on their assets. Not all this group of economists would agree with this suggestion, but most would agree that the better off should pay proportionately more tax than the poor. This suggestion, like so many in economics, derives from a value system which dislikes extremes of poverty and wealth in a society and seeks to use the fiscal system to reduce these differences.

The European Union budget

International organisations are different from national governments. One of the weaknesses of the United Nations is that it has to rely on countries paying their dues; many are in substantial arrears. When the European Community (now the European Union) was founded by the Treaty of Rome in 1957, this weakness was avoided; the Community was to have certain monies by right. However, there remained one big difference from the financing of a nation's government, because the rules said that the Community's expenditure was to equal its income. If the Community overspent in any one year, then the debt had to be eliminated in the next year. This rule still applies and means that there is no equivalent to a national public sector borrowing requirement.

As Table 15.4 shows, the Union receives its money from several sources. It receives all the tax revenues obtained from the common external tariff on imports, including levies applied to imports of agricultural products from outside the Union. Another source of income is the proceeds of a percentage rate of VAT up to a maximum of 1.4 per cent. This is the Union's main source of income. The EU can also receive additional payments related to the level of a country's GNP if the other sources are not sufficient to pay the bills. EU expenditure is dominated by agriculture. Although the proportion varies year by year, over half of the budget is spent supporting farmers. This proportion may fall in the future because efforts are being made to cut agricultural support, and also because there is strong support for money to be spent to help the poorer regions of the Union.

Table 15.4: *European Community* Budget, 1992*

Revenue	%	Expenditure	%
VAT	55	Agriculture and fisheries	53
GNP based	23	Regional	15
Customs duties	21	Social	8
Other	1	Administration	6
	100	Development	5
		Other	13
			100

*Now the European Union.
Source: Adapted from EC Commission, 1993.

Overall the Union's budget amounts to over 60 billion ECUs (an ECU is worth about 70 pence). Whilst this is a lot of money, it only amounts to about 1.8 per cent of the GDP of the member states, and is a small sum compared to the money spent on national governments. Put another way, the typical community citizen pays 55 times as much to domestic governments as to the EU.

Although there are strenuous efforts to control Union spending, the philosophy underlying the budget is firmly in the interventionist camp; this is shown by interventions to help farmers and poorer regions. This represents an acknowledgement that the equity argument is a strong one. Another principle is exemplified by the refund given to the United Kingdom. Largely because farming is a relatively minor industry in this country, the UK was a substantial net contributor and in 1984 an agreement was signed which gave the UK a refund equal to 66 per cent of the difference between what it receives and what is paid in VAT. This in effect reflects the view that to some extent there should be some relationship between the payments which a country makes and the benefits it receives. This principle is not consistently applied, Germany being a substantial net contributor to the EU whilst poorer countries such as Greece, Portugal and Ireland receive considerably more than they pay – the equity principle in action.

Conclusion

Over the years government spending has grown and, though tax receipts have also risen, in most years the government has had to borrow to make up the difference. These trends have led supply siders to argue that government spending and taxes should be reduced whenever possible in order to stimulate the ecopnomy. Interventionists respond by saying that markets often fail and that government spending is needed to correct these failures and to promote a more equal and caring society.

Data questions

Clarke declares war on state borrowing

Chancellor Kenneth Clarke, opening the first unified tax and spending Budget, said his first priority had been 'to sustain the economic recovery now under way and to create the right climate for growth and jobs'.

He continued, 'The over-riding need is to place the public finances on a sound footing... Business can plan ahead with confidence only if it knows that government borrowing is under control.' He said the measures he announced would cut PSBR from just under £50 billion this year to about £38 billion next year. 'It should eliminate borrowing to finance current spending by 1997-98 and eliminate government borrowing entirely by the end of the decade.'

Source: Chancellor's speech, reported in *The Guardian*, 1 December 1993.

Question 1

1. Explain (i) what is meant by 'PSBR' and (ii) how the government borrows money.
2. Which economic perspective is illustrated by these extracts from the Chancellor's speech?
3. Give examples of the kind of measures which could be used to cut government borrowing. Who would suffer from the introduction of such measures?

16 Money

● One of the central propositions of monetarist economics is that the control of inflation is the major goal of economic policy. Its supporters believe that the way to achieve this end is to control the money supply. Economists such as Milton Friedman argue that if the government keeps control of the money supply, prices in general cannot rise and money will be able to fulfil its necessary functions in the economy.

● Interventionist economists do not deny the importance of money – indeed the title of Keynes' major work was the *General Theory of Employment, Interest and Money* (1936). However, they argue that the supply of money in a modern economy is largely determined by the economy's need for money to undertake transactions, and that attempting to control the money supply leads to higher levels of unemployment and lower rates of economic growth. The interaction of the demand and supply of money can have a significant effect on the economy, and we need to examine what factors affect the demand and supply for money before considering the above perspectives.

The supply of money

Money and its functions

Money is often defined as anything which is generally acceptable for the purchase of goods and services or repayment of debt. This is a broad definition and in the past a wide range of objects have been acceptable as money. Gold and silver coins were the usual forms of money in many countries, but tobacco, cowrie shells and even dogs' teeth have served as money. What is important is not the precise form which money takes, but whether it is generally accepted. In a modern economy only a small part of the total money supply is in notes and coins. Most money is created by the banking system and moved around electronically. Cheques and credit cards are accepted as a means of payment, yet no notes or coins are involved when purchases are made using these methods. Whatever the precise form taken by 'money', it must fulfil four functions:

- It must act as a medium of exchange; that is, it permits people to exchange goods and services of different value. Without money an economy has to rely on barter and this has the same disadvantage as sex – it requires not only that someone has what you want, but also that the same person wants what you have! To use the jargon, barter requires the double coincidence of wants.
- It must act as a unit of account; that is, it is a standard of value that allows people to compare the relative worth of various goods and services.
- It must act as a standard of deferred payment. This is a way in which spending can be postponed, for example, when someone signs a contract or buys goods on credit.
- It must act as a store of value – a way in which today's wealth can be kept for use in the future.

If money does not fulfil all these functions, then the economy will suffer. For example, when there is inflation money ceases to be a good store of value. Some commodities fulfil some of the functions of money, but not all. Credit cards act as a medium of exchange and a way of making deferred payments, but do not fulfil the other functions of money.

Some forms of money – notes and coins – are supplied by the Bank of England. These are not 'backed' by any security, such as gold, but are in general printed in sufficient quantities to ensure the economy is not short of cash. The Bank of England can do this without there being severe consequences because most money in a modern economy is created by the commercial banks, such as Barclays and National Westminster, in a process usually called 'credit creation'.

Table 16.1: *The creation of credit*

	BANK Assets	Liabilities
Mr A deposits £1000	£1000 cash	deposit £1000
But the bank knows that he will withdraw only £100 so the rest may be lent to Ms B	£100 cash £900 loan	deposit £1000
Now Ms B deposits her new £900 with the bank	£1000 cash £900 loan	deposits £1900
But the bank realises that Ms B will withdraw only £90 of her deposit so the rest is lent to Mr C	£190 cash £1710 loans	deposits £1900
Now Mr C deposits his new £810 with the bank	£1000 cash £1710 loans	deposits £2710
But the bank realises that Mr C will withraw only £81 of his deposit so the rest is lent to Mr D	£271 cash £2439 loans	deposits £2710
Mr D deposits his new £729 with the bank	£1000 cash £2439 loans	deposits £3439

and so on . . .
Eventually the original £1000 will be held by the bank as the one-tenth it needs to cover withdrawals by its customers. If £1000 represents one-tenth, then total deposits must total £10,000, as follows:

	Assets	Liabilities
	£1000 cash £9000 loans	deposits £10,000

How do banks create credit?

When a bank receives a deposit from a customer, it keeps only part of the money in case the customer wants it back and lends out the rest. Since borrowers pay interest, the bank wishes to lend as much as possible, but is constrained by the need to maintain adequate assets. If we assume for simplicity that the bank keeps 10 per cent as security, it can lend out 90 per cent of each deposit received. Since most of the money lent will sooner or later be deposited in a bank, it follows that the bank receiving this deposit can then lend more money. The process is illustrated in Table 16.1.

If Mr A deposits £1,000 in a bank, the bank's assets will be £1,000 (the cash it holds) and its liabilities also £1,000 (the money it owes Mr A). The bank keeps 10 per cent as security and lends out £900 to Ms B who wishes to buy some furniture. The bank's assets are now £100 cash and £900 owed to it by Ms B. Ms B (or the furniture company) then deposits the £900 in the bank. Hence the bank's assets are now £1,000 cash(the £100 it kept as security on Mr A's deposit plus the £900 it received from Ms B or the furniture shop) plus the £900 owed it by Ms B. Its liabilities are also £1,900 (£900 deposited by the furniture shop plus the original £1,000 deposited by Mr A).

The next step is a repetition of the first, but with a smaller account. Since the furniture shop has deposited £900, the bank will keep 10 per cent of this, i.e. £90 and lend out the remaining 90 per cent, i.e. £810 to Mr C, perhaps to buy hi-fi equipment. In turn this will be deposited at the bank, which will keep 10 per cent and lend out 90 per cent to Mr D. The process will be repeated with ever decreasing amounts. Eventually the original £1,000 will have been turned into £10,000 by the banking system. If the banks keep 10 per cent of liabilities in reserve, then they can create 10 times their original deposit. This is known as the **credit multiplier**. If the bank keeps 25 per cent in reserve, it can only create 4 times the original amount deposited.

This account is simplified, but it does illustrate the way in which the banking system can create money. One simplification is that we have talked about 'the' bank when in reality there is a whole system. This complicates the process, but it does not invalidate the description. The account also assumes that money lent by the system is always returned to the bank as a deposit; in practice some will remain outside the banking system. Another simplification is the assumption that the banks keep 10 per cent as security. The real world is more complex than this.

However, banks do have to keep some deposits for their own security and in order to comply with Capital Adequacy Rules imposed by the Bank of

England. At present, banks have to keep a minimum capital ratio of 7.25 per cent. This 'capital ratio' is the bank's capital expressed as a percentage of its assets weighted in terms of risk.

What measure of money?

There is no single, universal definition of money. This is because, as we have seen, money fulfils a number of functions and some kinds of money fulfil certain functions better than others. This means that there is no single way to measure the money supply.

The two measures of money supply that are in most use in the United Kingdom are M0 and M4. M0 is composed of notes and coins in circulation and also bankers' balances with the Bank of England. M0 is therefore a useful measure of the transactions function of money and is often used as a good measure of changes in spending, since if people spend more, they will need more cash. M4 is much broader, and includes money in current and deposit accounts in banks and building societies. Table 16.2 shows the relationships between various monetary aggregates.

Figure 16.1: *The quantity of money, 1992*

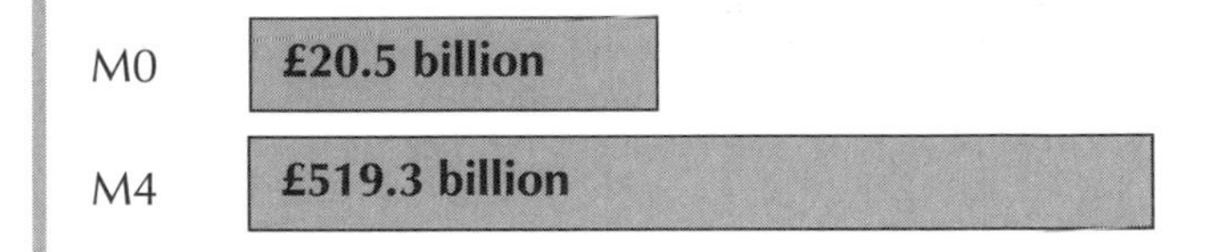

Source: Adapted from *Economic Trends*, HMSO, 1993.

Controlling the money supply

The amount of money in the UK measured in these ways is shown in Figure 16.1. Because there are several definitions of money, there is no one way in which the government can control the money supply. Indeed, because one type of 'money' can easily be converted into another, the authorities find that when they try to control one type people switch to another that is unregulated.

If 'money' is narrowly defined in terms of notes and coins, then the problem of how to control the

Table 16.2: *Relationships between the monetary aggregates and their components*

Notes and coin in circulation with the M4 private sector

plus M4 private sector non-interest bearing sterling sight bank deposits

Notes and coin in circulation outside the Bank of England

plus Bankers operational balances with the Bank of England

equals MO

plus M4 private sector interest bearing sterling sight bank deposits

plus M4 private sector interest bearing retail sterling deposits with banks and building societies

equals M2

plus M4 private sector sterling time bank deposits (including sterling certificates of deposit)

plus M4 private sector holdings of building society shares and deposits and sterling certificates of deposit

equals M4

Source: Adapted from *Financial Statistics Explanatory Handbook*, HMSO, 1992.

supply is relatively simple – just control the print run.

However, if broader definitions of money are used, the problem of control is more complex. The change in a broad money supply depends on such factors as:

- the public sector borrowing requirement,
- - the change in private sector lending to the public sector,
- + the change in bank lending to the private sector,
- + external flows,
- - the increase in banks' non-deposit liabilities.

Each of these will be discussed in turn.

The Public Sector Borrowing Requirement

The PSBR was discussed in the last chapter. Other things being equal, a rise in the PSBR, followed by increased borrowing from the banking sector through the sale of Treasury bills, will give the banks greater assets, allowing them to create credit. This will lead to a rise in the money supply. Hence economists who believe that it is important to have firm controls on the money supply tend to argue that government spending should be kept as low as possible. This is difficult to accomplish. There are often strong political pressures to increase spending and in any case, public expenditure next year is largely determined by spending this year. It is not possible to close a hospital suddenly, or make a battalion of soldiers redundant. Moreover, it is quite difficult to predict how much the government will have to borrow in any one year. Hence some economists argue that controlling the PSBR is not a good method to use to control the money supply.

Private sector lending to the public sector

A rise in public sector borrowing from the non-bank private sector will reduce the money supply. This is because when the public buy National Savings certificates, gilt edged securities or other government securities, they sign cheques payable to the government. (Gilt edged securities or bonds are a kind of IOU. To simplify, they say something like 'The government will pay the bearer the sum of £1,000 in January 2005 and £100 interest annually until that date'.) When these cheques are cashed by the Bank of England, money is withdrawn from the banks so their deposits fall. When their deposits fall the banks can create less money (this is the reverse side of the credit creation process described earlier). Hence a major way for the authorities to reduce the money supply is to sell more gilt edged securities. (You can see lists of these in the financial pages of some newspapers and they can be bought through banks or the Post Office.) This method of controlling the money supply is called 'open market operations' or funding the Public Sector Borrowing Requirement. One problem with this method is that an increase in government borrowing may push up interest rates which may be undesirable.

Bank lending to the private sector

A rise in bank lending to the private sector will tend to push up the money supply. There are a number of ways in which the authorities can attempt to reduce bank lending. One way is to push up interest rates so that some people are unwilling to borrow money. Unfortunately this also puts up costs to businesses. Moreover, it often requires large rises in interest rates before there is much effect on the willingness of people to borrow. An alternative approach is to require the commercial banks to make Special Deposits at the Bank of England. This means that the banks will then have less money to lend to the private sector.

External flows

External flows also affect the quantity of money. For example, when the balance of payments is positive (i.e. when UK exports exceed UK imports) money will flow into the country. It is possible for the authorities to intervene in the foreign exchange market in order to influence the flow of money, but this will have undesirable effects on the whole balance of payments.

Banks' non-deposit reserves

Increases in the banks' non-deposit reserves will also affect the money supply. If the banks choose to increase their capital base by retaining profits they will be transferring banks' liabilities into banks' assets. Such a transfer will reduce monetary aggregates since assets are not included in measures of the money stock.

An alternative way to control the money supply

The methods described above do not offer a trouble-free way to control the supply of money when this is broadly defined. An alternative way would be to control the monetary base. The idea is that the banks tend to keep a fairly stable ratio between their deposits and their reserves. They may do this because the law says that they must, or because they are prudent. If the law lays down requirements, then one way to influence the money supply is to change the requirements. If the banks are forced to keep bigger reserves, then their ability to create money will be reduced. In the credit creation example given earlier, a reserve of 10 per cent was used as an example. If this was increased to, say, 12.5 per cent, then much less money would have resulted from any increase in deposits (£8,000 instead of £10,000). However, this method of attempting to control the supply of money is criticised on a number of grounds. For example, if the reserve ratio is not fixed by law, then the banks may vary their reserves and so make it difficult to calculate the effect of any government sale or purchase of bonds. Even if a minimum reserve ratio is fixed by law, the effects of any intervention may be difficult to predict because prudential banks may keep more reserves than the law requires. Critics also claim that this method of monetary control would lead to very unstable interest rates, which are undesirable, particularly for firms wishing to borrow money to finance expansion.

The methods used to control the supply of money are complex. The detailed methods used by governments vary over time because no method is perfect, so as time passes governments look for improved techniques, but all have some disadvantages.

Key ideas

1. Money is anything that is generally accepted as payment for goods and services.
2. Because money has to carry out a number of functions, there are a number of different ways of measuring it.
3. Banks create most money by the process of credit creation.
4. There are several different ways to control the money supply. These include high interest rates, open market operations and controlling the banks' monetary base.

The demand for money

The phrase 'demand for money' has a curious ring to it; in commonsense terms we demand as much money as we can get. However, 'demand' has the same meaning here as it has in the context of the demand for goods. It is therefore important to find out what factors influence whether people wish to hold their assets as money or in some other form. One consideration is **liquidity**. Money is a perfectly liquid asset because it can be used immediately to buy goods or services. At the other extreme, a building may be very valuable but it is not very liquid – ownership of a house is no use if you want to buy an ice cream. Buildings are illiquid; it takes time to change them into a form which can be used to buy things and selling in a hurry may result in a capital loss.

The level of income

One factor which affects the demand for money is the level of incomes. This is because people need money to finance transactions (hence this is called the **transactions** motive for holding money). When incomes are high people buy more goods and services and hence need more money to finance these transactions than do people with low incomes.

There is also a precautionary reason for holding money. Because firms and individuals are not absolutely sure that future receipts and payments will occur as expected, they will wish to keep some money in reserve in case they need to make some payment quickly. The amount of money kept as a precaution will depend largely on the level of income. A rich person may wish to keep large sums of money available as a precaution; a poor person could not.

The rate of interest

Whilst the level of incomes is the chief determinant of the amount of money held for precautionary and transactions motives, the rate of interest may also play a part. That is because there is an opportunity cost of holding money. Particularly when interest rates are high, some people or firms may decide that it would be better to transfer their money into some other form of asset which would earn high interest. Hence high rates of interest may reduce the demand for money balances.

Figure 16.2: *The demand for money*

(i) Transactions and precautionary demand depend on the level of national income

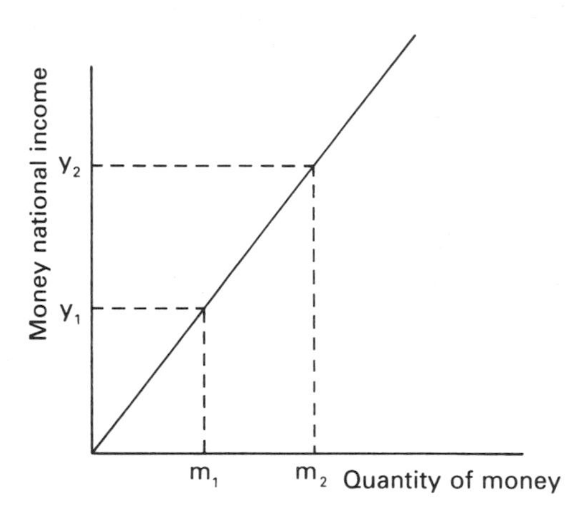

(ii) Speculative demand varies inversely with the rate of interest

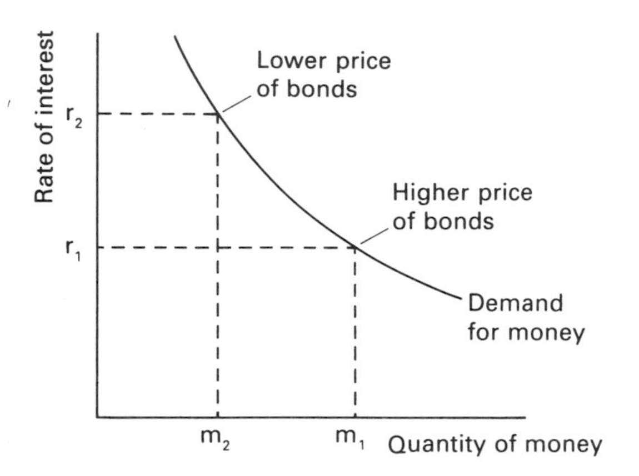

There is also a **speculative** motive for holding money. We have seen that there is an opportunity cost of holding money, and that this will encourage people to choose to hold other assets, such as bonds, instead. However, the price of bonds is not constant; speculators can gain or lose money if they buy bonds at the right (or wrong) time.

The price of bonds tends to vary inversely with the interest rate. When interest rates are expected to fall, the price of bonds will rise and vice versa. The reason is that bonds have a face value and pay a fixed interest. Hence a bond with a face value of £100 which pays £5 a year interest will be worth £100 when the current rate of interest in the economy is 5 per cent. However, when interest rates generally are 10 per cent no one would be willing to pay £100 for such a bond because they would only receive £5 interest on it compared to £10 on other assets. Hence the value of the bond would fall to £50; this would mean that someone with £100 could buy two bonds and receive £10 interest on their investment. Conversely if interest rates generally fell to 2.5 per cent the bond would be worth more than £100 because it would give much better interest than other assets. Its price would increase to £200 and the holder would receive £5, i.e. 2.5 per cent interest on the investment.

This account of the speculative motive for holding money is largely Keynesian. It suggests a negative relationship between the rate of interest and the demand for money. When interest rates are high and expected to fall, speculators will exchange money for bonds because the value of bonds will rise. When interest rates are low and expected to rise they will tend to sell bonds and hold money instead.

Figure 16.2 summarises the Keynesian demand for money function. It shows that there are two principal determinants of the demand for money: the level of national income and the rate of interest. A change in either of these will cause a change in the demand for money.

The monetarist approach to the demand for money

The modern monetarist approach to the demand for money differs from the Keynesian in that it considers assets other than money and bonds. Monetarists argue that money is only one of a whole range of assets and that if the supply of money exceeds the demand, then individuals and firms will not just buy bonds, but also other assets, such as buildings, shares, jewellery and consumer durable goods. If this view is accepted, then the level of incomes will still have a major effect on the demand for money. The rate of interest will also have an effect because when interest rates are high, the opportunity cost of holding money will also be high. However, monetarists argue that changes in interest rates have relatively little effect on the demand for money, and that the demand curve for money is inelastic.

The big difference between this view and that of Keynes is that the monetarist approach suggests that the demand for money is stable. Friedman claimed:

'A wide range of empirical evidence suggests that the ratio which people desire to maintain between their cash balances and their income is relatively stable over fairly long periods of time aside from the effect of two major variables.'

(These two variables are the level of real incomes and the cost of holding money – the opportunity cost in terms of interest forgone.) As we will see, this conclusion that the demand for money is stable has important implications for monetary policy.

Empirical evidence on the demand for money

In principle these differences could be resolved by research. Is the demand for money stable as monetarists argue, or does it fluctuate as Keynesians believe? After reviewing the evidence Gowland (1979) concluded:

'There seems to be a stable demand for money function.'

A few years later Howells and Bain (1985) concluded:

'The evidence seems now to favour the presumption that in Britain in the 1970s the demand for money function was decidedly unstable.'

A more recent summary of the evidence by Artis & Lewis (1991) concludes that one reason for these disagreements is that the demand for money may be more stable in the long run than in the short run. Moreover, the demand for some forms of money such as M0 seems to be more stable than the demand for broader measures of money such as M4. Finally, the evidence is inconclusive because economic behaviour changes over time. For example, financial deregulation, allowing building societies to compete with banks, and the growing use of credit cards may affect the way in which people use money. Consequently research may not be able to give a definitive answer to the question 'Is the demand for money stable?'

Equilibrium in the money market

In the market for goods and services equilibrium was brought about by changes in the price level. Similarly, in the money market equilibrium between the demand for money and the supply of money is brought about by changes in the rate of interest as shown in Figure 16.3.

In this Figure the money supply is drawn as a vertical straight line because it is assumed to be controlled by the authorities and does not vary with the rate of interest. The demand for money curve is labelled LP because it measures the liquidity preference of the population; at high rates of interest people will have a low liquidity preference – that is, they will desire bonds instead of money. The market will be in equilibrium when the interest

Figure 16.3: *Monetary equilibrium and the rate of interest*

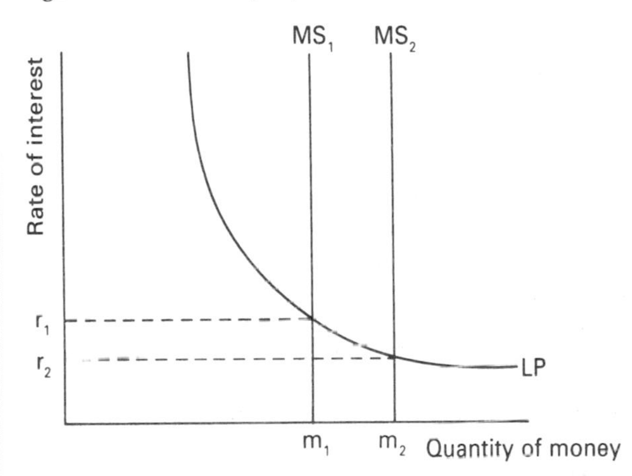

rate is r_1. If the interest rate was higher than this, the supply of money would be greater than the demand for money. Since people held more money than they wished, they would use this excess money to buy bonds and so cause the price of bonds to rise and the interest rate to fall until equilibrium was reached. When the demand for money is greater than the supply, people will sell their bonds to obtain money and this will push up the rate of interest.

A change in either the demand for money or its supply will affect the rate of interest, just as a change in the demand or supply of goods affects the price. An increase in the money supply will move the MS curve to the right and lower the interest rate, while a cut in the money supply will have the opposite effect. If there is an increase in the demand for money, caused, for example, by a rise in incomes, then the LP curve will move to the right, pushing up the interest rate. A fall in the demand for money will lead to a fall in interest rates.

The influence of government

So far this chapter has developed what is sometimes called the **liquidity preference theory of interest rate determination**. It is given this name because it focuses on people's desire to hold money or other assets. However, the theory as explained ignores an important influence – that of the government. In a modern economy governments are not content to leave important variables, such as the interest rate, to market forces and they often intervene to move the rate up or down. One reason for this is to influence the rate of exchange – the rate at which the pound is exchanged for other currencies. This is explained in detail in Chapter 21; for the present we will consider competing perspectives on monetary policy as it affects the domestic economy.

Key ideas

1. By 'demand for money' we mean the demand to hold money rather than other assets.
2. The Keynesian approach stresses three motives for holding money: transactions, precautions and speculative. The variables which affect these motives are the level of income and the rate of interest.
3. Monetarists consider money as one of a broad range of assets. This means that the demand for money is stable.

The monetarist approach

The quantity theory

The theory underlying the monetarist view is called the **quantity theory of money**. This theory is derived from an equation which is accepted by all economists:

$$MV=PT$$

In this equation:
M = the quantity of money
V = the velocity of circulation
(this is the number of times a year that money changes hands in order to purchase goods and services)
P = the average level of prices
T = the number of transactions, a measure of the quantity of goods produced by the economy in a year.
Thus the equation says that the quantity of money multiplied by its circulation will equal the number of goods produced multiplied by their price.

If this seems complicated, a simplistic example may clarify the point. Imagine a desert island where the quantity of money is 100 coins each worth £1. During the year each coin changes hands five times. Hence MV equals £500. If the economy produces £50 units of goods, then the average price of these goods must be £10, i.e.:

$$M \times V = P \times T$$
$$100 \times 5 = 10 \times 50$$

This equation is accepted by all economists because it is true by definition. In words it says that the total amount spent in the economy (MV) must equal the total amount received by producers (PT). The argument between economists arises not over the equation itself, but about how this equality comes about and whether this causal mechanism should be the basis for economic policy.

The essence of the monetarist argument is that if the government controls the money supply (M), then the result will be to prevent prices (P) from rising. This is because monetarists argue that the velocity of circulation (V) is fairly constant, since it is determined partly by social and institutional factors which do not change much in the short run (for example, if people are paid monthly instead of weekly, then they will tend to pay their bills monthly instead of weekly and this will reduce the velocity of circulation, but only very slowly and over a long period). Similarly, monetarists believe that real national income (T) is fairly constant because it depends on slowly moving variables such as productivity. Over a period of years it could be expected to rise by (say) 3 per cent a year. Hence if we look at the equation again we see:

M	x	V	=	P	x	T
controlled by government		constant		determined by M		rises slowly

From this analysis it follows that if the government keeps tight control over the money supply, then prices cannot rise. If a powerful union succeeds in obtaining a large wage increase this will not lead to inflation, unless the government allows the money supply to rise to fund the increase. Instead the wage rise will mean that there is less for others. This may be very undesirable, but it does not cause inflation. Hence in this view,

Figure 16.4: *The monetarist view of the transmission mechanism*

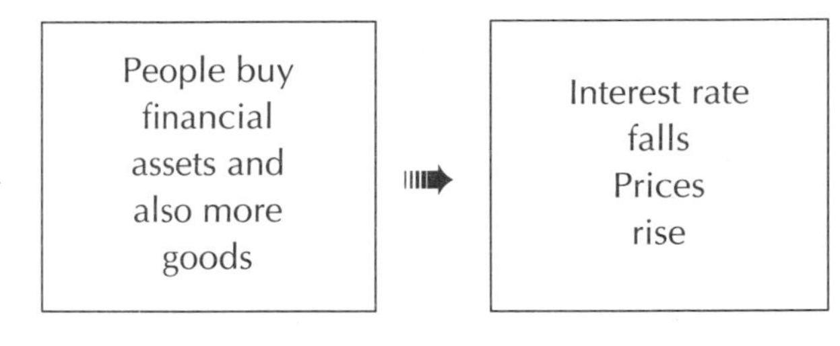

inflation is always a monetary phenomenon, caused by the government allowing the money supply to rise too rapidly.

In support of this line of argument, the monetarists have undertaken a good deal of research into the relationship between the money supply and the rate of inflation. According to Friedman (1966):

'There is perhaps no empirical regularity among economic phenomena that is based on so much evidence for so wide a range of circumstances as the connection between substantial changes in the stock of money and in the level of prices. To the best of my knowledge there is no instance in which a substantial change in the stock of money per unit of output has occurred without a substantial change in the level of prices in the same direction... instances in which prices and the stock of money have moved together are recorded for many centuries of history, for countries in every part of the globe, and for a wide diversity of monetary arrangements.'

Friedman himself has undertaken a good deal of this research and concluded that a change in the supply of money will lead to a change in the rate of inflation, but with a time lag. For example, if a government cut the rate of increase of the money supply from (say) 10 per cent to 5 per cent, the effect in the short run would be on T, the real level of national income. Firms and individuals would be short of money, interest rates would rise, and there would be a fall in the quantity of goods produced and a rise in the level of unemployment. But this would be temporary. Depending on the flexibility of the economy, in a year and a half or two years the period of readjustment would come to an end and the rate of inflation would start to fall.

One factor which could affect this relationship is the amount of money which the public desires to hold relative to its income. If the demand for money is unstable, then the velocity of circulation of money may also vary. This means that changes in the quantity of money would have little or no effect on the level of prices. However, if the demand for money is relatively stable, then changes in the stock of money will have a significant effect on the level of prices and monetary policy should concentrate on controlling the supply of money.

The transmission mechanism

By the phrase 'transmission mechanism' we mean the way in which changes in the money supply affect the economy. The monetarist view of the consequences of a rise in money supply is shown in Figure 16.4.

As can be seen, the increase in money supply means that the supply of money exceeds the demand for it. Since people have more money than they want, they use some of the money to buy financial assets such as bonds. This raises the price of bonds and brings down the rate of interest. They also use some of the excess money to buy more goods. However, since supply siders assume that the labour market is in equilibrium, there are no additional workers available to produce more goods. Hence the result is that prices rise, without any increase in output.

Key ideas – summary of the monetarist argument

1. Inflation is an economic phenomenon which must be eradicated.
2. The way to control inflation is to control the money supply. This is because the velocity of the circulation of money is fairly stable and national income tends to rise in the long run. Hence if M is controlled, P cannot rise.
3. In the short run, controlling the money supply will reduce the national income and increase unemployment, but this effect is only temporary.

Monetarist policies

The short summary of monetarist policy would be 'The government should control the money supply'. As we have seen earlier in this chapter, there are various ways in which this can be done, and there is also some dispute among monetarists about the extent of the control. Should the money supply be brought down quickly, or should its rate of growth be brought down gradually?

For most monetarists, the foundation of their ideas is the belief in the tendency of a free market economy to achieve economic efficiency. Hence monetary policy should be carried on in a way which will not disturb the real economy. This suggests that the money supply should be allowed to grow at a rate equal to the rate of growth of the productive capacity of the economy. If factors such as productivity and the labour supply suggest that the economy could grow at 3 per cent a year, then the money supply should also grow at this rate. The precise rate is less important than the principle that the growth should be steady, with governments given no discretion because they are likely to react to difficult circumstances by expanding the money supply.

The government should control the money supply by controlling the banks' ability to create credit, and this can be done by:

- Defining clearly which assets the banks can use as reserve assets.
- Controlling the issue of these assets.
- Having a minimum ratio of reserve assets to total assets.
- Keeping a close watch on banking practice.

Other policies can help achieve control over money supply . Because there is a link between government borrowing and the supply of money, control will be easier if the government controls its own spending. And, of course, the government should take whatever measures are needed to increase the efficiency with which market forces can operate in the economy.

Testing the theory

A simple view of monetarism would suggest that a change in the quantity of money will be followed by a change in prices. Table 16.3 gives some data from Spain. Does it support or refute the monetarist contention?

At first sight, the Table would seem to refute the monetarist argument – the rise in money supply after 1984 was followed by a fall in prices. However, the fall in money supply after 1988 was followed by a fall in prices. Moreover, there may have been changes in other variables such as PQ, i.e. the economy may have been growing rapidly so that the rise in money supply did not lead to high rises in prices. This simple example is an illustration of the fact that economies are very complex, so that it is often difficult to prove that a theory is correct or false.

Table 16.3: *Money and prices in Spain 1984-1992 (% changes)*

Year	M1	Prices
1984	10	9
1985	15	9
1986	16	5
1987	18	5
1988	20	5
1989	17	7
1990	17	7
1991	17	6
1992	6	6

Source: Adapted from *Economist Intelligence Unit, Country Report – Spain* 1993/94.

The Keynesian approach

Keynesian critique of the monetarist approach

Keynesian economists make a number of criticisms of the monetarist approach.

Control

Is it possible for the government to control the money supply? A policy which takes this as its central feature will not be successful if banks and firms can find ways to increase the money supply. As we have seen, 'money' can be defined in several different ways. Many Keynesians claim only money narrowly defined as notes and coins can easily be controlled by the government. In other cases, firms can borrow from abroad, make greater use of credit, or use 'near money' in order to avoid monetary controls. Keynesians go on to argue that the statistical links which monetarists have found between the money supply and the price level are only found in periods when the authorities have not tried to control the money supply. 'Goodhart's Law' says that:

'any observed statistical regularity will tend to collapse once pressure is placed on it for control purposes'.

This is because businesses find it relatively easy to switch into some other medium of exchange not under government control.

Table 16.4 illustrates the point. Even the Conservative government elected in 1979, which made control of the money supply a central feature

Table 16.4: *Monetary targets and out-turns*

Target Period	Target Range	Out-turn	Overshoot from Target Mid-Point
4.78- 4.79	8-12%	10.9%	+0.9%
10.78-10.79	8-12%	13.3%	+3.3%
6.79- 4.80	7-11%	10.3%	+1.3%
6.79-10.80	7-11%	17.8%	+8.8%
2.80- 4.81	7-11%	18.5%	+9.5%
2.81- 4.82	6-10%	14.5%	+6.5%

Source: Adapted from 'Financial Statement and Budget Reports', *Bank of England Quarterly Bulletin.*

of its economic policy, failed to achieve its target. Such targets were eventually abandoned, and changes in money supply considered merely as indicative. Consequently, monetary statistics are seen as useful information rather than precise targets to be achieved.

Velocity of circulation

Even if the government has some success in controlling the money supply, this will have little effect unless the velocity of circulation is reasonably constant. Keynesians claim that the velocity of circulation of money is unstable. A committee chaired by Lord Radcliffe as long ago as 1959 made the point:

'...during the last few years the volume of spending has greatly increased while the supply of money has hardly changed...we cannot find any reason for supposing, or any experience in monetary history indicating, that there is any limit to the velocity of circulation; it is a statistical concept that tells us nothing directly...'.

The reason for rejecting the monetarist view is simple; that if money is scarce, people will make greater use of the existing money supply. For example, if money is short then firms will cease to give a month's credit and insist on prompt payment. As a result the velocity of circulation will increase.

Every economist accepts that MV=PT, but there is disagreement about how this comes about. Whilst monetarists argue that controlling M will lead to changes in P, Keynesians argue that the line of causation is reversed – from P to M. In other words, they say the quantity of money responds to changes in the real economy; if individuals and firms need more money to finance their activities, then the sophisticated financial system will create more money, and this is why governments find it so difficult to control the money supply.

Effects

Finally, Keynesians disagree about the effects of attempting to control the money supply. Monetarists suggest that when the money supply is brought under control there will be a temporary effect on the 'real economy'. Keynesians believe that this will be permanent and that such a policy will lead to a fall in national income and employment. Hence the economic consequences of attempting to control the money supply will be worse than the original problem.

The Keynesian view of the transmission mechanism

The Keynesian approach agrees that money is important. The disagreement with the monetarists is in part about the time which the economy takes to react to changes. Monetarists tend to assume that markets adapt quickly and accuse Keynesians of only concentrating on the short run. To this Keynes retorted, 'In the long run we are all dead'. In other words, markets are often slow to react and changes that are predicted for the long run may never come about because new developments will have occurred and changed the entire position.

Keynesians focus on the link between the supply of money and aggregate expenditure; this is called the monetary transmission mechanism.

The first link is between the supply of money and the interest rate. As we have seen in Figure 16.3, an increase in the supply of money will lead to a fall in the rate of interest, just as an increase in the

Figure 16.5: *The supply of money and the level of investment*

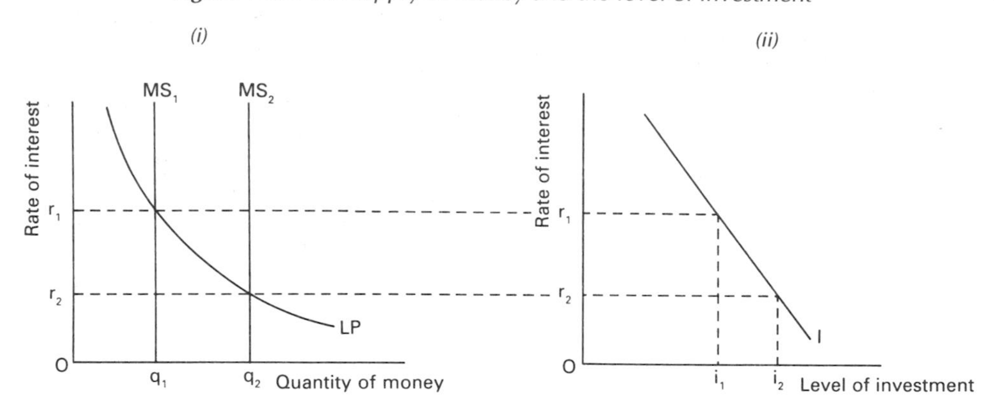

supply of a good would be expected to lead to a fall in its price.

The second link is between the interest rate and the level of spending on investment and consumer goods. Chapter 13 discussed the determinants of the level of investment and consumption; all we need to do here is summarise the main points. So far as consumption is concerned, a fall in interest rates will make borrowing cheaper and so encourage people to borrow money to finance the purchase of consumer durables. Similarly, lower interest rates will encourage firms to invest more. The links between money supply, interest rates and investment are shown in Figure 16.5. Original equilibrium is at interest rate r_1 and desired investment is i_1. When the money supply is increased from MS_1 to MS_2, the rate of interest falls to r_2 and desired investment rises to i_2.

The third link in the Keynesian explanation of the monetary transmission mechanism is that a rise in the level of investment will lead to a multiplied rise in aggregate demand, as shown in Chapter 13.

Putting the three links together, we see that a rise in the supply of money will lead to a rise in the aggregate demand and national income, the extent depending on such factors as the elasticity of the demand for money, the size of the multiplier and the interest elasticity of investment; that is the extent to which a fall in the rate of interest stimulates investment. A fall in the demand for money will have the same effect as shown in Figure 16.6.

However, there are limits to the expansion which can be achieved by this means. As the economy approaches full employment an increase in the supply of money will lead to a rise in prices because the T in the equation MV=PT will no longer rise (since the economy cannot produce more goods in the short run because there is full employment). Hence an increase in M will lead to rise in P.

Key ideas - summary of the Keynesian approach

1. Keynesian economists tend to concentrate on the short run.
2. The demand for money will be determined by the level of national income and expected changes in the rate of interest. When the rate of interest is expected to fall, there will be a fall in the demand for money because people will buy bonds.
3. Changes in the supply of money will affect the interest rate; a higher money supply will lower the interest rate and encourage investment.

Figure 16.6: *The Keynesian view of the transmission mechanism*

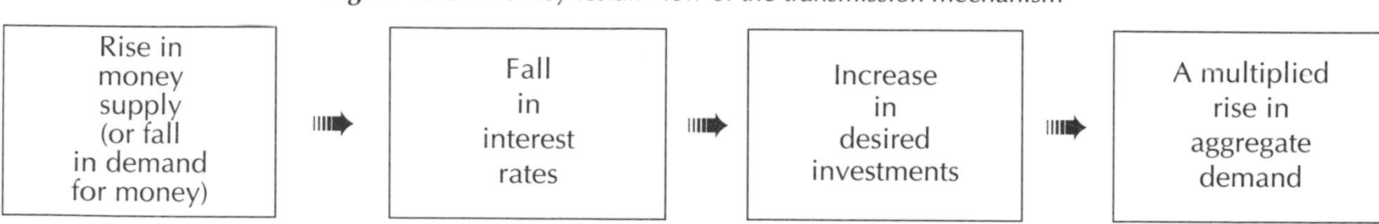

Keynesian policies

Keynesian policies tend to concentrate on the rate of interest rather than the money supply as such. This is because Keynesians tend to believe the money supply is difficult to control and that the attempt to control it will lead to a rise in unemployment. This does not mean that the money supply is unimportant. It must not be allowed to grow at an excessive rate and particular care must be taken as the economy nears the full employment level. In general, Keynesian economists believe the supply of money should be allowed to grow fairly freely so that it does not impose limits on the economy's rate of expansion. Moreover, the government should attempt to keep down the rate of interest so that firms are encouraged to invest more. However, this may be difficult.

As we will see when we discuss foreign trade and the rate of exchange, the rate of interest influences the value of the pound compared to other currencies (rich people and companies will switch their money to countries where interest rates are high and so force up the value of those currencies). Hence foreign trade and exchange rate considerations will sometimes determine policy on interest rates. Because these are interrelated, some Keynesian economists would adjust monetary policy so that it helped to achieve balance of payments and exchange rate goals.

Another policy associated with Keynesian economists is that they emphasise controlling **credit** rather than money supply. This is because there is a close link between the cost and availability of credit and the amount which consumers spend. Since Keynesians emphasise the importance of aggregate demand, it is not surprising that they advocate policies to control credit.

The European influence

The Maastricht Treaty committed most of the countries in the European Union to work towards the introduction of a single currency in the EU by the end of the decade, though the United Kingdom opted out of this requirement. In practice, however, it would be difficult for one country to be a member of the EU and to have a separate currency from all the others. The treaty proposed the introduction of a European Monetary Institute which would control the quantity of money in the EU, with the national central banks acting as its agent. However, the re-alignments of many currencies in 1992 and 1993 meant that progress towards a single currency was severely disrupted.

Conclusion

All economists agree that money matters; but there is not much agreement about other aspects of money - not even about how it should be measured. In essence, the difference between the two approaches depends in part on how they view markets. Keynesians believe that markets only adjust slowly; monetarists that the process is very quick. Monetarists believe that money affects prices because changes in money will affect asset switching behaviour which then affects all prices, including the price of goods. The real economy - the quantity of goods and services produced - is not affected by money in the long run because it is determined by supply side forces, such as changes in the working population and in productivity.

On the other hand, Keynesians tend to give less emphasis to monetary policy. Some Keynesians believe that the supply of money adjusts to the demand for it, and that attempts to control money supply lead to undesirable side-effects on output and employment. Some would argue that changes in the money supply affect the rate of interest and hence the real economy through changes in the level of investment. In turn this will affect the level of national income and employment. There will be little effect on prices, except when the economy approaches full employment. Keynesians also argue that it is often more important to control credit than the money supply since this has a strong effect on the level of consumer spending.

Data questions

Central Bank independence, fiscal policy and European Monetary Union

The case for central bank independence arises because in contrast to the political pressures that bear on elected governments, a constitutionally independent central bank has no incentive to depart from the socially optimal objective of price stability. The Maastricht Treaty requires that the European Central Bank (ECB) be constitutionally independent of elected governments and legally bound to maintain price stability within the EU. This will have implications for the governments of member states – not least it will end the ability of governments to use surprise inflation for election purposes. EMU will also affect national public finances in three other ways: first, the right to issue money will be transferred from national governments to the ECB; second, governments will lose the right of automatic unlimited access to central bank credit. Governments will be forced to cover deficits by the issue of securities; third, EMU will not only prevent national governments from using surprise inflation to affect inflation for electoral purposes, but it will also prevent surprise inflation being used to amortise outstanding debt by eroding its real value.

Source: Healey, N. & Levine, P., 'Unpleasant monetary arithmetic revisited', *National Westminster Bank Quarterly Review,* August 1992.

Question 1

1. Explain 'Surprise inflation being used to amortise outstanding debt'.
2. Summarise the argument in favour of independent central banks. What counter arguments do you think could be put?
3. What is the relationship between the supply of money and the rate of inflation?

The central propositions of monetarism

1. There is a consistent though not precise relationship between the rate of growth of the quantity of money and the rate of growth of nominal income.
2. It takes (a variable amount of) time for changes in monetary growth to affect income.
3. A change in the rate of monetary growth produces a change in the rate of growth of nominal income about six to nine months later.
4. A change in the rate of growth of nominal income typically shows up first in output and hardly at all in prices.
5. The effect on prices comes about six months after the effect on income and output, so the total delay between a change in monetary growth and a change in the rate of inflation averages around twelve to eighteen months.
6. Even after allowance for the delay in the rate of monetary growth, the relation is far from perfect.
7. In the short run, which may be as much as five or ten years, monetary changes mainly affect output. Over decades, monetary changes affect only prices; while output remains unaffected since, in the long run, output depends only upon such real factors as enterprise, ingenuity and thrift.
8. Inflation is always and everywhere a monetary phenomenon.
9. Government spending may or may not be inflationary. It will be inflationary if it is financed by creating money, i.e. by printing currency or creating bank deposits.
10. An increased rate of monetary growth raises the amount of cash which people and businesses have in relation to other assets. With the attempt to reduce cash balances, the effect spreads from one asset to another. This tends to raise asset prices and to reduce interest rates, which encourages expenditure on the production of new assets. It also encourages spending on current services rather than upon existing assets. Thus the initial impact on balance-sheets is translated into an effect upon income and spending.
11. Monetary expansion initially lowers interest rates, but, as spending and price inflation increases, it also produces a rise in the demand for loans which will tend eventually to raise interest rates. This two-edged relation between money and interest rates explains why monetarists insist that interest rates are a highly misleading guide to monetary policy. Moreover, rising (or falling), prices introduces a discrepancy between real and nominal interest rates which disturbs real sectors of the economy.

Source: Steele, G. 'Monetarism' in Atkinson, G.B.J. (ed). *Developments in Economics* Vol. 3, Causeway Press, 1987.

Question 2

1. Select three of the above propositions and develop arguments in favour of and against them.

17 Unemployment

Everybody knows what unemployment is, yet it is surprisingly difficult to define and measure, so that there are disagreements about the extent to which the published figures actually measure the level of unemployment. This chapter analyses the above problem and also the costs of unemployment – why unemployment matters to the individual and to society. It then discusses various types of unemployment and the theoretical approaches of supply siders, interventionists and Marxists.

- Supply siders urge more emphasis on market forces.
- Interventionists believe government action in order to increase aggregate demand is needed.
- Marxists argue that more radical changes are the only solution.

However, before we examine the topic in depth, we must first understand exactly what is meant by unemployment.

Defining and measuring unemployment

Defining unemployment

In everyday speech there is usually no need to make precise statements. If we say someone is unemployed, people will understand what we mean. In economics, however, we need to make precise statements and so precise definitions are needed. A useful simple definition of unemployment is someone who is willing to work, but cannot find a job. This approach is taken and developed by the International Labour Organisation, whose definition focuses on 'people without a job and seeking work for pay or profit'. However, this does not solve the problem of measuring unemployment because it is not always obvious if people are really seeking work. One reason for this difficulty is that people do not want any job; they want a job in a convenient place that pays reasonable wages. An unpleasant job in London, at a wage of £75 a week, would not appeal to many unemployed workers in Newcastle.

Measuring unemployment

There are two approaches to measuring unemployment. The first is to carry out a survey of the labour force in which a sample of members of the public are asked details of their work, or lack of it. This method is used in a number of countries, including the USA, Japan and Sweden. It gives a fairly accurate picture of the unemployment position on a national scale, but because the size of the sample in any one area is usually small, it does not give a clear picture of the position in particular parts of the country.

An alternative way of collecting unemployment statistics is to count people registering for work (or benefit) at state unemployment offices. This is the method used in the UK, where people are counted as unemployed if they register, are eligible for benefit and are actively seeking work. This gives a good picture of what is happening in small areas. The great weakness of the method is that if administrative arrangements change, then the statistics will show variations in the number registering as unemployed, even though there has been no change in the numbers actually unemployed. For example, in November 1982 the Department of Employment changed the system. Before that date the unemployment figures included all those seeking work, even if they were not entitled to benefit. Since November 1982 the basis of the figure has been the number of people entitled to benefit. The new system reduced the number of 'unemployed' by 100,000. In the decade following 1979 there were 24 changes in the way the unemployment statistics were compiled. According to the Unemployment Unit, an independent organisation which monitors the changing position, these changes have, to date, reduced the number of unemployed by over 900,000.

Do the statistics over or underestimate unemployment?

The measurement of unemployment is a political issue and people's views influence the way the unemployment figures are interpreted. Those who wish to emphasise other aspects of government policy, such as the need to reduce inflation, tend to argue that the official figures overestimate the size of the problem, whilst others (often on the political left) believe there are far more people out of work than the figures show.

The first group claims that there are many people who are registered as unemployed who are not really seeking work, or who are not in financial difficulties as a result of being out of work. For example, someone who is between jobs might be quite happy to be unemployed for a week or two whilst receiving benefit. Indeed, unemployed people sometimes take on work and 'forget' to declare the income so they continue to receive benefit. Some people do not really want work and there are some people who are so physically or mentally handicapped that however much they want a job, they have little or no chance of finding one. If all these were deducted from the unemployment figures, the number of unemployed – those who are really searching for work – would be much smaller and less effort would need to be devoted to solving the problem.

However, there are powerful arguments to suggest that the official figures underestimate the number of people seeking work. There are many people who are 'without a job and seeking work for pay or profit' but who are not counted as unemployed because they are not claiming benefit. Many married women are in this position, because if they have left paid employment to care for children they may be ineligible for benefit. Survey data suggests this group may number over half a million people. Other groups who are not counted as unemployed are those 'temporarily stopped' (that is those suspended by their employer but expecting to resume work) and workers on short time. Some people would also add those on special government schemes for the unemployed because they do not have a 'real' job. If this line of argument is accepted, then unemployment is much more serious than the official figures show and more effort ought to be devoted to solving the problem.

Stocks and flows

When unemployment is discussed, it is usually in the context of the number of people unemployed at a particular time. This can be misleading because it emphasises unemployment as a stock – a figure at a particular time. A more realistic approach is to view it as a flow, because each month many thousands of people become unemployed and thousands of others obtain work.

One explanation of the rise in unemployment at

***Table 17.1:** Jobless - the great divide*

Official total: 3,000,000

Left-wing critics ADD:		Right-wing critics SUBTRACT:	
Unemployed excluded by statistical changes	900,000	School leavers	150,000
Effect of special employment measures	400,000	Claimants who are not really looking for jobs	500,000
Unregistered unemployed	500,000	Severely disabled	20,000
		'Unemployables' - mentally or physically incapable	130,000
		'Job changers' - out of work for four weeks or less	350,000
		'Black economy' workers, illegally claiming benefit	250,000
Total additions	**1,800,000**	**Total subtractions**	**1,400,000**
TOTAL UNEMPLOYED	**4,800,000**	**TOTAL UNEMPLOYED**	**1,600,000**

Note: Approximate totals for 1993.
Source: Adapted from *The Daily Telegraph*.

Figure 17.1: *Number of 16 year olds available to enter the labour market*

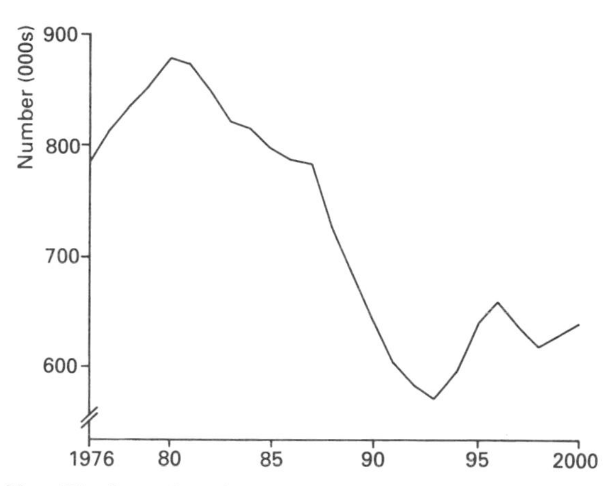

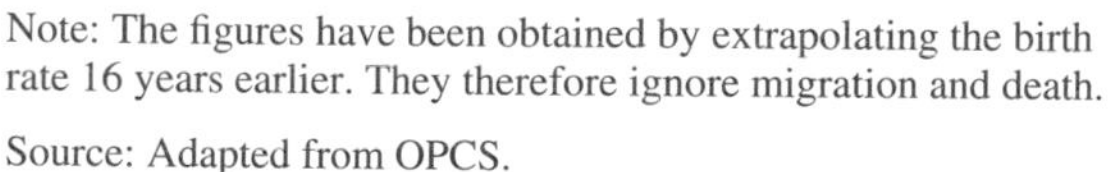
Note: The figures have been obtained by extrapolating the birth rate 16 years earlier. They therefore ignore migration and death.

Source: Adapted from OPCS.

the end of the 1970s focuses on the rise in the number of 16 year olds at this time, as shown in Figure 17.1. Whilst some of these young people continued in full-time education, a large proportion sought employment. As the number of jobs on offer did not rise at the same rate, the result was a rise in unemployment. There is not much that can be done about the age structure of the population, but governments can take measures to reduce its effect on the labour market. Thus youth training schemes take some people off the unemployment register and at the same time increase the level of skills in the labour force.

The government regularly surveys the labour force, and the information derived from these surveys can be combined with population statistics to give projections of the future size of the labour force. Figure 17.2 compares the civilian labour force in 1992 with estimates for 2001. As the figure shows, the labour force is expected to rise from 28 million to 29 million during this period. This implies that to keep the unemployment constant an additional million jobs will need to be created.

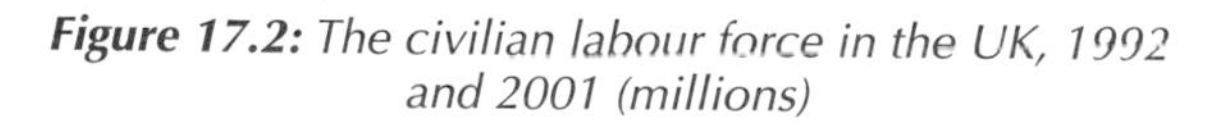
Figure 17.2: *The civilian labour force in the UK, 1992 and 2001 (millions)*

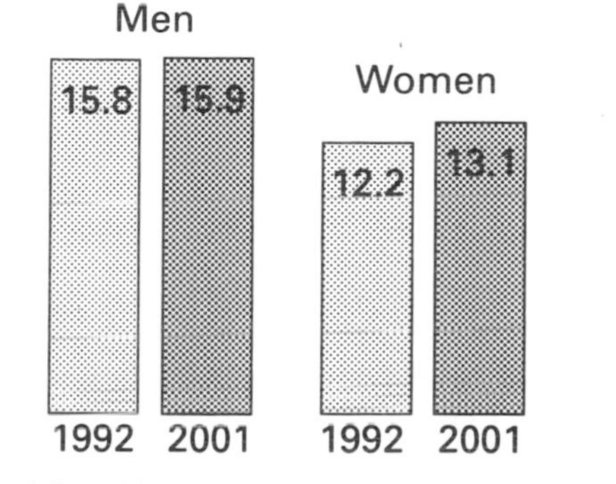

Source: Adapted from *Employment Gazette*, April 1993.

Key ideas

1. People can be regarded as unemployed if they have no job and are actively seeking work.
2. Unemployment is often viewed as a stock. A better approach is to consider the flow of people into and out of employment.
3. There are two ways to measure unemployment: the first is to survey the labour force; the second to count those registering as unemployed or seeking benefit. The UK uses the latter method.
4. Some people believe the official unemployment figures exaggerate the problem because certain people who register as unemployed do not want work, or could get a job if they were less 'fussy'. Moreover, some unemployed people are not in financial hardship.
5. Others believe that the real unemployment total is higher than the figures suggest because many people wanting jobs are not counted as unemployed because they are not eligible for benefit.

Does unemployment matter?

Everyone agrees that unemployment can be an unpleasant experience that imposes costs on the individual and on society, but there is disagreement about the size of these costs.

Unemployment and the individual

The obvious cost to the individual who is unemployed is relative poverty. Most unemployed people are poorer than those who are in work. It is true that for a few people social security benefits may mean they are better off unemployed than working, but they are exceptional. The extent to which people are poorer will depend on their particular circumstances, so that there are large variations from the average. However, a study by White (1983) into the long-term unemployed found that 59 per cent of men were receiving benefits which amounted to less than half of the amount they had earned in their last job, and that a further 25 per cent were receiving between 50 per cent and 75 per cent of their last net wage. Only 7 per cent were better off unemployed than working. Women's incomes followed a similar pattern.

A fall in a family's income affects its whole lifestyle; parents cannot afford to 'treat' their children as they would wish and Christmas may become a time of stress, when youngsters compare their meagre presents with those of their more fortunate friends. Social life is restricted and it is difficult to buy essentials, such as clothes. Unemployment leads to stress in the family. In most surveys, about one fifth of the unemployed report a deterioration in their mental health after becoming unemployed, and the longer they have been unemployed the more likely they are to report a deterioration. The unemployed tend to be more anxious, depressed, unhappy, suffer loss of self-esteem and sleep less than those with jobs. There is also evidence to suggest that the unemployed are more likely to have poorer physical health than the employed; they also have higher death rates. This type of evidence has its critics. It is difficult to prove cause and effect, and in some cases people may become unemployed because they have poor health rather than the other way round. Moreover, it is claimed that many unemployed people do not suffer very much from unemployment. In some cases their out of work income is not much lower than they would earn in work, particularly if additional costs of working, such as travel, are counted. In addition, the unemployed have more leisure time. And, the argument continues, if they really wanted work, they could find it if they were willing to be adaptable and accept low wages. This is examined in more detail later in this chapter.

The output costs of unemployment

The country is poorer as a result of unemployment. That is because if the unemployed had been working, they would have produced goods and services which would have benefited the country. However, it is not easy to measure this output loss. One reason is that it is not possible for everyone to have a job, so any estimate of the loss from unemployment has to guess what is the lowest practical level of unemployment. Some of the unemployed – for example, older workers – have effectively left the labour force and so their 'unemployment' does not involve any loss of output. One estimate of the output costs of unemployment calculated that when unemployment was just above three million the cost was about 10 - 12 per cent of GDP. This is a huge sum; it implies that if unemployment on a large scale persists at the level of the early 1990s, then the equivalent of a whole year's GNP would be lost in less than a decade.

Costs to the government

Unemployment increases government spending and cuts government revenue. Government spending increases because more public money is spent on unemployment benefits and on other social security benefits such as free school meals. Again, the costs of this are difficult to estimate because they will depend on the characteristics of the unemployed; the benefits paid to a young single person will be much less than those paid to someone with several children. Another difficulty is whether or not to include the exchequer costs of special employment measures, such as provision of work training programmes. Government finances also suffer loss of revenue because the unemployed do not pay income taxes; since their income is lower, they will also buy fewer goods and so pay less VAT.

The best estimates of these costs were done by Junankar and by Dilnot and Morris in 1983. Updated and adjusted to 1993, these suggest that the costs to the government were about £24 billion.

Costs to society

There has been considerable research on the link between unemployment and crime, and this research suggests a strong correlation between these two variables. For example, although crime rates have risen even when unemployment is low, they have risen fastest when unemployment is high and levelled off or fallen when unemployment falls. Another example, illustrated in Figure 17.3, comes from research by the Northumbria police, who found that in 1978, when the local unemployment rate was 8.8 per cent, 38 per cent of crimes involved unemployed people. The following year unemployment had risen to 12.1 per cent and 49 per cent of crimes involved unemployed people. This link between unemployment and crime is plausible; unemployed people may be more likely to commit crimes because they feel that they need money. They may also commit crimes because they are bored or frustrated. 'The devil finds work for idle hands', as the old saying goes. However, correlation does not prove that unemployment causes crime. Crime rates rise for many reasons, and continue to rise even when unemployment falls. Nevertheless it does seem probable that part of the reason for the rise in crime lies in persistent unemployment.

Figure 17.3: *Unemployment and recorded crime, England and Wales, 1971-1991*

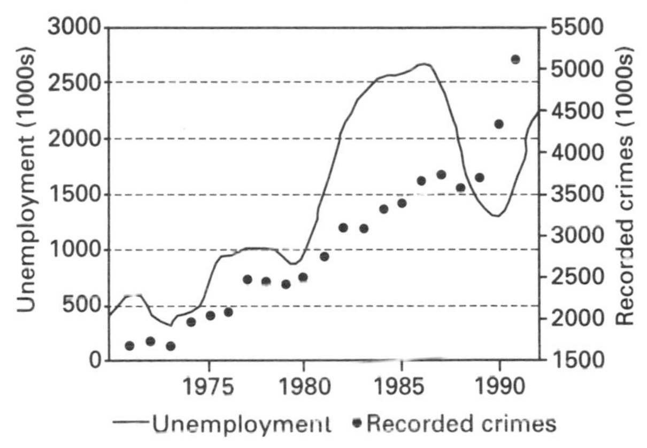

Source: Adapted from *New Statesman and Society*, January 14 1994.

There may be other social costs. Unemployment may lead to a rise in selfishness and disillusionment with society which makes people less willing to contribute their services to good causes, and may also lead to a less caring society. These sort of external costs are impossible to calculate.

Key ideas

1. Unemployment imposes costs on the unemployed, their families, the community, the government and society as a whole.
2. Individuals and their families suffer from lower incomes, poorer health and a lower status in society.
3. The government loses tax revenue and has to spend more on benefits.
4. National output falls as a result of unemployment.
5. High levels of unemployment may be one cause of crime.

Types of unemployment

One approach to the study of unemployment is to analyse the different types of unemployment. Over a period of time the relative importance of each type will change. There is some disagreement about the relative importance of each type.

Seasonal unemployment

More people are unemployed in January than in July. This is because some industries are affected by the weather. In agriculture, tourism and construction, employers tend to take on more workers as the summer approaches and to reduce employment in winter. Consequently unemployment in these industries rises in the winter months.

This has implications for measuring unemployment. In a particular winter, the actual number of unemployed people may rise, but this may be due entirely to seasonal factors; the long-term trend may be falling. The opposite may apply in summer. Hence the employment figures are sometimes presented as 'seasonally adjusted'. This means that the actual figures have been adjusted to eliminate seasonal influences.

Whilst seasonal unemployment can be painful for the individuals concerned, it is not a major problem. This is just as well, because there are no easy cures for it. One approach is to attract new industries to tourist areas, or to extend the tourist season.

Frictional and search unemployment

Everyone agrees that the labour market has special characteristics which make it different from other markets. In the market for consumer goods, for example, buyers and sellers can usually exchange information quickly and purchases can be made immediately. However, in the labour market both firms and workers need to search for information. Firms need information about the supply of labour and prevailing wage rates, whilst workers also incur costs when looking for work. Time is spent looking for appropriate posts and there may be travel and postage costs too. Sometimes workers have to decide between accepting a job now or waiting in the hope that a better one will become available in the future. The unemployment which occurs as a result of these search costs is called search unemployment. A key to understanding this type of unemployment is that people are ignorant about job opportunities. Some supply side economists believe it is a primary cause of the length of time that certain people are unemployed.

A closely related type of unemployment is frictional unemployment. Like search unemployment, this is present even when the economy is booming. In the twenty years after the Second World War, UK unemployment averaged less than 2 per cent; most of it was frictional. As its name implies, this type of unemployment is caused because people do not move smoothly from one job to the next. It is not a serious problem because workers who are frictionally unemployed obtain jobs fairly quickly. Indeed, a rapidly developing economy may have relatively high levels of frictional unemployment.

Structural unemployment

There is a good deal of agreement between economists about the existence of structural unemployment, but disputes about the causes and measures appropriate to deal with it. As its name implies, structural unemployment is caused by changes in the structure of the economy. In other words, there is dis-equilibrium in individual labour and product markets. Changes take place and the labour market is slow to adjust, causing unemployment. Thus changes in technology can cause unemployment. To give just one example of technological unemployment, for centuries dockers loaded individual items on to ships. When containers were introduced, items for transit were put into containers at the factory and far fewer people were needed on the docks because standard sized containers could be easily loaded on to specially designed ships.

Foreign competition can also cause structural unemployment. Britain used to have a substantial industry which manufactured motor cycles, but this was destroyed by competition from Japan. Changes in demand can have the same effect. At one time, almost every adult used to wear a hat or cap. This is now very rare, so employment in the hat making industry has declined substantially.

In all these events, the labour market was affected by changes and unemployment was the result. The most spectacular examples arise from the decline of manufacturing industry in the UK, so that industries such as steel and coal have experienced huge falls in employment. Thus the British Steel Corporation (later British Steel) employed 254,000 people in 1968/69; twenty years later the number had fallen to less than 50,000. Since declining industries are highly concentrated in particular areas, the effects can be very severe. This was the heart of the discussion of the regional problem in Chapter 8.

Policies for structural unemployment

Disagreements arise when policies are being suggested. Supply siders suggest policies which would emphasise market forces. Thus they believe that removing rent controls would lead to more houses becoming available for rent, so making it easier for people to move from areas where jobs have been lost to those where they are relatively plentiful.

Critics of this view argue that even if more houses did become available, the rents would be so high that those seeking jobs would be unable to afford them. These critics believe that market forces need to be curtailed by government action if much progress is to be made in reducing structural unemployment. Both groups would agree that one approach to reducing structural unemployment is that workers should retrain. However, supply siders would put the responsibility for this on individuals and firms. Interventionist economists would place more emphasis on government initiatives. This debate was discussed in more detail in Chapter 8.

Cyclical unemployment

Over a period of years, the level of unemployment rises and falls. This is sometimes called 'cyclical unemployment', though the term is not precise, because 'cyclical' implies a regular pattern and changes in unemployment are not regular. The rest of this chapter is largely concerned with explaining these changes in the level of unemployment. In order to do that, we need to develop theories about causation. Such theories are important, because policies develop from theories. Supply siders explain changes in unemployment by looking at changes in the demand and supply of labour, paying special attention to supply side factors. Keynesian economists argue that fluctuations in the level of unemployment are largely caused by changes in aggregate demand. Marxist economists argue that they are caused by conflicts which are inevitable in a capitalist society.

Key ideas

1. Frictional unemployment is a short-term unemployment which occurs when people change jobs. Search unemployment is caused by costs involved in looking for work, and is given particular emphasis by supply siders.
2. Seasonal factors are important in some industries, such as tourism.
3. Structural unemployment occurs when changes take place in the structure of the economy. These structural changes often have a strong regional impact.
4. Cyclical unemployment is the name sometimes given to fluctuations in the level of unemployment. It is the subject of competing explanations. Some economists emphasise supply side factors, whilst Keynesians focus attention on changes in aggregate demand.

The supply side approach

Although this section is headed 'supply side approach', it could equally well have been called the 'market forces approach' or even the 'monetarist approach' because all these phrases identify particular aspects of a fairly common approach to unemployment. It represents a return to pre-Keynesian economics and is also known as 'neo-classical economics'. One of the popularisers of supply side economics, an American called Arthur Laffer (1983), has explained the position:

'Supply side economics provides a framework of analysis which relies on personal and private incentives. When incentives change, people's behaviour changes in response... the role of government in such a framework is carried out by the ability of government to alter incentives and thereby affect society's behaviour.'

The starting point of this approach is the labour market. As in any other market, the forces of demand and supply determine the quantity of the good or service bought and sold. The factors which determine the demand and supply of labour were discussed in Chapter 9. All we need to do here is repeat the central supply side argument; that the demand and supply of labour are primarily determined by the price of labour and that a fall in the real wage rate will cause firms to take on more workers. It will also lead to a decline in the number of people wanting work so that there will be fewer people wanting jobs who could not find them.

The natural rate of unemployment

This is one of the most important concepts in the supply side analysis of unemployment.

The natural rate of unemployment is the rate of unemployment which exists when the labour market is in equilibrium. Alternatively, it can be defined as the amount of unemployment which still exists when the labour market has cleared, that is, when the demand for labour equals the supply, because real wages are at a level which will bring about equilibrium. This implies that at the natural rate of unemployment the rate of inflation will be constant. Hence it is sometimes given the clumsy title of NAIRU – the Non-Accelerating Inflation Rate of Unemployment. (Some economists would distinguish between the natural rate of unemployment and NAIRU, but for practical purposes it is a distinction without much difference.)

The implication of this approach is that involuntary unemployment does not exist. If some people are unemployed it is because they choose not to take up employment at the going wage rate. They prefer unemployment to work at existing wages. The argument is illustrated in Figure 17.4. In this Figure, I d shows the demand for labour. Lf is the size of the labour force and Ww the number of workers willing to take jobs at any level of real wages. The difference between Lf and Ww is that some workers are between jobs and some are unwilling to take jobs at the existing wage rate, perhaps because they are hoping for better offers. The labour market is in equilibrium at E, and ED is the measurement of natural unemployment.

If this supply side argument is accepted, then it is necessary to find out what factors determine the natural rate and then take appropriate measures to reduce it. According to Milton Friedman (1966) the natural rate is determined by:

'the actual structural characteristics of the labour and commodity markets, including labour imperfections... variability in demands and supplies, the costs of gathering information about job vacancies and labour availabilities, the costs of mobility and so on'.

Consequently the crucial factors on which this group of economists focus are the composition of the labour force, mobility of labour, costs of employing workers and imperfections in the labour market caused by government 'interference' and trade unions. Factors which shift the demand curve for labour to the left, such as a reduction in productivity, will increase the natural rate of unemployment. Factors which shift the supply curve to the left, such as increased unemployment benefits which might increase the time people spend between jobs, will also increase the natural rate.

Whilst the idea of the natural rate of unemployment has become influential, there is considerable difficulty in measuring it. According to one of the leading supply siders in the UK, Patrick Minford (1985), the natural rate was low until 1965 when 'there was a sharp rise in union power, in benefits and in taxation' so that the rate rose to a maximum of 13.5 per cent in 1980. However, Layard, Nickell and Jackman (1991) estimate that the natural rate in 1980 was only about 8 per cent. These differences are significant, because if Layard and his colleagues are right the government could have stimulated the economy without causing inflation. More recently Layard estimated the natural rate to have been 8.7 per cent in the period 1987 - 1990, compared to the actual rate of 7.3 per cent.

Figure 17.4: *The natural rate of unemployment*

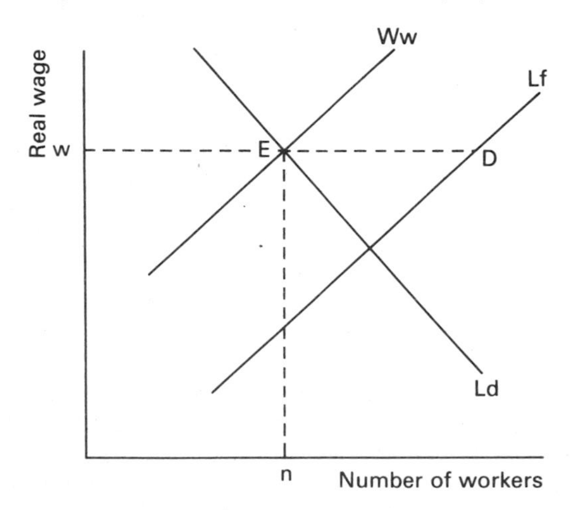

The natural rate of unemployment approach is criticised by some economists. In the first place, the word 'natural' seems to imply that it is 'God given' and that nothing can be done about it. In addition, they point out that the amount of natural unemployment is impossible to measure precisely. However, the main criticism they make is that the natural rate approach assumes the labour market is in equilibrium at the full employment level of output, and therefore any attempt by government to cut unemployment by stimulating the economy is doomed to fail. This assumption is criticised by Keynesian economists, who argue that the economy can be in equilibrium at less than full employment. Hence governments should intervene to stimulate the economy.

Unemployment benefits

Supply siders argue that government intervention reduces the effectiveness of market forces by keeping the real wage above the point where the demand and supply of labour are in equilibrium. This prevents the labour market from clearing. According to Minford (1985):

'The first and fundamental cause of unemployment is the operation of the unemployment benefit system.' Anyone who is unemployed will receive benefits and *'Such a man will very naturally expect to be re-employed at a wage after tax and work expenses which is at least as high as this benefit, and probably somewhat higher because he may not wish to "work for nothing"... Hence wages cannot effectively fall below this level for even the most unskilled worker. This level then acts as a floor under the whole wage structure...It follows that shifts in economic conditions which would warrant a fall in real wage costs will have only a limited effect on them and unemployment will result instead.'*

The argument is illustrated in Figure 17.5. Without any social security the market will clear at

Figure 17.5: *The effect of social security on employment*

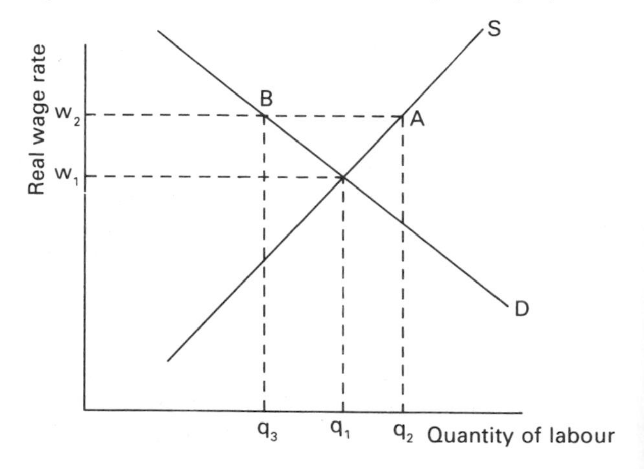

wage w_1 and q_1 units of labour will be employed. If a social security system is then put into operation so people can receive an income of w_2 when on the dole, then no one will work if wages are less than this. Hence the supply of labour is zero for wages below w_2 and the new supply of labour curve is w_2 BAS. At this level of wages the supply of labour exceeds the demand by AB. The social security system has created unemployment.

The replacement ratio

The amount of social security an unemployed person receives depends on family circumstances, so that a married person with a large family receives much more than a single person. The relationship between income when not in work and that received when working is called the replacement ratio. When this is 1.0 a person would receive the same income whether at work or unemployed. The rational person would therefore choose to be unemployed – why work when you can obtain the same income from being unemployed? Very high replacement ratios of 0.8 or 0.9 are found in cases where people only receive low incomes when at work and whose family circumstances would mean they receive high levels of social security. At the opposite end of the spectrum some single people earning high wages will have low replacement ratios. The way in which replacement ratios vary with previous earnings and family size is illustrated in Figure 17.6. At one extreme, a married couple with no children earning £50 a week would be 15 - 20 per cent better off when unemployed. At the other extreme, a couple with two children earning £180 a week would be 55 per cent worse off.

The supply side approach suggests that for many people the replacement ratio is high and that this gives them an incentive to choose unemployment. Minford (1985), for example, believes that replacement ratios are very high in the UK, exceeding 0.90 for over one in five single people and one in ten married people. Inserting this data into his model of the UK economy leads him to the conclusion that a 10 per cent cut in benefits would lead to a fall in real wages of 2.1 per cent and cause unemployment to fall by 500,000 and output to rise by 2.5 per cent.

Very different results have been obtained by other researchers making different assumptions about family circumstances and behaviour (for example, Minford assumes that married women do not go out to work and also that people claim all

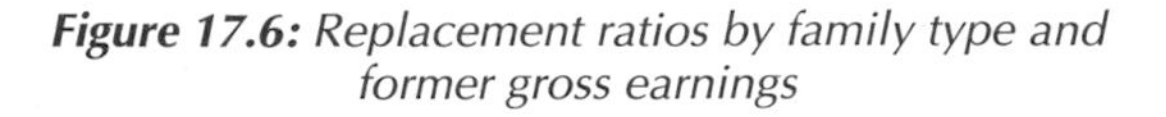

Figure 17.6: *Replacement ratios by family type and former gross earnings*

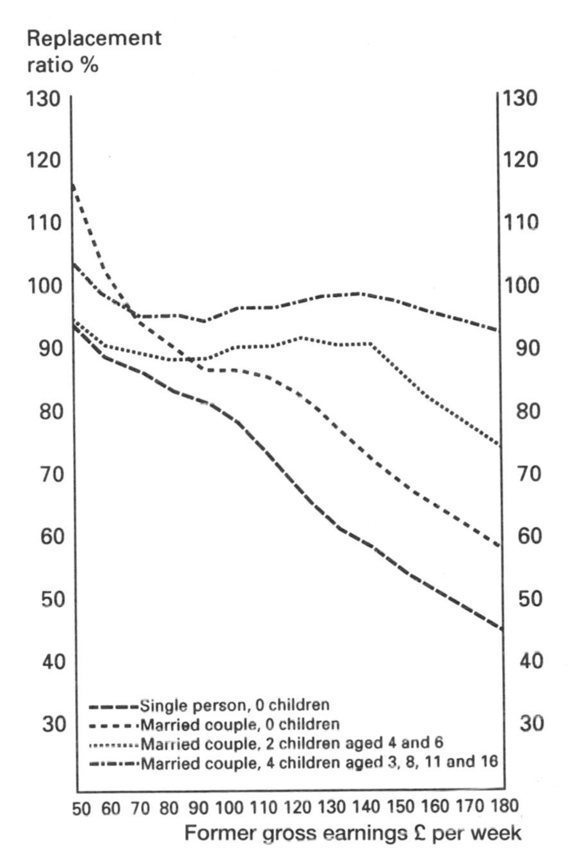

Source: Adapted from Dawson, G., *Inflation and Unemployment*, E. Elgar, 1992.

the benefits to which they are entitled). Nickell and Andrews (1983) developed a computer model and concluded that for the long-term unemployed the replacement ratio was quite low – only 0.56. They concluded that they were unable to find any strong replacement ratio effects and that the level of unemployment benefit had only a marginal impact on unemployment.

One reason for these differences is that the calculation of replacement ratios can be complex because detailed analysis is needed to discover precisely what social security benefits an individual would be entitled to in different circumstances. For example, the birth of a child or an increase in rents may lead to an increase in benefits. This argument is about the extent to which the existence of unemployment benefits raises unemployment. Everyone agrees that for some people the possibility of receiving benefits will encourage them to go on the dole. The consensus seems to be that the effects are smaller than strong supply siders, such as

Minford, would suggest. The policy implications of his approach are that radical reforms are needed to the social security system because:

'the current system of unemployment support is dangerously inefficient because it does not limit replacement ratios as work incomes fall'.

He therefore proposes that individual social security benefits should be limited so that, in all cases, net income whilst out of work would be substantially below net income whilst in work.

Tax rates

Supply siders also claim that high tax rates increase unemployment. This is because high rates discourage initiative. On the other hand, when income tax is low entrepreneurs will have more incentive to invest because they will be able to keep more of the profits. In this way, low tax rates help to develop an enterprise economy and so more people will be employed.

Trade unions

Supply siders dislike trade unions. Hayek (1984), a Nobel Prize winning economist, claims that the:

'powers of the unions have become the biggest obstacle to raising the living standards of the working class...They are the prime source of unemployment. They are the main reason for the decline of the British economy...'

The main reason for this dislike is the belief that unions distort the working of market forces. If labour is mobile, wages will rise in expanding industries and in profitable firms and fall when industries decline and firms make losses. Trade unions attempt to prevent such wage cuts. They also attempt to maintain high levels of employment in declining industries. Such activities introduce rigidities into the labour market and increase the natural rate of unemployment. Even where the economy is expanding and level of employment is rising, supply siders claim that unions cause unemployment by pushing up the level of wages for their members. This cuts employers' demand for labour, causing unemployment. If unions do manage to maintain jobs for their members, then it is argued that the burden of unemployment falls on those not in unions.

The effect on the labour market of unions succeeding in an attempt to raise real wages is shown in Figure 17.7. Original equilibrium is at wage w_1, when q_1 units of labour will be employed. If real wages rise then the quantity of labour employed falls to q_2. Note that this analysis assumes that unions can push up real wages and not just nominal wages. If firms raise prices in line with wages there will be no rise in real wages. Moreover, even if there was a fall in employment in the unionised sector of the economy, some of those displaced would drift to the non-union sector. This increase in supply would force down wages and increase employment in that sector so that the overall result may be no change in the employment level.

Figure 17.7: *A shift in supply due to union action*

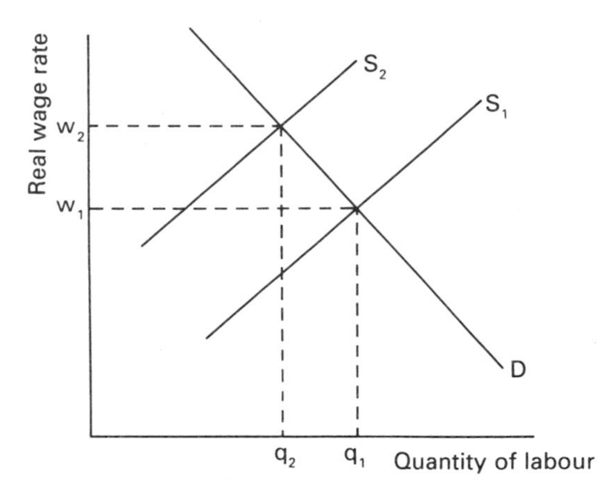

A number of estimates have been made of the effects of union power on employment, though all such studies lack precision, if only because it is difficult to quantify 'union power'. One measure often used is the number of people in unions, though this is not entirely suitable because the statistics of union membership are not very accurate and because numbers may not necessarily measure power or militancy.

Minford's model of the economy makes use of the unionisation rate and suggests that, other things being equal, a fall in the unionisation rate would lead to a fall in real wages of 0.8 per cent, a fall in unemployment of 170,000 and a rise in output of 1 per cent.

Other economists obtain very different results, even where they agree that unions do push up unemployment. Nickell and Andrews (1983) calculated that since the Second World War unions have pushed up unemployment by about 400,000.

However, they also believe that it would be wrong to attempt to weaken the power of unions because they help the less privileged sections of society. Another estimate, this time by Layard and Nickell (1985,) suggests that only 8 per cent of the rise in unemployment after 1979 could be explained by union activity. They also calculate that in the post-war period the direct impact of unions on employment has been about 2 percentage points. One reason for the difference between this result and that of Minford is that Layard and Nickell use different measures of union militancy.

Key ideas – summary of the supply side approach

1. The labour market responds to market forces. If real wages are cut then employers will take on more workers.
2. The level of unemployment cannot be reduced below its natural rate.
3. Unemployment is largely voluntary; people could obtain work if they were willing to accept lower wages.
4. People need incentives to work. Social security payments and high tax rates reduce the incentive to work.
5. Trade unions distort the working of the labour market and cut employment.

Supply side policies

Policy proposals in this area follow from the basic belief that the labour market should be free of all restraints on competition and that any action which causes workers to join unions to fix the terms of their employment is a restraint of competition. Therefore it follows that laws should be passed which weaken the unions, for example, by making them liable for damages to employers who suffer losses as a result of strike action. Such legislation is opposed by those who believe that union power is necessary because otherwise individual workers would be powerless against the huge financial resources available to employers. According to the supply side argument, governments intervene in the labour market in a number of ways, causing unemployment to rise. They believe that high rates of income tax act as a disincentive to effort, so that some people will choose not to work. This is

because rational people will consider the net effects of any action. High tax rates will shift the relative advantages against work causing people to choose leisure. National Insurance contributions paid by employees will also have the same effect.

But National Insurance contributions are also paid by companies on each employee. It is therefore argued that they act as a tax on jobs – the more people employed, the more tax which has to be paid. (This line of reasoning is also accepted by economists from other schools of thought.) The difficulty is that National Insurance contributions bring in large sums of money to the government which would find it difficult to raise the revenue in other ways. According to one estimate, the rise in employers' National Insurance costs since the 1960s has increased unemployment by about 2 per cent.

Governments also impose several non-wage labour costs on employers. Employment protection legislation may help workers to avoid unfair dismissal, but it also makes it more expensive to dismiss workers so employers are more reluctant to take on workers in the first place. Redundancy payments have the same effect. If the government imposes costs which make it more expensive to take on new workers, then employers will tend to encourage overtime among existing employees instead of increasing the number of jobs. However, empirical investigation suggests that whilst government legislation may be annoying to firms, it has relatively little effect on unemployment. In any case, these non-wage labour costs are usually lower in the UK than in other comparable countries.

Other policies favoured by supply side economists include measures to reduce the replacement ratio, for example, by cutting social security payments. They also favour cuts in income tax and other measures to improve industrial efficiency.

The Keynesian approach

The 1930s, like the 1980s, was a decade when unemployment was high and when economists disagreed strongly. The supply side analysis was the orthodox approach, but to the younger economists this failed to explain the high levels of unemployment. Their leader, John Maynard Keynes, believed that it was possible for the economy to be in equilibrium at less than the full employment level of output because markets fail to ensure that all those who want work can obtain it. He claimed:

'The system is not self-adjusting and, without purposive direction, it is incapable of translating our actual poverty into our potential plenty.'

His basic idea can be put simply. The number of people employed by a firm will depend on the demand for its products. If demand for shoes rises, more people will be employed in shoe factories and in shoe shops. If people buy more books then employment in publishing will rise. For the economy as a whole, the level of employment will depend on the level of aggregate demand. As was seen in Chapter 13 this is made up of consumer spending, investment, government spending and exports. Variables such as investment and exports are not easily manipulated by the government. Consequently, governments attempting to increase aggregate demand either cut taxes, so that consumers spend more, or preferably (because consumers will save some of their extra take home pay or spend it on imports) increase their own spending. If the government spends more on schools, hospitals or housing, then employment in these industries will rise and unemployment will fall.

There are many theoretical and practical difficulties which this brief outline has ignored, but the basic idea is clear. The government should intervene in the market to ensure a satisfactory level of aggregate demand.

Modern Keynesians

Contemporary Keynesian economists have adapted and developed his original analysis to take account of modern conditions. For this group of economists the basic cause of mass unemployment remains too low a level of aggregate demand. Thus Layard and Nickell (1985) found that about a quarter of the increase in unemployment between 1966 and 1977 was caused by falls in aggregate demand, whereas almost three-quarters of the rise since then was caused by inadequate aggregate demand. Similar results were obtained by Junankar and Price (1983) who estimated that in the period between 1979 and 1981, when unemployment rose very rapidly, 67 per cent of the increase in unemployment was caused by falls in aggregate demand. However, even if this theoretical analysis is accepted, there

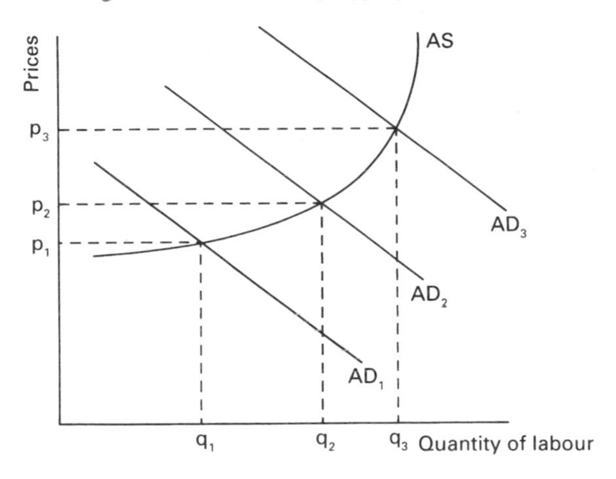

***Figure 17.8:** Increasing aggregate demand*

***Figure 17.9:** Supply side approach to an increase in aggregate demand*

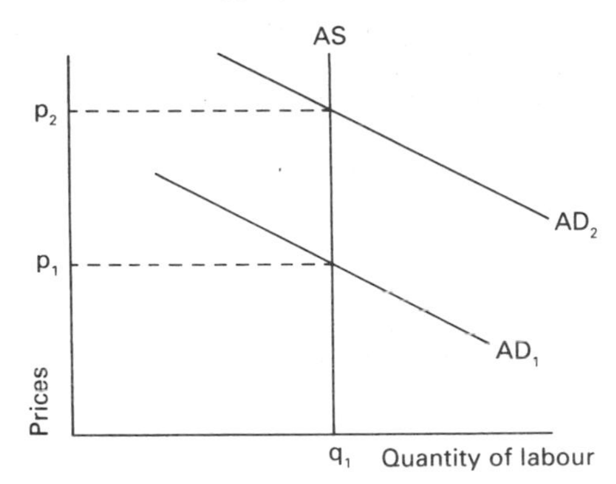

may be complications when attempts are made to implement the theory.

Complication 1: Inflation

One complication is the danger of inflation. Keynesian economists accept that as the economy nears the full employment level of output some prices will rise. If demand rises some firms will be able to increase output without putting up prices because they will be able to take advantage of economies of scale.

Other firms will be in a very different position. To increase output they will have to pay overtime rates of pay or increase wage rates in order to attract new staff. This will push up prices and cause inflation, particularly when there is only a relatively small number of unemployed workers. This effect will be greatest in those regions of the country where unemployment rates are low. The position is shown in Figure 17.8. This shows the aggregate demand and aggregate supply curves for the economy. At the original equilibrium position the average level of prices in the economy will be p_1 and the quantity of labour employed q_1. The government then expands aggregate demand to AD_2 and the result is an increase in the quantity of goods and services produced and hence in employment. However, prices also rise to p_2. If the government continues to increase aggregate demand to AD_3 the result is a much greater rise in prices and a relatively small increase in output and employment.

The Keynesian approach to this dilemma is to attempt to shift the aggregate supply curve to the right. This can be done in part by adopting some of the supply side measures discussed in the last section. Thus Layard (1986) titles one of his chapters 'Cutting Unemployment with Both Blades of the Scissors: More Demand and Improved Supply'. If these policies are successful they will encourage firms to produce more goods without putting up prices. This example illustrates that economists do sometimes agree!

A more typically Keynesian response is to adopt an incomes policy. This can take many forms, but all seek to control increases in wages. If these policies are successful then firms will be able to attract more workers without putting up wages and so increase output and employment without putting up prices.

This line of argument is rejected by supply siders. Strict supply siders believe that the long-run aggregate supply curve is vertical as shown in Figure 17.9. The reasons for this conclusion were discussed in Chapter 14. If the aggregate supply curve is this shape, any attempt to reduce unemployment by increasing aggregate demand will fail. The only result will be a rise in prices.

Complication 2: The balance of payments

A second problem which may occur when attempting to implement a Keynesian policy towards unemployment is that the economy will run into a balance of payments problem. As the circular flow of income diagram in Chapter 13 shows, the prime determinant of the level of imports is the level of incomes in the economy. If incomes rise, many people respond by taking a foreign holiday or buying foreign-made goods, such as compact disc players or video recorders. Thus the result of an increase in aggregate demand may be a fall in unemployment, but the rise in incomes which accompanies this will suck in imports and lead to a balance of payments deficit. There are a number of ways in which such a deficit can be tackled, and these are discussed in Chapter 20. However, none are particularly effective except the imposition of a deflationary policy which requires the imposition of higher taxes and cuts in government spending – precisely the measures which will cause unemployment to rise.

In recent years the balance of payments problem in the British economy has been eased by the flow of North Sea oil, but as the economy expanded in the 1980s the problem returned. Keynesian economists accept that there is no easy solution to this problem. One approach is to cut the value of the pound compared to other currencies. For the reasons given in Chapter 21, this will mean there is a fall in the price of British goods in overseas markets which will encourage exporters and increase employment in exporting industries. A fall in the value of the pound will also mean that imports are more expensive. This will help domestic manufacturers fight off foreign competition.

Key ideas – summary of Keynesian ideas

1. The level of income and employment is largely determined by the level of aggregate demand.
2. The government should vary its spending and taxation policies in order to obtain the full employment level of aggregate demand.
3. Two problems which may arise are the likelihood of inflation or a deficit on the balance of payments. Appropriate measures to solve these problems include an incomes policy and a fall in the value of the pound.

Keynesian policies

Keynesians accept that there is no easy solution to the problem of unemployment. Their policies derive from the theoretical analysis which suggests that aggregate demand is the prime determinant of the level of employment.

Since some components of aggregate demand are not under government control, Keynesians focus their policy measures on government spending and taxation. Cutting taxes may help, but some of the extra income received by consumers will be saved or spent on exports. Therefore a

better measure is to increase government spending, which should be targeted on sectors of the economy which require few imports – health, education and construction are examples. Expenditure on training is another example; this would also make industry more competitive. Governments' spending should also be targeted on those regions where unemployment is highest. If theses measures lead to inflation, an incomes policy will mitigate this. Similarly, a fall in the value of the pound will help keep British exporters competitive.

The Marxist approach

The Marxist approach is very different. Both supply siders and Keynesians are attempting to make the existing system work better. Underlying the Marxist approach, however, is the belief that conflict and crises are inevitable in any capitalist system and that, in the long run, problems such as unemployment will only be overcome by a change in the nature of the system itself.

From this it follows that, for Marxists, the Keynesian analysis is inadequate. They accept that stimulating aggregate demand would relieve unemployment, but believe the improvement would not solve the basic problem which is inherent in the system itself. For example, they criticise the Keynesian view of the way the state is supposed to operate. For most Keynesians, the state – the government, civil service, police etc. – is politically neutral. For Marxists the position is very different. They argue that the state and its institutions are the instruments of the ruling class and the aim of the state is the continuance of the system. Thus when unemployment rises, as it did after 1979, they are not surprised to see this accompanied by large increases in spending on the police and the armed forces which will then be in a position to crush any trouble arising from increased unemployment.

So far as Keynesian economic policies are concerned, some of these would be supported by Marxists, some would not. If the effect of a Keynesian reflation was a fall in unemployment, this would strengthen the power of the workers relative to that of the employers. This power shift would be opposed by the capitalists and since in the Marxist view these control the state, the state apparatus would ensure that such reforms did not succeed; for example, many capitalists would move their money overseas, thus causing a sterling crisis. Hence any improvement in unemployment resulting from Keynesian policies would only be temporary because it would be followed by a new crisis. Some other Marxist-orientated economists are rather more sympathetic to certain elements of Keynesianism so long as it is coupled with structural reforms, for example, the nationalisation of key industries, which would weaken the power of the capitalists and could be used by a socialist government to increase investment and employment.

Marxist analysis of crisis

In a capitalist society the aim of the owners of capital is to increase profits rather than production. Decisions will be made using the criterion of profitability. This will lead to conflict. There will be conflicts with other firms as they all compete for markets and there will be conflicts with workers, as employers try to keep down wages and workers try to raise them. Because these conflicts are integral to the system, they inevitably produce crises from time to time.

Falling profits

These crises can originate in a number of ways. Marx believed there was a long-run tendency for the rate of profit to fall. That is because the search for profits forces business people to accumulate more and more capital goods, such as machinery. The process of accumulation will lead to a relative increase in the amount of capital power compared to labour power. However, in the Marxist view profits arise because the value of the output produced by the workers is higher than the wage received by the workers. This is called 'surplus value' and, since it is produced by workers, the rate of profit will decline over time because the ratio of workers to capital will decline.

Consequently Marxist economists frequently produce evidence of the falling rate of profit. This decline is a long-run phenomenon, countered in the short run by other factors, such as increased productivity or wage cuts. However, from time to time the rate of profit will fall and for some firms this will mean losses and bankruptcies which will lead to a rise in unemployment. This creates a 'reserve army of labour' which is beneficial to employers. This reserve army provides an easily-available supply of workers which can be used when the economy starts to expand again. It also helps to keep down wages and makes those in work less militant because they know there are others who would like their jobs. As Marx put it, the reserve army of labour:

'creates, for the changing needs of the self expansion of capital, a mass of human material always ready for exploitation.'

In this way unemployment is beneficial to capitalists and it is not surprising to Marxists that it is a characteristic feature of such economies.

Contradictions in the system

The desire to keep down wages leads to a basic contradiction within capitalism. On the one hand, workers are buyers of goods and services and the money they spend is necessary if profits are to be maintained. On the other hand, higher profits also require low wages in order to keep down costs. If employers succeed in keeping down wages the result will be a crisis of overproduction (under-consumption). This is very similar to the Keynesian notion of unemployment caused by insufficient aggregate demand. For Marxists, the crisis is one of **realisation**; the capitalist cannot sell sufficient goods to realise the full surplus value. Profits fall and so will investment, causing problems in firms which produce investment goods. For Marx this was a crucial cause of unemployment:

'The last cause of all real crisis always remains the poverty and restricted consumption of the masses compared to the tendency of capitalist production to develop the productive forces in such a way that only the absolute power of consumption of the entire society would be their limit.'

Translated into intelligible English, Marx is saying that the system forces firms to compete by investing in more and more machinery, but workers' incomes will not grow fast enough to enable them to consume all the goods that could be produced!

Criticisms of the Marxist approach

These Marxist ideas are criticised on a number of grounds. Both supply side economists and Keynesians reject the basic Marxist belief that

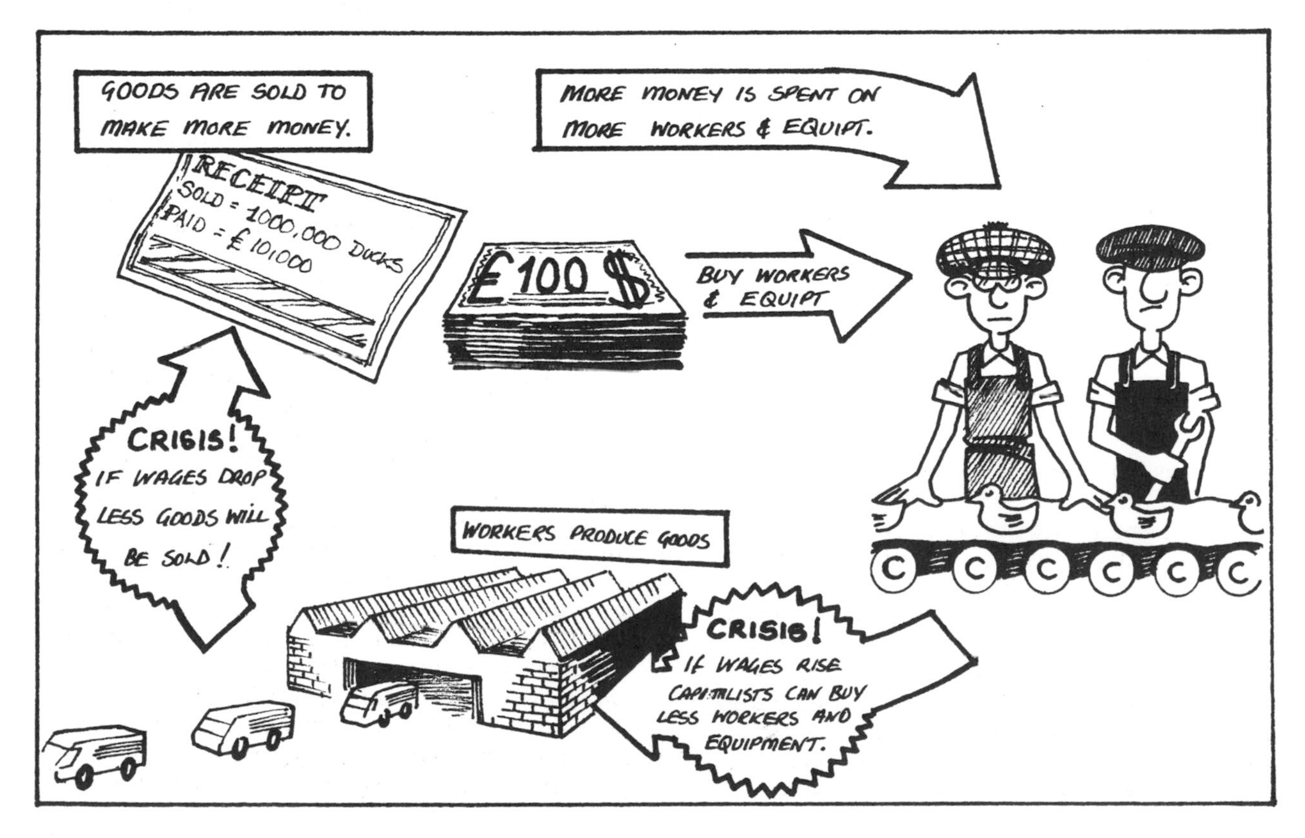

unemployment is inevitable in a capitalist system. They argue that appropriate policies can solve the problem – though, of course, they disagree about the policies. In other words they want to improve the working of the present system, not change the entire system. Moreover, both groups would be likely to reject the amount of state intervention which the Marxists would like (though some radical Keynesians would advocate an increase in public ownership). They tend to argue that state intervention is inefficient, leading to a waste of resources because large numbers of bureaucrats would be needed to run the system. The notion of a falling rate of profit is also criticised. Empirical evidence is inconclusive because it is possible to measure profit in several ways and the data is not always accurate. Critics of the Marxist position argue that the rate of profit will rise and fall over time, rising when the economy expands and falling in periods of depression.

Key ideas - summary of the Marxist approach

1. Economic crisis is inevitable in a capitalist society. If wages are too high, owners will suffer from low profits. If wages are too low, sales will fall and so will profits.
2. In the long run, unemployment can only be wiped out by a revolutionary change to a socialist society.
3. The basic causes of unemployment are exacerbated by structural factors, such as low investment and the international monetary system, both of which lead some countries to build up huge debts.

Marxist policies

There is some disagreement between Marxists about the precise policies which should be adopted in the short run because they believe that unemployment is caused by the nature of the system itself and can only be overcome by changing it. For these Marxists, what is needed is that production should be organised for need, not profit. This implies that about 200 of the largest firms should be nationalised in order that the state can control output and employment. Other Marxists suggest less radical measures, many of which are along Keynesian lines of increased public expenditure. Marxists would reinforce this by including some nationalisation, for example, of part of the banking sector in order to ensure cheap loans for industry.

'To ensure that financial resources are fully used for the programme of industrial regeneration, key sectors of banking and finance would become part of a publicly owned system'

argues the Marxist economist Aaronovitch (1981).

Many Marxists also favour some measure of import controls so that the economy can expand without running into a balance of payments problem. Some radical Keynesians also advocate such measures. Marxists also argue that unemployment can also be reduced by measures which reduce the supply of labour, for example, a reduction in overtime so that existing work could be shared out more evenly.

Behind all these proposals is a belief that radical state intervention is required to reduce unemployment. Planning output and employment is needed to bring stability into the system.

Recent developments in employment theory

The prolonged periods of high unemployment of recent years, combined with the difficulties which both Keynesian and supply side economists have in giving complete explanations, have caused economists to review their theories. One recent development concerns **efficiency wages**. This is an attempt to explain why wages do not fall to the level at which 'involuntary' unemployment will be eradicated, as explained on page 189. One reason is that firms may set wages above this level as a way of disciplining workers. If wages were at the competitive level, workers would be indifferent between working and losing their job since they could easily find alternative employment at a similar wage. However, if firms pay more than the competitive wage, workers will lose if they move jobs, and this gives employers a disciplinary lever. Firms may also be willing to pay over the odds to keep their workers, since the costs of a rapidly changing workforce can be considerable. Consequently, firms prefer to pay wages above the equilibrium rate, and unemployment results.

A variation of this approach is the **insider -**

outsider hypothesis, developed by two economists, Lindbeck and Snower (1989). In this theory, workers are divided into two groups, 'insiders' who have stable jobs, and 'outsiders' who are unemployed or whose jobs offer little security. When insiders continue to be employed, the firm saves on turnover costs. This means that insiders can command higher wages and earn an economic rent. Insiders can increase their bargaining power by not co-operating with the training of new entrants, so pushing up training costs and reducing the productivity of new entrants. One result of this is that firms offer low wages to new entrants, causing them to be reluctant to accept jobs. The insider-outsider model helps explain why unemployment tends to be persistent, but it does not explain what causes unemployment in the first place.

Another recent approach to unemployment is called **hysteresis**. This is a term borrowed from physics, and refers to the process whereby a variable is determined by its past history and where there is no tendency for it to return to its former value. In the case of unemployment, it helps explain the fact that once unemployment rises, it is very slow to return to its old level. One reason for this is the 'discouraged worker'. People who have been unemployed for some time may become discouraged by the failure of repeated job applications and consequently their resolve to work may diminish. Moreover, employers are often reluctant to employ the long term unemployed either because their skills are eroded or because they believe such people are lazy.

There is some evidence to support this argument. A rising unemployment rate implies that inflows into the register of unemployed workers exceeds outflows so that short term unemployment is high. If unemployment is hysteretic it is the *change* in unemployment, not the *level*, that affects wage inflation. Research by Coe (1988) suggests that this is the case in the UK, Austria and Spain, but that there is no support for the hysteresis theory in Japan or the USA.

This analysis has policy implications. Unemployed people who have been out of work for only a short period of time can obtain jobs if they are willing to work for lower wages. The long term unemployed cannot do this – they may lack the initiative to seek jobs, and employers may be unwilling to offer them work. Consequently, governments should intervene with special measures for the long term unemployed. One suggestion is a job subsidy; for example, offering employers a subsidy equal to the benefits which would be received by an unemployed person when they employ such a person. In 1993 the government initiated four pilot schemes offering employers average benefits (about £50 a week) when they provided jobs for people who had been unemployed for two to four years.

Conclusion

The three approaches to unemployment discussed here have been presented as three separate and distinct theories. Whilst this is largely true, it should be remembered that it is something of an oversimplification. There is disagreement within each group and some overlap of views. Thus some Keynesians accept the need to improve the supply side of the economy whilst some would agree with Marxist views about the need for an increase in public ownership.

Nevertheless, it is possible to identify three distinct strands of thinking, each with its own policy proposals. The economists who are here called supply siders focus on the market and on incentives. Their strategy leads to less government intervention and cuts in taxation and public spending, particularly on social security benefits. Keynesians believe government intervention is necessary, particularly to ensure an adequate level of aggregate demand and help hard hit regions. Marxists would like a much greater degree of government intervention in the economy and a substantial increase in the public sector. These three views are not compatible; it is not possible to select the 'best' of each approach and advocate this package because the policies are often contradictory. For example, supply siders argue that cuts in real wages will increase employment, whilst many Keynesians would oppose such cuts because they believe that they lead to a fall in aggregate demand and hence in employment.

Data questions

Charter for jobs

1. We believe that the present level of unemployment is economically wasteful and socially corrosive. The Government can and must stimulate the creation of more jobs.
2. There is useful work crying out to be done. With extra spending we could renovate our cities and improve the health of our people, while lower taxes on jobs would raise private spending power and make us more competitive. To make this possible there has to be some increase in Government borrowing. Government borrowing should normally rise in a depression. When there is useful work to be done, it is as sensible for the Government to borrow money as for firms or families to do so.
3. The Government has a special responsibility for the million and a quarter people who have been unemployed for over a year.

These people should be guaranteed the offer of a job on socially useful projects, such as the Community Programme supports.

We can cut unemployment.

Source: Charter for Jobs, London.

Question 1

Examine the 'Charter for Jobs'.

1. Explain why unemployment can be 'economically useful and socially corrosive'.
2. Which economic theory lies behind these public proposals?
3. What problems could result from such a policy proposal?

Pay versus jobs in the 1990s

The last ten years have seen significant changes in UK government policy towards labour markets and in labour market legislation, designed to make markets more efficient. Trade union power has been reduced, official intervention in wage setting (for example on minimum wages) has declined, the tax and benefit system has been revised to improve work incentives, companies have been encouraged to link pay to performance (for instance through profit-related pay) and increased emphasis has been given to training.

Source: *Lloyds Bank Economic Bulletin* No 175, July 1993.

Question 2

1. What effect would (i) supply siders and (ii) Keynesians suggest that these measures would have on unemployment?
2. The extract suggests that work incentives have improved. What effect might supporters of the efficiency wage argument suggest that this would have on unemployment?

Unemployment and figures of speech

Many people have challenged the accuracy of the unemployment statistics. A recent study by John Wells at Cambridge University has estimated that the true level of joblessness is much nearer four million than the 2.8 million estimated by the statisticians at the Department of Employment. The main criticism of the official jobless count is that it is purely an administrative tool to count the number of people claiming benefits, and not intended to measure the social and economic cost of unemployment. To this charge, ministers respond that the total closely corresponds to the internationally accepted survey of joblessness by the International Labour Office.

Dr Wells argues that this is coincidence. On the ILO measure (a survey of 60,000 households who have looked for a job in the last four weeks and have not had any paid work) there were over a million people who were unemployed but not claiming benefit. When these are added to the core of 1.8 million which is common to the ILO and the government measures, the ILO total unemployed comes to 2.9 million – very similar to the government total. However, Dr Wells argues that the ILO approach also underestimates the number of unemployed because it excludes many people who combine low part time casual earnings with state benefits to make a living wage. The ILO definition also excludes 140,000 discouraged workers – people who have given up hope of finding a job though they would take one if it was offered to them. Finally, the study suggests that the 300,000 people on a variety of work related training schemes should also be counted as unemployed.

Source: Adapted from *The Guardian,* 10 January 1994.

Question 3

1. Outline 'the social and economic costs of unemployment'.
2. Contrast the methods used by the ILO and the government to measure unemployment. What are the advantages and disadvantages of each method?
3. What criticisms might the government make of Dr Wells' arguments?

18 Inflation

When prices are more or less steady there is little interest in inflation; but when they do rise it becomes the prime focus of economic attention. Everyone recognises that when inflation gets out of control it can have severe consequences.

- Monetarists believe that inflation is the supreme economic evil and that the government should give top priority to eradicating it. The background to their methods was discussed in Chapter 16. For these economists, the only way to conquer inflation is to control the money supply.
- Keynesian economists argue that the undesirable effects of inflation are often exaggerated, though they do recognise that high inflation rates cause problems. They put forward two possible causes of inflation. In the first place they suggest that excess aggregate demand can lead to rising prices. Secondly, they point to supply factors, such as wage increases or rises in the price of raw materials like oil, as the causative factors. A variation of this approach comes from sociologists who suggest that inflation derives from social conflict. As this increases, disadvantaged groups seek to improve their position by forcing up their incomes, and this leads to inflation.

How accurate are the measures of inflation?

Inflation can be defined as a **persistent** increase in the general level of prices. Hence a rise in the price of one or two goods is not called inflation; nor is a once and for all increase in the general price level.

There is no perfect way to measure inflation. In practice, the first step is to find out what goods and services people actually buy. This is done through a survey of about 7,000 households. The items purchased are given 'weights' according to their importance. This is because it does not matter much to most people if there is a rise in the price of drawing pins or shoe laces, but rent or food price increases will have a significant effect. Table 18.1 shows the weights used in the Retail Price Index. Their precise importance varies over time. This version suggests that 16.4 per cent of the typical household spending went on housing and 14.4 per cent on food. Over the last few years we have spent **relatively** less on food and more on transport and housing. From this survey, the authorities derive a notional 'basket' of goods which represents the spending pattern of a typical household. However, since few households are typical, these average figures will not be an accurate measure of the inflation rate for particular households. This is because some families spend much more on, say, cars so a rise in the cost of motoring would have a much bigger effect on them than on others who rely on public transport. The second stage is to find out the prices of these goods and services. For some items, such as electricity, this is done nationally, but the prices of most goods are found by officials visiting a range of shops. The information is then used to calculate the cost of a notional basket of goods. This is repeated each month, making it possible to compare the change in prices over time.

The Retail Price Index

In order to make comparisons easier, the actual price of the basket is translated into an index number. Essentially this involves comparing the cost of the basket of goods in one year with that in a base year which is given the value of 100. That is:

$$\text{Price index} = \frac{\text{Cost of basket today}}{\text{Cost of basket in base year}} \times 100$$

Hence if the cost of the basket of goods rose by 50 per cent over a period of time, then the price index would rise from 100 to 150. Percentage changes in the Retail Price Index (RPI) for the UK in recent years are shown in Figure 18.1.

The Retail Price Index is only one way in which

Table 18.1: *Weights used in compiling the Retail Price Index*

Food	144
Catering	45
Alcoholic drink	78
Tobacco	35
Housing	164
Fuel and light	46
Household goods	79
Household services	47
Clothing and footwear	58
Personal goods	39
Motoring	136
Fares	21
Leisure goods	46
Leisure services	62
Total	**1,000**

Source: Adapted from *Employment Gazette*, HMSO, May 1993.

the level of inflation can be measured. A separate index is calculated for pensioners, since this group has different spending patterns to the population as a whole. Another index takes into account changes in tax and National Insurance and is called the Tax and Price Index. This attempts to measure the changes in income after tax which the average person would need to maintain their purchasing power.

Two more indexes can be mentioned. The Producer Price Index measures changes in the cost of primary products and is, therefore, a useful predictor of future changes in the Retail Price Index. Finally, the GDP deflator takes account of changes in the cost of non-marketed goods, such as health and education. It is used when economists want to eliminate the effects of inflation when comparing changes in national income over time.

All price indexes have limitations. We have already mentioned that the RPI only measures the goods bought by the average family, and few people are average. Moreover, it is difficult to take proper account of the effect of new goods that appear on the market, since these will not appear for some years in the 'basket' of goods used to construct the index. During this time their price may fall. This is what has happened to the prices of items such as calculators and computers.

Another limitation arises because the RPI is concerned with changes in prices. If the quality of goods improves or deteriorates this will not be reflected in the index. If the price of cars rises by 5 per cent but their quality improves by 10 per cent, consumers will be better off, but this will not be reflected in the index. Finally, problems arise when making international comparisons. In the UK mortgage repayments are included in the 'basket', so when interest rates rise so will the measured rate of inflation. In most other countries these payments are not included. Consequently, inflation rates are now sometimes quoted as 'the underlying rate'. This means that mortgage payments are excluded.

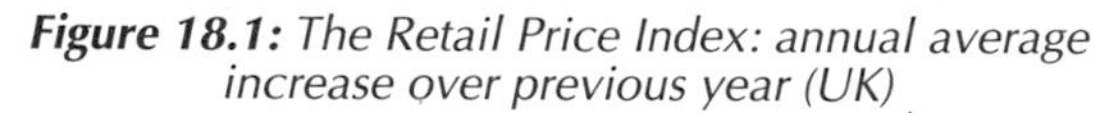

Figure 18.1: *The Retail Price Index: annual average increase over previous year (UK)*

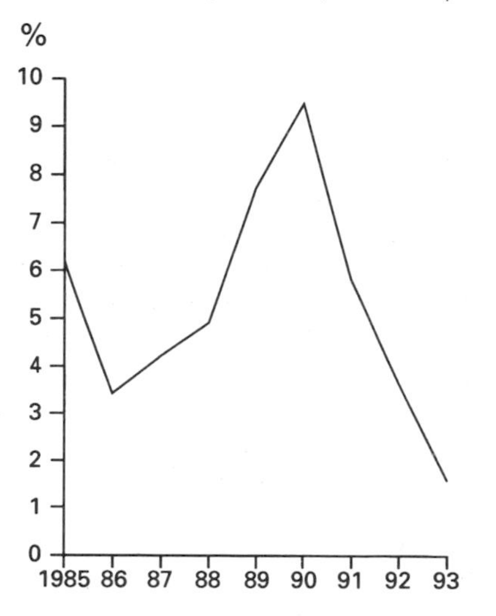

Source: Adapted from *Employment Gazette*, HMSO, 1994.

Key ideas

1. Inflation is a persistent increase in the general level of prices.
2. In the UK, the Retail Price Index measures the change in the price of a basket of goods bought by the average family. Other measures include the producer price index and the GDP deflator.

Does inflation matter?

What are the effects of inflation on the economic life of the community? In everyday life, people tend to assume that inflation is undesirable, but it is necessary for economists to be more precise and analyse the exact effects. This is easier to say than to do. One reason is that the effects depend to a large extent on whether the inflation is anticipated. If people expect inflation to be 10 per cent and it is 10 per cent, then they can change their behaviour to take account of this. However, if they expect a zero or low rate of inflation and the actuality is a high rate, then the effects are much more serious.

Perfectly anticipated inflation

If we assume that people can anticipate inflation perfectly, then the main costs will tend to be relatively minor because people can change their behaviour to minimises the undesirable effects; for example, they can save their money in index-linked accounts.

Shoe leather costs

This takes two forms. Since not all prices rise at the same rate, people spend time shopping around for the lowest price. Secondly, money loses its value in inflationary times, so the rational individual holds little money and consequently has to make frequent trips to the bank to withdraw money.

Menu costs

Firms have to spend time and money changing price tags, altering vending machines and so on.

Psychological costs

Even though people anticipate rises, they can still be annoyed when they find that prices have actually gone up. This cost is much greater when the inflation is unexpected. For example, some people will find they have not enough money to pay the bill when they reach the supermarket till.

Unanticipated inflation

If people do not anticipate the rate of inflation perfectly, then the effects are more severe.

Redistributional costs

These take several forms. In the first place, people tend to pay more in tax. This is because many incomes rise with inflation so that some people will move into high tax brackets (unless tax allowances are increased at the rate of inflation). Also, as prices rise, the government will obtain more money from a standard rate of VAT.

Secondly, inflation reduces the real value of the National Debt. Hence the government benefits, but people who have lent money to the government lose out. This is a specific example of a general point; inflation benefits borrowers while lenders lose. That is because the money paid back by borrowers is worth less than the money which they borrowed. One group of losers is people on fixed incomes. Those receiving state pensions do not lose because these are increased to take account of inflation, but some people receive incomes which do not rise with inflation and risk sinking into poverty.

These redistribution effects are undesirable because they are arbitrary. Whether they are serious is open to debate. The extent of the gains and losses is unclear. In some cases the redistribution may be from rich to poor (which some people may think is desirable), though some will be from the less well-off to those with greater resources.

Balance of payments

When prices rise in a country it tends to become more difficult for that country to export because its goods are less competitive. Moreover, the high prices which can be charged will encourage foreigners to send more goods to that country. Hence it can be argued that inflation will worsen the balance of payments. However, this assumes that the rate of exchange remains the same. If prices in country A rise by 10 per cent more than those in the rest of the world, but the value of A's currency falls by 10 per cent, then this balance of payments effect will disappear.

Investment

Monetarists tend to argue that inflation will lead to a decline in investment because it makes entrepreneurs less certain about the future. However, it may encourage investment if firms see their profits rising (even though they may be constant in real terms). In addition, since firms often borrow money to invest, they will benefit as borrowers, and so be encouraged to invest. The overall effect is uncertain. In most cases it may be that the effect of inflation is small compared to the other influences on investment.

Unemployment

According to supply side economists, such as Milton Friedman, inflation is likely to increase the level of unemployment. That is partly because he believes it will reduce investment as mentioned above. An indirect reason is that he believes inflation leads to a fall in efficiency, since firms and workers find it difficult to judge if price rises result from inflation or from an increase in demand. In other words, inflation prevents the price system from working as well as it should. Misleading messages replace the clear signals of the price system. Efficiency falls, with the result that unemployment rises. Friedman also argues that inflation can lead to stronger trade unions and to governments introducing inappropriate policies, such as prices and incomes policies. Both these developments weaken the market and cause a less efficient allocation of resources and possibly higher unemployment.

These claims by Friedman are not universally accepted by economists. The relationship between inflation and unemployment is discussed in the next section in more detail.

Hyper-inflation

Some economists believe that inflation can lead to political and social disintegration. In part this depends on the rate of inflation. In the First World War, several countries suffered from very high inflation and this led Keynes to write:

'There is no subtler, no surer means of overturning the existing basis of society than to debauch the currency'.

This is an opinion of Keynes with which Friedman heartily agrees.

There is little evidence to suggest that 'ordinary' rates of inflation lead to the overthrow of society.

Table 18.2: *The depreciation of the German mark, 1921-23*

Date	Price index	Currency in circulation (billion marks)
1921 July	1	123
1922 July	7	1,295
1923 January	195	
1923 July	5,230	
1923 August	66,017	
1923 September	1,674,755	
1923 October	496,209,790	2,500,000
1923 November 15	54,448,000,000	92,000,000

Source: Jefferson, M., *Inflation*, Calder, 1977.

Countries as diverse as Brazil and Israel have experienced inflation rates of over 100 per cent per annum and show no signs of disintegration. However, hyper-inflation can accelerate and destroy a currency's usefulness as a means of exchange. The best known example of this was the depreciation of the German mark in the period 1921 - 1923, as shown in Table 18.2. A change such as this means that people can find their life savings become worthless, and as a result they turn to political extremists.

Key ideas

1. The effects of inflation differ according to whether or not it is anticipated.
2. Even when inflation is anticipated, there are shoe leather, menu and psychological costs.
3. Unanticipated inflation can affect income distribution, the balance of payments, investment and employment.
4. Hyper-inflation destroys a currency's usefulness as a means of exchange.

Inflation and unemployment

In the 1950s A.W. Phillips compared the rate of change of money wages in the UK with the rate of unemployment over 100 years. Since there is a closes statistical link between the rate of change of money wages and the rate of inflation, money wages are sometimes used as a proxy for inflation and used to analyse the relationship between inflation and unemployment. The link between these variables found by Phillips is called the Phillips curve and is shown in Figure 18.2.

The curve suggested a trade-off between these two variables. This meant the government had a choice between a position such as A where unemployment is low, but wage rates (and hence inflation) are rising quickly, and B where unemployment is high but wage rates (and inflation) are rising very slowly. Note that the terms of the trade-off vary over the length of the curve. To the right of B, for example, unemployment has to increase substantially in order to achieve only a small fall in the rate of inflation. To the left of B a much bigger fall in inflation is achieved for a relatively small rise in unemployment.

A number of explanations were put forward to

Figure 18.2: *The Phillips curve*

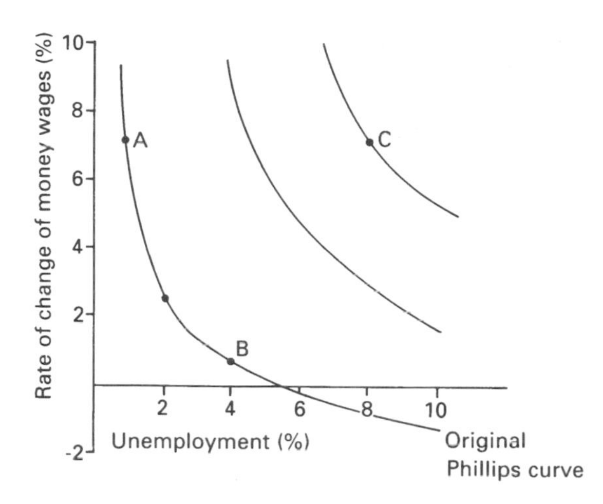

explain this relationship. At a position such as A, unemployment is very low, so many people have money to spend, aggregate demand is high and this pulls up prices. Moreover, at A there will also be a shortage of labour in some areas and this will push up wages (and prices).

Phillips' analysis of the relationship between inflation and unemployment was published in 1958 and the relationship seemed to hold true for a decade after that. Then it broke down; the economy suffered high rates of inflation and unemployment at the same time. The Phillips curve had moved to the right to a position such as C, with relatively high levels of both inflation and unemployment. These reasons are discussed in detail later in this chapter, but briefly the monetarists suggested that people had come to expect higher rates of inflation and so claimed higher wages, and that the government financed the inflation by allowing the money supply to rise. Keynesian economists, on the other hand, stressed changes in costs, such as the rise in oil prices and the strength of trade unions. These pushed up prices, irrespective of the unemployment level.

In 1985, Lewis attempted to identify the main sources of inflation and considered five categories, as shown in Table 18.3. He found that increases in wages accounted for over a third of the rise in prices, but that the relative importance of each factor varied over time. Hence in 1973/74 import prices (particularly oil) were the most important source of inflation.

An analysis such as this identifies possible sources of inflation, but it does not offer a coherent theory of why inflation occurs and why the rate of inflation varies over time. It will come as no surprise to discover that economists have competing theories about these matters.

Key ideas

1. The Phillips curve suggested a statistical relationship between the rate of change of money wages (which was used as a proxy for inflation) and unemployment.
2. Many economists interpreted this relationship to imply a trade-off between the two variables.
3. Subsequently the curve shifted to the right, showing high levels of inflation and unemployment.

The monetarist approach

The monetarist approach to the control of inflation has three elements: the quantity theory of money, expectations and the Phillips curve, and the system of exchange rates.

The quantity theory of money

This has been extensively discussed in Chapter 16.

Table 18.3: *Components of inflation in the UK, 1970/71-1982/83*

Components of inflation rate	1970/1	1971/2	1972/3	1973/4	1974/5	1975/6	1976/7	1977/8	1978/9	1979/80	1980/1	1981/2	1982/3
Labour costs	2.5	4.1	2.7	7.2	11.2	3.5	3.2	3.9	5.6	7.6	3.8	1.5	1.2
Capital costs	3.2	3.9	2.6	0.8	4.3	5.0	7.4	3.4	2.6	3.0	2.5	2.8	2.7
Imported goods	0.8	0.6	5.0	9.0	3.0	4.7	3.0	0.6	1.6	2.0	1.1	1.6	1.7
Indirect taxes	0.2	0.4	-0.1	-0.3	3.8	3.1	4.4	1.6	4.7	3.8	3.1	1.8	0.2
Residual	1.7	-2.4	-1.6	0.6	1.3	-0.6	-2.8	-0.7	1.7	0.1	0.4	0.8	-0.4
Inflation rate	8.4	6.6	8.6	17.3	23.6	15.7	15.2	8.8	12.8	16.5	10.9	8.5	5.4

Source: Lewis, M., Money and the control of inflation in the UK', *Midland Bank Review*, Summer, 1985.

Here we can examine it in a slightly different way. If we assume that the supply of money is unaffected by the demand for it (an assumption which non-monetarists would not accept), then for the monetary sector to be in equilibrium the demand for money must equal the supply and we can write:

$$\Delta Md = \Delta Ms$$
and
$$\Delta Md = a\Delta Y - b\Delta R + \Delta P$$

where Δ = change in. This equation says that the change in the demand for money (ΔMd) has three parts. In the first place, it depends on changes in the level of national income (aΔY), a rise in which will lead to a rise in the demand for money for transactions purposes. The a in the equation measures the income elasticity of the demand for money, that is the extent to which a rise in incomes will lead to a rise in the demand for money.

The second element in the equation says that the demand for money will depend on the rate of interest (bΔR). A rise in the rate of interest will increase the opportunity cost of holding money and so lead to a decline in demand for it. The b in the equation measures the interest elasticity of the demand for money, that is, the extent to which a rise in the rate of interest will lead to a fall in the demand for money. The final element says that a rise in the rate of inflation (ΔP) will lead to a rise in the demand for money – as prices rise people will want more money to finance their transactions. The monetarist argument is that any increase in the supply of money will lead to a rise in the demand for money in order to maintain equilibrium. In the short run, the effect will be on Y and on R, but in the longer term, Y – the level of national income – is determined by 'real' factors, such as productivity and the size of the labour force. Monetarists also argue that b (the size of changes in the demand for money resulting from changes in the rate of interest) is very low. Hence it follows that, in the long run, changes in the supply of money will affect the price level.

Expectations and the Phillips curve

As we saw earlier, the original Phillips curve suggested an inverse relationship between the rate of inflation and the level of unemployment, but in the 1970s the relationship broke down and the economy was faced with high rates of inflation and unemployment. Monetarist critics, such as

Figure 18.3: *Expectations-augmented Philips curve*

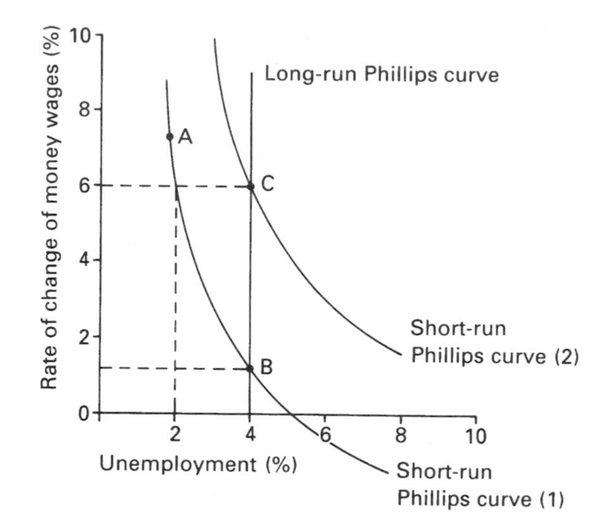

Friedman, claimed that the reason why this relationship broke down was because there was no trade-off in the long run. His argument was that workers were interested in **real** wages. If they expected prices to rise by 5 per cent, they would demand wages which increased by at least this amount.

The effect of including expectations is to shift the curve to the right. If at a position such as B in Figure 18.3 workers expect inflation to be 5 per cent, they will demand an extra 5 per cent in wages; this will push up prices by an extra 5 per cent, and the result will be a point on a new Phillips curve (at C). In fact, this is a point on a **vertical** Phillips curve. For this group of economists, there is no trade-off and the long-run curve is vertical.

Their reasoning is this. If at a point such as B the economy is in equilibrium, but the government tries to stimulate the economy, the immediate result will be an increase in the money supply which will increase aggregate demand. This causes an increase in the demand for labour to produce the extra goods. However, since this group of economists believes that the labour market is in equilibrium, the only way for firms to attract more workers is to put up wages. But this then pushes up prices by an equivalent amount. This means the real wage falls so the extra workers drop out of the labour market leaving production at its original position. The only effect of the attempt to stimulate the economy has been a rise in prices and wages, with output and unemployment unchanged. The Phillips curve will be vertical at the natural rate of unemployment.

The exchange rate

This is discussed more extensively in Chapter 21. Here it is sufficient to note that in a system of fixed exchange rates (that is one where the value of a currency is fixed against other currencies so that the pound always equals, say, $1.50) a balance of payments surplus or deficit will affect the supply of money. For example, a surplus will mean that money will flow into the country, and so increase the money supply. However, if the exchange rate is floating – so that the value of the currency varies each day – the authorities have more control over the money supply because they can allow the value of the currency to vary if there is a surplus or deficit in the balance of payments. This means that if money is flowing into the country as a result of a balance of payments surplus, they can allow the value of the currency to rise, so making exports more expensive and reducing the surplus.

Non-causes of inflation

In *Free To Choose* (1980), Milton and Rose Friedman list factors which non-monetarists sometimes suggest as causes of inflation, and which they claim are not causal factors:

- Unions may provide useful services for their members. They may also do a great deal of harm by limiting employment opportunities for others, but they do not produce inflation. Wage increases in excess of increases in productivity are a result of inflation, rather than a cause.
- Similarly, businessmen do not cause inflation. The rise in the prices they charge is a result or reflection of other forces. Businessmen are surely no more greedy in countries that have experienced much inflation than in countries that have experienced little.
- Neither is inflation imported from abroad. If it were, how could the rates of inflation be so very different in different countries?

They conclude:

'We return to our basic proposition. Inflation is primarily a ***monetary phenomenon,*** *produced by a more rapid increase in the quantity of money than in output...Many phenomena can produce temporary fluctuations in the rate of inflation, but they can have lasting effects only insofar as they affect the rate of monetary growth.'*

Key ideas - summary of the monetarist approach

1. The quantity theory of money provides the basic explanation of inflation. Inflation is always caused by an increase in the quantity of money.
2. Government attempts to expand the economy will only lead to rises in wages and prices. This is because people cannot be fooled; they will expect prices to rise and modify their behaviour accordingly. Hence the long-run Phillips curve is vertical.
3. Trade unions and foreigners do not cause inflation, though they may put pressures on governments, which cause permissive and misguided governments to allow the money supply to increase.

Monetarist policies

The essential feature of a monetarist policy towards controlling inflation will come as no surprise – the government must keep the supply of money under control. The quantity of money should only be allowed to increase at a steady rate linked to the rise in the output of the economy. If output is expected to increase by 2 per cent a year in the long run, then the money supply should also be increased by 2 per cent a year. However, there are pressures on government to increase the money supply. Three causes in particular lead government to do this. In the first place governments can 'import' inflation if they attempt to maintain fixed exchange rates. An expansion in the role of government and its spending, and government's attempt to increase the level of employment by expanding aggregate demand will also encourage weak governments to increase the money supply.

It follows that governmental attempts to control the money supply will be made easier if flexible exchange rates are adopted, government spending is cut and supply side measures are used to improve employment prospects.

Some monetarists, such as Friedman, also suggest that it can be made politically more feasible to end inflation if measures are taken to reduce the side-effects which result from **unanticipated** inflation and can be reduced by 'escalator clauses'. These are devices to increase wages, pensions and benefits in line with the rise in prices. This is already done in some cases; for example, state old age pensions are raised each year as prices rise. Friedman would also like tax allowances to rise with inflation (this is also done in some cases), and he would also like these types of arrangement to become more common in the private sector. For example, financial transactions involving borrowing and lending should contain clauses linking the interest to the rate of inflation. Friedman believes that measures such as these would reduce the ill-effects of inflation and make it easier for the government to take the essential measures needed to end inflation. Some monetarists disagree with him on this and argue that escalator clauses make inflation easier to live with, thereby reducing the government's incentives to control the money supply.

The Keynesian approach

All economists accept that large increases in the quantity of money will lead to rises in prices. If £20 notes showered down from the skies like rain at an Old Trafford test match, then some of the money

Figure 18.4: *Demand pull inflation*

(i) An increase in aggregate demand leads to a rise in price

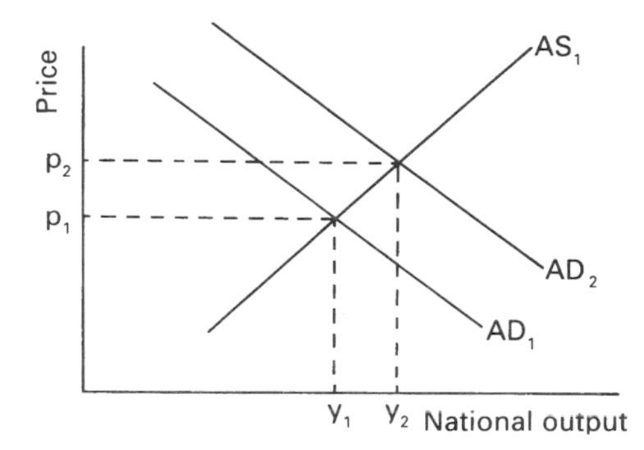

(ii) The rise in price leads to a fall in aggregate supply and a further price rise

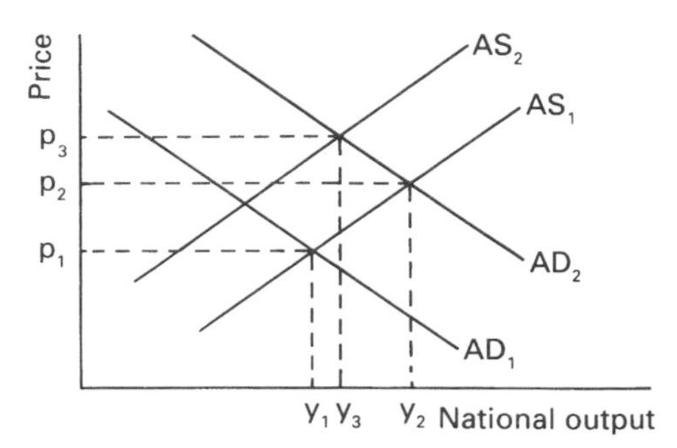

Figure 18.5: *The wage-price spiral*

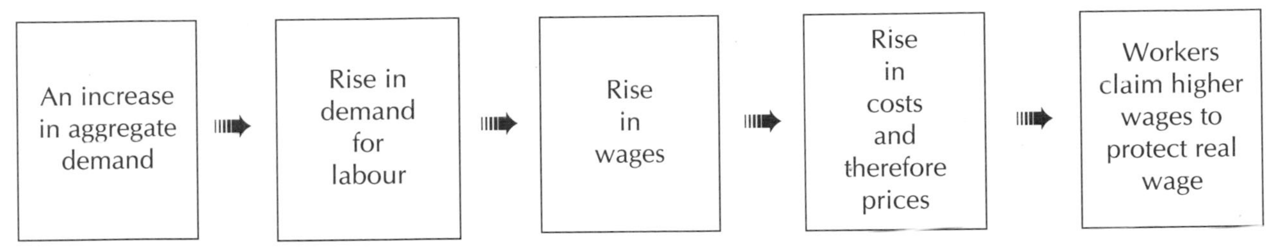

would increase demand for goods and push up prices. However, no government is likely to increase the money supply, in this way. The argument is about what factors cause inflation in the real world and what policies should be adopted to reduce the likelihood of it happening. As was seen in Chapter 16, non-monetarists believe that attempts to control the money supply will fail since the supply of money responds to the demand for it. Moreover, attempts to control the money supply may have undesirable side-effects, such as higher unemployment. Instead they stress two causes: inflation caused by excess aggregate demand and inflation resulting from increased costs of production.

Demand pull inflation

This explanation of inflation begins with an increase in aggregate demand. This can occur in any of the components of aggregate demand. Consumers may spend more on goods or services, firms invest more, government increases its spending, or exports increase. If this is accompanied by a rise in the money supply then the result will be an increase in prices, as shown in Figure 18.4. However, this does not explain inflation, which implies a *continuing* rise in prices. In order to explain this we need to describe a process. In this case, the rise in prices makes workers less well off; they respond by demanding higher wages. This rise in real wages will put up costs and cause the aggregate supply curve to shift to the left (just as in micro-economics a rise in costs causes the supply curve to move to the left). This will push up prices, lead to a new demand for higher wages and so on. This wage-price spiral is shown in Figure 18.5.

Cost push inflation

This is the second Keynesian explanation of inflation and is also the reason they put forward to explain the movement of the Phillips curve to the right. The explanation starts with an increase in costs. One reason this can occur is because of a push by trade unions for higher wages. Several economists have attempted to test this theory by linking rises in wages to the strength of unions, but monetarist critics say that union strength does not vary enough to explain the considerable variations in the rate of inflation over time. An alternative source of the increase in costs can occur because of a rise in the price of raw materials, such as the huge rise in oil costs in 1973/74 and again in 1979. This is sometimes called a supply side shock. Alternatively, the rise in prices can occur because of a push for higher profits by business people. The effect of an increase in costs on prices is shown in Figure 18.6. This original rise in prices then leads to a wage-price spiral. The rise in prices leads to a demand for higher wages, a further rise in prices and so on. Note that this argument suggests that there is still a trade-off between inflation and unemployment.

Figure 18.6: *A supply side shock*

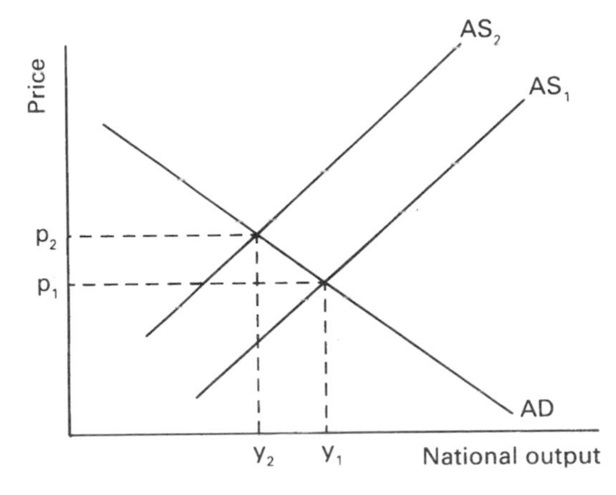

A sociological approach

This can be considered as a quite separate perspective, or as a variation of the Keynesian emphasis on the costs of production approach, as it is here. Some sociologists, such as Rowthorn (1977), see inflation as the outcome of conflict between workers and capitalists over the share of wages in the economy. According to Rowthorn:

'The working class can shift distribution in its favour by fighting more vigorously for higher wages, although the cost of such militancy is a faster rate of inflation, as capitalists try, with only partial success, to protect themselves by raising prices.'

This view rests on an increase in social conflict. This may occur because the old social order has been replaced by one in which workers feel less socially inferior, recognise their power and are prepared to use it. This power rests on the ability of workers to cause disruption due to the increased interdependence of a modern economy.

Behind this approach is a view that wages are not set by the forces of demand and supply because the labour market never reaches equilibrium. Instead they are set by collective bargaining and hence by sociological and political pressures. It follows that changes in political factors (such as a change in government or in a dominant ideology) can lead to a rise or a fall in wages and hence in prices.

Key ideas – summary of the Keynesian approach

1. The supply of money tends to respond to changes in the demand for money. The velocity of circulation varies and will nullify control measures. Hence attempts to control the money supply will probably fail. Moreover, such attempts will have severe effects on the economy.
2. One cause of inflation is a rise in aggregate demand (consumer spending, investment, government spending or exports). This pulls up prices.
3. In addition, inflation can be caused by increases in costs (for example, wages and raw materials). This pushes up prices.
4. Many Keynesian economists argue that the labour market does not clear. Hence wages are not determined by demand and supply, but by collective bargaining. This means that changes in wages are caused by political and social factors.

Keynesian policies

Since Keynesian economists identify two main causes, their polices focus on two areas.

One set of policies seeks to reduce aggregate

demand. One way to do this is to cut government spending or increase taxes. This would mean that consumers would have less money to spend. Both measures would shift the aggregate demand curve to the left. A disadvantage of this is that it would probably increase unemployment.

A variation on this approach would be to control consumer credit, for example, by putting up interest rates. However, this seems to have little effect and has undesirable effects on industry, perhaps reducing investment. Alternatively, the government can try to pass laws which restrict the ease with which people can obtain credit, or which makes them pay back loans more quickly. This has become more difficult in recent years because of the expansion of credit cards and the diversification of building societies into institutions which provide personal loans for the purchase of consumer goods.

The other approach seeks to cut costs, or at least to slow down the rate at which they rise. One way in which this can be done is through an incomes policy. This attempts to reduce public sector incomes in the hope that these will then set levels which the private sector follows. Teachers feel that they have often been used in this way. Such measures reduce morale in the public sector and then lead to strikes and other action designed to ensure parity with the private sector. In the past, governments have adopted formal prices and incomes policies. These have sometimes been voluntary, for example, by making agreements with the TUC, or imposed by law, for example, outlawing any wage increase over a certain amount. Such policies have been criticised on the grounds that they distort the allocation of resources, for example, by making it difficult for growing firms to attract more workers by putting up wages. Moreover, it is claimed that these policies have only a temporary effect, so that after a while the policy breaks down and wages catch up to where they would have been without a policy.

These criticisms have led to new ideas. James Meade (1984) has suggested a compulsory system of 'pendulum' arbitration. This means that the arbitrators would not be able to split the difference between claim and offer, but have to choose one or the other. This would prevent unions making excessive claims. Moreover, the arbitrators would have to make their decision bearing in mind the effects on the level of employment.

Another new idea is associated with Richard Layard (1986). This is a tax-based system, whereby companies paying excessive wage increases to their workers would have to pay higher taxes. The rationale is that this would force companies to resist high wage increases, and the workers would also realise that sales and employment might fall if companies' costs were increased, not only by large wage increases but also by higher taxes. They would therefore reduce their wage demands.

Conclusion

For monetarists, inflation is a major economic disaster. Hence strong measures have to be taken in order to bring it under control. Since they believe that the basic cause of all inflation is that the money supply is rising faster than national output, it follows that the essential policy is that the money supply should be brought under control. In addition, measures should be taken to reduce pressures on the government to increase the money supply; hence the government should cut its spending.

Keynesians take a very different view. They also believe that inflation is undesirable, but perhaps not so bad as monetarists claim. They see two causes of inflation. The first is too much aggregate demand; hence this must be cut, for example, by putting up taxes or cutting government spending. Another cause is that costs rise and so push up prices. The usual response to this is some form of prices and incomes policy.

In principle it ought to be possible to test these two approaches, but in practice this is very difficult. In the real world it is not possible to undertake economic experiments to see what happens. Hence much economic investigation takes the form of statistical investigation. In the USA, Friedman and Schwartz provided a comprehensive statistical case in favour of monetarism. However, Hendry and Ericsson (1983) reviewed Friedman's evidence and concluded that the evidence did not support his claims. Instead they suggested that the velocity of circulation of money was very variable, so that a policy of controlling the money supply would have little effect. One reason why investigations such as these can come to different conclusions is that some of the variables are difficult to quantify. For example, which measure of money supply should be used? Or how should investigators measure union strength? Moreover, different time lags give different results. If the money supply and prices are both rising, it is not easy to test whether the money supply is causing prices to rise, or if rising prices lead to increases in the money supply.

Data questions

Year	M4 (£ billion)	Retail Price Index 1985=100
1980	111	70.7
1981	129	79.1
1982	154	85.9
1983	170	89.8
1984	192	94.3
1985	218	100.0
1986	252	103.4
1987	290	107.7
1988	343	113.0
1989	404	121.8
1990	464	133.3
1991	495	141.1
1992	515	146.3

Source: Adapted from *Economic Trends*, HMSO, 1993.

Question 1

1. What is meant by the Retail Price Index?
2. (i) From the data, calculate the rate of change of M4 and the Retail Price Index.
   (ii) Is there any relationship between the two variables?
3. If time lags were taken into consideration, how would this affect your answer to 2(ii)?
4. What economic theory could be used to explain the figures? Use examples from the table to support your answers.

Brazil under pressure to curb mounting inflation

The inexorable rise in Brazil's monthly inflation, expected to top 33 per cent this month, has led to growing demands for drastic action to tackle the problem, even a new 'shock plan' of economic measures.

Prices of food have risen particularly quickly, and in an apparent sign of desperation, the government have reinstated Sunab, the prices watchdog body previously associated with enforcing price freezes and pressure for a freeze is growing. The government has promised the International Monetary Fund that it will reduce monthly inflation to 25 per cent by December, but companies have revised predictions upwards for this year to 1,900 per cent, Brazil's highest ever.

Despite making $6 billion in cuts, the government's most optimistic figures for next year's budget put the operational deficit at a record $31.5 billion, partly because the federal payroll has jumped from $14 billion to $18 billion. To the Finance Minister's dismay, Congress approved a new wage policy requiring monthly real wage adjustments, though this would be highly inflationary.

Source: Adapted from *Financial Times*, 12 August 1993.

Question 2

1. Explain why a rise in the Federal payroll might cause inflation.
2. What would be the monetarist approach to reducing inflation in this context? What would they think of the idea of a price freeze?
3. Which groups in society would favour 'monthly real wage adjustments'?

Serbs issue 50m dinar note as inflation hits 48pc a day

The price to Serbia of two years of war, international pariah status, years of economic mismanagement and 14 months of a trade embargo, was spelt out yesterday when the Yugoslav national bank said it will issue a 50 million dinar note next week.

The highest dinar note now buys five German marks (£2), but by the time the new note is on the streets, perhaps only one. Inflation in Sebia used to be calculated in annual terms, then in monthly figures. In the past few weeks, statisticians and economists have almost given up trying to compute a figure that is soaring as fast as they can count. The inflation yesterday was calculated at 48 per cent (for the day).

Source: *The Guardian*, 28 July 1993.

Question 3

1. Explain how inflation rates are calculated in the UK. What difficulties will arise in calculating the rate of inflation in conditions such as those in Serbia?
2. What economic consequences do you think will follow from an inflation rate of 48 per cent a day?
3. Calculate the annual inflation rate in Serbia, assuming that the daily rate continues at 48 per cent.

19 International Trade

Debates about international trade focus on the extent to which complete free trade – trade without any barriers – is desirable

- One group of economists, who favour market forces and dislike government 'interference', tend to argue that trade between countries should be free from all, or almost all, restrictions. They argue this will give consumers a greater choice of goods at lower prices and that they will gain from the benefits of specialisation.
- Critics of free trade suggest it can have substantial disadvantages. They argue that barriers to trade can help new and also declining industries. They can protect industries from dumping by foreigners, and barriers may be needed to help essential defence industries.

Finally, some economists believe that trade restrictions may be needed if a country suffers from a deficit on the balance of payments.

The case for free trade

Three hundred years ago, the prevalent theory of foreign trade was mercantilism. This suggested that a country should do all it could to increase exports, but should restrict imports and so build up 'treasure'. This view was criticised by Adam Smith in *The Wealth of Nations* (1776). He argued that restrictions on foreign trade limited the benefits which could be obtained from market forces. In essence, the case for free trade is the case for markets on a larger scale. If complete free trade were introduced the market would consist of the whole world and consumers would benefit from a huge choice of goods. Moreover, international competition would force domestic firms to keep down prices. Innovations in production techniques and product design would spread more rapidly, so benefiting consumers.

Absolute advantage

Smith argued that trade should be based on absolute advantage. This phrase describes the position when one country is absolutely more efficient at producing good A, whilst another country is absolutely 'better' at producing good B. Both countries would benefit if they specialised in producing the good at which they have the advantage and then exchanged their products. Thus Britain has an absolute advantage compared to Jamaica in the production of cars whilst Jamaica has an absolute advantage in the production of tropical fruits. It will benefit both countries if they specialise and trade. Absolute advantage is a specific example of the advantages of specialisation and the division of labour. In Smith's words:

'It is the maxim of every prudent master of a family, never to attempt to make at home what it will cost him more to make than to buy. The tailor does not attempt to make his own shoes, but buys them off the shoemaker. The shoemaker does not attempt to make his own clothes, but employs a tailor... What is prudence in the conduct of a private family can scarce be folly in that of a great kingdom... If a foreign country can supply us with a commodity cheaper than we ourselves can make it, better buy it off them with some part of the produce of our own industry...'

Comparative advantage

Smith's argument about absolute advantage was developed by David Ricardo in 1817 in his book *On the Principles of Political Economy and Taxation.* Ricardo was concerned about the position where a country was able to produce every commodity at an absolutely lower real cost than another country. He suggested that in this case each country should specialise in the production of those goods where its comparative advantage was greatest. This can be explained by using the division of labour as an example; if A is ten times more efficient than B as a surgeon and twice as efficient as a road sweeper, then A should devote all his efforts to surgery (particularly if I am the patient!) and leave all the road sweeping to B.

Table 19.1: *Comparative advantage*

Country	Amount of labour (man hours) required to produce 1 unit	
	wine	cloth
Portugal	80	90
England	120	100

Ricardo developed his theory by comparing two countries, England and Portugal, and two commodities, wine and cloth. Table 19.1 shows that Portugal was more efficient in the production of both goods, but Ricardo argued that both countries could benefit if they specialised where their advantage was comparatively greater and then traded. Portugal's labour costs were lower than England's in both cloth and wine, but the comparative advantage was greater in wine. The cost ratios were 9:10 for cloth and 8:12 for wine. Thus it cost England roughly 1.1 times as much labour to produce cloth as it did Portugal, but 1.5 times as much to produce wine.

Ricardo showed that both countries would benefit if England specialised in cloth and Portugal in wine and they then exchanged a unit of wine for a unit of cloth. England would gain 20 hours since it costs her 100 hours to produce cloth but 120 to produce wine. Portugal would also benefit because she would trade a unit of wine which took 80 hours to produce and receive a unit of cloth which would have taken her 90 hours to produce. Hence Portugal gains 10 hours. In Ricardo's words (referring to Portugal):

'It would be... advantageous for her to export wine in exchange for cloth... she would obtain more cloth from England than she could produce by diverting a portion of her capital from the cultivation of vines to the manufacture of cloth.'

Ricardo's model is a simple one. It ignores factors such as transport costs and assumes that goods are homogeneous. It also ignores intra-firm trade, such as that between subsidiaries of a multi-national firm. Nevertheless, its conclusion is clear. Countries should specialise where their advantage is comparatively greatest (or comparative disadvantage is least) and then trade.

This principle has been restated in various ways, for example, by including all costs and not just labour costs. Another approach uses the terminology of opportunity costs to reach the same conclusion. In the example above, the opportunity cost to Portugal (what is given up) is minimised if Portugal concentrates on producing wine.

Factor endowments

In order to improve Ricardo's theory, two Swedish economists, Heckscher and Ohlin (Heckscher, 1919 and Ohlin 1933), developed a theory which stressed factor endowment as the basis for international trade. They suggested that countries such as India, with a huge supply of relatively cheap labour, would specialise in labour-intensive products and countries such as the USA, with abundant capital, would specialise in the production of capital-intensive products. However, an investigation by Leontief (1954) found a paradox. His research showed that the USA actually exports labour and land-intensive products rather than capital-intensive goods. Despite this paradox, more sophisticated versions of Heckscher and Ohlin's ideas still provide the most widely accepted theories of international trade.

The terms of trade

The extent to which countries benefit from trade depends on the price at which the goods are exchanged. Ricardo's example simply assumed that one unit of cloth was exchanged for one unit of wine; in the real world both would be sold for a price.

Because world trade involves many goods and many prices, the terms of trade are compiled as an index. This index is itself compiled by making use of two other index numbers, one for the price of exports and one for the price of imports:

$$\text{Terms of trade} = \frac{\text{Index of the price of exports}}{\text{Index of the price of imports}}$$

In the base year the terms of trade will be $\frac{100}{100} = 1$.

Thus if the index of export prices changes from 100 to 150 and the index of imports price changes from 100 to 50, then the terms of trade will be $\frac{150}{50} = 3$.

The terms of trade are said to have become favourable when the index rises; that is when the price of exports rises relative to the price of imports. This means more imports can be bought for a given quantity of exports. However, 'favourable' can be misleading because a rise in the price of exports may make them more difficult to sell abroad. The precise effect will depend on the price elasticity of demands for exports.

Gains from large-scale production

The extent to which a firm can specialise depends on the size of the market. When this is large, firms can employ specialised machines and labour and obtain the benefits of other economies of scale. Free trade extends the potential market and so permits extensive specialisation. This benefit is greater for small countries such as Ireland or Switzerland than for larger countries like the USA, where the market is already large. Moreover, the potential benefits will differ between industries; in cases such as personal services there are no advantages to be gained from free trade. In others, however, there are substantial benefits from being big, as was shown in Chapter 5.

Key ideas – summary of the case for free trade

1. Free trade extends the market and so brings consumers the benefits of competition, such as lower prices and greater choice.
2. When two countries each have an absolute advantage in producing products, it will pay both to specialise and then to exchange. Britain could grow oranges, but it would be a waste of resources; hence Britain should specialise in other products and then exchange these for goods it cannot produce efficiently.
3. Ricardo's theory of comparative advantage shows that even where a country is better at producing several goods than another country, both will benefit when they specialise in products where their advantage is comparatively greater (or their disadvantage is comparatively least). The extent to which each benefits will depend on the prices at which the goods are exchanged.
4. Ricardo's theory has been developed by later economists such as Heckscher and Ohlin.
5. Free trade makes possible greater economies of scale.

Free trade policies

Free traders wish to see the removal of all, or nearly all, barriers to trade. For them, life is a constant struggle against special interest groups which seek to protect their industry against foreign competition by introducing new restrictions on imports. Hence at one level their policy involves a defence of the present position.

To extend free trade is difficult. The growth of the European Community extends free trade within its area, but puts up substantial barriers to those outside the Community, especially in agricultural products.

On a world arena, much of the struggle takes place at meetings of GATT (the General Agreement on Tariffs and Trade). This is a body which, since the Second World War, has negotiated substantial reductions in customs duties and helped to remove other barriers to international trade. Economists who support freer trade would like this to be given more emphasis.

The case for protection

Criticisms of the case for free trade

Some economists criticise the case for free trade on a number of grounds. According to Joan Robinson in her book *Reflections on the Theory of International Trade* (1974):

'...the models imply trade between countries of equal weight and at the same level of development. This rules out imperialism and the use of power to foster economic advantage. In Ricardo's example Portugal was to gain as much from exporting wine as England from exporting cloth, but in real life Portugal was dependent on British naval support, and it was for this reason that she was obliged to accept conditions of trade which wiped out her production of textiles and inhibited industrial development...'

Moreover:

'Investment in expanding manufactures leads to technical advance, learning by doing, specialisation of industries and accelerating accumulation (of ***profits*** *and* ***capital****), while investment in wine runs up a blind alley into stagnation. In a similar way the British cotton industry grew up under protection from superior Indian exports. When it was developed, free trade was imposed on India and the Indian textile industry decimated.'*

Infant industries

Joan Robinson's views underlie one of the arguments put forward in favour of protection; that many less developed countries have the conditions necessary to compete successfully, but lack experience and expertise which take time to acquire. The infant industry argument suggests that new industries should be given protection for a time in order to allow them to build up this experience. This argument applies where the industry is small and young, and where costs are high but fall as the industry grows. Critics of this line of argument claim that most infant industries never grow up; that they continue to demand protection so their customers continue to pay high prices. Once protection is given to such industries, it is very difficult, politically, to remove it.

Protection to improve the terms of trade

Countries can improve their position when they are the sole (or dominant) buyer of a world commodity. This is rare, but if British importers of tea agreed with each other to restrict imports, then the world price would fall. Of course this would lower the incomes received by the producers of tea and so might be thought undesirable as they are mostly poor countries.

Protection against low-cost imports

This line of argument takes a number of forms. One suggests that declining industries need a period of protection in order to allow the decline to take place gradually, so that workers can retrain and new industries develop. This would apply to industries in the UK such as cotton, coal mining and shipbuilding.

A variation on this approach says that industries in high-wage countries should have protection against goods made by low-paid labour. This, of course, denies the advantages of comparative advantage which derive from lower costs. Instead, the argument is that if foreign firms pay low wages, this is a form of unfair competition and domestic firms should be protected. This would safeguard the position of British workers. Critics argue that this would, in fact, reduce the wages of workers in poor countries and would make British consumers pay higher prices.

Protection against unfair foreign competition

'Unfair' competition can take various forms. Sometimes foreign governments can subsidise their export industries. This means that domestic industries cannot compete fairly. Similarly, foreign firms may 'dump' their products overseas, either because they cannot be sold on their domestic market, or in order to destroy competitors. They could then increase their prices and make large profits.

In some cases what is seen as dumping is no such thing. Firms can sometimes sell abroad at low prices because their domestic sales cover high fixed costs and allow prices abroad to reflect the low marginal cost of production.

Macro-economic arguments for protection

So far we have considered economic arguments which have suggested protectionist measures to help particular industries. However, some economists have suggested protection on a much wider scale. One of the problems of the British economy is that, as the economy expands, the level of imports rises, leading to a deficit on the current account. This can then force the government to deflate the economy by putting up taxes and cutting government spending. As an alternative to this it is suggested that the government should take measures to restrict the overall level of imports. This would then allow the economy to be expanded without the constraint of a balance of payments problem. A variation on this approach is to target the protection against a particular country which has a huge surplus on its trade with the country concerned. In recent years this has usually been Japan. There is no doubt that in the past Japan employed many protective devices to build up its industry and that a few of these still exist. What is also clear is that Japan is so successful as an exporter because it is efficient.

Critics of this argument for protection say that it would contravene many international agreements. They also argue that protectionist measures would lead to retaliation from other countries, so the ultimate effect would be to reduce the level of world trade and increase unemployment in many countries. That is what happened in the 1930s when world trade plummeted as a result of the growth of restrictions on imports.

Non-economic arguments for protection

The economic arguments used to support free trade usually assume that it is desirable to maximise national income. However, other objectives may also be desirable. For example, the people of a country may wish to preserve a way of life that is desirable, such as a certain way of farming or traditional crafts. If these are threatened by foreign competition it may be desirable to protect them. Similarly, politicians may suggest that defence requirements necessitate the protection of an industry; for example, that Britain needs a shipbuilding industry. Such arguments depend on political grounds and not on economic considerations.

Key ideas – summary of the protectionist argument

1. The case for free trade using comparative advantage arguments is oversimplified. In particular it rests on the assumption that power is spread equally so the strong do not impose on the weak. In the past, countries such as Britain and the USA have used their power to force poor countries to concentrate on producing raw materials and to exchange these for manufactured goods.

2. Countries should be able to use protection to acquire comparative advantage, for example, by helping infant industries.

3. Protection can help countries improve the terms of trade, particularly where they import a large part of the world's output of a commodity.

4. Declining industries should be helped to decline in an organised way so that new industries can be developed to replace them.

5. The level of imports should be controlled in order to prevent balance of payments problems developing. This would allow countries to expand their economies more rapidly.
6. There are also non-economic arguments, such as the protection of a way of life, or the safeguarding of essential defence industries.

Protectionist policies

There are a number of ways in which protectionist policies can be introduced.

Tariffs

Tariffs are a traditional way to help particular industries and also to reduce the level of imports as a whole. They are a tax on imports and can be **specific,** that is so much per item, or **ad valorem,** that is a percentage of the value of the good. Another advantage of tariffs is that they raise money for the government.

Figure 19.1 illustrates their effect. The tariff shifts the supply curve upwards because it puts up the costs of the foreign producer. In the Figure the new supply curve S_2 is above the original curve by t - the amount of the tariff. Imports fall from q_1 to q_2 and the price rises from p_1 to p_2.

Figure 19.1: *Effect of a tariff*

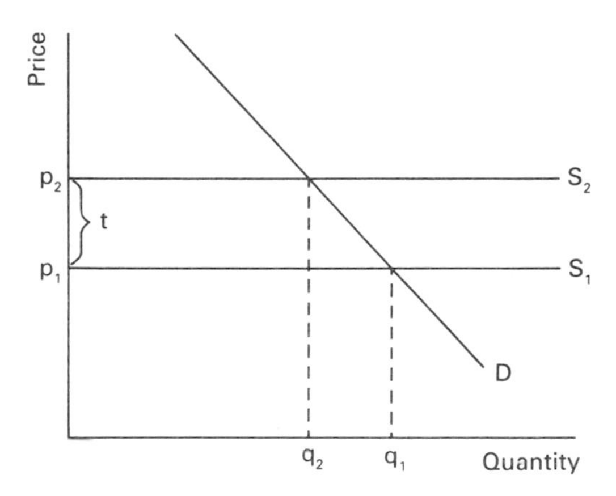

Quotas

Quotas can also be used to restrict imports. A quota is a limit on the number of goods that are allowed to enter the country; thus a country may say that only 10,000 video recorders will be allowed to come into the country during the year. The effect is shown in Figure 19.2. The original equilibrium is at price p_1 and quantity q_1. The quota shifts the supply curve so that it becomes vertical, and the new equilibrium is at price p_2 and quantity q_2.

Both these methods will reduce imports. Comparing the two we see that in both cases there is a rise in price. A tariff benefits the Treasury, whilst a quota may benefit foreign suppliers because they can charge a higher price for their product.

Figure 19.2: *Effect of a quota*

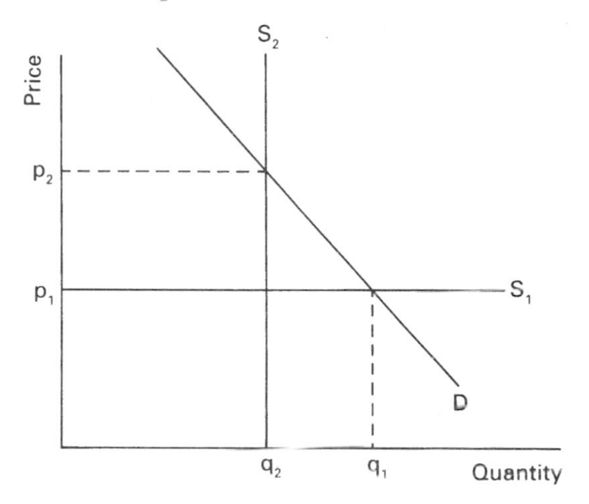

Non-tariff barriers

Imposing tariffs and quotas will certainly reduce imports, but they are illegal under many international agreements. Hence in recent years they have become less important as barriers to trade. However, there has probably been an increase in non-tariff barriers. There are a number of such devices. Some are uncontroversial, such as the imposition of strict quality controls in the form of regulations to reduce the likelihood of food poisoning in imported foodstuffs.

Sometimes governments insist that importers need a special licence before they are allowed to import goods. Another variation occurs when two or more governments come to an agreement that imports should be limited. This is usually referred to as voluntary export restraint, for example, an agreement restricting the number of Japanese cars which are allowed to enter the UK. The 1993 Uruguay Round of GATT attempted to reduce the use of these restraints. For example, the Multi-Fibre Agreement, which restricts the import of textiles from less developed countries, was due to be phased out over a ten year period. Their advocates say that barriers such as these can be used to reduce unfair competition. Such barriers do work in the sense that the level of imports is reduced. Their opponents say that they restrict trade in ways which make it very difficult for foreign companies to overcome, and so reduce consumer choice.

Devaluation

Devaluation means cutting the value of a currency when measured against other currencies. This means that the price of exports falls as shown in Figure 19.3. Consequently firms will be able to sell more goods abroad. At the same time the price of imports rises. This can also help the balance of payments since it may lead to fewer goods being imported. However, there is an undesirable side effect; the higher price of imports will cause inflation. It may also make matters worse in the short run because people will often continue to buy imports even though their price has risen. Hence this is a long term measure.

Figure 19.3: *Effect of a fall in the value of the pound*

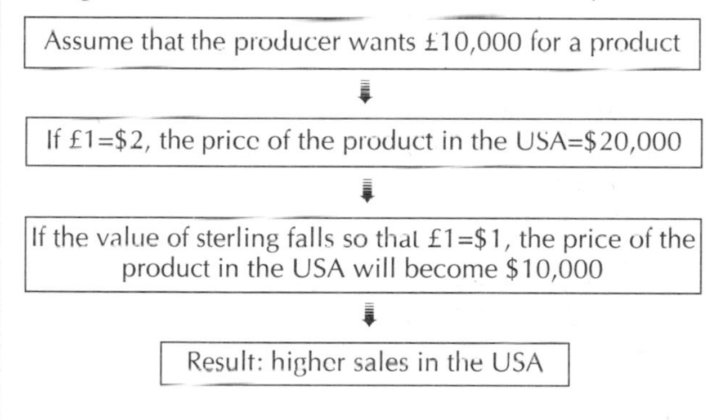

Interest rates

An alternative way to reduce the demand for imports is to increase interest rates. This will make borrowing more expensive and so discourage those consumers who borrow to buy goods. It will also mean that those people buying houses with mortgages will have less money to spend on goods, many of which would have been imported. However, higher interest rates make domestic industry less competitive because they push up costs. The CBI estimates that a 1 per cent increase in interest rates puts up industry's costs by £250 million; hardly the way to encourage exports.

Higher interest rates will also tend to push up the rate of exchange. This is because people with money to invest will tend to move it to those countries with high interest rates, and this will push up the value of those currencies. A high exchange rate will have the opposite effect to a devaluation.

Deflation

The certain way to improve the balance of payments is to deflate the economy. Since the prime determinant of the level of imports is the level of income, then a cut in incomes will reduce imports. Hence governments with balance of payments difficulties often cut government spending and increase taxes. These measures succeed in their purpose, but the side-effects are extremely undesirable. National income falls (or rises more slowly) and the level of unemployment rises.

There are therefore a large range of policies which can be used to restrict imports. The precise measures advocated to restrict imports will depend on the circumstances. If the aim is to help a particular industry, measures to restrict the importation of specific goods should be adopted. If the aim is to rectify a balance of payments deficit, more general measures are needed.

The European Single Market

The EEC, which came into existence on 1 January 1958, was based on the idea of a common market; member states had to remove customs duties and quotas on goods they sold to each other. The Treaty of Rome, which set up the EEC, also required member countries to abolish restrictions on the freedom to supply services such as banking and insurance.

However, restrictions on trade in both goods and services persisted. Sometimes countries used health and safety regulations to reduce competition. These particularly affected industries such as engineering, chemicals and food. Services such as banking continued to be regulated by domestic governments, making it difficult for foreign banks to compete.

Hence, in 1986 the twelve member states of the European Union (as it has now become) signed the Single European Act. One part of this Act caused governments to remove restrictions on trade. For example, although some barriers to trade had been removed before this date, checks at frontiers continued and there were about a hundred export, import and transit documents in existence. These were replaced by a single administrative document. Similarly, technical standards were harmonised so that goods which met the requirements of one country could be sold in another.

The creation of the single market will lead to many benefits such as those resulting from greater competition which will force companies to cut costs and improve consumer choice, from the exploitation of economies of scale which are possible when firms can sell to a huge market and from the removal of bureaucratic barriers at border points. These benefits were investigated by an official report (Ceccini 1988). This estimated that the benefits from reducing trade barriers would vary from 2.5 per cent to over 6 per cent of EU GDP.

Conclusion

Economists who support freer trade claim that world trade brings consumers the benefits of the market; lower prices and greater choice. They are supported by research from organisations such as The Organisation for Economic Co-operation and Development (OECD), which surveyed research in this area in a book called *Costs and Benefits of Protection* (1985) and concluded:

- The spread of protection has yielded few benefits, but imposed substantial costs.
- Protection has not proved to be an efficient means of sustaining employment. Jobs saved in the industries protected are often offset by viable jobs foregone elsewhere in the economy.

However, this research would be criticised by those who favour an element of protection. Some would suggest that free trade favours the powerful and that industries in less developed countries are not able to compete on fair terms. Even in developed countries they suggest that some protection should be given to declining industries to allow adjustments to take place in an orderly way. On the macro level, they suggest that imports should not be allowed to rise when the economy expands because this leads to a balance of payments crisis. This may force the government to impose deflationary measures, which would have the effect of reducing imports, but in an uncontrolled way.

Data questions

The Uruguay Round

The period since the Second World War has seen a huge reduction in customs duties and a corresponding expansion of world trade. Much of the credit for this goes to the General Agreement on Tariffs and Trade (GATT). But trade is still restricted, less by duties than by other restrictions, and the difficulties in dealing with these are exemplified by the GATT negotiations which were started in Uruguay in 1986 and only completed in December 1993. That is because 108 countries were trying to negotiate the best deal for themselves, so many compromises had to be agreed. The agreement finally reached included measures to free trade in agriculture so that, for example, EU farm subsidies will be reduced by 21 per cent, the Multi-Fibre Agreement which restricts trade in textiles will be phased out, and it includes measures to protect 'intellectual property' such as copyright in books and computer programs. Many countries do not recognise these at present and reproduce without payment to the authors. In addition tariff cuts will average 38 per cent on more than 20,000 products worldwide.

Question 1

1. Show, using a diagram, how customs duties restrict international trade.
2. Explain what other restrictions limit international trade.
3. What advantages and disadvantages do you think will result from the GATT agreement?

The greening of protectionism

It has never been easy to persuade ordinary voters that free trade is a cause worth defending. Its huge economic benefits are easily ignored when local jobs are threatened by foreign competition. Now trade liberals face a tougher challenge. American environmentalists are building a coalition around the argument that free trade policies seem appropriate. The environmentalists argue that:

- trade liberalisation encourages economic growth and so damages the environment;
- GATT does not allow countries to keep out a product because of the way it is produced or harvested;
- Gatt prevents countries imposing export bans which they might wish to impose to protect, say, their own forests or elephants.

In response to these arguments, many economists (and *The Economist*) would argue that free trade is often 'green'. Give markets a bigger role, and equally important, put strong environmental policies in place, and resources will be used more efficiently.

Source: *The Economist*, 27 February 1993.

Question 2

1. Outline the work of the GATT.
2. Explain how free trade can cause resources to be used more efficiently.
3. Why do some environmentalists object to freer trade? Do you think that these objections are justified?

20 The Balance of Payments

The balance of payments is a statement of a country's transactions with the rest of the world. The most useful way to approach this topic is to consider the flow of funds into and out of a country. For example, when someone in the UK buys a foreign car, money flows out of the UK. When someone from abroad comes to the UK for a holiday, money comes into the country. Over a period of several years, these flows into and out of the country should at least balance. If the flow of money out of the country is greater than the flow into it, a balance of payments crisis may result and force the government to take unpleasant measures to remedy the position. Since none of the measures is guaranteed to work, and the most successful have undesirable side-effects, there are considerable arguments between economists about which policies to adopt.

- Some economists believe that no government intervention is necessary because market forces will solve the problem by cutting the value of the currency.
- Others argue that government intervention, for example to deflate the economy, is needed to solve a deficit.

Components of the balance of payments

There are two main areas of the balance of payments: the current account, and transactions in assets and liabilities.

The balance of payments of any one country must always balance. The central bank will hold assets in the form of foreign currencies and gold, and these reserves increase or decrease according to changes in the current or asset accounts. For example, if there is a surplus on the current account, the foreign exchange reserves will rise by the amount of the surplus. In this sense the balance of payments must always balance, because the change in the reserves always equals the change in other items.

When the accounts do not balance, then a **balancing item** is introduced in order to make them balance. This is another name for errors and omissions.

Language can be confusing in this context because economists sometimes talk about 'a deficit on the balance of payments'. When they use this phrase they usually mean a deficit on the current account of the balance of payments, but the phrase 'current account' is often omitted. A deficit on the current account can be serious if it is prolonged because it will lead to a fall in the reserves; foreigners will demand payment in foreign currency and the government may be forced to adopt new policies to remedy the position. A deficit on capital items such as investment abroad may be less serious, because it can be seen as building up a nation's assets abroad. If this is the position, foreigners may be happy to accept payment in domestic currency.

Table 20.1: *UK balance of payments, 1992*

		£ million
CURRENT ACCOUNT		
Visible balance		-13,406
Invisibles:		
Services balance	4,069	
Interest, profit & dividends	5,777	
Transfers	-5,060	
Invisible balance		4,786
CURRENT BALANCE		-8,620
TRANSACTIONS IN EXTERNAL ASSETS AND LIABILITIES		
Transactions in assets		-84,976
Transactions in liabilities		93,295
NET TRANSACTIONS		8,319
BALANCING ITEM		301

Source: Adapted from *Economic Trends*, HMSO, 1993.

Table 20.1 shows the UK balance of payments. The precise figures vary each year, but the overall picture does not change rapidly.

The current account

This includes all international payments which are deemed to be related to income. It covers money received from the sale of goods and services to other countries, and also money in the form of receipts and payments from property and gilts. Overall the current account in the UK amounts to about 50 per cent of GDP (goods 25 per cent of GDP, services 7 per cent, property incomes 16 per cent, transfers 1 per cent). The UK tends to run a surplus on the current account when the economy is doing badly. This is because, when unemployment is high, we spend less on imports. However, as the economy expands we tend to go on foreign holidays and buy imported consumer goods, such as electronic equipment and, as a result, the current account goes into a deficit. The current account in the UK can be sub-divided into various components.

Figure 20.1: *Current account (£ million)*

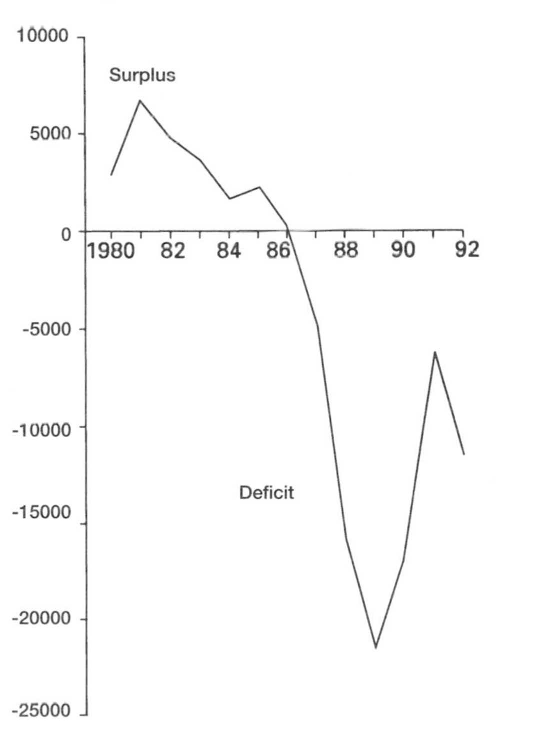

Source: Adapted from *Economic Trends*, HMSO, 1993.

Trade in goods

This is sometimes called 'visible trade' because it refers to goods passing through customs barriers. It includes such things as the import and export of manufactured goods such as cars, chemicals and computers. The UK used to have a surplus of these items, but now runs a deficit on manufactures. Raw materials, such as iron ore and food, are also 'visibles', and the UK always runs a deficit on this item. Finally, trade in oil appears in this section. The UK always used to run a deficit in the trade in oil, but North Sea oil has changed this into a surplus. Overall, the UK runs a deficit on trade in goods.

Table 20.2: *UK Trade in goods, 1992 (£ million)*

Exports	
Finished manufactured goods	57,144
Semi-manufactured goods	30,354
Food, drink and tobacco	8,673
Oil	6,556
Other	4,320
Total	**107,047**
Imports	
Finished manufactured goods	63,691
Semi-manufactured goods	31,157
Food, drink and tobacco	12,609
Oil	5,079
Other	7,917
Total	**120,453**

Source: Adapted from *UK Balance of Payments*, HMSO, 1993.

Invisible trade

The other components of the current account are often called 'invisibles', because they (usually) cannot be seen:

- Services. The UK earns money from the activities of its insurance companies in other countries. Shipping, banking, air travel and tourism are other examples of trade in services. The UK runs a surplus on its trade in services.
- Interest, profits and dividends. Some individuals and firms in Britain own property abroad and this gives rise to incomes which then come into this country. Similarly, foreigners own assets in this country and send the income they receive abroad. Some of the profits Nissan receive from their factory in the UK will be sent back to Japan and will therefore appear as a deficit on the UK current account and as a surplus on the Japanese current account.
- Transfers. These include international gifts from

governments or individuals and also payments to bodies such as the European Community.

Transactions in assets and liabilities

This is the second main component of the balance of payments. It includes payments which are made, not from income, but from capital. It covers such things as money spent and received on the sale of shares in foreign companies (as when Nestlé bought Rowntrees in 1988). This is known as portfolio investment. This account is also affected when domestic firms build factories overseas, or when foreign firms build here (as when Nissan built a factory in the North East of England. In this case some of the money to pay for the construction came from Japan.) Short-term lending by banks is also included. The published figures for this part of the balance of payments are often inaccurate because the people concerned do not always notify the authorities.

Some people believe that a deficit in capital transactions is not a bad thing because it builds up the country's assets abroad. The total value of the UK's overseas assets is about £700 billion, whilst external liabilities are about £100 billion less.

Foreign exchange reserves

Part of the assets of a country are in the form of foreign exchange reserves. These can be regarded as the nation's savings. In principle, foreign exchange reserves can be used to pay for imports in a crisis, but their total is small compared to the amount spent on imports so they could not really fulfil this function. Instead their real use is to enable the government to intervene in the foreign exchange market. Put another way, the reserves mean that the government can buy and sell currencies in order to obtain a desirable value for the pound. The reasons they should do this are discussed in the next chapter.

How accurate are the figures?

In some cases, there is a widespread feeling that the authorities adjust the basis of the statistics in order to obtain better results. Unemployment figures are the best example of this. In other cases the figures are known to be inaccurate, not because of government alterations, but because of genuine difficulties in obtaining accurate figures. One reason for this is that almost all governments are concerned about the possibility of a substantial deficit on their current accounts and so pay particular attention to imports – which often bring in tax revenue from tariffs. One consequence of such action is that world imports exceed world exports. This should not take place in theory as the combined balance of payments deficits of all countries should be equal to the combined surpluses that exist in other countries. Since it is unlikely that creatures from outer space are trading with the earth, it follows that the figures are inaccurate. One reason is that the people responsible for making the transactions are more concerned with the success of their business than with sending accurate figures to the authorities.

This means that it is difficult to test the accuracy of predictions made about future movements in the balance of payments and therefore it is hard for the government to decide if corrective measures need to be taken to prevent future deficits. In any case, predictions in this area are extremely difficult. This is not surprising because any deficit (or surplus) is the difference between a huge sum for imports and a huge sum for exports. A small percentage error in either of these will lead to a large error in forecasting the difference between them.

Key ideas

1. The balance of payments statistics have two main areas: the current account and transactions in assets and liabilities.
2. The UK now runs a deficit on trade in manufactures, but has a surplus on invisibles.
3. The UK has substantial assets abroad.
4. Balance of payments statistics are very inaccurate and are also difficult to forecast.

What factors determine imports and exports?

A short-term deficit on the current account is not significant; there are large swings from month to month in the figures and a deficit in one month may well be corrected in the next without any action from the authorities. A deficit can be pleasurable; a country in deficit is receiving more goods than it is sending abroad. However, a large deficit which seems likely to continue over a period of years can lead to serious problems. Foreigners will demand payment in a 'hard' currency – one which is acceptable anywhere in the world. A persistent deficit will cause reserves of such currencies to fall and the authorities will be forced to take action to correct the position. In order to discuss possible government action we first need to discuss the determinants of the level of imports and exports.

The rate of exchange

As shown in the last chapter, a fall in the value of the pound will make it easier for firms to sell their products abroad. It also makes imports more expensive. The extent to which this benefits the balance of payments depends on the price elasticity of demand of imports and exports. If this is high, then a relatively small fall in the exchange rate will have a substantial effect. However, if demand for imports and exports is inelastic, a fall in the exchange rate will make matters worse. The reason for this is that the country will not sell many more goods abroad and these will be at a lower price. Moreover, it will continue to import nearly as many goods, and at a higher price.

Inflation rate

If a country has a higher rate of inflation than its competitors, then this will attract imports and at the same time its products may be too expensive to sell abroad. However, a fall in the exchange rate can compensate for this. For example, if the inflation rate in country A is 5 per cent greater than in other countries, a fall in the value of its currency of 5 per cent will maintain the original price in real terms and eliminate the effect of inflation on imports and exports.

Competitiveness

This refers not only to price, but also to such factors as reliability, design, reputation and ability to deliver on time. These are not variables which the government can control and are difficult for individual firms to change in the short run.

Barriers to trade

These include a variety of measures, such as tariffs, quotas and various administrative barriers which were discussed in the last chapter.

Figure 20.2: *Imports, exports and the circular flow of income*

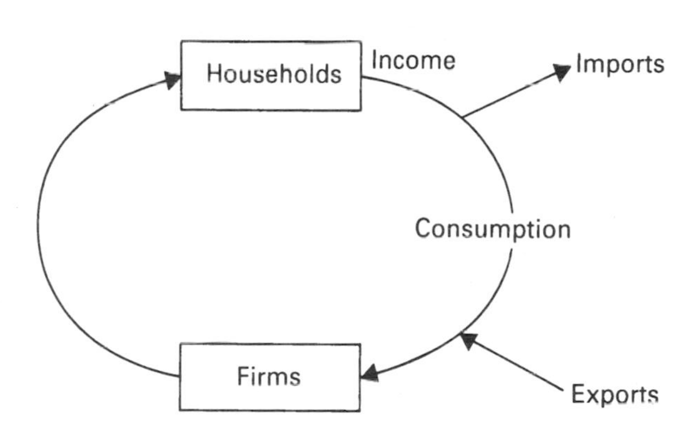

Levels of income

This is perhaps the most important factor. Figure 20.2, a simplified version of the circular flow of income model, shows that the main determinant of imports is the level of incomes. As incomes rise, people are more likely to go on foreign holidays and to buy goods such as electronic equipment which are made abroad. The relationship between the level of incomes and the balance of payments on the current account is shown in Figure 20.3. As domestic incomes rise, imports also rise, but exports are largely unaffected by the level of

Figure 20.3: *Income and the current account*

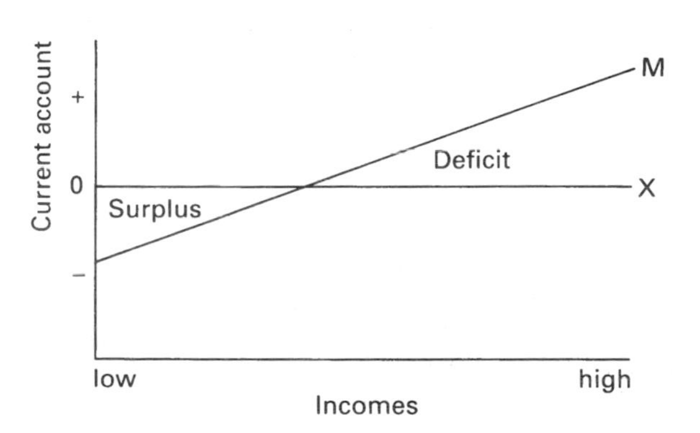

domestic incomes. Instead the quantity of exports depends largely on the level of foreign incomes.

Key ideas

1. A fall in the rate of exchange will make exports cheaper and imports more expensive, and so will help the balance of payments if demand is price elastic.
2. An inflation rate higher than in competing countries will worsen the balance of trade unless there is a compensating fall in the country's currency.
3. Rising incomes lead to an increase in imports.
4. Competitiveness and barriers to trade also affect the balance of payments.

Policies to reduce a deficit

There is no easy solution to a severe balance of payments problem. This is not surprising because the factors affecting exports and imports also affect the economy as a whole so that policies to improve the current account will also affect many other things, such as the level of unemployment.

Because it is so complex, a wide range of policies is possible.

Market forces approach

One approach to a deficit on the current account is to leave any adjustment to market forces. If there is no government intervention, then any country whose imports exceed its exports will find that the value of its currency falls. This is because people in the country will be exchanging their own currency for foreign money in order to buy foreign goods. Since more people are selling the currency than are buying it, its price will fall. This will make exports cheaper, so that the country will export more. The fall in the value of its currency will also make its imports more expensive, so less will be imported. This argument assumes that imports and exports are sensitive to price changes – that demand is price elastic.

This argument is explored in detail in the next chapter; here it is enough to say that many economists believe that adjustments do not take place so easily and that the government needs to intervene to solve the problem. Hence most of the argument is about the precise form any intervention should take.

However, if the market forces approach is adopted, its supporters claim that not only will a fall in the exchange rate end any deficit on the balance of payments, but the country will benefit because market forces will encourage it to specialise in those industries where it has comparative advantage. In the UK, for example, the deficit in manufacturing would continue because the UK cannot compete successfully with other countries. Instead resources would be concentrated on services, such as insurance and banking, where the UK has comparative advantage. This would enable resources to be used more efficiently.

Key ideas – summary of the market approach

1. Without government intervention, market forces will automatically cause a fall in the exchange rate of a country with a balance of payments deficit. This will make exports cheaper and imports more expensive.
2. Market forces will also encourage countries to specialise in economic activities where they have a comparative advantage.

Interventionist approach

Several of the protectionist measures discussed in the last chapter are relevant here. Some, like tariffs and quotas would probably succeed, but are impossible to implement because this would break international agreements such as GATT. They would also break the rules of the European Community.

The effects of a devaluation would be similar to the consequences following from a decision to leave adjustment to market forces. The difference is that devaluation implies that the fall in the value of the currency is determined by the government. Supporters of devaluation suggest that this gives a more controlled fall and prevents the uncertainties which result from a policy of leaving everything to the market. The consequences of a devaluation are discussed in the next chapter.

One undesirable consequence of a fall in the value of the currency is that the price of imports rises and makes any inflation worse. In order to avoid this, the British government in the second half of the 1980s adopted a policy of high interest rates. They argued that this would reduce domestic demand for goods since borrowing would be more expensive, and people buying houses on mortgage would have less money to spend on consumer goods because they would be paying more on their mortgage.

A less painful way would be for the government to encourage exports. However, this is not easy. British embassies abroad provide potential exporters with information, and the Export Credit Guarantee Department provides insurance cover for exports. New ways in which the government can increase exports are not easy to find.

In the past the UK government imposed controls on the movement of money out of the country. For example, tourists were limited in the amount of money they could take abroad. This reduced invisible imports. People have also argued that firms should be prevented or discouraged from investing abroad since this helps other countries. Instead they should be forced, or encouraged, to invest their money at home. Supporters of market forces dislike such restrictions on the capital market and argue that entrepreneurs should be allowed to invest where they wish. Moreover, in recent years the electronic transfer of funds has made it much easier to transfer money, and government controls would be bureaucratic and relatively easy to avoid. An alternative suggestion is to give tax advantages to firms which keep money in the UK.

Another approach involves deflating the economy. Since incomes are the prime determinant of imports, deflating the economy would reduce incomes and hence imports. Moreover, if domestic markets declined, some firms would be encouraged to make bigger efforts overseas. Deflation does work, but at a price. Since incomes fall, people are poorer, output falls, and unemployment rises.

Key ideas – summary of the interventionist approach

1. Government should plan the value of a currency and devalue when needed to correct a balance of payments deficit.
2. In certain circumstances, restrictions should be made on people's ability to transfer currency out of the country.
3. Deflating the economy may be necessary to correct a deficit, but it has undesirable side-effects such as an increase in unemployment.

Recession and the balance of payments

One of the uses of economic theory is to make predictions. Figure 20.4 is an extract from the more detailed circular flow of income model which was discussed in Chapter 13. As the Figure shows, the main determinant of imports is the level of income. As incomes in a country rise, people buy more imported goods and services. We would also expect that as incomes fall so will imports and the result will be an improvement in the current account of the balance of payments.

Figure 20.4: *Income and Imports*

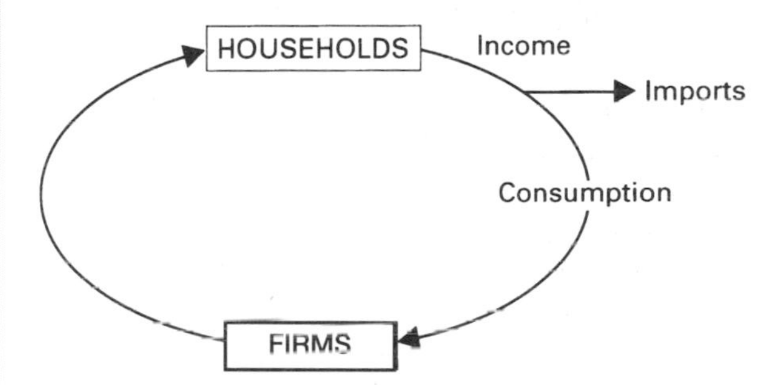

However, in the early 1990s, the UK economy was characterised by severe recession, and it also had a substantial deficit on the balance of payments as Figure 20.1 makes clear. So how can we explain this apparent contradiction?

One explanation is that the recession did indeed lead to an improvement in the balance of payments, but that this was not large enough to wipe out all the deficits. This is worrying to many economists because it implies that as the economy expands the UK economy will be faced with very large deficits on the current account and will be forced to take measures to correct this deficit. More optimistic economists hope that although rising living standards will cause a rise in imports, this factor might be overpowered by rising productivity which will lead to rises in exports. Moreover, as other countries also come out of recession, they will buy more British goods. These two factors might then wipe out any deficit.

Conclusion

The balance of payments has been a persistent problem for the British economy. When the economy expands, imports are sucked in causing a deficit on the current account. To remedy this problem, the government deflates the economy leading to a fall in living standards and a rise in unemployment. Eventually the current account moves into surplus and the economy expands, leading to another balance of payments crisis. This sequence was called 'stop-go' and was only interrupted by the advent of North Sea oil which greatly reduced imports. The crisis re-appeared in the late 1980s after several years of economic expansion. The root cause of the problem is probably that the UK economy is often not as competitive as it should be.

Supporters of free markets would argue that the problem will only be resolved when government intervention is reduced. Interventionists would retort that government measures such as devaluation and deflation are needed to correct a persistent deficit.

Data questions

UK Balance of Payments: current account (£ million)

Year	Visible trade	Invisibles
1988	-21,480	5,302
1989	-24,683	2,956
1990	-18,809	1,778
1991	-10,290	4,050
1992	-13,771	2,225

Source: Adapted from *Economic Trends,* HMSO, 1993.

Question 1

1. Calculate the current balance for these years and comment on the UK position.
2. What measures could the government take to achieve a balance or surplus on current account? What disadvantages would these have?

The importance of the balance of payments

The importance of the balance of payments for economic performance can be stated quite succinctly. If a country gets into balance of payments difficulties as demand expands, before the short term capacity growth is reached, then demand must be curtailed, capacity is never fully utilised, investment is discouraged, technological progress is slowed down and a country's goods compared with foreign goods become less desirable, so worsening the balance of payments still further, and so on. A vicious circle is initiated.

By contrast, if a country is able to maintain demand up to the level of existing productive capacity, without balance of payments difficulties arising, the pressure of demand on capacity will raise the capacity growth rate. There are a number of possible mechanisms through which this may happen: the encouragement to investment, the supply of labour may increase from both inside and outside the country, factors of production may move from low to high productivity sectors and so on. This is the argument behind the advocacy of export led growth.

Source: Thirlwell T., Adapted from 'The balance of payments and economic performance', *National Westminster Bank Quarterly Review,* May 1992.

Question 2

1. Explain why you might expect countries to get into balance of payments difficulties as demand expands.
2. Why is export led growth desirable?

21 The Exchange Rate

Just as potatoes are sold in a supermarket, so are currencies such as the pound sterling bought and sold in the foreign exchange market. However, arguments arise about the extent to which the foreign exchange market should be allowed to operate without government intervention.

- Some economists argue that the foreign exchange market should be allowed to operate like any other; that the forces of demand and supply will operate efficiently to bring about equilibrium, and that this equilibrium will reflect the underlying strength of the currency. Consequently, the value of the currency will alter to bring about equilibrium in the current account of the balance of payments.
- Critics of this approach suggest that, left to itself, the market will produce great fluctuations in the value of a currency. Hence the value of a currency should be fixed, either by government intervention or by establishing an international system of fixed exchange rates. This will provide stability for international traders.
- A variation on these approaches is provided by those who advocate that Britain should join the European Monetary System (EMS) which provides a stable relationship between the values of most of the currencies within the European Union. If Britain joined this system, the value of the pound would be fixed against other European currencies, such as the French franc. However, the European currencies as a whole would continue to fluctuate against the currencies outside the EMS.

Before considering these approaches, we need first to explain what factors determine the rate of exchange.

Determinants of the rate of exchange

Defining and measuring the exchange rate

Every time someone from the UK planning a foreign holiday goes to a bank and asks for (say) some Spanish pesetas, that person is selling pounds and buying pesetas. If many people do this, the bank will sell pounds in order to buy pesetas required by customers, but on a much bigger scale. Such transactions take place every day and determine the value of currencies such as the pound. If more people are selling pounds than are buying them, the value of the pound will tend to fall.

The price which the pound sterling is worth in terms of foreign currency is called the exchange rate for sterling.

Because the American dollar is the most important world currency, the exchange rates of most currencies are usually expressed in terms of the dollar. If we read that £1 = $1.50, we know the price in dollars of one pound sterling – that it costs $1.50 to buy £1. The same information can also be expressed in reverse – that it costs £0.667 to buy $1. When the pound falls in value so that it costs more pounds to buy a dollar (or fewer dollars to buy a pound), we say it has appreciated.

A currency such as the pound sterling is exchanged for many other currencies. Some of these exchanges are on a huge scale; others with small countries, such as Burma or Burundi, are of relatively little importance. Hence when calculating the value of sterling compared to all other currencies, these other currencies are weighted according to their importance. The **trade**

weighted exchange rate is an average of the exchange rate between the pound sterling and the UK's main trading partners. Figure 21.1 shows the changes in the value of the pound as measured by this index.

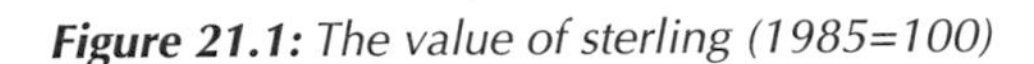

Figure 21.1: *The value of sterling (1985=100)*

Source: Adapted from *Economic Trends*, HMSO, 1993.

Demand and supply

The value of a currency will be determined by the forces of demand and supply. The demand and supply curves for currency are the same shape as those for goods. Other things being equal, a fall (depreciation) in the price of one currency against another will cause more of that currency to be demanded, but less to be supplied. Other factors can also affect the quantity demanded and supplied. These will cause a shift in the curves.

The demand for sterling will be determined in part by the desire of foreigners to buy British goods. If they buy more British cars or whisky, or come to the UK as tourists, then they will want sterling. They will also want sterling if they wish to invest in the UK. This increased demand will cause an appreciation in the value of the pound.

Similarly, the supply of sterling will depend in part on the amount of foreign goods and services which UK residents wish to buy. Hence imports and exports of goods and services, and the movement of capital into and out of the country will influence the exchange rate.

There are two other important influences. In recent years there has been a large growth in currency speculation. Individuals and institutions try to buy a currency cheap and sell it for a higher price. If they think the pound is going to rise in price, they will buy pounds. If they believe that the pound will fall compared to the dollar, they will sell pounds and buy dollars. Tourists sometimes do this on a much smaller scale, when they decide to exchange pounds for a foreign currency prior to departure in the hope that more foreign currency will be obtained that way. This speculation tends to increase the extent of the fluctuations in the value of a currency. Indeed, the quantities of currency traded by speculators greatly exceed the amount bought and sold to pay for imports and exports, so speculation can be regarded as a major determinant of the value of a currency.

The government also affects the value of a currency. If the government wants the pound to rise in value (say because it wishes to cut the price of imports) then it can use its reserves of foreign exchange to buy pounds, so restricting their supply and forcing up the exchange rate as shown in Figure 21.2(i). On the other hand if the government sells pounds, then the value of the currency will fall as shown in Figure 21.2(ii).

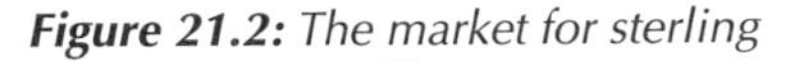

Figure 21.2: *The market for sterling*

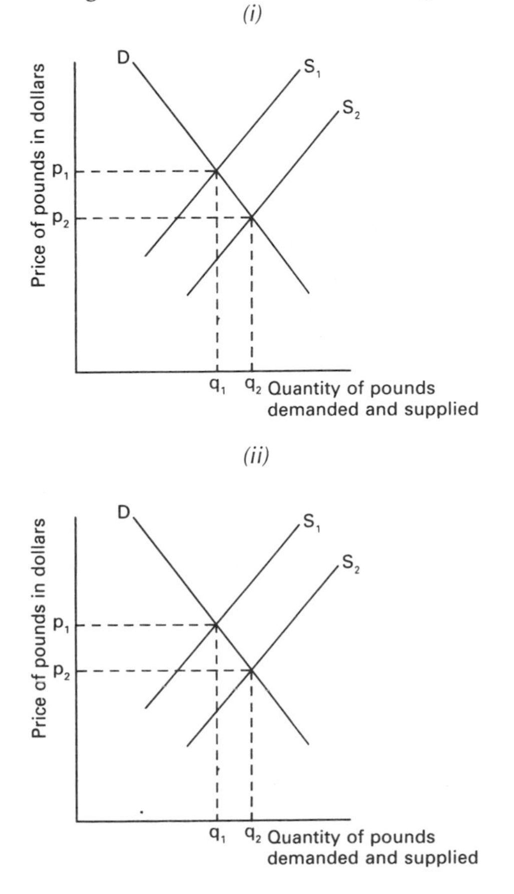

The government can also influence the value of the pound by changing the rate of interest in the country. A high rate of interest in the UK will cause some people to buy sterling, thus raising the rate of exchange. For example, if a firm has some money to invest for a short period and the interest rate is 10 per cent in the UK and only 5 per cent in the USA, its managers may move the money to the UK – unless they believe that the pound will fall in value. Hence expectations also play a part in determining the value of a currency.

Purchasing Power Parity (PPP)

The factors discussed above will often affect the value of a currency in the short run. But what factors will be important in the long run?

One approach to this is called Purchasing Power Parity (PPP). This suggests that the long-term value of the exchange rate will vary according to the cost of buying a representative basket of traded goods in competing countries. If prices in the UK rise by x per cent more than in its competitors, then the theory predicts that the value of the pound will fall by x per cent compared to the value of the currencies of competing countries.

Table 21.1: *Hamburger prices in several countries*

	Price in local currencies	Implied purchasing power parity of the dollar	Actual exchange rate	Percentage over and under valued
Britain	£1.74	0.79	0.57	-28
France	FF18.10	8.26	5.55	-33
Ireland	I£1.45	0.66	0.61	-8
USA	$2.19	–	–	–
Germany	DM4.50	2.05	1.64	-20
Australia	A$2.54	1.16	1.31	+13

Note: (1) Foreign price divided by dollar price.
Source: Adapted from *The Economist*, April 18, 1992.

The essence of this theory is that changes in relative price levels change the PPP rate. If the actual exchange rate between two countries mirrors the PPP rate, then neither will have a commercial advantage over the other. This is because each country's goods would have the same prices as the other's. This would cause each country to export the goods it can produce at home at a relatively low price and to import those goods that it would otherwise produce at a relatively high price. There is some evidence to support the theory that the long-run exchange rate will reflect changes in PPP. However, there are many variations from this rate. One reason is that international competitiveness is not determined solely by price, but by factors such as design and reputation.

A simple way to test if exchange rates reflect PPP is to compare the price of a particular product in several countries. If the exchange rate reflects PPP, such a product will have an identical price in each country. In 1992 *The Economist* did this for a Big Mac. Their results are shown in Table 21.1. In the UK, *The Economist*'s representatives had to pay £1.74 for a Big Mac. Dividing this by the dollar price gives a Big Mac PPP of 1$ = 79 pence. The actual rate was 57 pence, suggesting that the dollar was undervalued against the pound sterling (and indeed against most other currencies). Picking one product is clearly a very simplified way of deciding whether or not a currency is under or over valued, but the example illustrates the principle of PPP very well.

Key ideas

1. The price which a particular currency is worth in foreign currency is called its exchange rate.
2. In a free market, the exchange rate of a currency will be determined by demand and supply.
3. The demand for a currency will depend in part on demand by foreigners for goods produced in the country.
4. The supply of a currency will depend in part on the amount of foreign goods which the people in the country wish to buy.
5. Speculation, interest rates and government intervention will also affect the value of a currency.
6. In the long run, the main determinant may be Purchasing Power Parity.

What are the effects of changes in the rate of exchange?

Effect on the balance of payment

The rate of exchange affects the prices of imports and exports. A fall in the value of a currency will make imports more expensive and exports cheaper. Hence we should expect a sterling depreciation to lead to a fall in the quantity of goods imported and to a rise in the quantity of goods exported. The extent of the change will depend on the price elasticity of these goods. If (say) the demand for imports is inelastic (so that people are not deterred from buying imports even though the price has risen), then a country will continue to import nearly as many goods and to pay a higher price for them. The result will be a worsening of the balance of payments. If demand is elastic, then a fall in the value of the currency will lead to an improvement in the balance of payments because the rise in import prices will lead to a sharp fall in the quantity of imports.

The same analysis also applies to exports. If the demand for exports is elastic, then a fall in the exchange rate will lead to a large increase in the quantity of goods exported. This analysis has been formulated as the 'Marshall-Lerner condition'. This states that a fall in the exchange rate will improve a trade deficit if the sum of the price elasticities of demand for imports and exports is greater than one.

Figure 21.3: *Effect of a currency depreciation over time*

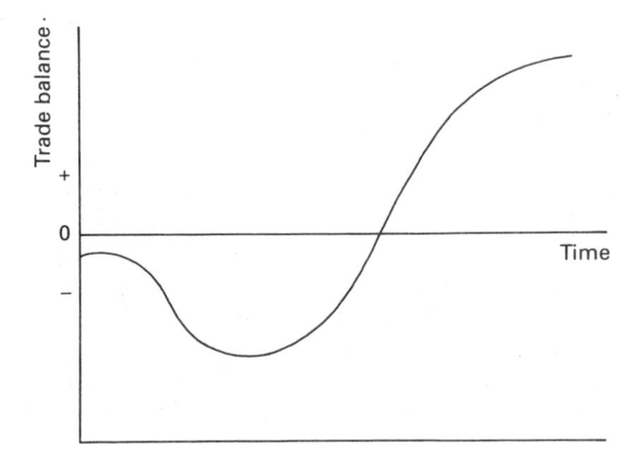

There will be a time lag before these changes take effect and, in the short run, a fall in the value of a currency may make things worse as shown in Figure 21.3. The reason for this is that, for a while, people will continue to buy the goods they have always bought and domestic manufacturers will take some time to replace imported goods; imports may therefore remain high and will also cost more. For example, when the price of oil rose in the period 1973/74, it took some time before car manufacturers could develop models which used less petrol per mile. Until this occurred, the quantity of oil imports fell very little after the price rose. After a while, a depreciation in the value of the currency should lead to an improvement in the current account. The length of the lag will vary according to the circumstances, but for an economy such as the UK, it will probably be well over a year before a currency depreciation leads to a significant improvement in the current account, and the full effect may not be felt for two years.

Effect on inflation

A rise in the value of a currency will cut the price of imports. Does this suggest a good way for the government to reduce inflation?

The extent of the fall in the Retail Price Index will depend on a number of factors. For example, will producers use the fall in import prices as a way to increase their profit margins and not pass the price cut on to consumers? Secondly, the effect may be very small in a country which imports relatively little, and the effect may be only temporary unless the fall in prices leads to a slowdown in the rate at which wages rise. Even if all these factors are favourable, it must be remembered that a rise in the exchange rate will probably lead to a worsening in the current account of the balance of payments. Hence this method can only be used to bring down inflation by those countries which have a strong surplus in their foreign trade.

Effect on unemployment

Another reason for not using the exchange rate to fight inflation is that a high rate of exchange for sterling will make exports more expensive and therefore cut output and employment in industries which export a large proportion of their production. It will also encourage imports and therefore lead to

***Table 21.2:** Effects of a change in the value of a currency*

Direction of change in value of the currency	**Effect**		
	On current account of the balance of payments	On inflation	On output and employment
Rise	Fall in exports and rise in imports	Lowers prices	Fall in output and rise in unemployment
	Improvement if demand and supply are inelastic		
	Deterioration if demand and supply are elastic		
Fall	Rise in exports and fall in imports	Raises prices	Rise in output and fall in unemployment
	Improvements if demand and supply are elastic		
	Deterioration if demand and supply are inelastic		

job losses in firms which face competition from abroad.

As can be seen from Figure 21.1 above, the pound rose rapidly in value around 1980 and this was followed by a collapse of output and employment in manufacturing industry. This suggests that there may be a trade-off between objectives. A high exchange rate will help bring down the rate of inflation, but it will also lead to a worsening of the balance of payments and a fall in output and employment. A low rate will have the reverse effects. Hence car manufacturing firms such as Rover Group and Jaguar do very well when the pound is falling, but consumers may be faced with higher prices for imported goods. Table 21.2 summarises the overall position.

Key ideas

1. A fall in the value of a currency will make imports dearer and exports cheaper. This should increase the quantity of exports and reduce imports, the extent depending on how consumers react to price rises. A rise in the value of a currency will have the opposite effect.

2. Since a fall in the exchange rate makes imports more expensive, it will make inflation worse.

3. A fall in the value of a currency will cut export prices and so help exporters. It may lead to an increase in employment in these industries.

The market approach – floating exchange rates

A system of floating exchange rates treats a currency as a commodity which is bought and sold in the market place and its supporters tend to be those economists, such as Milton Friedman, who are enthusiastic about markets in general.

For most of the nineteenth century most international transactions took place under the gold standard system. The price of each major currency was fixed in terms of gold and therefore was also fixed in terms of other currencies. The system tended to be self adjusting. Countries which had a surplus on their foreign trade received payment in gold. This increased their money supply and incomes, which in turn led to a rise in imports and

Figure 21.4: *Self-equilibriating function of free exchange rates*

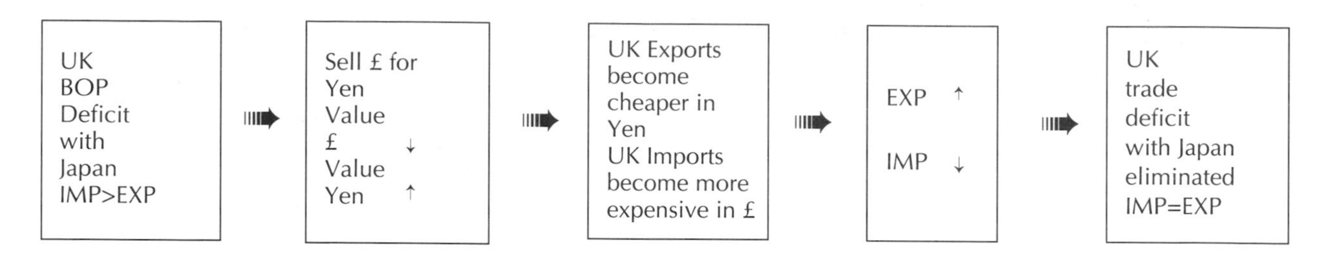

eliminated the surplus. A deficit led to an outflow of gold, a fall in incomes and hence in imports. Again the deficit was eliminated. In other words the system – output and employment – adjusted to the balance of payments. This system broke down about the time of the First World War, which had an enormous disruptive effect on world trade. After that, countries were not willing to allow their economies to be dominated by foreign trade considerations.

Since about 1970, most world trade has taken place under a system of floating exchange rates in which the value of a currency is determined by the forces of demand and supply. However, this has not been a period of pure floating exchange rates because governments intervene to increase or decrease the value of their currencies; this is known as 'dirty floating'.

Benefits of floating rates

Under a system of floating exchange rates, the forces of demand and supply determine the value of a currency. Supporters of markets argue that these forces give a truer valuation of a currency than could a government. The rate of exchange will vary quickly to bring demand and supply into equilibrium. Put another way, the system is self-regulating. If the UK has a deficit in its trade with Japan, then the pound will fall in value because UK importers will sell pounds in order to obtain yen to buy Japanese goods. This fall in the value of the pound will cause British exports to Japan to become cheaper and imports from Japan will become more expensive. The fall in the value of the pound will only cease when trade between the two countries comes into equilibrium.

Another advantage claimed for floating exchange rates is that there is no need for government to hold large quantities of gold or foreign currency reserves. More important, since the balance of payments ceases to be a problem requiring government action, the government can concentrate its efforts on other problems. For example, a system of floating exchange rates makes monetary policy more effective. This is because a cut in the money supply will increase interest rates which will attract money from abroad and push up the exchange rate. In turn this will cut import prices and deflate the economy. Flexible exchange rates combined with a tight monetary policy therefore offers a good combination of policies for economists who favour a tough monetary policy. Some economists have argued that floating exchange rates will tend to be stable because they will not deviate much from the PPP level. Since this can be forecast fairly accurately, speculators will only do so within narrow margins. However, experience does suggest that without any government intervention there will be relatively large fluctuations in the value of a currency; hence no government allows its currency to float unhindered. Instead they practice 'dirty' or 'managed' floating whereby the government buys and sells currency and varies interest rates in order to iron out fluctuations and obtain a desirable level for the currency. Managed floating therefore attempts to get the best of both worlds by letting the exchange rate float in order to obtain a payments balance, while maintaining some stability in the value of a currency.

Key ideas – summary of the case for floating rates

1. Markets can judge the worth of a currency better than governments. Demand and supply will quickly bring the foreign exchange markets into equilibrium.
2. Freely floating exchange rates will automatically bring about a balance between imports and exports, so eliminating the possibility of a balance of payments crisis.
3. Floating exchange rates make monetary policy more effective and so help eliminate inflation.

4. Some economists in this group prefer perfectly free floating. Other want managed floating to reduce fluctuations in the value of the currency.

Policies associated with floating exchange rates

These can be described very briefly; the government should not try to influence the value of the currency. Instead it should allow the forces of demand and supply to determine the value of the currency. Other economists would modify this generalisation to suggest that the government should intervene discreetly in the market to reduce the extent of fluctuations. The government can do this by buying and selling currency on the foreign exchange market.

The interventionist approach – fixed exchange rates

Critique of the case for floating rates

Supporters of the case for fixed rates of exchange point to experience in the last few years to suggest that, even with managed floating, exchange rates fluctuate considerably. Figure 21.1 showed the annual variations in the rate of exchange of sterling over the last few years – a period when the government was 'managing' the float. This conceals the extent of the variations in the value of the pound because within any one year the currency fluctuates considerably.

Do these fluctuations matter? Critics suggest that they do. International trade flourishes best in conditions of certainty. If currency fluctuations mean entrepreneurs do not know how much they will receive for their products, trade will suffer. This is because an import order may become more or less profitable between signing the contract and the final payment. Individual consumers are also affected when firms pass unexpected costs on to the customer. A good example of this is the surcharges which travel firms pass on to travellers when variations in the exchange rate put up their overseas costs. For these reasons it is argued that floating exchange rates are destabilising and so harm international trade. Supporters of floating would respond to this criticism by pointing out that firms can avoid this destabilising effect by buying currencies in futures markets.

Another criticism is that floating rates pass their destabilising effects on to other countries. If the balance of payments of country A is brought into equilibrium by cutting the level of imports from country B, there will be a rise in unemployment in B. The home country will have exported its unemployment. Similarly, if the exchange rate falls the price of imports will rise causing inflation.

Benefits of fixed rates

So far the case for fixing rates has been put in terms of the disadvantages of floating; but there are positive advantages claimed for fixing exchange rates.

The International Monetary Fund System (IMF) was set up after the Second World War. Currencies were fixed against each other, but could be adjusted ('devalued' or 'revalued') when a country had a deficit or surplus on its balance of payments, causing market forces to put pressure on the existing value of the currency. International liquidity was increased by the provision of a pool of money to which all countries contributed and from which they could draw when in trouble. The IMF system of fixed exchange rates worked well for many years and contributed to a large rise in world trade, but this system broke down at the end of the 1960s, partly as a result of rising inflation. Despite this, supporters of fixed rates claim that this period was one in which the world economy expanded faster than ever before, and that this was made possible by the IMF system which gave the stability needed by international traders.

Supporters of fixed rates claim that they help to prevent speculation. Since the rate of exchange is fixed, there is no point in buying currencies in order to speculate. However, critics point out that this advantage disappears when it becomes obvious that a currency is over or under-valued, because then the government will be forced to change the value of the currency – to devalue or revalue. Speculators can forecast such developments and benefit from them. Proponents of fixed rates also claim that one cause of economic depression in the

1930s was that countries pushed down the value of their currency in order to obtain lower prices for their exports. This caused other countries to retaliate and caused confusion on the foreign exchange markets. Fixed exchange rates would prevent such policies. Critics of fixed rates deny these advantages. Firms can guard against future losses by buying currencies in advance. And even under a system of fixed rates of exchange, some countries do devalue their currencies in order to obtain competitive advantage.

Key ideas – summary of the case for fixed rates

1. Part of the case for fixing exchange rates rests on the disadvantages of floating rates. These include destabilisation caused by large variations in the value of a currency and speculation.
2. Positive advantages include the encouragement of international trade arising from stable rates, a reduction in speculation and less likelihood of competitive devaluations.

Policies associated with fixed rates

The essence of the policies associated with this point of view is that the rate of exchange should be kept stable at a desirable level. What is meant by 'desirable' will depend on the circumstances. Some would argue that the value of a currency ought to correspond more or less with its PPP. Others would argue for a value which reduced the cost of imports and hence brought down inflation. Perhaps the largest group would favour a level which was low enough to stimulate exports and hence employment.

Whatever the actual value chosen for the rate of exchange, the government would buy and sell currency in the foreign exchange markets in order to maintain the value. Hence if the pound was falling below its desired level, the government would intervene to buy pounds and so push up the price. Often this intervention would be done in conjunction with foreign governments who would sell their currency and buy pounds. If the value of the pound was thought to be too high, then the government would sell pounds and buy foreign currency. One difficulty which might be faced is that the government's ability to buy pounds depends on the amount of foreign exchange reserves. If these are too low compared to the level required to buy pounds, then the government will be unable to buy enough pounds to keep up the value, and will be forced to devalue. This will destroy the stability which is the prime reason for the policy.

Governments may be forced to devalue if the long term trading position of the country deteriorates compared to that of its competitors. This can happen if competitors are more efficient, or if their inflation rate is lower. In both cases the country would be unable to compete and would have to make unpleasant decisions, such as devaluing the currency or deflating the economy in order to reduce demand for imports. A more pleasant solution would be to increase efficiency, but it is difficult to improve the efficiency of a country's industries.

The European Monetary System (EMS)

Both fixed and floating exchange rates have costs and benefits, but in the European Union there has been a strong commitment towards fixed exchange rates, partly because these are seen as a step towards a single currency. If this is achieved, then there will be no exchange rate problems within the Union, but the value of the European currency would vary against other world currencies such as the dollar.

The EMS has a number of functions. It makes use of the ECU (European Currency Unit). This is used within the EU as a unit of account in European Union transactions and the central banks use it to buy each other's currencies and to settle debts. Another element in the EMS is the European Monetary Co-operation Fund, which lends money in ECUs to members in difficulties. This organisation is seen by some as a prototype of a future European central bank.

So far as exchange rates are concerned, the most important part of the EMS is the exchange rate mechanism (ERM). This system began in 1979 and its main role was to stabilise exchange rates. However, partly because of lack of political will, combined with very different inflation rates, there were several realignments of exchange rates. From

1982 these became much rarer. The European economies tended to converge, and most of the currencies were almost fixed against each other since only small percentage fluctuations were allowed. This gave the system stability, which firms liked and which stimulated trade. Opponents of the system disliked it for a number of reasons. Some argued that it reduced the freedom of individual countries to determine policy (for example, to stimulate their economies by letting the value of their currency decline), whilst others argued that market forces should determine the value of exchange rates.

The period of relative stability came to an end in October 1992 when currency speculators came to the conclusion that sterling was overvalued. This was partly because inflation was relatively high in the UK and economic growth was low. Consequently, they sold sterling and bought other European currencies. Although the government tried to maintain stability, it could not succeed, and the UK was forced to leave the ERM, though it continued to participate in other aspects of the EMS. When the UK left the ERM the value of the pound fell in a few days from 1£ = 2.95DM to 1£ = 2.40DM. This was only the prelude to a number of realignments, and in 1993 the EMS was reformed to allow currencies to vary by 15 per cent from their official values. This gives some stability to the system and supporters of monetary union hope that it can be reformed to bring about this goal by the end of the century. Critics argue that the forced realignments show that monetary union is impossible because the European economies are too diverse to achieve union.

Supporters of UK membership of the ERM argue that it linked the UK to Germany and so helped bring down the rate of inflation, and that the stability it provided also helped exporters. Critics argue that there was a high price to pay for these benefits because keeping the pound at 2.95DM required very high interest rates which caused recession and unemployment.

Key ideas

1. The EMS makes use of a common unit of account, the ECU. It also has a monetary co-operation fund.
2. Participants in the EMS exchange rate mechanism have fixed exchange rates against each other, but the currencies as a whole float against non-member currencies.
3. Supporters of the exchange rate mechanism say that it helps European business. Critics argue that it reduces the freedom of individual countries to determine economic policy.

Conclusion

The basic question to be faced when discussing the foreign exchange market is the extent to which the governments should intervene in the market. One group of economists suggests that the market will work best without any action from government. The market will determine the value of the currency and will bring about a balance between imports and exports. It will also increase the effectiveness of monetary policy. Critics of markets suggest that government intervention will prevent excessive fluctuations in exchange rates and will encourage international trade.

The EMS can be seen as an attempt to get the best of both systems, but the real goal of many of its supporters is European monetary union. Consequently EMS is opposed by those who dislike greater Union influence in the domestic economy.

Data questions

Rise in sterling presents Chancellor with interest rate dilemma

The relentless rise in the pound in recent weeks presents the Chancellor with a tough test. The decision on whether to cut interest rates to stem the rise of sterling is a real dilemma and will determine the future course of economic policy.

In recent weeks the pound has crept up to levels not seen since the UK left the ERM. Left to its own devices it could conceivably be back within its old ERM band, eroding all the gains in competitiveness which have underpinned the pick-up in exports since the devaluation.

Source: Adapted from *The Guardian*, 17 January 1994.

Question 1

1. Explain what is meant by 'ERM' and 'devaluation'.
2. How will a cut in interest rates stem the rise in sterling?
3. Why is a rise in sterling thought to be undesirable?

Reasons for EMS stability

Economic fundamentals lie behind the instability of the EMS:

1. Slower than expected economic growth. With weak economic growth in most European countries, and with some countries already in recession, disenchantment about the costs of economic convergence has grown.
2. More prolonged than expected tightness of German monetary policy. ERM pressures have been boosted further by growing concern in some countries that the interest rates required in Germany to offset the costs of reunification are too high elsewhere to prevent recession or allow recovery.
3. Good inflation outlook. The ERM may be a victim of its own success. Now that countries have used the system to achieve low inflation there will be less commitment in some countries to maintaining existing parities at any costs.

Source: Adapted from *Lloyds Bank Economic Bulletin* No. 168, December 1992.

Question 2

1. Explain what is meant by 'the costs of convergence'
2. Why do events in Germany affect other European countries?
3. Should the UK rejoin the ERM? Discuss the arguments for and against.

22 Economic Development

There are a number of controversies in the field of development economics: indeed this is such a broad area that it is only possible here to outline some of these arguments. Many of them focus on the efficiency of market forces.

- Some economists suggest that the incentives provided by an unhindered system of markets will stimulate economic development. Low wages in poor countries will attract capital and new technology, and development will result.
- Others suggest that most poor countries need intervention from domestic governments and from the international community in the form of aid, cheap finance and trade advantages if they are to develop at an acceptable pace.
- Many Marxists argue that the real cause of poverty in less developed countries is the direct result of the wealth found in richer countries; that rich countries exploit poorer ones, and that revolutionary change is needed.

What is development?

It is both true and an over-simplification to say that the world is divided into rich and poor countries. It is true because some countries, such as Haiti or Burma, are poor by any standards, whilst others, such as Sweden or Switzerland, are clearly rich. The statement is also an over-simplification because some people in poor countries are quite rich whilst there are poor people in rich countries. Moreover, between the two extremes there are many countries which have some characteristics usually found in rich countries but also some features common to poor countries. For example, some countries have low incomes per head but relatively high levels of education. In other countries the position is reversed. Hence we need to begin by exploring the problem of defining and measuring economic development. Terminology is important because it colours the way we think about problems. For example, to call countries 'backward' implies that they are uncivilised. In this chapter we will use the expression 'less developed countries' (LDCs) when we refer to those countries with low levels of income per head.

Classifying development

There are a number of ways to classify development. One method is to construct some measure of welfare. This could include measures of life expectancy, infant mortality and levels of education and also take into account the distribution as well as the average level of income. This is a valid approach to the study of development, but it does raise questions about which measures should be included. There are other problems: for example, it is not possible to add an infant mortality rate to a low literacy rate to obtain a single measure of development. Hence in this chapter we will use the conventional measure of national income per head. As you may recall from Chapter 12, this is far from a satisfactory measure for a number of reasons. The figures are often inaccurate, they say nothing about the distribution of income and unpaid activities are excluded. Moreover, international comparisons are particularly difficult because this requires data on national income for different countries to be converted into a common currency, usually US dollars. Since exchange rates vary daily, this would imply daily changes in living standards, which is nonsense. Moreover, prices are usually lower in LDCs. The figures suggest that a country such as Mozambique has a per capita income of only $80 per annum. In a country such as Britain, people would clearly starve to death on an income as low as this. Clearly comparisons between countries with very low incomes and those with high ones can be misleading.

Diversity among LDCs

There is enormous variation between countries conventionally described as 'less developed'. Some, such as China, cover a huge geographical area, whilst others are tiny. Some have large populations, others small. Some are densely populated, in others the population is sparse. Similarly, as Table 22.1 shows, some have low levels of education and health whilst some have high standards. Certain countries rely on markets to allocate resources whilst others have extensive planning mechanisms. Despite this massive diversity, the division of the world into rich and poor countries is real. The 75 per cent of the world's population who live in poor countries such as China, India, Pakistan and sub-Saharan Africa produce only 20 per cent of the world's output.

Table 22.1: *Diversity in less developed countries*

	Life expectancy at birth (years)	Adult illiteracy (%)
Somalia	48	88
Bangladesh	51	67
Sierra Leone	42	71
India	59	71
China	70	45
Sri Lanka	71	17
Phillipines	64	14
UK	76	less than 5

Source: Adapted from *World Development Report 1991*, World Bank.

The development record

Table 22.2 summarises recent world economic development. Over the period as a whole living standards have been rising, but there are substantial differences between areas. African economies have done relatively badly and this is likely to continue. The reason for this is that they tend to have high rates of population growth, unsatisfactory domestic policies and poor export performance. Oil exporting countries did relatively poorly in the 1980s because of the low price of oil. On the other hand the major exporters of manufactured goods (countries such as Brazil, Korea, Singapore and the Phillipines) have developed rapidly.

Table 22.2: *Gross Domestic Product*

	GDP per capita (dollars 1989)	Average annual growth (%) 1965-89
Low income economies		
Mozambique	80	n.a.
Ethiopia	120	–0.1
Tanzania	130	–0.1
Somalia	170	0.3
Bangladesh	180	0.4
Nigeria	250	0.2
India	340	1.8
China	350	5.7
Pakistan	370	2.5
Middle income economies		
Egypt	640	4.2
Thailand	1220	4.2
Jamaica	1260	–1.3
Turkey	1370	2.6
Greece	5350	2.9
High income economies		
Ireland	8710	2.1
UK	14650	2.0
France	17820	2.3
USA	20910	1.6
Japan	23810	4.3
Switzerland	29880	4.6

Source: Adapted from *World Bank Development Report 1991*, World Bank.

Factors affecting economic development

Economists do not possess a generally accepted theory of economic development. If such a theory existed it would be possible to predict growth and, indeed, to adopt policies which would ensure growth. In the meantime it is possible to note some of the factors which seem to be associated with rapid development.

Natural resources

Britain's development at the time of the industrial revolution was helped by the possession of coal and iron ore. Similarly, oil has helped the development of countries such as Saudi Arabia and Kuwait. However, countries such as Japan have had rapid economic growth despite the lack of natural resources.

Political stability

Countries in political turmoil, such as Somalia, do not develop, if only because investors have little confidence in the future. However, stability on its own is not enough. Salazar ruled Portugal for nearly forty years from the 1920s, but this stable government was used to oppose change and the country stagnated.

Investment

Investment today leads to future growth. A resource consumed today cannot also be used to increase future consumption. Put another way, the opportunity cost of an investment such as a dam may be houses that are urgently needed to accommodate the homeless. Hence investment requires saving, but this is difficult in countries where incomes are low.

Skilled labour force

The quality of the labour force is a crucial factor in economic development. The human capital approach to development approaches the problem by analysing people as they would an ordinary capital investment and asking 'Would this be a good investment?'

In general this line of approach suggests that investment in education is worthwhile for developing countries. An educated labour force tends to be more productive than one which is ignorant. Good health also helps increase productivity, and in turn this is improved by education as well as by factors such as suitable diet and pure water.

Attitudes towards change

For centuries China seemed to have all the requisites necessary for development, but remained desperately poor. It had long periods of stable government, a tradition of scientific investigation, mineral resources and a hard working people. The reason that it remained poor was that the whole ethos of the society opposed change. Business people had a low status in society and the government did little to encourage growth.

Some societies, such as Japan, do not question the need for constant change and are rewarded by rapid growth; others are less willing to adapt and consequently develop at a slower rate.

Appropriate government policies

Countries grow quickly if the government adopts appropriate policies. Of course, economists being economists, there is room for considerable argument about which policies are correct! (President Roosevelt of the USA once asked his advisers to find him some one-handed economists. When asked to clarify his request he said 'I'm tired of economists saying "on the one hand this, but on the other hand that".') This debate is expanded later in the chapter when policy alternatives are analysed.

Key ideas

1. Economic development is conventionally measured by using national income statistics, though these have considerable limitations.
2. LDCs vary considerably in size, economic characteristics and rates of growth.
3. Factors influencing development include the extent of natural resources, political stability, the level of investment, the quality of the labour force, attitudes towards change and appropriate government policies.

Some controversies in development economics

Development economics is a large subject and it is not possible to cover all the controversies here. However, it is possible to focus on some particular issues.

Costs and benefits of development

Change can be painful. People have to adapt to new working methods, existing skills become obsolete and traditional products may disappear, being replaced by mass produced goods which lack individuality. Some people may have to move in order to obtain work, so breaking up families. This can cause a fall in the welfare of old people who in LDCs are cared for at home by their children, but who in advanced countries often have to go into 'homes'.

There are other costs associated with development. As industries grow, the problems of pollution increase and there is more congestion on the roads. Moreover, when people move into cities they suffer from overcrowding as huge slums develop, and there is often a rise in crime.

Despite all these costs, the potential benefits of economic development are enormous. Rising levels of national income do not only mean more goods, they also permit higher standards of education and health. Rising incomes also give people greater choice, not only in goods, but in the whole way of life. For example, in richer countries people have a much greater choice of jobs than they do in poor countries.

Population

At the birth of Jesus, the population of the world was about 300 million people. It took 1,500 years to double. It then grew rapidly and by 1900 it had reached 1.7 billion. The rate of growth continued to increase and in the thirty years after 1950 the world's population doubled again. Estimates now suggest that it has reached about 5 billion.

Attitudes towards population are strongly affected by religious beliefs and by nationalistic feelings. Some people argue that it is wrong to limit the number of births. In some countries, leaders advocate more births because they believe that this increases the importance of the country. In addition some economists would argue that the size of population is not a constraint on growth; more people means more workers and more demand for goods and services. However, most economists would probably support the argument that a rapidly rising population hinders growth. In many LDCs half the population is aged under 20, and this means that they cannot afford to provide adequate education. Consequently the labour force remains poorly qualified. In addition, an increasing population means that there are fewer capital resources per head of the population, and simple arithmetic shows that if GNP increases at 3 per cent a year and the population also rises by 3 per cent, then the average person is no better off.

Agriculture and industry

For many LDCs industrialisation is a prime objective. They see the path of development as one in which their countries move from a position where agriculture is the dominant sector to one where industry predominates. One reason is that this was the path by which more developed countries increased their national income. They also argue that industrialisation will raise output per head and help their balance of payments by reducing the need for imported manufactured goods. In order to develop their industries many countries have used scarce funds to build up large-scale, capital-intensive factories and have protected their industries with high tariff barriers. Critics of this approach argue that it is wasteful to build industries which cannot compete and that the money should be used instead on less glamourous small-scale developments in agriculture. Since most people live in rural areas, the prime objective should be to improve living standards of small farmers. Thus in many LDCs, the quality of life would be improved if peasants could afford to keep a few chickens. The provision of pure water would have a similar result. Rising rural living standards would also stem the rush to the towns which has created huge slums in many countries.

Key ideas

1. Economic development can have undesirable side-effects, but it increases living standards.
2. World population is growing rapidly. Some people welcome this, but it causes problems such as a large number of young people who have to be educated.
3. Many LDCs have emphasised industrial development, but some critics say that agriculture should have greater priority.

The case for intervention

The conventional view of most development economists is that positive action by both domestic and foreign governments is needed if development is to be stimulated. And official international organisations, such as the World Bank and the Food and Agriculture Organisation, must also play a part. The reason for such policies being advocated is that these economists believe market forces are inadequate to the task of fostering development.

Criticisms of market forces have already been discussed in detail, particularly in Chapter 2, but there are special reasons why intervention is advocated in the case of LDCs. When we say that a country is poor we mean primarily that its inhabitants have a low standard of living. But we also mean much more than this. One assumption behind the market forces approach is that people are knowledgeable and so are able to make informed decisions. In most LDCs, however, the standard of education is low and people do not have the sources of information – for example, about new crop possibilities – which would allow them to make reasoned judgements about new initiatives. Consequently the incentives which provide the stimulus for change in market economies may not work in LDCs. Moreover, since many people live in a subsistence economy, growing their own food and building their own houses, the price system may only operate to a very limited extent. Hence it is argued that the necessary conditions needed to make markets work efficiently are not met in these countries.

Investment

Poor countries need to spend a huge part of their income on the basics which are necessary for life. There is little left over to finance extensive investment, whether in infrastructure such as roads, education or health, or in new factories or farms. Hence government and even international help is needed. This is largely given in the form of aid, sometimes through bilateral (that is state to state) help, sometimes through international agencies and sometimes through the efforts of the voluntary sector. The rationale behind long-term aid is that funds made available in this way will provide investment which poor countries could not afford and enable them to break out of a circle of poverty. This exists when poor countries cannot afford to invest; consequently they cannot compete with other countries, so that incomes and investment remain low.

Balance of payments

Most LDCs face chronic balance of payments problems and owe huge sums of money. Some LDCs have huge debts and consequently pay large sums in interest. Hence in the world as a whole there is a transfer of funds from poor countries to rich, as illustrated in Figure 22.1.

One reason for this debt is that in the 1970s the price of oil increased enormously and there was little they could do in the short run to reduce the level of oil imports. Then in the 1980s world interest rates rose and debts which had been manageable could no longer be financed.

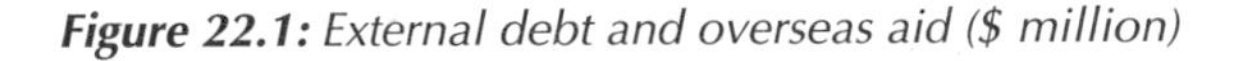

Figure 22.1: *External debt and overseas aid ($ million)*

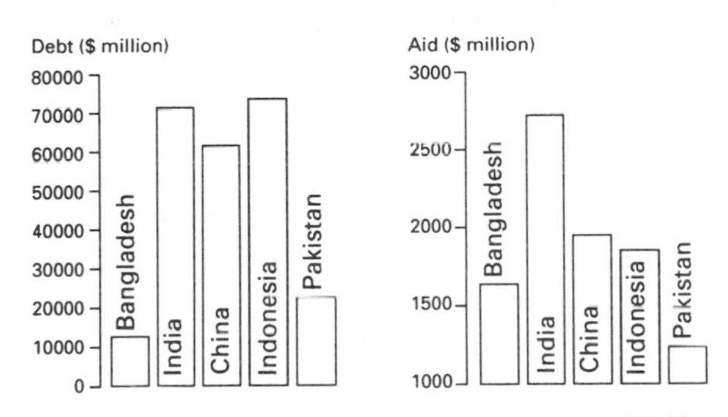

Source: Adapted from *World Bank Development Report*, World Bank, 1993.

There is another reason why many LDCs face persistent balance of payment problems – that is because they tend to export agricultural products. One characteristic of most of these products is that demand for them does not rise much with income, i.e. income elasticity of demand is inelastic. When we become richer we do not increase our consumption of tea, nor eat more bananas or sugar. Because many LDCs have attempted to solve their problems by increasing the output of cash crops such as these, world production has increased substantially whilst consumption has remained fairly static. This has caused the price to fall as shown in Figure 22.2. Hence the value of exports from LDCs has fallen compared to the price they have to pay for imports – that is the terms of trade have become more unfavourable.

Figure 22.2

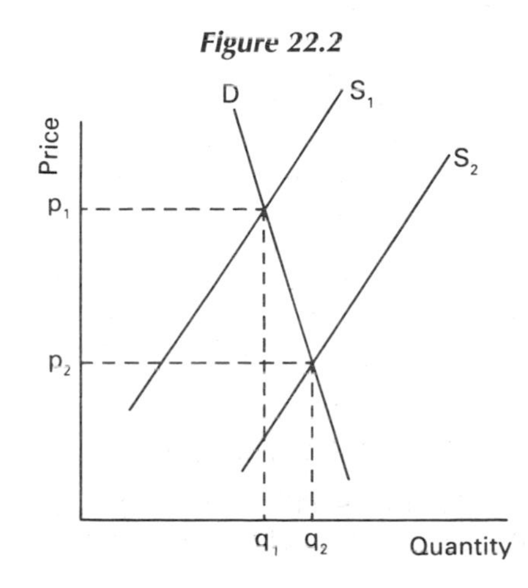

Trade in manufactures

One way out of this dilemma is for LDCs to produce manufactured goods to sell in the richer countries. Over the last two or three decades LDCs have developed their manufacturing industries, so that exports of manufactures now amount to nearly a quarter of their total exports. For some countries, such as South Korea or Singapore, the proportion is much higher than this. However, it is easier to suggest that countries should increase their exports of manufactured goods than it is to achieve this goal. In the first place there is only a limited market in rich countries for products such as textiles or other manufactured goods that do not require highly skilled labour or expensive machinery and so can be easily made in LDCs. Moreover, countries that are already industrialised often take measures to prevent competition from LDCs – look in almost any shop selling textiles and very few will come from poorer countries. Hence it is suggested that governments should remove these barriers to trade. (This argument is also supported by economists who advocate the use of market forces to allocate resources.)

The reason why markets in richer countries are barred to many products from the LDCs is that vested interests keep up these barriers. An additional reason is that many poor countries do not have the ability to produce goods of the quality that is required to sell in advanced countries. Hence some economists suggest that aid in the form of experts or machines is needed in order to help raise standards.

Population control

Without government intervention many LDCs would be faced by rapid growth in population. The problems this can cause have already been mentioned, and these have caused many economists to urge government intervention to reduce the rate at which population grows. This can take many forms. In some countries governments run publicity campaigns urging people to have fewer children. Some provide cheap contraceptives. In others, such as China, individuals with large families have faced official disapproval and lose social benefits.

Key ideas – summary of the case for intervention

1. As in developed countries, market forces sometimes fail to achieve satisfactory ends.
2. However, these inadequacies are exacerbated in LDCs; for example, low educational standards mean that people lack knowledge of the opportunities which may be present.
3. LDCs face particular problems in accumulating capital and in balancing their external payments. This needs government intervention and international aid.

Interventionist policies

A long list of policies could be produced; those that follow are largely taken from *Common Crisis* (1983), the report of an international commission chaired by Willie Brandt, formerly the Chancellor of the German Federal Republic:

- Finance. The International Monetary Fund should make more credit available to LDCs which face balance of payments problems. Similarly, more resources should be made available to the World Bank so that it can lend more to poor countries. In addition, individual developed countries should increase their aid so that it amounts to 0.7 per cent of GNP.
- Trade. Developed countries should resist protectionist pressures and encourage imports from LDCs.
- Agriculture. There should be increased food aid and more research into agriculture, especially in an African context.
- Energy. A new international agency should be established in order to increase self-reliance in developing countries. This could provide advice and expertise, not only on how to produce more energy, but also on energy saving methods.

The case for non-intervention

The case against government intervention is essentially an extension of the case favouring market forces as the way to allocate resource. Economists such as Bauer and Yamey, in their book *The Economics of Underdeveloped Countries* (1957), argue that decision making should be

decentralised in order to extend choice:

'The role of the state is seen primarily as that of making it possible for individuals to have access to a wider range of alternatives and to more adequate knowledge of them.'

They believe that this can only be achieved by using the forces of demand and supply to allocate resources through the market.

One reason for this approach is that they believe politicians and civil servants are not competent to take decisions in the interests of the country as a whole and so make decisions which are in their own interest. This often includes expanding the public sector because it extends the power and patronage of politicians. Bauer (1982) also claims that:

'Third World rulers use economic controls primarily to promote their own political and financial purposes, including the undermining or destroying of opponents and rewarding of supporters.'

In this view the functions of government should be limited to activities such as maintaining law and order, providing public goods such as defence, helping in catastrophes, providing an institutional framework which encourages individual initiative, and breaking down monopoly power.

In support of their approach, economists such as Bauer would argue that the rapid economic growth of countries such as Singapore and South Korea has occurred because their economies have been driven by entrepreneurs and not politicians.

Aid

Foreign aid plays little or no part in this approach. According to Bauer:

'If the conditions for development other than capital are present, the capital required will either be generated locally or be available commercially from business... If the required conditions are not present, then aid will be ineffective and wasted.'

Note that this line of argument assumes that capital is not a constraint on development because it is mobile and will switch from rich to poor countries if economic opportunities arise. This assumption is not accepted by advocates of aid. There are other arguments against aid. Bauer argues that aid is often wasted on unproductive projects because it is not expected to yield a commercial return. Moreover, aid goes to governments which are inefficient. It increases the politicisation of life, the power of politicians and encourages the development of the state sector. Thus many LDCs spend large sums of money on armaments which contribute nothing to development.

International debt

As Figure 22.1 shows, many LDCs have extensive debts to richer countries. This is sometimes used as an argument to support an increase in aid or cancellation of debts. However, the debts arose because of the transfer of real resources and any failure to repay is clear evidence that the capital was wasted by the governments that received the resources. Cancelling such debts therefore favours the incompetent and the dishonest. Critics of this would claim that debts have built up because of factors outside the control of LDCs, such as the rise in oil prices, and because rich countries have put up interest rates after loans have been agreed.

Key ideas – summary of the case against intervention

1. Markets are the best way to allocate resources. Interference with market forces will delay economic growth.
2. Governments should limit their activities and instead stimulate the local private sector by providing incentives for innovation.
3. Foreign aid is not needed because private sector capital will flow automatically to economically desirable projects whilst aid will encourage the growth of the inefficient public sector.

Policies advocated by economists opposed to intervention

The group of economists who dislike intervention favour measures which will limit the role of government to relatively few activities, such as defence, law and order, and the provision of incentives which will stimulate private sector

entrepreneurial activity. Hence government should cut both taxes and public spending. They should also encourage the private ownership of land because private owners will be more efficient than co-operatives or other forms of ownership. This group also favours the elimination of barriers to international trade. Indeed, the best way in which the richer countries can help the poor is by removing the barriers which restrict the opportunity of poor countries to export their goods.

The Marxist approach

A third alternative is put forward by Marxist economists. They suggest that a 'Marxist' economic system should be established in order to promote development. Evidence in support of this approach can be found in countries such as Cuba, where there has been a huge fall in the infant mortality rate and a large expansion in education since Marxist methods were adopted. In addition, some countries such as Tanzania have adopted Marxist ideas and used a 'socialist' approach, for example, encouraging peasants to move into co-operative villages where facilities such as health centres can be provided.

For Marxists, the process of development is dialectical. This means that development produces disequilibrium as well as equilibrium; conflict as well as harmony. In the long run, conflict will lead to the break up of existing capitalist states and their replacement with socialist ones, where the people own the capital. It follows from this that the process of development cannot be one of smooth progress; instead it is characterised by conflict and frequent crises.

Most Marxists would accept that the capitalist accumulation process produces both poverty and wealth, and that the wealth found in the richer countries was largely the result of the destruction of living standards in poorer, exploited countries. This will continue until the system itself is changed. In Marx's words:

'...only then will human progress cease to resemble that hideous pagan idol, who would not drink the nectar but from the skulls of the slain.'

An example will illustrate the point. Until the Industrial Revolution in Britain – when power passed to the capitalist class – India had a large textile industry. As a British colony, India was forced to accept textiles made in British factories and this decimated the Indian industry, causing enormous poverty, whilst the profits led to rising standards in Britain. Consequently the wealth of the West rests on the poverty of the world's poor.

Other examples of this exploitation can be given. Marxists claim that economies such as Mexico are organised in the interests of the USA, supplying cheap labour and providing a market for the products of American industry. The products produced in Mexico tend to be those requiring low wages or those which cannot be easily produced in the USA. Similarly, international capitalists move production of products such as electronic goods to a few LDCs where wages are low and governments keep down business taxes and discourage trade unions. South Korea is an example. Production in countries such as these maintains profits and stimulates growth in one or two countries, but this cannot be spread to others – there is only a limited number of video recorders which are needed by the developed world. Hence capitalist investment in the less developed world does little to raise living standards there because it is organised in the interests of the capitalists who live in the richer countries. The profits are expropriated by foreign capitalists or squandered on luxury consumption by domestic elites who form an alliance with foreign capitalists and, in return, reap some of the benefits.

The prevalent Marxist view of the 1960s and 1970s argued that LDCs experienced under-development (or dependent development) because they were part of the international capitalist system. This made them vulnerable to fluctuations in the price of primary products which they produced, to penetration and exploitation by trans-national companies, to dependence on international capital markets, and to a subservient military position.

More recently, some Marxists have suggested that capitalism can spread to LDCs and that it can be a progressive force. By this they mean that it can replace more backward economic systems as it did in Europe in the nineteenth century. This group of Marxists argues that LDCs are able to absorb imported technology and that they can negotiate on strong terms with transnational companies. In this view there are good possibilities for sustained development.

Key ideas – summary of the Marxist approach

1. The general Marxist position since the War has been that the poverty of LDCs is a direct result of the wealth found in richer countries.

2. In this view the wealth found in rich countries is caused by the exploitation of poorer countries whose economies are geared to supplying the needs of the rich countries, such as raw materials and markets.
3. A different Marxist approach suggests that LDCs can take the capitalist path and become wealthier, at least in the short term.
4. Both groups believe that economic crises are inevitable in development and will continue until the whole system is changed.

Marxist policies

In the long run Marxists believe that revolutionary change is needed; this can be peaceful in certain circumstances. In the shorter run they advocate the strengthening of workers' organisations, such as trade unions, and the growth of public ownership. Since resources are particularly scarce in poor countries, government intervention is needed to prevent them being wasted on the pleasures of the rich. Instead, more money should be spent on education, providing basic health facilities and on building up the economic infrastructure such as roads, electricity and pure water. Government farms and factories can also be set up to force the pace of development.

The Asian Tigers

'Asian Tigers' is the name given to those Asian countries such as Korea, Singapore and Taiwan which are following in the footsteps of Japan by achieving very high rates of economic growth. Following the Second World War, the Japanese economy grew at 10 per cent a year for twenty years. Between the mid 1960s and the mid 1980s GDP grew in South Korea by 8.6 per cent a year and in Taiwan by 9.8 per cent a year. So does their experience support the market forces or the interventionist approach?

Interventionists could point to many factors supporting their arguments. The governments of both countries had virtually complete control over their entire banking systems, primarily through public ownership of the banks. Both countries had development plans, five year plans in South Korea and four year plans in Taiwan, and these plans mapped out government commitment to a well defined path of development. For example, the first five year plan in South Korea emphasised light industry whilst the second established and developed a heavy chemical industry. Government investment amounted to about a third of all investment and both countries had strong public sectors. For example, in 1972 Korea's public sector accounted for seven-eighths of value added in finance, for two thirds of electricity, water and sewage and for a third in mining, transport and communications (Wu Qi, 1988). Moreover, both countries made extensive use of protection to help domestic industries develop; for example, average tariffs in Taiwan were over 30 per cent in the 1970s. So there is ample evidence of government intervention.

However, supporters of markets can also claim support for their arguments. There was very strong competition between firms, there were low rates of personal taxation, wages were low and the labour force was flexible. Moreover, the governments made considerable use of incentives such as tax holidays, and grace periods for firms which invested. These are all characteristics of a supply side approach.

So the case of the Asian Tigers can be used to support both interventionists and market supporters. What seems to be important is the right mix of government and private sector activity.

Conclusion

Economists agree that there are large differences in living standards between rich and poor countries. Arguments arise when the causes and significance of these differences are considered and when policies are suggested. The debate centres around the role of government. Those who admire the efficiency of market forces seek to limit the role of government to a relatively few essential activities. Interventionists argue that market forces cannot cope with the circumstances found in many LDCs and that intervention is needed from domestic governments and from the international community if development is to be stimulated. Finally, Marxists believe that strong government action is needed to prevent exploitation.

Data questions

While rich men talk

It is time for the rich world to overhaul its thinking on helping the poor. In the case of much of the aid rich countries give to the poor, the main motive has not been to end poverty, but to promote the self interest of the giver, by winning useful friends or promoting the donor's exports. One glaring example is that almost half of America's aid budget has been earmarked for Egypt and Israel. And about half of all aid is tied to the purchase of goods and services from the donor country. This is a particular folly. It costs developing countries some 15 - 20 per cent of the value of the aid because they pay higher prices.

An even better way for the rich to help the poor is to buy the poor world's goods. If the rich countries abolished all their barriers to third world goods, the increase in developing nations' exports would be worth twice what they receive in aid. The rich would benefit too. Which is why free trade is the best aid policy of all.

Source: Adapted from *The Economist*, 10 July 1993.

Question 1

1. What principles do you think should determine donors' aid policies?
2. Explain 'the barriers to third world goods'.
3. Explain how rich countries would benefit from lower barriers to developing countries' imports.

Health systems and their problems

Although health services are only one factor in explaining past successes, the importance of their role in the developing world is not in doubt. Public health measures brought about the eradication of smallpox and have been central to the reduction in deaths caused by vaccine - preventable childhood diseases. But there are major problems with health systems:

- **Misallocation.** Public money is spent on health interventions of low cost-effectiveness, such as surgery for most cancers, at the same time that critical and highly cost-effective interventions such as treatment of tuberculosis remain underfunded.
- **Inequity.** The poor lack access to basic health services and receive low-quality care.
- **Inefficiency.** Much of the money spent on health is wasted: brand name pharmaceuticals are purchased instead of generic drugs, health workers are badly supervised.
- **Exploding costs.** In some developing countries health care expenditures are growing much faster than income.

Source: Adapted from *World Bank Development Report 1993*, World Bank.

Question 2

1. Why do you think that health is an important factor in economic development?
2. Use the points in the text to argue the case a) for government intervention in health, and b) the use of market forces.
3. Explain what is meant by 'cost-effectiveness' and explain how it can be used to improve health care.

23 Conclusion - Economic Models and Theories

Facts don't speak for themselves. They have to be interpreted. If two cars collide, the interpretation of the facts offered by the drivers will often vary considerably. Their perspective will alter the way they perceive the events and their perspectives will probably be determined by their self-interest. In economics the position is much more complicated. The number of possible facts surrounding any economic problem is so large that no individual – and no computer – can comprehend them all. Therefore the economist has not only to interpret the facts, but also to decide which facts are important. In order to do this economists build models.

Economic models

An economic model is a simplification of reality which abstracts from the complexities of the real world in order to explain economic phenomena and to make predictions. In everyday life we build and make use of models all the time. Most people have a simplistic model of how a television works. If they press a certain button, the result will be a particular programme. This model has simplified reality by ignoring everything inside the set. If something goes wrong, people have to call a repairer who has a much more sophisticated model which allows them to make predictions about the causes of television failure.

Models can be expressed in various ways. The most obvious is to use words; most of the models in this book are verbal models. They can also be expressed diagrammatically. The circular flow of income model is a good example. In this model reality is simplified so that just six variables are considered; but this is sufficient to allow predictions to be made. Professional economists would extend the model, bring in more variables, and probably specify their relationships mathematically. The Treasury model of the British economy has some 600 equations which make it possible to forecast the consequences if some variable, such as the money supply, is altered. Despite its complexity, even this model is a considerable simplification of reality.

Testing models

In order to use models we usually have to be able to **quantify** the variables involved. In principle this may seem an easy task. In practice it is quite difficult. Statistics are often not available or are inaccurate. If we are investigating income, for

Figure 23.1: *Theorising in economics*

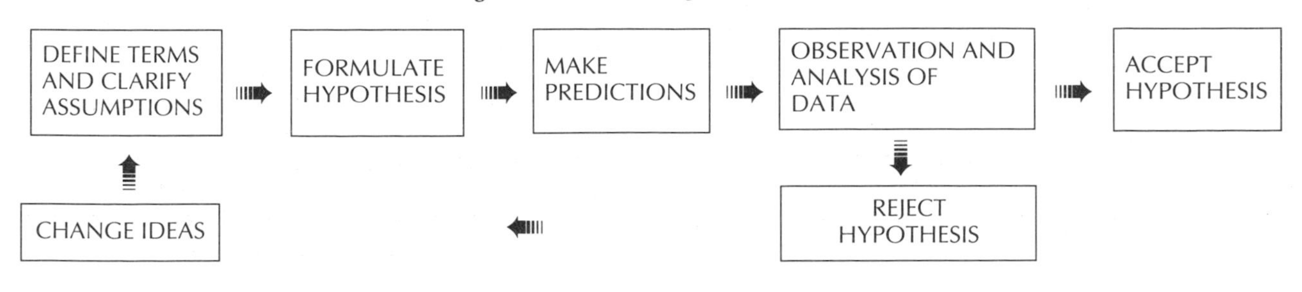

example, most data comes from the Inland Revenue and people have been known to give inaccurate information to the tax authorities! If we knocked at doors asking people their income we would be more likely to get a black eye than accurate information. Take another instance; there is no perfect way to measure 'housing conditions', so we have to use **proxies**, such as overcrowding or lack of facilities.

Economic method

According to Keynes:

'The theory of economics does not furnish a body of settled conclusions immediately applicable to policy. It is a method rather than a doctrine, an apparatus of the mind, a technique of thinking which helps its possessor to draw correct conclusions.'

This economic 'way of thinking' has been used throughout this book and is closely related to the methods used by other scientists, particularly other social scientists. However, there are special difficulties which occur when scientific method is applied to people.

One difficulty is that most economic analysis assumes people behave rationally and this manifests itself in an attempt to improve their utility. However, people can be capricious, behaving differently in the same circumstances, perhaps just because they feel like a change. This makes it difficult to predict how individuals may behave.

The position is different when we consider large groups of people because of the 'law of large numbers'. This suggests that while particular individuals may behave in odd ways, this will be offset by the behaviour of others. Hence it may be impossible to predict whether a particular individual will buy an ice cream on a particular day, but it is predictable that more ice cream will be bought when the weather is hot than when it is cold. Similarly, a 'Scrooge' may spend only tiny amounts of money whatever his income, but it is safe to suggest that on average people will spend more when their income rises.

Evaluating theories

Theories can never be proved correct because it is not possible to check a theory against every possible observation. A statement such as 'Every person will eventually die' cannot be **proved** correct until every person is dead – and then there would be no one to confirm the accuracy of the prediction. Consequently, instead of trying to prove theories true, social scientists seek evidence to refute them. Again, this can never be done with complete certainty, if only because people are not perfect and are liable to make mistakes. However, if data is accumulated which suggests that a theory does not accord with the evidence, it is discarded or amended. To test a theory, economists ask questions such as 'Does it account for all the evidence?' and 'Does it predict the consequences of a change more accurately than the alternative theory?'

From this viewpoint, a good theory is one that makes wide ranging claims which can be tested, while leaving itself open to falsification. Newton's theory of gravity is such a theory. It allowed scientists to make predictions about the orbits of planets as well as about the way objects would fall to the ground. Scientists could therefore make many predictions and test them. The theory therefore gave rise to many opportunities for falsifying it. The more it resisted attempts to falsify it, the more likely it was to be true. However, because of the special difficulties facing social scientists it may never be possible to achieve this amount of certainty in economics.

Values

Some economics textbooks begin by distinguishing between **positive** and **normative** economics. Positive economics deals with what is; with **objective explanations** of the working of the economy. Normative economics is about what ought to be; it puts forward views based on **personal value judgements**. Thus positive economics deals with questions which, in principle at least, are testable. 'Students taking A level economics are better looking than those taking physics' is a testable statement, though there might be a problem in deciding how to measure 'good looking'. 'Students taking 'A' level economics ought to be grateful to their teachers' is a normative statement concerned with values. Similarly, 'A tax on a good will raise its price' and 'Business people will invest more when interest rates are low' are positive statements about economics. Normative statements would include 'Britain ought to give more aid to poor countries', and 'Unemployment is a more serious problem than inflation'.

In practice the distinction between positive and normative may not be so clear. People's values can have a substantial effect on their economics. The issues examined by economists – poverty, money and unemployment – are ones where people have strong views. These views influence the areas which economists choose to investigate; for example, someone who believes in greater equality may investigate the causes of poverty. This belief will affect the way the researcher perceives the problem, the way it is investigated and the way the results are interpreted and reported. Similarly, in investigating world poverty Marxist economists would focus on explanations which emphasised exploitation, while supply siders would emphasise evidence which supported their views that inappropriate government intervention retarded development. The **facts** are the same, but the facts which are seen as significant differ between perspectives. The explanations given by economists reveal their values and affect the way they perceive the facts.

The assumptions underlying research are often not made clear. Marxist economists would make very different assumptions about the nature of economics in a capitalist economy than someone who believed in the virtues of the private ownership of the means of production. These differing assumptions would influence their methodology and their findings.

Differing values and assumptions are one reason why economists disagree and give rise to the old jibe that 'if all the economists in the world were laid end to end they would not reach a conclusion'. Readers of all economics texts should be aware that however much the authors may try to present a value–free science, they cannot do so.

The problem of relativism

Some philosophers, such as Kuhn (1970), do not see science as a rational activity. He emphasises the importance of groups of scientists with shared ideas to which their members are committed and which they do their best to defend. When individuals or groups switch from one set of beliefs to another it is because there have been changes in social forces. Thus the competing perspectives discussed in this book represent groups of economists with similar beliefs who seek to justify their ideas. Changes in these ideas only occur when there have been significant social and economic changes. Kuhn's ideas highlight a problem. If knowledge is shaped by social forces and defended by groups of scientists, how can we distinguish between genuine knowledge and mere belief? This problem of 'cultural relativism', as it is called, has no easy solution. One answer is to accept that economic perspectives are value laden and that what is needed is a clarification of the values of disputing parties. If these are made explicit then readers are in a position to make better judgements about policies. However, in practice it is often difficult to do this. One reason is that many people take most note of facts and theories which support their own values. In addition, economists often conceal their values and present their work as impartial and authoritative.

Conclusion

Economists often claim to use scientific methods of investigation. These involve the use of models which can be tested against the evidence. When the evidence contradicts a theory, then the theory is abandoned or modified. However, some critics say that this is too simplistic. They claim that impartial investigation is impossible and that economists are often concerned to defend perspectives which reflect their values. The reader should try to ascertain these values in order to be able to judge the policies which are advocated.

Data questions

Question 1

Examine the photographs.

1. (i) Prepare two competing hypotheses for photograph A.
   (ii) Prepare two competing hypotheses for photograph B.
2. In each case, suggest what type of evidence could be put forward to support these conflicting hypotheses and the perspectives which lie behind them.

Theorising in science

Admittedly, science suffers from our human fallibility, like every other human enterprise. And although we are doing all we can to find our mistakes, our results cannot be certain. But we learn from our mistakes: scientists turn our fallibility into objectively testable conjectural knowledge. They are continuing to do so this very moment. And I trust they will continue to do so, for many years to come.

Ladies and Gentlemen, all I have said so far has been an attempt to introduce myself to you as a valiant lover of science who has the greatest admiration for the marvellous and often true results of science, without believing these results to be certain. The results of science remain hypotheses, which may have been well tested, but not established: not shown to be true. Of course, they may be true. And, at any rate, they are splendid hypotheses, showing the way to still better ones. Our theories, our hypotheses, are our adventurous trials. Admittedly, most of these turn out to be errors: under the impact of our tests they turn out to be false. Those theories that we cannot refute by the severest tests, we hope to be true. And indeed, they may well be true. But new tests may still falsify them.

This method of bold, adventurous theorising, followed by exposure to severe testing, is the method of life itself as it evolves to higher forms. Just as life conquers new worlds, new lands, the ocean, the air, space; so science conquers new worlds: new lands, the ocean, air and space. What we aim to know, to understand, is the world, the cosmos. All science is cosmology: it is an attempt to learn more about the world: about atoms, about molecules, about living organisms, about the riddles of the origin of life on earth.

Source: Sir Karl Popper, *The Guardian,* August 29, 1988.

Question 2

1. What conclusions does the article draw about theory? What implications do these conclusions have for economists?
2. How would the values of an investigator influence the choice of hypotheses to be tested, and the way in which the results were presented?

References

Aaronovitch, S. *et al* (1981), *The Political Economy of British Capitalism,* Pluto, London.

Artis, M. & Lewis, M. (1991), *Money in Britain,* Philip Allen, Hemel Hempstead.

Atkinson, G.B.J. ed. (annual), *Developments in Economics,* Causeway Press, Ormskirk.

Bain, J. (1958), *Barriers to New Competition,* Harvard University Press, USA.

Bauer, P. T. & Yamey, B. (1957), *The Economics of Underdeveloped Countries,* Cambridge University Press, Cambridge.

Bauer, P. T. (1982), *Equality, the Third World and Economic Delusion,* Methuen, London.

Baumol, W. J. (1958), 'On the Theory of Oligopoly', *Economica.*

Baumol, W. J. (1959), *Business Behaviour, Value and Growth,* Macmillan, New York.

Brandt Commission (1983), *Common Crisis,* Pan, London.

Brown, C. V. (1983), *Taxation and the Incentive to Work,* Oxford University Press, Oxford.

Buzzel & Gale (1997), *The PIMS Principles,* Strategic Planning Institute, London.

Ceccini, P. C. (1988), *The Economics of 1992,* Oxford University Press, Oxford.

Coase, R. H. (1937), 'The Nature of the Firm', *Economica.*

Coe D. T. (1988), 'Hysteresis Effect' in Cross, R.B. (ed) *Unemployment, Hysteresis and the Natural Rate Hypothesis,* Basil Blackwell, Oxford.

Curry, B. & George, K. D. (1983), 'Industrial Concentration - a Survey', *Journal of Industrial Economics.*

Dickens, R. *et al* (1993), 'Wages councils: was there a case for abolition?" *British Journal of Industrial Relations,* vol 31 no 4 pp. 515-529.

Ferguson, P. (1988), *Industrial Economics: Issues and Perspectives,* Macmillan, London.

Friedman, M. (1966), *The Optimum Quantity of Money,* Macmillan, London.

Friedman, M. & R. (1980), *Free to Choose,* Harcourt Brace Jovanovich, USA.

Gaitskell, H. (1956), *Socialism & Nationalisation,* Labour Party, London.

Galbraith, J. K. (1952), *American Capitalism,* Penguin, London.

Galbraith, J. K. (1983), *A Life in our Times,* Corgi, London.

Gowland, D. (1979), *Modern Economic Analysis,* Butterworth, London.

Greenhalgh, C. A., Layard, R. & Oswald A. J. eds (1983), *The Causes of Unemployment,* Clarendon, Oxford.

Hattersley, R. (1987), *Choose Freedom,* Michael Joseph, London.

Hayek, F. A. (1984), *1980s Unemployment and the Unions,* Institute of Economic Affairs, London.

Heckscher, E. (1919), 'The Effects of Foreign Trade on the Distribution of Income', reprinted in A. E. A. (1949), *Readings in the Theory of International Trade,* Blakiston, Philadelphia.

Hendry, D. F. & Ericsson, N. R. (1983), *Assertion without Empirical Basis: An Economic Appraisal of Friedman & Schwartz,* Bank of England, London.

Howells, P. G. & Bain, K. (1985), *Introduction to Monetary Economics,* Longman, Harlow.

Junankar, P. & Price, S. (1983), 'The Dynamics of Unemployment', *Economic Journal.*

Kay, J. A. & Silberston, Z. A. (1984), 'The New Industrial Policy - Privatisation and Competition', *Midland Bank Review.*

Keynes, J. M. (1936), *General Theory of Employment, Interest and Money,* Macmillan, London.

Kuhn, T. S. (1970), *The Structure of Scientific Revolutions,* University of Chicago, Chicago.

Laffer, A. (1983), Letter to the Los Angeles Times, USA.

Layard, R. & Nickell, S. (1985), 'The Cause of British Unemployment', *National Institute Economic Review.*

Layard, R., Nickell, S. & Jackman, R.(1991), *Unemployment,* Oxford University Press, Oxford.

Layard, R. (1986), *How to beat Unemployment,* Oxford University Press, Oxford.

Lewis, M. J. (1985), 'Money and the Control of Inflation in the UK', *Midland Bank Review.*

Leontief, W. (1954), 'Domestic Production and Foreign Trade: The American Captial Position Re-examined', reprinted in A.E.A. (1968), *Readings in International Economics,* Irwin, Homewood, Illinois.

Marx, K. & Engels, F. (1848), *The Communist Manifesto,* various editions.

Marx, K. (3 vols. 1867), *Capital,* various editions.

Maude, A. (1977), *The Right Approach to the Economy,* Conservative Party, London

Meade, J. (1984), *Wage Fixing Re-visited,* Institute of Economic Affairs, London.

Millward, R. and Parker, D. M. (1983), 'Public and Private Enterprise' in Millward, R. *et al, Public Sector Economics,* Longman, Harlow.

Minford, P. (1985), *The Causes of Unemployment in the UK,* Blackwood, Edinburgh.

Nickell, S. J. & Andrews M. (1983),'Unions and Unemployment in Britain', in Greenhalgh *et al,* op cit.

Ohlin, B. (1933), *Inter-regional and International Trade,* Harvard University Press, USA.

Pearce, D. W. & Turner, R. K. (1990), *Economics of Natural Resources and the Environment,* Harvester Wheatsheaf, Hemel Hempstead.

Phillips, A. W. (1958),'The Relationship between Unemployment and the Rate of Change of Money Wage Rates in the UK, 1861-1957', *Economica.*

Powell, J. E. (1969), *Freedom and Reality,* Elliot Right Way, Tadworth.

Pratten, C. (1971), *Economies of Scale in Manufacturing Industry,* Cambridge University Press, Cambridge.

Prest, A. R. & Turvey, R. (1965), 'Cost-Benefit Analysis: A Survey', *Economic Journal.*

Rawthorn, R. (1977), 'Conflict, Inflation and Money', *Cambridge Journal of Economics.*

Ricardo, D. (1817), *On the Principles of Political Economy and Taxation* (various editions).

Robinson, J. (1974), *Reflections on the Theory of International Trade,* Manchester University Press, Manchester.

Rowley, C. K. (1978), *Liberalism and Collective Choice: A Return to Reality?,* Manchester School.

Savas, E. V. (1983), 'Private and Public: the Record' in Shenfield A. ed., *Public Services and the Private Alternative,* Adam Smith Institute, London.

Scherer, F. M. (1980), *Industrial Market Structure and Economic Performance,* Rand McNally, USA.

Schumacher, E. F. (1974), *Small is Beautiful,* Sphere, London.

Schumpeter, J. (1943), *Capitalism, Socialism & Democracy,* Allen & Unwin, London.

Skinner, R. C. (1970), 'The Development of Selling Prices', *Journal of Industrial Economics.*

Smith, A. (1776), *The Wealth of Nations* (various editions).

Stewart, M. (1981), *Relative Earnings and Individual Union Membership in the UK,* London School of Economics.

Stuckley, J. A. (1983), *Vertical Integration and Joint Ventures in the Aluminium Industry,* Harvard University Press, USA.

Taylor, J. (1988), 'Unemployment: Causes and Policies' in *Developments in Economics* vol. 4, Atkinson, G. B. J., ed.

Taylor, J. & Armstrong, H. (1988), 'Regional Policy and the North-South Divide' in Atkinson G. B. J. (ed.) *Developments in Economics* op cit.

White, M. (1983), *Long Term Unemployment and the Labour Market,* Policy Studies Institute.

Whittington, G. (1976), 'Rate of Return on Assets for Large Firms' in Meeks, G. & Whitton, *The Financing of Quoted Companies in the UK,* Royal Commission on the Distribution of Income and Wealth, London.

Wren, C. (1990), 'Regional policy in the 1990s', *National Westminster Bank Quarterly Review,* London.

Qi, Wu (1985), *South Korea and Taiwan: A Comparative Analysis,* Institute of Development Studies.

Yarrow, G. (1985), 'Privatisation in Theory and Practice',*Economic Policy.*

Index